Sut Lovingood's
Nat'ral Born Yarnspinner

Sut Lovingood's
Nat'ral Born Yarnspinner

Essays on George Washington Harris

Edited by
James E. Caron and M. Thomas Inge

The University of Alabama Press

Tuscaloosa and London

Copyright © 1996
The University of Alabama Press
Tuscaloosa, Alabama 35487-0380
All rights reserved
Manufactured in the United States of America

∞

The paper on which this book is printed
meets the minimum requirements of
American National Standard for
Information Science-Permanence of Paper
for Printed Library Materials,
ANSI Z39.48–1984.

Library of Congress Cataloging-in-Publication Data

Sut Lovingood's nat'ral born yarnspinner : essays on
George Washington Harris / edited by James E. Caron
and M. Thomas Inge.
        p.   cm.
Includes bibliographical references and index.
ISBN 0-8173-0821-0 (alk. paper)
1. Harris, George Washington, 1814–1869—Criticism
and interpretation.   2. Dialect literature, American—
Tennessee—History and criticism.   3. Humorous stories,
American—Tennessee—History and criticism.   4. Lovingood,
Sut (Fictitious character)—Bibliography.   5. Lovingood,
Sut (Fictitious character)   6. Tennessee—In literature.
I. Caron, James Edward, 1952– .   II. Inge, M. Thomas.
        .   PS1799.H87Z88   1996
   813'.3—dc20   95-46293

British Library Cataloguing-in-Publication Data available

Contents

New Perspectives

An Editorial Note

Reprinting commentary on Harris, some of it over 100 years old, presents a number of editorial choices. Obvious errors have been corrected silently, but we have tried, as far as possible, to represent the material as it was. The major exception to this rule comes with any reference to or quotation from Harris's works. For the old as well as the new essays in this collection, *"Sut Lovingood. Yarns": A Facsimile of the 1867 Dick and Fitzgerald Edition,* ed. M. Thomas Inge (Memphis: Saint Lukes Press, 1987), and ed. M. Thomas Inge, *High Times and Hard Times: Sketches and Tales by George Washington Harris* (Nashville: Vanderbilt University Press, 1967) have been our authorities. In some cases the references to these editions have been placed in the text in square brackets, which we have used throughout to indicate any editorial insertion. Insertions in braces indicate additions made by an article's author. In other cases changes have been made to endnotes. Footnoted material at the beginning of each reprinted contribution in this volume indicates original publication information. Finally, the title of Harris's only book has been rendered either as *Sut Lovingood. Yarns Spun by a "Nat'ral Born Durn'd Fool"* or with the abbreviation *Yarns,* unless otherwise noted.

Acknowledgments

The editors would like to thank the contributors to "New Perspectives" for their efforts in furthering scholarship on George Washington Harris. A special thanks to Sandy Pinsker for his patience. Thanks to Ben Fisher, Bill Lenz, and Noel Polk for revising their work for the collection. We also wish to acknowledge our debt to Carolyn Brown for allowing us to "borrow" part of the title of her article for this collection's title.

Thanks to the staff of The University of Alabama Press for all their hard work on a manuscript full of quotes in dialect.

For permission to republish, we acknowledge the following:

"George Washington Harris" from *Native American Humor, 1800–1900* by Walter Blair, copyright 1937 by Alfred A. Knopf (reprinted by permission of the estate of Walter Blair).

"Sut Lovingood: A Nat'ral Born Durn'd Yarnspinner" from *The Tall Tale in American Folklore and Literature* by Carolyn S. Brown, copyright 1987 by the University of Tennessee Press (reprinted by permission).

Donald Day, "The Life of George Washington Harris," *Tennessee Historical Quarterly* 6, pp. 3–38, copyright 1947 by the Tennessee Historical Society (reprinted by permission).

Benjamin Franklin Fisher IV, "George Washington Harris and Supernaturalism," *Publications of the Mississippi Philological Association* 1, pp. 18–23, copyright 1982 by Mississippi Philological Association (reprinted by permission).

Elmo Howell's "Timon in Tennessee: The Moral Fervor of George Washington Harris" originally appeared in *The Georgia Review* 24, no. 3 (Fall 1970), copyright by The University of Georgia (reprinted by permission of *The Georgia Review* and Elmo Howell).

M. Thomas Inge, "Sut and His Illustrators," *The Lovingood Pa-*

pers, 1965, pp. 26–35, copyright 1965 by the University of Tennessee Press (reprinted by permission).

William E. Lenz, "Sensuality, Revenge, and Freedom: Women in *Sut Lovingood's Yarns* [sic]," *Studies in American Humor* 1:3 (n.s.), pp. 173–80, copyright 1983 by *Studies in American Humor* (reprinted by permission).

"Man in the Open Air" from *The American Renaissance* by F. O. Matthiessen, copyright 1941 by Oxford University Press, Inc. (reprinted by permission).

Ben Harris McClary, "The Real Sut," *American Literature* 27:1, pp. 105–106, copyright 1955 by Duke University Press (reprinted by permission).

Noel Polk, "The Blind Bull, Human Nature: Sut Lovingood and the Damned Human Race," from *Gyascutus: Studies in Antebellum Southern Humorous and Sporting Writing,* ed. James L. W. West III, copyright 1978 by Humanities Press (reprinted by permission of James L. W. West III).

"The Fool as Point of View" from *George Washington Harris* by Milton Rickels, copyright 1965 by Twayne Publishers (reprinted by permission of Milton Rickels).

Brom Weber, "A Note on Edmund Wilson and George Washington Harris," *The Lovingood Papers, 1962,* pp. 47–53, copyright 1962 by the University of Tennessee Press (reprinted by permission).

"Poisoned!" from *Patriotic Gore* by Edmund Wilson, copyright 1962 by Oxford University Press, Inc. (reprinted by permission of Farrar, Straus & Giroux, Inc.).

Sut Lovingood's
Nat'ral Born Yarnspinner

Introduction

James E. Caron

Reprinting old commentary and collecting new perspectives on George Washington Harris as the twentieth century moves toward its end are sure signs that Harris and his character Sut Lovingood will survive into the twenty-first century—at least in academic circles. The accolade from a select readership implied by this volume continues a long critical tradition of sifting through the popular culture of the nineteenth century not only for what is usable from the past but also for what can be claimed as the best. As well as probe-and-employ agendas to make ideological claims of what is usable, part of the job of academics is to make aesthetic claims of "good," "better," and "best." However, when the academy examines popular culture, inevitably a tension emerges: the reader by definition is elite while the material by definition is not. Thus it is always curious when work defined by its appeal to a general readership is discussed seriously by college professors, that select readership paid to read and discuss and write on Literature.

The curious nature of academic debate about popular culture is perhaps compounded when the material is also comic. Those who profess an abiding interest in comic writing and its authors are forever reminded that analysis of a joke kills it. E. B. White best phrases the warning: "Humor can be dissected, as a frog can, but the thing dies in the process and the innards are discouraging to any but the pure scientific mind."[1] Yet professors take that risk to learn about what makes people laugh and about what popular culture can reveal of the culture as a whole. Such issues inform this introduction, which will discuss scholarship on George Washington Harris within the context of how Americans have read their comic writers. My account of such a large topic will of course be sketchy, but placing commentary on Harris briefly within this larger picture reveals some reasons why his work has been passed down from its original readers to readers today. My discussion will also suggest what enables the academy to read authors like Harris at all. We will find more than a little irony in E. B. White's wry admonition, for unlike his dissected frog, popular comic writers live on only when elite readers no longer read them as comic but begin to dissect them. This formulation is not the whole truth, but it is enough for a start. I want to begin my narrative with five items published in 1846. This constellation of texts represents *the* framing issue for any discussion of comic tradition in the United States: the entanglement of, even the clash between, elite and popular ideas of culture.

The first of these publications is Margaret Fuller's critical collection *Papers on Literature and Art*. In "American Literature," one of the essays in her volume, Fuller states that the United States would not produce a true national literature until the physical continent had been tamed. She advises that those who were then writing could but prepare the ground for the glorious future harvest that would be called American literature. As with most of the nation's educated class in 1846, Fuller overlooked the comic material the popular writers of the day were producing in the popular media of the day, newspapers and magazines, when she elaborated her vision of what constituted culture. Given Fuller's education and her propensity to think in terms of European cultural models, her neglect of popular writings, especially funny ones, is not surprising. In the long antebellum debate about whether or not the United States had its own literature, a debate that was the background for Fuller's essay, the elite readership that Fuller represented rarely considered newspapers or most magazines as a source of any culture worthy of the name.

Fuller, however, was one of the rarities. Despite the appeal to a learned audience in her list of writers who have or are contributing something worthy to the project of building an American literature, she makes an astonishing claim: "The most important part of our literature . . . lies in the journals, which monthly, weekly, daily, send their messages to every corner of this great land."[2] Two years working on Horace Greeley's *New York Tribune* as a literary critic had obviously affected Fuller, the one-time editor of the transcendentalist journal the *Dial*, for in this passage she acknowledges a connection between high culture and popular culture. Yet she does not pursue her claim, suggesting just how weak that connection is for the educated reader. As a literary critic for a large New York City daily, Fuller herself symbolizes a tension—rather than a connection—between a highbrow American readership eager to discover it has its own literary culture (yet is all too imitative in its taste) and a general American readership whose ideas about culture are raw and unformed (yet whose taste may contain a truly original element). Understanding how a comic writer like George Washington Harris was and is read—how any American comic writer was and is read—means understanding that tension, which amounts to an ambivalence on the part of ordinary American citizens about culture with a capital *C* in a democracy.

Except for such a rare notice of popular writing in general, writing and reading American-produced comic material remained for the most part outside the purview of cultural elites in the nineteenth century. Emerson wrote that the "Kentucky stump-oratory, the exploits of Boone and Crockett, the journals of western pioneers, agriculturalists and socialists . . . are genuine growths, which are sought with avidity in Europe, where our European-like books are of no value"—and even he bypasses the comic.[3] Unless the humor was modeled on English writers, such as Addison and Steele or Goldsmith—vide Washington Irving[4]—comic texts were generally banished from the parlor. This attitude existed despite James Russell Lowell's *Biglow Papers,* also published in 1846, which made use of Yankee dialect and comic characters and represents the highest ascent on Parnassus achieved by American comic material before the Civil War. But Lowell's effort, heir to the political satire of another New Englander, Seba Smith, was the exception that proves the rule.

More typical of the production and consumption of antebellum comic writing were the Crockett almanacs that had already been enormously successful for a decade by the time they ran concurrently with the *Biglow Papers* during the Mexican War. Crudely produced and written by hacks, the almanacs during the war used David Crockett's hero status in a jingoistic campaign to portray fantastic American triumphs over all enemies.[5] Written largely by men and for men, such antebellum humor more often appeared in newspapers first, the exchanges widely circulating individual items, thus guaranteeing their popularity. Such spontaneous syndication meant not only that a sketch could reach into every town whose newspaper subscribed to the exchanges but that it could also call forth from local pens stories with the same motif or other comic tales to match the latest from elsewhere. Many tales probably circulated orally first

before a local wag scribbled them down, but no doubt many racon-
teurs who read "a good one" would not hesitate to recast the narrative into oral form. This interpenetration of oral and printed modes
of narrating meant that the swapping of yarns that went on everywhere was matched by the copying of printed material that nearly all
newspaper editors exploited. This preindustrial network hummed
with activity in the antebellum period, creating a new kind of "folklore."[6]

Stories like those found in the Crockett almanacs meant that by
1846, well before the physical continent had been tamed, an event
unique in history was already under way: a written popular culture
was being produced by the people and for the people—and some of
it was written to amuse the people. Indeed, in 1846 Lewis Gaylord
Clark, editor of the *Knickerbocker,* would offer a pronouncement to
stand alongside Fuller's: "The present age is emphatically the Age
of Fun. Everybody deals in jokes, and all wisdom is inculcated in a
paraphrase of humor."[7] But should examples from Clark's "Age of
Fun" be included in an itemized list of American literature? Despite
their sense of the potential for such material, Fuller and Emerson
effectively said no. Antebellum humor at the time of its production
was ephemeral, made so by a self-fulfilling prophecy wherein the
radar of culture is built only to scan briefly (if at all) popular comic
writing because it cannot be a serious contender for inclusion in
American literature.

Of course, other periodicals than newspapers published the characteristic material from the new style of "folk," material generally
ignored by print outlets with a pretension to culture. A pair of magazines from New York—the *Knickerbocker; or, New York Monthly
Magazine* and the *Spirit of the Times: A Chronicle of the Turf, Agriculture, Field Sports, Literature and the Stage*—were the longest-lived
antebellum magazines regularly printing American comic material.
But while the *Knickerbocker* was widely imitated for the regular
comic miscellany of its best-known editor, Lewis Gaylord Clark, the
editor of the *Spirit,* William T. Porter, made his magazine famous
for printing original comic tales from American authors. Porter was
probably one of the best judges in the period of comic tales. Not
only did he edit the *Spirit of the Times* for more than thirty years,
but he also compiled two popular anthologies of comic American
writers. The second one, *A Quarter Race in Kentucky,* was published
in 1846.[8]

Porter's anthology is very much in the fun-loving spirit of the times announced by Clark, and though Clark might have included *Biglow Papers* in the fun, Porter's repeat effort was more: a sign that publishers knew there was a market for the fun, knew books of comic material produced by Americans could make money. Another sign that people saw gold mines in native wit—especially in the early 1850s, at about the same time they found gold in California—was the proliferation of magazines devoted exclusively to humor.[9]

Though some of Harris's early work was originally printed in two such periodicals, *Yankee Notions* and *Atlas,* he had his first "hit" when William T. Porter published "The Snake-bit Irishman" in his widely distributed *Spirit of the Times.* The story was printed in 1846—of course—and, along with Porter's anthology of comic stories, glosses Lowell's comic poetry just as Clark's "Age of Fun" quip glosses Fuller's learned discussion. The conjunction of these five items suggests the interplay of various degrees on the high/low spectrum of culture—not only the American Renaissance and what was comic and so "beneath" it, but also other popular cultural productions in the antebellum United States as well, some of them by highbrows and some still in the canon today, such as the poetry of Lydia Sigourney and Henry Wadsworth Longfellow, or the novels of E. D. E. N. Southworth and James Fenimore Cooper. Scholars today see such interplay as representative of the full spectrum of antebellum American culture.[10]

Comic material, then, took its place in the burgeoning marketplace that characterized the publishing industry of the 1840s and 1850s, an indication that the reading public for such material continued to build throughout the period. This readership did not worry if it was culture or not, while the highbrows ignored it, Lowell excepted.[11] It was not until a less-exclusive comic from New England, Charles Farrar Browne, achieved a breakthrough success in London in 1866 with his showman character Artemus Ward that more select audiences in the United States began to think there was more to American humor than just laughs. The English had noted as early as 1838 that American comic writers were part of a truly American culture, but it required Browne's enormous popularity in London to make well-educated Americans take notice.[12] Browne's achievement followed the pattern established by Washington Irving and James Fenimore Cooper. As Artemus Ward, Browne initially created his success as a regular contributor to the *Cleveland Plain Dealer,* then as a touring "phunny phellow" in the late 1850s who mocked the style of the serious lecture circuit. Browne's popularity spread as far west as Virginia City, Nevada, where Mark Twain saw him perform.

At about this same time, the American comic tradition achieved another breakthrough when Abraham Lincoln was elected president. Lincoln brought to national attention through his own writings and utterances the habit of homespun philosophy that American comic writers had long featured. Moreover, he made well known his habit of reading those comic writers, such as David Ross Locke—who created a caricature of northerners in sympathy with the South, the wonderfully named Petroleum Vesuvius Nasby—and Robert H. Newell, whose comic creation, Orpheus C. Kerr (office seeker), sported a moniker equally apropos for the times.[13]

Into this antebellum world of commercialized "folk culture" and its neglect by cultural elites stepped George Washington Harris. Remarkably, from their first printings the sketches and tales of Harris have been read as clear standouts in what was by 1846 a crowded field of comic writings. The popularity of the sketches and tales is suggested by the repeated entreaties to Harris from Porter to write again for the *Spirit.*[14] Moreover, Harris's most important creation, Sut Lovingood, who first appeared in 1854, enjoyed a popularity strong enough to survive the Civil War and to enable him to publish his book, *Sut Lovingood. Yarns Spun by a "Nat'ral Born Durn'd Fool,"* printed in New York in 1867 by Dick and Fitzgerald. Mark Twain's review of the book recalls for readers the outstanding antebellum sketches the fan of Harris would expect to find in the volume. *Yarns* apparently sold well enough so that two years later Harris journeyed to Lynchburg, Virginia, with another manuscript of Sut stories for publication. Unfortunately, Harris died on the return trip and the manuscript was lost.

The span of time from Harris's death in 1869 to the demise in 1928 of the original plates for his only book saw a great many changes in the United States and in its perception of its own culture, but comic writing remained popular. One indicator of its continuing popularity was the proliferation of anthologies of comic material that march through the period alongside the work of certain comic authors, like Henry W. Shaw (Josh Billings) and David R. Locke (Petroleum Vesuvius Nasby), whose books sold well. Money could be made with such compilations, a fact that enticed even Samuel L. Clemens to produce *Mark Twain's Library of Humor* in 1888, when his abilities had already placed him in the forefront of best-selling comic writers.

Another indicator of the popularity of funny material is that numerous comic writers were attached to specific newspapers, a phenomenon that grew during the second half of the nineteenth century. Whereas in the past newspapers had been content to reprint the popular comic writer as he appeared, postbellum newspapers began to keep a man on staff whose job was to produce comic copy. The result is a long list of writers who were well known in their day though forgotten now—men such as Melville D. Landon (Eli Perkins), C. H. Clark (Max Adeler), Eugene Field, Edgar W. Nye (Bill Nye), and James M. Bailey ("Danbury News Man").[15]

A third indicator is the fact that editions of some antebellum humorists were reissued throughout the rest of the century. Henry Clay Lewis's *Swamp Doctor* was republished in 1881, as was Johnson J. Hooper's *Simon Suggs*. Hooper's burlesque campaign biography appeared as late as 1928. Augustus B. Longstreet's *Georgia Scenes*, often said to have started the golden age of antebellum comic writing, had a reprint edition in 1897; William T. Thompson's *Major Jones's Courtship* in 1901; Joseph Baldwin's *Flush Times* in 1908. George Washington Harris's *Yarns* topped all of them, for the Dick and Fitzgerald version did not go out of print at any time in the nineteenth century, selling steadily until 1928 and beyond, when that firm's successor, the Fitzgerald Publishing Corporation, continued to market an edition.[16]

Some postbellum comic energy was also engaged by what has come to be known as "local color writing," a set of representations of regions epitomized by a fondness for an America that no longer existed. Typical examples are Harriet Beecher Stowe's *Oldtown Folks* (1869) and Mary N. Murfree's *In the Tennessee Mountains* (1884). However, the nature of the comic material changed. Whereas antebellum humor was often rough-and-ready and far from acceptable in parlors, the humor of the local colorists was gentler and tinged with sentimentality.

A significant confluence of writing local color and anthologizing comic material can be found in Henry Watterson's *Oddities in Southern Life and Character* (1882).[17] Watterson employs the ready and recognizable format of an anthology of comic writers but not simply to exploit the commercial possibility of reprinting funny stories. In effect, he also promotes regional culture, in this case the culture of former Confederate states. Watterson's anthology thus functions as local-color writing too, though its use of rough-and-tumble antebellum comic writers such as George Washington Harris makes it exceptional. Using comic material to represent a culture is ground breaking. Many of the best American antebellum comic writers came from southern states, but until Watterson their achievements were not deemed to be a source of regional pride.

Despite the popularity enjoyed by comic writers in the postbellum United States, the intense commercialization of their work meant that to the elite readership, those who thought and wrote about culture, the material was subliterary and so remained mostly beneath notice, as it had been before the Civil War. After the Civil War ended, reviewers and analysts had discovered a critic whom they could follow in any dismissal of comic writers: that well-known English arbiter on culture, Matthew Arnold, who excluded Chaucer from the roll call of the best English writers because he "lacks the high seriousness of the great classics." To be funny was to lack the dignity assumed by many to be the basis for Literature and Culture.[18]

On a practical level, the condescension toward the comic in the latter half of the nineteenth century by those with their hands on the levers of culture's machinery means that for today's scholar there is not much contemporary commentary on many comic writers who flourished on either temporal side of the Civil War other than biographical sketches or reviews of books. This paucity of comment is especially true for antebellum comic writers. The scant three reviews extant for Harris's *Yarns* reprinted in this volume are typical of this lack of critical attention. Although one might imagine that there is a great deal of commentary on American humor in periodicals as antebellum writers are reprinted or as anthologies are published, in general, scholarship has not looked for it.[19] With one exception, that lack of critical commentary is the hallmark of the history of the American comic tradition until a virtual orgy of retrospection elicited by the close of the nineteenth century included something as seemingly unimportant as comic stories. That one exception to this history of neglect was, of course, Mark Twain.

A brief look at the critical fortunes of Mark Twain's career can be useful for a general discussion of how Americans read their comic writers. Commentary on Mark Twain first executed the maneuver that reveals how popular comic culture can be discussed by academics, the maneuver indicated already by E. B. White's frog story: one must see past the fun to the point. The maneuver originally served the claim that Mark Twain is a great writer. This claim reached an early plateau in 1912 with Albert Bigelow Paine's three-volume biography of Samuel L. Clemens, which implicitly argued that Mark Twain deserved a niche in the pantheon of Great American Writers, but it was first developed in 1882 when William Dean Howells urged that those who would truly know Mark Twain needed to acknowledge the earnestness existing alongside his humor.[20]

Howells's basic strategy in claiming that Mark Twain deserved to be seen as an artist and not just as a professional funnyman reversed the popular view of Mark Twain's strengths. Howells first separated the humor from artistic qualities such as dramatic presentation and story telling and then argued that those qualities guarantee that the humor will be remembered (58). This subordination of the comic element to such privileged categories as "the artistic" or "earnest seriousness" was a crucial move for Howells as well as for the critics who followed him and added other qualities to which the comic element is subordinated—such as "courage," "honesty," "a broad humanity." Moreover, when Howells did focus on the humor, he said, "I cannot remember that in Mr. Clemens's books I have ever been asked to join him in laughing at any good or really fine thing." This restraint was necessary for the task of claiming a cultural importance for Mark Twain. And the price for that claim was essentially a denial of his less-than-literary roots: "Before 'John Phoenix,'" said Howells, "there was scarcely any American humorist—not of the distinctly literary sort—with whom one could smile and keep one's self-respect" (56–57).

The argument by Howells and other cultural critics who deny or repress links between culture and comic popular culture has in mind the two audiences that have dominated our discussion. One audience includes the members of the general public who need no one to convince them to read Mark Twain but who are perceived as unlikely to grasp the artistic depths of the humorist. The second audience comprises the best-educated readers, those who think that professing a taste for Mark Twain admits that one has no taste, a belief the Englishman Andrew Lang joked about in his 1891 essay,

"The Art of Mark Twain." It is to this second audience that Edmund Yates pitched his essay, "Mark Twain at Hartford" (1877), when he assured his English readers (in the *London World*) that Mark Twain was no frontier joker but a gentleman. Yates necessarily dwelt on the tasteful Clemens house and the "richly-furnished library, to whose beauty and artistic completeness half the lands of Europe have contributed." Both audiences must be convinced of the same thing: they must see past the fun that established the popularity of Mark Twain's writings.[21]

Howells's 1882 essay is thus pivotal to an understanding of how popular comic authors of the nineteenth century, like Harris, have been passed on to a select group of readers in the twentieth century, namely, some academic readers today. The essay in effect is a first step in that transmission because it asks readers to read comic writers as more than merely funny; it enables that reading by implicitly highlighting a basic assumption of a select group of readers in the nineteenth century—writers, reviewers, and editors mostly—that "literary greatness" and "popular frontier roots" were mutually exclusive categories. This assumption colors most of the early commentary on Mark Twain and, by extension, frames an attitude toward popular antebellum humor with its obvious frontier, that is, "folk" or unpolished qualities.

The Howellsian gambit does not, however, bury the links among "literature," "the frontier," and "popular culture." William P. Trent asserted in 1901 that the humor of Mark Twain may not yet claim kinship with that of Augustus B. Longstreet and Johnson J. Hooper, "but this is mainly due to the fact that the family tree has not been drawn." When Trent, a Columbia professor of literature, published these remarks in his essay "A Retrospective of American Humor," American comic writers from the first half of the century like Harris, who most obviously embodied the frontier, must have seemed quaint at best or fading completely from view at worst, despite reissues and reprintings in anthologies. Yet Trent's few remarks on Mark Twain in the essay anticipate an important strand of modern scholarship on the American comic tradition, recognition of the frontier antecedents of Mark Twain. Most importantly, Trent elsewhere in the essay, and in an earlier piece, "Mark Twain as an Historical Novelist" (1896), also makes the claim Howells made: Mark Twain is a great writer.[22]

Trent's pair of essays, then, represent a second step in the transmission of nineteenth-century comic material to the twentieth century. Because Trent did not represent "literary greatness" and "frontier roots" as mutually exclusive, his essays bear implications not just for Mark Twain scholarship but also for ideas about the American comic tradition as a whole. Howells's argument in effect placed comic writing on culture's radar and maintained that place long enough for academics like Trent to contemplate it, even as they began to recast ways of thinking about the relation between "artistic" and "frontier," between literature and popular culture.

Despite Trent, the need on the part of well-educated readers to ignore the comic (and thus its popularity and commercialization) remained strong. That need can be found in the two essays in this collection from the beginning of this century, by George F. Mellen and J. Thompson Brown, Jr. Mellen was professor at the University of Tennessee at Knoxville and clearly a partisan of Harris, yet the passages he chose to reproduce reflect his bias toward gentility and local color. Brown's essay is earnest throughout—and decidedly ambivalent, for Brown by turns deplores elements of Harris's work and adds his own far less than effusive praise. Thus, Sut is "not fraught with a single virtue" and is presented "in perfect *unloveliness*," and Mary N. Murfree is "far and away the better artist." The best that can be said about Sut is that he "has touches that in realism exceed the ordinary." And for Harris there is even less, with Brown claiming that what good description exists in the book comes because "the author forgets himself." As part of the multivolumed *Library of Southern Literature,* which is clearly meant to symbolize the cultural achievement of that region—and thus represents an elaboration of Henry Watterson's anthology—the whole entry reads as though Brown himself cannot understand why he was asked to write on Harris at all. Nevertheless, the editors of the *Library of Southern Literature* did include George Washington Harris in 1907. Apparently, some cultured people at the turn of the century like Mellen and Brown, which is to say people who believed in Literature, laughed in spite of themselves when reading the *Yarns* and thus felt compelled to acknowledge that power by attempting to discuss its literary merits. Yet their assumptions about what constitutes literary merit precluded a full appreciation of Harris. The criteria by which comic writers were judged remained very much the product of a time that was dominated by the aesthetics of the genteel tradition, which guaranteed that a certain kind of humor would be praised, a humor that is, more often than not, very different from George Washington Harris's and probably more like Mary N. Murfree's.

The detailed commentary on the work of Samuel L. Clemens in his lifetime dovetails with the more meager early twentieth-century commentary on Harris, both showing clearly how a comic author becomes an object worthy of contemplation by anyone of discernment: ignore the humor. With that strategy, Mark Twain might be seen as artistic, though a writer like Harris could at best hope to earn a spot in anthologies like Watterson's *Oddities* or the *Library of Southern Literature,* where a sense of regional place overshadows the comic element. Comic writers by the early part of this century thus had achieved some progress from the marginal status given them within the confines of literature during the antebellum period, but that progress was ambiguous. For Harris and Clemens, the price of that progress is clear. Making important cultural claims for humor obscured the sense of what makes the material funny—and thus popular—in the first place. The comic element is necessarily subordinated to ideas about artistry, earnestness, region, and gentility. Brown's and Mellen's commentary on Harris, coupled with Howells's and Trent's on Mark Twain, indicates a tentative acceptance of comic writers by elite readers at the outset of the twentieth century, an acceptance that is a tacit acknowledgment of the material's original power with a popular audience. There is more than one way to kill a frog.

The same ambivalent acknowledgment of the power of Harris's work can be found in the comments of one of the pioneering studies on American humor. In *Crackerbox Philosophers in American Humor and Satire,* Jeannette Tandy's remarks on Harris suggest that she was not one of his fans, yet she felt the need to include him in her book. Tandy also noted that *Yarns* was still current in her Indiana of 1925. From the same time, we have another tantalizing hint of Harris's popularity with audiences other than academic, in Indiana and elsewhere. In a letter to his mother written in 1925, William Faulkner refers to Sut Lovingood in a casual way that implies her general knowledge of Harris's work. Is Mrs. Faulkner's knowledge typical of southern women of her generation? As Faulkner made clear in an interview, Sut was one of his favorite fictional characters. His letter and Jeannette Tandy's testimony suggest that Harris continued to be read by a general public at least through the 1920s.[23]

If the academy even into the 1920s was tentative at best in accepting writers like Harris as significant while the general public still enjoyed him, that partial acceptance was nevertheless a significant departure from the outright dismissal that characterized so much commentary from the nineteenth century. But if the general public in the 1920s still enjoyed Harris, that would soon fade. Indeed, one of the most remarkable features of how the United States has read its comic writers is the fact that the historical polarity of elite indifference and general acclaim was reversed in the years between the world wars. On the one hand, the public taste for the laughable was steadily overtaken by new media, first by silent moving pictures and their slapstick clowns—Sennet, Arbuckle, Chaplin, and Keaton—and their successors in talkies (the Marx brothers, for example) and by radio, with comic shows such as Jack Benny's. These new comic forms and new comic stars guaranteed that the written comic material from a previous century, which had apparently held its own through the generation of Jeannette Tandy and William Faulkner, would be eclipsed.

On the other hand, conditions in and out of the academy were shifting so that this same nineteenth-century material became an object worthy of increasingly intensive study. First, as William Clark and W. Craig Turner note in the introduction to their collection, *Critical Essays on American Humor* (5–6), the foundation for serious study of American humor had already been laid by academicians such as Brander Matthews and William P. Trent. This serious contemplation of humorists reflects part of the growing acceptance of American literature as part of the curriculum in American universities at the turn of the century.[24] Popular comic material was also increasingly integrated into a university setting. Longstreet had been the subject of master's theses and doctoral dissertations written as early as 1917. Starting in 1929 that narrow range expanded, with Baldwin, Hooper, Thorpe, and Harris being added to the list of graduate students' theses.[25] By the time of World War II, some American universities were regularly granting degrees to students who had written on comic authors. The scholarship included a folklorist interest in humor both oral and written, exemplified in 1939 by Richard Dorson's anthology on Davy Crockett. This steadily growing academic interest in nineteenth-century popular culture was complemented by an antiquarian interest the United States officially took in its folkways as the Works Progress Administration sought out and recorded contemporary folk artists during the 1930s.[26] In addition, scholars throughout the early twentieth century were mulling over Frederick Jackson Turner's frontier hypothesis as an important way to interpret American culture. The debate about Turner's emphasis on the frontier sparked a post–World War I interest in any writing that could be characterized as "frontier."[27]

This interest in the frontier's function in American culture yielded important results for studies of the American comic tradition. Franklin J. Meine's *Tall Tales of the Southwest* (1930) and Constance Rourke's *American Humor* (1931) presented comic material as integral to understanding the frontier America of a previous era.[28] Meine's book, by collecting and reprinting a number of comic narratives, indicated that circulation of the tales among the public had largely ceased; the reversal of interests between general and select readerships was nearly complete.

The importance of the American frontier for comic authors was probably most clearly seen, however, in the Van Wyck Brooks/ Bernard DeVoto controversy over the role the frontier played in the artistic life of Samuel L. Clemens. Brooks in *The Ordeal of Mark Twain* (1920) saw it as crippling while DeVoto in *Mark Twain's America* (1932) claimed it as enabling.[29] Brooks was essentially revisiting the Howellsian gambit of dividing the work of Mark Twain into two categories—the "frontier" (read "folk," "popular," and "comic") and "artistic"—but with a very different purpose. DeVoto's counterattack was crucial because he argued strenuously that the frontier was a positive factor by discussing and celebrating the rich interplay among three levels of cultural production: the oral culture of the folk; the written but popular culture of newspapers, cheap periodicals, and almanacs; the written and polished culture of literary tradition. Championing the frontier, the people who lived in it, and their taste for comic writing was the third step in the transmission of nineteenth-century comic writing to the twentieth century. By elevating the role of the frontier in American culture generally, and in the work of Samuel L. Clemens specifically, a select group of readers, mostly within the academy, had established an institutional place for all popular comic writing.

The 1930s also saw, in Walter Blair's *Native American Humor* (1937), the first attempt at systematizing, summarizing, and supplementing previous commentary on American humor. More than any other single effort, *Native American Humor* defined the field of study for scholars of American comic writers: slighting most women writers; leaving David Crockett and Charles F. M. Noland out of the section on humorists from the Old Southwest; following Watterson's lead and using region as a prominent tool to categorize; and following Trent's hint and DeVoto's polemic by making clear just how much Mark Twain owed to the frontier (Blair crowned him king of American humorists). The organization of Blair's book laid down tracks so authoritatively that scholars looking over the terrain today either follow, thus etching the tracks again in deepening grooves, or contend with them, trying to maneuver their vehicles out of what have now become the ruts of scholarship on American humor.

Blair's book was not just a marvel of scholarship; like Franklin J. Meine's *Tall Tales of the Southwest,* it also was meant to recirculate the writers themselves by reprinting selections from a number of nineteenth-century writers. The pairing of Blair and Meine is crucial in any consideration of scholarship on George Washington Harris, for amid all of their discussion about the larger issues of the role of comic writers in American culture, of how American or "native" the humor was, both Meine and Blair single out George Washington Harris as the best of his kind. Blair's assessment is included in this volume. Meine's view of Harris's only book, *Sut Lovingood. Yarns Spun by a "Nat'ral Born Durn'd Fool,"* was emphatic: "for vivid imagination, comic plot, Rabelaisian touch, and sheer fun, the *Yarns* surpass anything in American humor."[30]

The first repercussion from such high praise, which came as the academic field of American humor studies was achieving its initial configuration, was heard a few years later in F. O. Matthiessen's *The American Renaissance* (1941). Here was a monumental effort to discuss the writers who even today form the core of any canon of American literature before the Civil War—Emerson, Thoreau, Hawthorne, Melville, and Whitman. Published by Oxford nearly a hundred years after Margaret Fuller's *Papers on Literature and Art, The American Renaissance* was another learned volume on canonical writers written for an elite readership. But there was a difference too. Matthiessen finished his book with a section entitled "Man in the Open Air," a brief meditation on the popular culture during the time period he designates as the American Renaissance, with all the echoes of high European culture that phrase suggests. In some ways, this section deconstructs his designation, functioning as a supplement to the writers chosen as representative. By discussing the connection between culture and popular culture more completely than Fuller or Emerson, Matthiessen in effect exposes the tight circle of writers elected to the Renaissance to the open air of popular comic writing and acknowledges the arbitrary nature of the category "masterworks." Relying heavily on Walter Blair and Constance Rourke, Matthiessen chose Davy Crockett and Sut Lovingood to represent American popular culture in his discussion. Meine's and Matthiessen's books, then, established the importance of popular American comic writing, not just through links with such obvious authors as Mark Twain and James Thurber, but also through links with writers who occupy some of the largest niches in the American cultural pantheon, such as Herman Melville.

Though the voltage within this circuit of Meine/Rourke/Blair and Matthiessen is obviously high, its significance to scholarship on George Washington Harris needs to be emphasized. Harris is highly lauded at both the beginning and the end of the circuit. Few writers who were truly popular manage to receive the accolades of serious critics. Though Mark Twain had enjoyed that distinction at least since the final decade of the last century, by 1941 the same can be said of George Washington Harris. The influence of that circuit for Harris scholarship can also be seen in the enormous increase of academic interest that follows. Bibliographies on American humor reveal that since Matthiessen's book scholarly interest in Harris consistently exceeds that given to any other antebellum comic writers, beginning with the publication in 1940 of three items by Donald Day, who had written his dissertation on Harris. No other humorist from Harris's era receives as much attention in print in the 1940s. One of Day's three items was his biography of Harris, reprinted in this volume. Up to that point, only Longstreet among the Old Southwest humorists had been the subject of a biography. Day's other two essays, on Harris's satires and humorous tales, began the task of reevaluating segments of his work.

Day's basic spadework was augmented when Brom Weber decided in 1954 to publish a collection of Harris's stories, including most of the original *Yarns* plus three satires on Abraham Lincoln written early in 1861. In retrospect, what became most important for scholarship on Harris was Weber's decision to modernize Sut's dialect in order to reconnect *Yarns* with a broad audience. In a review of the edition for the *New Yorker*, Edmund Wilson chided

Weber for changing the dialect, saying he had produced "something that is not of much value to the student of literature." The truth, as Weber later pointed out, was that even Harris's champions in the 1930s had modified the dialect with the goal of making Harris easier to read, once again suggesting how writers like Harris had lost their general audience somewhere around 1930. (Both Wilson's review and Weber's rebuttal are reprinted in this volume.)

Wilson's phrase "the student of literature" hides within it the controversies under discussion here, recapitulating the tension between a general readership—implied in a style rooted in the popular imagination—and an elite readership, one that gives the style its serious attention. The phrase suggests how George Washington Harris (and writers like him) have become the sole property of professional readers—"the student." The term *literature* and Wilson's admonition about the dialect also suggest the possibility that Harris's work should be considered as literature. But Wilson's objections to Harris in the review echo earlier objections associated with Literature, thus invoking the bone of contention this introduction has been worrying over all along: what are the grounds for elevating popular comic writing into the canonical status of Literature? That Wilson admonishes Weber for fiddling with the dialect, the most obvious sign of the comic and the popular in Harris's work, adds an ironic twist.[31]

Weber's edition and Wilson's attack—on it and on Sut Lovingood—prompted a number of events in the 1960s, guaranteeing that Harris's work, already marked out as superior to its peers, could be thoroughly evaluated. First, the Sut Society was formed and began publishing *The Lovingood Papers* (1962–67), the bulk of which was devoted to reprinting, with extensive commentary, the uncollected sketches of Harris. This work cleared the way for another edition of Harris's *Yarns* in 1966, edited by M. Thomas Inge and with the dialect intact, and an edition of Harris's uncollected material in 1967, again edited by Inge and with extensive annotations. In 1965, Milton Rickels published a study of Harris in the Twayne's U.S. Authors Series, taking the first book-length assessment of Harris as an artist. The final piece of all this basic scholarship came in 1987 when Professor Inge edited a facsimile edition of *Yarns*. This edition brought things full circle from Weber's modifications in 1954, but by 1967 all the essentials were in place for the extensive and deliberate evaluation of all aspects of Harris's writings, an evaluation represented by the reprinted essays in this collection and continued by the new essays.

It is always dangerous to generalize about a body of scholarship, even one relatively contained such as that on George Washington Harris. In some measure, the selection of items made for reprinting is already such a summary, suggesting patterns and encouraging interested parties to investigate further. Nevertheless, some useful generalizations can be made.

Running throughout the last thirty years of scholarship are favored points of discussion—Sut's dialect, Sut as storyteller, Harris as satirist, Harris's use of language—that clearly raise complex and vital issues. However, a crucial topic for scholarship on George Washington Harris is the character of Sut Lovingood. Moreover, it may be that the single most important point for evaluation of Sut's character is how one interprets Sut's epithet for himself, "a nat'ral born durn'd fool." Walter Blair compared Sut to the European trickster Till Eulenspeigel, and M. Thomas Inge broadened this idea in discussing facets of Sut's foolishness, speaking of him in terms that emphasized the fool's role as the unintentional speaker of truths and dispenser of justice. Milton Rickels devoted a chapter of his book on Harris to discussing Sut's point of view as that of the traditional fool, claiming that Sut is closest to the Renaissance court fool and comparing him to some of Shakespeare's fools.[32]

Starting with the general premise, then, that Sut's character cannot be understood without some discussion of what it means to call him a fool, commentators have branched out into other topics that depend upon, or at least are connected to, this initial premise and discussion. There is, for example, Sut's link to folk tales, tall tales, and folk culture, which in turn brings up, on the one hand, the violence and ribaldry of Sut's stories and, on the other, the recording of folkways that was in some instances clearly a goal of Harris, along with many other antebellum comic writers.

But Sut as the natural numbskull that is the folk fool (born an idiot) or as the wise fool that is most in evidence during the Renaissance (used as a mask to critique the world) brings up a basic question that critics have wrangled over in various specific ways. Is Sut generally an ignorant lout simply hell-bent for fun and thus someone who is mostly not to be taken seriously, or is Sut conscious of his abilities, such as they are, a backwoods philosopher who is thus more than he seems?

This basic question ramifies in a number of ways. It bears, for example, on the issue of whether or not there is a moral center in Sut's tales, for it is difficult to discover morality, assign blame, demand responsibility, and so forth if Sut is mindless like an idiot. Claiming a set of morals exists in Sut's world or saying it does not exist in turn argues for or against the notion that there is a rationale to Sut's victimizing, for or against the notion that Sut is more than merely subversive of social order, for or against the notion that Harris is writing satire as well as rollicking tall tales. These oppositions yield at least four ways of conceptualizing Sut, which of course may be combined in a number of ways: (1) he is unredeemable and silly, coarse and foolish without intent; (2) he has no intent behind his coarseness and foolishness, but Harris does, giving rise to a situation of dramatic irony in which Sut is unconsciously either subversive or supportive of social norms; (3) he is a conscious reformer of social norms; (4) he is a conscious supporter of social norms. In any case, deciding what Sut is and how he functions, as well as evaluating Harris as a satirist (or just master of invective?), or why Sut's tales seem to compel laughter, in some measure would seem to depend upon the meaning given to Sut's phrase "a nat'ral born durn'd fool."

Related to the central issue of Sut's character is the persistent charge against Harris that the tales are simply coarse, crude without any real purpose, like a nasty schoolyard joke. Mark Twain's assessment of Harris's book—"it will sell well in the West, but the Eastern people will call it coarse and possibly taboo it"—and the reluctance of the genteel tradition early in this century to accept Harris as more than a schoolyard jokester both suggest this attitude. Two of Edmund Wilson's complaints against Sut are that he is always malevolent and that "his hatred is directed against anybody who shows any signs of gentility, idealism, or education." Brom Weber's rebuttal of Wilson's review charges that Wilson is merely a latter-day proponent of the genteel tradition and thus incapable of "a sensitive appreciation of American humor in its full range, . . . frolicsome and serious all in one." Weber is probably right about Wilson; much of his disgust with Sut Lovingood misses the complexity of Harris, but it is of course not enough to label those who object to Sut's yarns and other, similar material with the phrase "defender of the genteel tradition." Presenting Harris in the classroom today quickly alerts one that the ambivalence of J. Thompson Brown, Jr., and Edmund Wilson represents an enduring feature within an array of possible responses to Sut Lovingood. In some ways it is ironic that, even though Harris appears regularly in anthologies of American literature as one of two authors representing antebellum comic writers, the tales of Sut Lovingood have tough sledding because the classrooms of today may be tuned to what is politically correct. The genteel tradition has not so much gone away as it has transformed.

The claim that political correctness is a latter-day form of the genteel tradition would be itself a worthy topic of future investigations of the reception of George Washington Harris's work. Scattered throughout the yarns that Sut spins are remarks about and representations of minorities and women that would today be pounced upon as racist and sexist. Of course Sut and Harris would not even recognize the category "minorities." African Americans are simply childlike, gullible niggers, Native Americans are Injuns, and Jews are "Christ-killin" and "hog-hatin . . . followers of Moses" with prominent noses. And Sut's version of the division of labor between the sexes is equally beyond the pale: "Men wer made a-purpus jis' tu eat, drink, an' fur stayin awake in the yearly part ove the nites: an' wimen wer made tu cook the vittils, mix the sperits, an' help the men du the stayin awake."[33]

Sut's comic incorrectness, one should note, is Whitmanesque; it contains multitudes. He berates, makes fun of, teases, and/or terrorizes other groups perceived as outsiders, such as the Irish and Yankee folks of all sorts, especially when they come to Tennessee to peddle encyclopedias and grind razors. But even when Sut encounters them on their own turf, they turn out not just to have the wrong set of political ideas but also to be unmanly dandies. Indeed, Sut derides anyone who has the wrong politics, referring to a convention of southerners who opposed the Democratic candidate for governor of Tennessee in 1860 as a "love feast ove varmints," which included "pole cats, coons, groun-hogs, minks, house-cats, hoss-cats, hell-cats, weazels, mus-rats, wharf-rats, bull-bats, owls, buzzards, water-dorgs, wild boars, bell weathers, possums, moles, grub-worms and tumble-bugs."[34] This willingness on Sut's part to lambaste even those who seem to be of his community also extends to any hypocrites, especially if they are sanctimonious, like Mrs. Yardley or Mrs. Rogers ("Hen Baily's Reformation"), or in positions of authority, like Sheriff Doltin or Parson Bullen. Even the presidency is not exempt once Lincoln is elected. In one sketch he shows Honest Abe as a flea-ridden, whiskey-guzzling coward who is a bigger fool than Sut. Sut is so ashamed that a man like Lincoln is president that he contemplates cutting Lincoln's throat.[35] Sut's scapegoating and tongue-lashings are truly ecumenical. While that may not excuse Harris in the eyes of some of today's politically sensitive readers—students as well as professional critics—it does suggest that Harris is an equal opportunity purveyor of derision.

Any analysis of Harris's political incorrectness will have to deal with the "incorrectness" of all comic material, however. Jokes in Freud's terms represent hostility displaced onto a verbal plane and presented in a manner designed to evoke that notoriously most politically incorrect of human gestures, laughter.[36] The problem with jokes and, arguably, all comic forms is that they are inherently unstable and ambiguous utterances. Like laughter itself (and smiles), comic forms resist boundaries. And like the child's jack-in-the-box, laughter and the comic forms designed to evoke it will continually pop up to disconcert and surprise us as we crank the handle of serious and correct discourse.

Comic invective like George Washington Harris's against Lincoln or Rush Limbaugh's against feminists ("feminazis") measure how close to the bone an issue cuts or how high the stakes within an issue are perceived to be. Because Freud has taught us that all jokes are tendentious, such rhetorical flourishes as "feminazi" are one way of gauging the depth of aggression felt by some on certain topics. Moreover, because comic material is always ambiguous, some readers will respond seriously while others will not.[37] Laughing at jokes signifies that the locution or representation has been processed as ambiguous, that the listener or audience or reader recognizes the playful, artful "packaging" that does not erase the serious contents but does obscure them, does place them in an ambiguous zone where the serious is being played with, where one plays at being serious. The matter in effect is both serious and not serious—and thus can be responded to in a serious or not-serious way.

Arguably, this dynamic is part of the artistry of authors like George Washington Harris. A more elaborate future analysis of Harris's invective could explore how his comic aggression played with serious issues of his day as well as come to grips with why today's student audience (the only general audience Harris is now likely to have) often resists it. Such analysis would move us past Weber's "genteel tradition" epithet.

Moving past epithets and the ideas embedded in them is necessary to further scholarship on Harris. After all, the charge of coarseness merely recapitulates the critical argument about Sut as fool, for coarseness and foolishness both manifest a fatal flaw from the viewpoint of a polite and ordered society. The dominant scholarly view about Harris has conceptualized Sut as symbolizing all forces arrayed against such a society. Three of the new essays in this volume, however—my own as well as those by Nancy Walker and Pascal Covici—discuss Sut in just the opposite terms, as far more implicated on the side of normality than is usually suspected. This emphasis on the conservative elements of Harris's work suggests that while Sut may usefully be projected as Harris's madcap alter ego, Sut also speaks for Harris's sober, fastidious side. Donald Day's biography shows that Harris did not mind displaying both facets and that close friends of Harris appreciated him accordingly. The fact that Harris, a strict churchgoer, did not mind being called Sut seems to confirm the point.

Walker's examination of Harris vis-à-vis two female comic writers, Frances M. Whitcher and Marietta Holley, shows how all three writers took deliberate satiric aim at similar targets and how they are concerned with a clash of the real and the ideal. My essay suggests how Sut's foolishness constitutes a comic sermonizing about human nature and how such mock preaching both reinforces and ridicules social authority, making Sut a comic champion of southern values. Covici takes the issue of gentility head on, demonstrating how Sut, for all his trickery, represents key concepts of a genteel viewpoint, thus creating a tension between order and disorder. Each of these essays should provoke further debate on how Harris expected his contemporary readers to see Sut in relationship to social norms and customs: supporting them or coarsely and foolishly subverting them (whether intentionally or not).

One aspect of Harris's work that has been explained unsatisfactorily is the function of the violent, repellent, and grotesque elements and their connection with laughter. It is not enough to observe, in trying to explain the darkly comic quality of Harris's work, that the ritually repetitive mayhem of cartoons is similar to Sut's tales, but such links to today's popular culture could be helpful in a continuing discussion. Sanford Pinsker begins an exploration of such linkage by charting Sut's subversiveness not only in comparison with Washington Irving's Rip Van Winkle but with Andrew

Dice Clay's contemporary stand-up comic persona, "the Dice Man." Such links suggest why *Yarns* continued to be printed long past the time when other Southwest humorists were no longer read, but more work is needed here. If we are to gain a hold on Harris's extraordinary talent for invective and other forms of comic hostility, more efforts like Pinsker's will be needed. Further exploration could focus on sketches that did not go into *Yarns* or could compare the book with those uncollected items.

Shelley Armitage also moves into unfamiliar critical territory. Playing off the critical attention that has usually been paid to Harris's gift for imagery and vivid metaphor, Armitage discusses the connection between Harris's use of pictorial qualities to structure and to rhythm his art and attempts by illustrators to re-present visually the feel of the tales. Her analysis is also suggestive, like Pinsker's, of Harris's ability to appeal to emotional levels deep within a psyche.

Yet, for all the analysis by select readers that this volume represents, the basic questions brought up earlier about how Americans read their comic writer return. Why has the work of George Washington Harris survived? Why is it still read? Two facts are crucial in formulating answers. First, the original, uncollected tales were very popular in the 1840s and 1850s, so popular that not even the hiatus of the Civil War could extinguish their appeal, thus guaranteeing that when *Sut Lovingood. Yarns Spun by a "Nat'ral Born Durn'd Fool"* was issued in 1867 it would sell. Next, the momentum from that popularity meant that *Yarns* remained in print throughout the nineteenth century, maintaining its visibility until the field of "American humor" was established in the 1930s as a legitimate academic subject. The time between the waning of that initial popular appeal and modern academic interest was the uncertain moment, and two additional facts that kept Harris relevant seem crucial alongside Harris's initial popularity and the continuous printing of *Yarns*. One was the incorporating of Harris into projects designed to establish a sense of southern culture and pride in its accomplishments, of which *Oddities in Southern Life and Character* (1882) and *Library of Southern Literature* (1907) are examples. The other was the academic discussion at the turn of the century about the role of the frontier in American culture, a discussion that turned all available popular "frontier" writing into potentially valuable documents.

The foregoing overly neat description masks another uncertain "moment" in the survival of George Washington Harris we can glimpse with more questions: Why amid the academic interest in popular comic writers from the nineteenth century has Harris been judged as one of the best of his kind? Why have subsequent scholars reconfirmed Meine's and Blair's early assessments? A start toward answering those questions could be that whatever doubts some individuals may have about Harris's artistry, no one has disputed the three-dimensional comic vitality of Sut Lovingood, a quality that only a handful of fictional characters possess. Certainly before the Civil War only Davy Crockett of the almanacs could match Sut as a source of unrepressed ridicule and hostility—for example, when Davy encounters Mexicans or Sut meets Abe Lincoln. Sut seems particularly good at reminding all readers how close laughter is to hostility. Perhaps that is why Sut has been so popular; it may also account for some of his detractors, both from the genteel tradition and the politically correct.

But Harris's skill in representing Sut is so clearly beyond the anonymous hacks who produced the almanac stories of Davy Crockett that even that comparison pales, for Sut's wondrously comical lack of restraint goes well beyond a willingness to display hostility. For one thing, Sut is unabashed when it comes to yarning about sexuality. For a genre that in general was relatively freewheeling for its time, American comic writings in the nineteenth century were remarkably shy about the basic facts of life. But not Sut. With a gusto and a realism closer to medieval fabliaux than Victorian comic sketches, Sut's tales illustrate both the frustrations and the pleasures of sex. Then there is a feature always celebrated by Harris's advocates—Sut's speech. Unfazed by standards of grammar and pronunciation and unconvinced about the superiority of "proper" ways of talking, Sut speaks in his own east Tennessee dialect, as he demonstrates when he interrupts George's sentimental and literary way of telling a tale to "talk hit all off in English."[38] As pure comic energy, Sut Lovingood may be without peer at any time in the American comic tradition. Moreover, when scholars looked past the fun, as scholars do, they found much to talk about in terms of dialect, folk ways and traditions, narrative traditions, satiric impulse, imagery, and links to regional culture as well as to subsequent American writers.

In short, scholars found Harris was good in the sense that he was truly a frontier artist, with all the historical and folkloric implications attached to that aesthetic judgment. But the other answer must be that scholars reaffirmed the uncritical judgment of the general public. Elite readers, too, find appealing that fantastic representation of id-chaos and ego-community, that fool and fool-killer, Sut Lovingood. Harris is good in the sense that he is downright funny. We may not learn much from that assertion, but it does mean the frog from time to time escapes alive.

Thus, whatever future discussions of George Washington Harris entail, a valuable point of departure is given to us by Hershel Parker, whose essay begins this volume's section of new commentary. Conducting us through a series of reader-response questions that explore Harris's narrative strategies in the Sheriff Doltin sequence, Parker reminds us of *the* most basic, most important point about George Washington Harris: the delight one experiences when being mastered by a natural born yarnspinner.

Notes

1. "Some Remarks on Humor," in *Essays of E. B. White* (New York: Harper and Row, 1977), 243–49. Adapted from the preface to E. B. White and Katherine S. White, eds., *A Subtreasury of American Humor* (New York: Coward-McCann, 1941).
2. Bell Gale Chevigny, *The Woman and the Myth: Margaret Fuller's Life and Writings* (Old Westbury, N.Y.: Feminist Press, 1976), 193.
3. *Dial*, 3 (April 1843), 511–12. Certainly Emerson made no mention of contemporary popular comic writing in his essay "The Comic."
4. See Lewis Leary, "Washington Irving," in *The Comic Imagination in American Literature,* ed. Louis D. Rubin, Jr. (New Brunswick: Rutgers University Press, 1973), 63–76.
5. Two examples of this jingoistic use are "Crockett's Trip to Texas and Fight with the Mexicans" and "Crockett Playing Death with the Mexican Pirates," reprinted in Richard Dorson, ed., *Davy Crockett: American Comic Legend* (New York: Spiral Press, 1939), 93–96. Reprints of other almanacs are Franklin J. Meine, ed., *The Crockett Almanacs: Nashville Series, 1835–1838* (Chicago: Caxton Club, 1955), and Michael A. Lofaro,

ed., *The Tall Tales of Davy Crockett: The Second Nashville Series of Crockett Almanacs, 1839–1841, An Enlarged Facsimile Edition* (Knoxville: University of Tennessee Press, 1987). For critical commentary on the almanacs, see John Seelye, "A Well-Wrought Crockett: Or, How the Fakelorists Passed through the Credibility Gap and Discovered Kentucky," in *Davy Crockett: The Man, The Legend, The Legacy, 1786–1986,* ed. Michael A. Lofaro (Knoxville: University of Tennessee Press, 1985), 21–45.

6. Richard Dorson, "Print and American Folktales," in *American Folklore and the Historian* (Chicago: University of Chicago Press, 1971), 173–85.

7. Clark published his remark in August 1846. Quoted in Frank Luther Mott, *A History of American Magazines,* 4th ed., 3 vols. (Cambridge: Harvard University Press, 1966), 1:424.

8. Norris W. Yates, *William T. Porter and the "Spirit of the Times": A Study of the "Big Bear" School of Humor* (Baton Rouge: Louisiana State University Press, 1957). The stories in both anthologies were gleaned from the pages of Porter's own *Spirit.*

9. Mott notes that in the period 1825–50, "all except the most serious [periodicals] now have their 'Fun Jottings' or 'Joke Corner,' or something analogous" and that between 1850 and 1865 "two score comic periodicals were begun" (*History of American Magazines,* 1:424, 2:179). He has a partial list in n. 132, 2:185.

10. I deliberately echo the titles of two books of scholarship whose publication dates suggest how the slant away from the popular and the comic found in the example of nineteenth-century critics like Fuller dominated twentieth-century academic discussion of the antebellum period: F. O. Matthiessen, *The American Renaissance: Art and Expression in the Age of Emerson and Whitman* (New York: Oxford University Press, 1941), and David S. Reynolds, *Beneath the American Renaissance: The Subversive Imagination in the Age of Emerson and Melville* (Cambridge: Harvard University Press, 1989).

11. See Walter Blair, *Native American Humor* (1937; reprint, with new material, New York: Harper and Row, 1960), 109, n. 2.

12. See H. W. "Slick, Downing, Crockett, Etc.," originally in the December 1838 *London and Westminster Review.* An excerpt is

reprinted in *Critical Essays on American Humor,* ed. William Bedford Clark and W. Craig Turner (Boston: G. K. Hall, 1984), 19–22. For Browne's success, see John J. Pullen, *Comic Relief: The Life and Laughter of Artemus Ward, 1834–1867* (Hamden, Conn.: Archon Books, 1983), 163–67.

13. "Introduction," in Paul M. Zall, ed., *Abe Lincoln Laughing: Humorous Anecdotes from Original Sources by and About Abraham Lincoln* (Berkeley and Los Angeles: University of California Press, 1982).

14. After "The Snake-bit Irishman" was published, Porter praised Harris in print and/or asked for more material on at least three separate occasions: 17 January 1846; 3 March 1849; 14 October 1854. See Donald Day's biography in this volume.

15. Walter Blair and Hamlin Hill provide a long list of such writers in *America's Humor: From Poor Richard to Doonesbury* (Oxford: Oxford University Press, 1978), 289.

16. Willard Thorpe, "Suggs and Sut in Modern Dress: The Latest Chapter in Southern Humor," *Mississippi Quarterly* 13 (1959): 169–75. Nancy Snell Griffith, *Humor of the Old Southwest: An Annotated Bibliography of Primary and Secondary Sources* (Westport, Conn.: Greenwood Press, 1989).

17. Henry Watterson, *Oddities in Southern Life and Character* (1882; reprint; Boston: Houghton Mifflin, 1910).

18. From "The Study of Poetry," in *The Works of Matthew Arnold,* 15 vols. (London: Macmillan, 1903), 4:26, originally published in 1880 as the general introduction to *The English Poets,* ed. T. H. Ward. E. B. White notes that the world "decorates its serious writers with laurel, and its wags with Brussels sprouts" ("Some Remarks on Humor," 244). Mott, *History of American Magazines,* says that in the late 1860s and early 1870s both American and English critics complained about the plethora of comic material and its vulgarity (3:264).

19. A recent exception to this rule is Gwendolyn B. Gwathmy, "'Who will read the book, Samantha?': Marietta Holley and the 19th century Reading Public," *Studies in American Humor,* n.s. 3, 1 (1994): 28–50.

20. Howells, "Mark Twain," in *Critical Essays on Mark Twain, 1867–1910,* ed. Louis J. Budd (Boston: G. K. Hall, 1982), 54–60. I do not think it accidental that Howells claims Mark Twain has what Matthew Arnold says Chaucer lacks—that

underlying earnestness so prized within Anglo-American Victorian culture.

21. Lang (87–90) and Yates (42–45) in Budd, *Critical Essays on Mark Twain.*

22. William P. Trent, "A Retrospect of American Humor," in Clark and Turner, *Critical Essays on American Humor,* 42, and "Mark Twain as an Historical Novelist," in Budd, *Critical Essays on Mark Twain,* 118–21.

23. Jeannette Tandy, *Crackerbox Philosophers in American Humor and Satire* (New York: Columbia University Press, 1925), 93–94. Faulkner's letter is published in James G. Watson, ed., *Thinking of Home: William Faulkner's Letters to his Mother and Father, 1918–1925* (New York: W. W. Norton, 1992), 191–93. The interview was in 1956 and is printed in Malcolm Cowley, ed., *Writers at Work: The "Paris Review" Interviews* (New York: Viking Press, 1958), 119–42.

24. Gerald Graff, *Professing Literature: An Institutional History* (Chicago: University of Chicago Press, 1987).

25. Griffith, *Annotated Bibliography,* 34–40, 53–57, 95–109, 122–27, 142–47, 202–08.

26. Jerre Mangione, *The Dream and the Deal: The Federal Writers' Project, 1935–1943* (Boston: Little, Brown, 1972), 263–77.

27. For an overview of debate on Turner's frontier thesis, see Gerald D. Nash, *Creating the West: Historical Interpretations, 1890–1990* (Albuquerque: University of New Mexico Press, 1991). Examples of early scholarly interest in the frontier's relationship to literature are Jay Hubbell, "The Frontier in American Literature," *Southwest Review* 10 (1925): 86–92, and Lucy L. Hazard, *The Frontier in American Literature* (New York: Thomas Y. Crowell, 1927). Vernon Parrington, *Main Currents in American Thought,* vol. 2, *The Romantic Revolution in America, 1800–1860* (1927; reprint, New York: Harcourt, Brace, Jovanovich, 1954), includes a section called "The Frontier in Letters," which discusses Longstreet and Crockett.

28. Franklin J. Meine, ed., *Tall Tales of the Southwest: An Anthology of Southern and Southwestern Humor, 1830–1860* (New York: Alfred A. Knopf, 1930); Constance Rourke, *American Humor: A Study of the National Character* (1931; reprint, New York: Harcourt, Brace, Jovanovich, 1959).

29. Van Wyck Brooks, *The Ordeal of Mark Twain* (New York: E. P. Dutton, 1920); Bernard DeVoto, *Mark Twain's America* (1932; reprint, Boston: Houghton Mifflin, 1967).

30. Meine, *Tall Tales*, xxiv.

31. For an extended discussion of dialect as a sign of the comic, see Neil Schmitz, *Of Huck and Alice: Humorous Writing in American Literature* (Minneapolis: University of Minnesota Press, 1983).

32. Blair's and Rickels's comments are in the selections for this volume. Inge's can be found in "Sut Lovingood: An Examination of the Nature of a 'Nat'ral Born Durn'd Fool,'" *Tennessee Historical Quarterly* 19 (1960): 231–51.

33. Quotes taken respectively from "Sut Lovingood's Hog Ride," in M. Thomas Inge, ed., *High Times and Hard Times: Sketches and Tales by George Washington Harris* (Nashville: Vanderbilt University Press, 1967), 157; and "Sicily Burns's Wedding," in George Washington Harris, *"Sut Lovingood. Yarns": A Facsimile of the 1867 Dick and Fitzgerald Edition*, ed. M. Thomas Inge (Memphis: Saint Lukes Press, 1987), 88.

34. "Sut Lovingood's Love Feast Ove Varmints, I," in Inge, *High Times*, 238.

35. "Sut Lovingood Lands Old Abe Safe at Last," in ibid., 274.

36. Sigmund Freud, *Jokes and Their Relation to the Unconscious*, ed. and trans. James Strachey (1960; reprint, New York: W. W. Norton, 1963), 93.

37. For a serious discussion of political correctness, see Judith Frank, "In the Waiting Room: Canons, Communities, 'Political Correctness,'" in *Wild Orchids and Trotsky: Messages from American Universities*, ed. Mark Edmundson (New York: Penguin Books USA, 1993), 125–50. Frank makes the point that the term "political correctness" is used ironically by activists "as a kind of check to *themselves* in their political zeal" (128).

38. Harris, "Eaves-dropping a Lodge of Free-masons," in *"Sut Lovingood. Yarns,"* 116.

Section One
Historical Background

The Life of George Washington Harris

Donald Day

I. The Early Years

There is little information extant on George Washington Harris's ancestors and early life. This has necessitated garnering from letters and newspaper material which, when placed together, form only a fragmentary picture.

George Harris, father of George Washington, was probably born in Virginia and left there for North Carolina in the troubled days following the Revolutionary War. There, he became associated with Samuel Bell and accompanied him to Washington County, Pennsylvania, at an unknown date. Either in North Carolina or in Pennsylvania, Samuel married and a son, Samuel, Junior, was born on July 15, 1798. Subsequently Samuel Bell, Senior, died and George Harris married his widow. To this union George Washington was born on March 20, 1814, in Allegheny City (now a part of Pittsburgh), Pennsylvania.[1]

Young Samuel Bell was apprenticed to an arms factory at the outbreak of the War of 1812, and at once "giving evidence of his deftness he was put to work making swords for use in the struggle."[2] When the war was over he continued his apprenticeship, receiving a thorough training in metal working. In 1819, having served his apprenticeship, he yielded to the attraction of the boundless Southwest

Tennessee Historical Quarterly 6 (1947): 3–38.

and traveled down the Ohio. Eventually he reached Knoxville, on the upper Tennessee River, and decided to settle in that city.

What prompted Samuel to make this decision is not known. Knoxville was then a straggling frontier village with fewer than a thousand inhabitants, although the country around was well settled. Perhaps its location at the confluence of the Holston and French Broad rivers, which form the Tennessee, convinced him that the city might have a commercial future. Creeks were plentiful, and within a space of half a mile on First Creek, three mill ponds furnished power to small but thriving mills.[3] Perhaps he was attracted by the natural beauty of the place. Lying in the foothills of the Clinch and Chilhowee mountains and in the valley between the Cumberland and the Great Smoky Mountain ranges, Knoxville offered easy access to almost every variety of scenery. Or, perhaps, the slow tempo of the sleepy village in the "peaceful valley" may have been a relief from the hurly-burly that had already enveloped Allegheny City.[4]

Samuel went back to Allegheny City, married, and returned to Knoxville with his bride and half-brother, George Washington Harris. In Knoxville, he established a combined dwelling and work shop at the corner of Main and Prince (now Market) streets.[5] Whether the mother of the two boys and George Washington Harris's father accompanied them is not known. The records simply do not reveal what became of them.

Samuel soon attained a wide reputation in Knoxville and the surrounding country for his skill and workmanship. Dr. Mellen said:

> The skill he exhibited as a workman with precious metals was equally displayed in the fashioning of pistols, swords, dirks and other weapons. Old Tennessee families still have in their possession specimens of his handiwork to which they refer with pride. The impress of Sam Bell's on any article was a guarantee of its genuineness and durability.[6]

Undoubtedly Samuel Bell's skill influenced George's development as a worker in metals. Life in the little village, with its frontier amusements that followed the pattern of the day, might be inferred as a causal factor in his development, yet Harris gives little hint in his writings that these things played an important part in his life. . . . George was disturbed very little by the schoolroom. He received not more than eighteen months of schooling, probably spaced over a period of three years.

In 1826[7] when George was twelve, a steamboat made its way for the first time through the "Suck" where the Tennessee River cuts through the Cumberland Range, and tied up at Knoxville. If the daily coming of a steamboat could awaken sleepy Hannibal to such a frenzy,[8] what must have happened to Knoxville when the *Atlas* put in its appearance? Little inference and less imagination is needed to picture George staring at it with wide-open eyes and asking countless questions about its operation. The commander, Captain Conner, was given an ovation by the citizens of Knoxville and a company was immediately formed for the purchase of a steamboat to ply the river. W. B. A. Ramsey was dispatched to Cincinnati to contract for the building of the boat, which arrived a few months later and was christened the *Knoxville*.[9]

George soon thereafter began building a miniature steamboat of his own. Perhaps Samuel Bell helped him. If not, Samuel must have been a sympathetic taskmaster or he would not have permitted the boy to take time from his other duties for something that many men would have considered a foolish waste of energy and time. When the little steamboat was finished, George announced that on a certain day he would give a public exhibition on the "flag pond," a wide shallow pond in the center of the village. Report has it that the boat worked well and excited the interest and admiration of the spectators.[10]

This anecdote shows that George was a skillful worker. At least Samuel Bell was so impressed with his ability that he apprenticed him in his jewelry shop.[11] But more important than the skill shown was the early emergence of a creative desire and a capacity for showmanship. . . .

While George was learning under the careful eye of Samuel Bell, Knoxville plodded along with little change. Most of the settlers heading for the West streamed around or through Knoxville to the more fertile lands of Middle Tennessee and Northern Alabama. However, in 1835 a canal was completed to Lynchburg, Virginia, and about the same time steamboats began plying regularly between Knoxville and Decatur, Alabama, thereby making Knoxville the center of an important wholesale trade in drygoods and groceries.[12]

Soon after finishing his apprenticeship, Harris married Mary Emeline Nance, daughter of Peter Nance of Knoxville, on September 3, 1835.[13] Apparently he continued his interest in steamboats and steamboating, for in the same year he was made captain of the *Knoxville*.[14] Such responsibility, reposed in a boy who had just reached his majority, cannot be taken lightly. It is true that capable men were being drawn away constantly by the lure of the West, yet Harris must have evidenced a more than ordinary sense of responsibility or he never would have been entrusted with this important position.

Captain Harris was small of stature, active and alert, but quiet and sedate. He was always neatly dressed, and was kind, and scorned both the officious person and the bully.[15] His adequacy as a captain is shown by the fact that he commanded the *Knoxville* until 1838, when it was rechristened the *Indian Chief*. At that time, Harris was commissioned to help move the Cherokee Indians farther west.[16] Three anecdotes which grew up around him in this period are worth recording since they throw light upon his character. During one of Harris's trips as captain of the *Indian Chief*, the Cherokees were packed and jammed on the boat and a barge which the boat was towing. Day by day the Indians evidenced an increasing discontent that showed signs of breaking out into open rebellion at any moment. Captain Harris had received orders that under no circumstances was he to permit the drinking of intoxicating liquors by the Indians. One afternoon the *Indian Chief* tied up on the bank of the river in order to permit the Indians to go ashore. Captain Harris had watched a big sullen brave all day and as this man crossed over the gangplank, he saw that something was hidden under the blanket which draped his shoulders. He followed the Indian and found him behind some bushes, surrounded by a number of braves, taking a drink from a jug. He shouldered his way up to him, eyed him sternly, and ordered the jug to be broken. Growls and muttered curses came from the Indians. The brave raised the jug angrily, paused momentarily at the look in Captain Harris's gray eyes, then broke it. Captain Harris said later that if he had ordered the Indian to give the jug to him rather than to break it, he would have been a dead man. There was no more drinking on that trip, at least by the Indians.[17]

A second anecdote was related by the late Colonel John Bell Brownlow, son of the famous "Parson" Brownlow, to J. Cleveland Harris, of Knoxville:

> The boat {*Indian Chief*} was lashed in the willows at the mouth of First Creek {now in the center of this city} with a gangplank lying from the shore to the gunwale of the boat. A stranger in civilian garb, without any announcement of his authority or purpose, was about to pass onto the boat when Capt. Harris raised his hand above his head and ordered the stranger to "Halt!" The stranger proceeded across the gangway heedlessly, and when he had stepped aboard the boat, Harris lay upon him, beat him mercilessly, and threw him

bodily overboard and into the river. Much to Capt. Harris' surprise, but maybe not to his chagrin, it soon developed that the stranger was none other than an officer of the United States Navy Department on a tour of survey and inspection.[18]

A better known anecdote was told to Dr. George F. Mellen by Dr. James Park, pastor of the Presbyterian church to which Harris belonged for many years:

> As a highranking officer of the United States Army, Gen. Winfield Scott had to do with the supervision of the removal of the Cherokees. While Harris, with his steamboat and barges, was on the way, Gen. Scott came on board down the Tennessee River, near Ross' Landing now Chattanooga. The sobriquet, "Old Fuss and Feathers," was eminently appropriate to General Scott. He criticised severely the arrangements of Capt. Harris, and peremptorily ordered changes. Harris, a little fellow whose steps measured about fifteen inches, in his quick, nervous way, stepped up, informed the pompous Scott that he himself commanded the boat, and wanted to know the authority for interference. Looking disdainfully upon the insignificant youngster, Scott asked him who he was. Harris, without preliminaries or apologies, told him that he was entrusted with that boat, with the barges and all on board, and that he could manage it to suit himself. Thereupon, Scott took off his hat, apologized, and refrained from intruding with his {sic} own orders.[19]

A dangerous Indian, an officious stranger (perhaps Harris was aware of his identity), and "Old Fuss and Feathers" himself, all looked alike to Captain Harris. This trait of independence in Harris is significant for an understanding of his character.

In 1839 Harris quit steamboating, and soon thereafter contracted for a sizable tract of land in neighboring Blount County, where he began farming. This land was on a branch of Nails Creek and the waters of Little River close to "Tuckalucky" (Tucaleeche) Cove, at the gateway to the Great Smoky Mountains.[20] No doubt as a boy Harris had made many trips into the region, but close proximity certainly gave a leisurely opportunity for its topography and people to influence his development.

It was while living on this farm that Harris first entered the "comedy of the pen," writing political articles for the Knoxville *Argus and Commercial Herald,* the official organ of the Democratic party in East Tennessee under the editorship of Elbridge G. Eastman. The file of the *Argus* is extant but none of the many political articles in it bears indelibly the stamp of Harris's pen, and other papers published at the same time, unfortunately, give no clues.[21]

Harris had bought the farm on credit, agreeing to make annual payments for the next four years.[22] In December, 1840, shortly after his first note on the farm came due, an indenture was made on his household goods and farming implements to Peter Nance and Pryor Nance, who had endorsed his note, for nonpayment.[23] A listing of the personal property covered by the indenture shows several important things:

> Seven bedsteads, three beds and bedding, two bureaus, one book case, 75 books, one Bible, 1 dressing table, 1 kitchen Do, 2 dressing Do, 1 candle stand, 1 fire screen, 1 fine looking glass, four trunks, 1 dozen of windsor chairs, 7 split-bottom, one fine carpet (32 yards), one map of the world, 1 corner cupboard, 1 tin safe, 1 cradle, one rifle gun, 2 pr fire dogs, 1 pr shovel and tongs, one fine wire fender, 7 pots & ovens, 2 skillets, 1 grid iron, 1 wash kettle, one set of cupboard ware, 1 cross-cut saw, 6 hogs-heads, ten barrels, 1 straw cutter, 1 wheat fan, 2 harrows, 5 ploughs, 1 wagon and harness for horses, one gray horse, one gray mare, one sorrel colt, 7 head of cattle, 6 head of hogs, 10 head of sheep, 1 Irish sow, one vise, one anvil, worn, 1 set of carpenter's tools, 2 cradles and blades, 2 mowing scythes, 2 mattocks, one spade, one shovel, 2 dung forks, 4 pitch forks, one frow, 4 troughs, 1 hand saw, 4 augers, 1 hand saw, 1 saw set.

First, this was a great deal of equipment for a young farmer buying a farm on credit. Secondly, if it showed poor financial management, it also pointed to the significant fact that Harris wanted to do things well and wanted the equipment for so doing. Third, he desired good things for his family and himself. One dozen windsor chairs in addition to ordinary chairs, a "fine looking glass," thirty-two yards of "fine carpet,"—these things were not for a struggling young farmer trying to get a start. Lastly, his ownership of seventy-five books pointed to some interest in literature. Couple these deductions with his interest in politics, the location of the farm on Nails Creek and Little River, both good fishing streams, the proximity of good hunting, quiltings, cornhuskings, and an increasing family, and the indenture is easily understood.

But there were other debts. On the 24th of December, 1840, Harris gave a bill of sale on a Negro boy slave named Jasper to cover a hundred dollars which he had borrowed from William Wallace on the 22nd of August of that year.[24] On the 31st day of December, 1840, he gave another bill of sale on the same boy to cover debts due to merchants in Maryville.[25] On December 29, 1840, he made an indenture on a "certain bay mare now about five years old" in order to secure the payment of one hundred dollars due William Swan of Knoxville.[26] Records of this sort are not available on Harris for his later life, but perhaps a statement made by Mr. E. Y. Chapin of Chattanooga, a great lover of Harris's stories who knew many men personally acquainted with Harris, is correct:

"Sut" (Harris) showed the aptitude for business which a reader of his yarns might expect; yet he was always ready to tackle it; and his financial condition was always a spur toward income from any source.[27]

What a tragical combination of qualities in a man! Spurred on always by ambition and desire; capable, but caught by a world that rewards those who can gear their capacities to an entirely different order of things.

Harris lost the Negro boy Jasper on February 7, 1842,[28] but the records do not show what became of the farm, nor is it known definitely when he left it and moved back to Knoxville. However, the Knoxville *Argus* carried the following advertisement under date of February 1, 1843:

NEW WORK SHOP
IN THE METALS GENERALLY
Corner of Prince and Cumberland Streets
Knoxville, Tenn.

———

GEORGE W. HARRIS,

Has commenced business at the above stand, with the best of *Tools and Machinery,* where he will be ready at all times to execute work cheap, workmanlike and at the time promised, in the following branches:

JEWELRY AND SILVER WARE,

Copper-plate and Wood Engraving, and stereotyping; County and Corporation Seals, die sinking in a style equal to any; *Models* of new inventions for the Patent office or exhibition, with or without drawings. Every variety of turning in *Steel, Iron,* or *Brass.* Screws cut of any number, from 8 threads to 65 per inch, right or left handed, and as long as 5 feet. Surgeons' and Dentists' instruments; Mathematical and Philosophical ditto; model Steam-engines for Colleges, &c.

RACING CUPS,

from the latest English models, in gold or silver, and in fact almost any work in metals. Clocks, watches, jewelry, silverware, guns, pistols, &c., carefully repaired.

He respectfully asks a trial from the people of East Tennessee who have heretofore been compelled to send their orders abroad for such work as he now offers to do.[29]

Again Harris "commenced business . . . with the best of *Tools and Machinery*." There is evidence that he used this equipment skillfully. The Knoxville *Register* said:

> Capt. George W. Harris . . . {is} well known in these parts for his ability to shape the metals at his pleasure into any form that can possibly be conceived—ranging from a tenpenny nail up to a high-pressure steam engine. Well aware of the exceeding modesty of the captain, and not desiring to put him to blush, we will not say (what we nevertheless firmly believe), that, both in regard to design and execution, he has a most remarkable genius, and that he is one of the cleverest fellows we have ever known.[30]

The Knoxville *Standard* added: "The Captain has executed this work (an engraving) as well as it could be done at any other place—just as he does all work sent to his shop."[31]

In July, 1843, Harris joined with the mechanics of Knoxville in complaining about the practice of allowing the training of convicts in the penitentiary and the sale of their products in competition with the products of other mechanics. An open letter was addressed "TO THE MECHANICS OF EAST TENNESSEE,"[32] through the medium of the press over the signature of a committee of three, headed by George W. Harris. Their outcries were heard in the legislative halls at Nashville and the general assembly of the state (1843–4) redressed their wrongs.[33] In the same series of acts the "Mechanic's Library Association" of Knoxville was incorporated, naming George W. Harris as one of its members.[34]

II. Earlier Writings

Knoxville offered no outlet for writing other than in the field of politics or an occasional article in the "polite" fields of education, manners, or sentiment. Fortunately, a medium existed in William T. Porter's New York *Spirit of the Times*, which filled the gap between the local papers and the literary journals. The *Spirit*, as its subtitle indicates, was a weekly *Chronicle of the Turf, Agriculture, Field Sports, Literature and the Stage*. Started originally as a sporting journal, it had expanded its field until by 1845 it had an international circulation.[35] Its readers and contributors were scattered over the face of the earth "from Hudson's Bay to the Caribbean Sea, from the shores of the Atlantic to the Pacific,"[36] and included every conceivable occupation and interest. The influence of such a medium was cumulative. Readers of the journal became contributors when they saw their neighbors "in print," and they, in turn, encouraged other readers to try their hands. As a result story telling that had been mostly oral heretofore began to find its way into print and was further encouraged by a boisterous, highly appreciative audience, presided over by "York's Tall Son"—Porter. These factors fostered and brought into focus the humor of the frontier, with the *Spirit* as its "principle mouthpiece."[37]

Naturally, some of the widespread readers of the *Spirit* were in Knoxville. The Knoxville *Times* for August 23, 1839, said of the *Spirit*: "To those who wish a periodical, comprising excellent literary selections, valuable agricultural information, and all the sporting news of the day, we most cheerfully recommend it." Horse racing, the chief sporting interest of the *Spirit*,[38] was so popular in Tennessee that in 1840 Porter announced that he had special paid reporters for the meets in that state.[39] Harris may have become acquainted with the *Spirit* through an interest in horse racing, an interest which he may have had from youth, since he said in a story about himself at fifteen: "I was gently plying my horse on the off side with my heel and hickory to stir him up a little. I had ridden a few quarter races in my time, and was pretty well up to the dodge."[40]

In 1843 Harris began writing "sporting epistles" for the *Spirit* over the pseudonym of "Mr. Free."[41] These epistles are valuable sources of biographical information in that they give hints of his activities and interests outside of his "metal working" shop. In the first epistle, dated from Knox County, East Tennessee, January 23, 1843,[42] Harris bemoaned that in these times of "scarcity and pressure" the sporting men around Knoxville "have to amuse themselves with the cheaper sports: such as Quarter racing, Cockfighting, Deer-driving, Fox, Coon and 'Possum-hunting, Turkey-shooting, and Partridge-netting." He described the "very pleasant sport" of partridge-netting, then recounted his experiences on a coon hunt with Tom D., who "is known a hundred miles round, as the owner of 'Old Turkey Reacher'; the best rifle you ever heard tell of!" The second epistle was dated from "'Possum Knob, East Tenn.," March 27, 1843,[43] and describes a quarter race that took place at the Stock-Creek Paths, near where Harris had lived on the farm. His third epistle, dated June 6, 1843,[44] has a mournful note because the spring racing meet in Knoxville had not materialized. He added that "at the present time preaching thrives and matrimony is all the go. Such is always the case in times of pecuniary distress." The epistle ends with an invitation to Porter to visit Knoxville, and after setting forth the inducements, Harris concluded that "here lies open a wide field, on which the lover of sport can roam at his pleasure and never tire; that is, if seeing an occasional race, hunting, fishing, contemplating the beauties of nature and seeing humanity in all its varieties, possess for him any charms."

The fourth and last epistle, dated August 15, 1843, shows that Harris was still interested in politics. He said:

> I have been so *monstrous* busy, riding about, making so many speeches, soliciting votes, cajoling the husbands, shaking hands with the wives, kissing the children, and giving them dimes and half dimes, treating temperance men to watermelons, and topers to *old Bald-face*, that it was not possible for me to attend that Quarter Race on the 4th of July, in Tuck-a-lucky Cove, between those notorious crowders, *Terrapin and Snapping Turtle*. . . .[45]

Evidently, Harris had offered for an office, but he was saved from inglorious defeat by having "drawn back a few days before the election, and giving the other candidates a 'clear field.'" His colleagues "fought the battle manfully, but were all conquered, save one."

Harris immediately put this defeat behind him and described a "'log-rolling' and 'quilting' in Tuck-a-lucky" and a "corn-shucking" in Morgan, where "things are done up brown!" He ended by assuring his readers that "any gentleman wishing for 'variety,' which you know, is the 'spice of life,' can have the pleasure of being shucked into one end of Morgan County, and danced out at the other, by applying to Your humble-cum-tumble, MR. FREE."

Certainly, Harris spiced his life with plenty of variety during this period unless one is naive enough to assume that he sat in his shop and imagined pictures like this [from his 15 August epistle]:

> The music sounds high, and the wild woods ring; the feet of the company fly thick and fast; reels, cotillions and waltzes, are all so mingled and blended together that it is a dance without a name. The mirth becomes uproarious, the men jump high, "cut the pigeon wing," and crack their heels together; the women shed their brogens—here they fly and there they go—and now in nature's slippers they feel more "at home," and "joy unconfined" continues as long as breath and toenails last.

In addition to sporting and social activities, Harris had time for more serious interests. The Knoxville *Register* for June 19, 1844, carried the following notice:

THE YOUNG MEN'S LITERARY SOCIETY

At its meeting on Tuesday evening of last week, elected the following offi-cers for the ensuing three months:

Dr. Jas. W. Paxton, President
Jno. L. Moses, Vice President
A. R. Crozier, Recording Secretary
Geo. W. Harris, Treasurer
Dr. F. A. Ramsey, Librarian

This society, although it has but just entered upon the third year of its exis-tence, is probably second to no institution of a similar character in the State. Its library, which already contains many Standard works—and its museum, are constantly receiving valuable acquisitions; and among its members—of whom there are now about thirty-five—are many of our most worthy and intelligent citizens.

Certainly, Harris devoted a portion of his busy life to his family. His daughter, Mrs. Raymond, said that he was always considerate as a husband and a father, thoughtful, and seemed to relish keenly his family life.[46] She has a silver spoon with which she keeps the fol-lowing memorandum written in her father's hand:

Made by David L. Hope in Knoxville, Tenn. One dozen of these spoons were my Christmas gift to my wife, 1844. I engraved the stamps for Hope, with which they were stamped. I also engraved the M.E.H. on them—my wife's initials. The silver out of which they were made was the saddle mountings and belonged to Tippo Sahib.[47] Bought by me from Doct. Black of Amster-dam. I am satisfied of the authenticity of this.[48]

An epistle that appeared in the *Spirit of The Times* on June 21, 1845, over the pseudonym of "The Man in the Swamp," next excited Harris to write. This correspondent made the statement that he had never heard the expression "don't crowd the mourners" ex-cept in East Tennessee, and concluded the epistle by saying that East Tennessee had degenerated until the old time fun had been re-placed by "politics and religion." Harris replied [in the same issue of the *Spirit*] with his first full length story entitled "The Knob Dance—A Tennessee Frolic," prefacing it with some jabs at "The Man in the Swamp," and wondering if that worthy was at "'ar-a-frolick' while he was in East Tennessee." Then Harris described the "frolic" as proof-positive that "The Man in the Swamp" was mis-taken about his deductions as to amusements in East Tennessee. This story indicates that Harris was still interested in fun, "from a *kiss* that cracks like a wagin-whip up to a *fite* that rouses up all outdoors." He submitted it over the pseudonym "Sugartail," which he was sure to use for a number of years. Mr. Robert T. Quarles, assistant archivist of Tennessee, explained that "Sugartail" is a designation given in the mountainous regions to a donkey because of the resemblance of its tail to a stalk of sugar cane.[49]

"The Man in the Swamp" lashed back at Harris in "Fun in East Tennessee" [*Spirit*, 6 September 1845] and reiterated his position that "unless a man takes delight in politics or religion he will find East Tennessee a dull place." He admitted that in out-of-the-way places frolics like that described by "Sugartail" might be found, "but they don't do them up brown like they used to." He then proceeded to tell of the good old days:

> I can recollect when the Natives met from the North and South side of Bay's Mountains, at the county seat of little Massachusetts, and sometimes there would be twenty couples fighting at one time. One of my ancestors figured at one of those pitched battles. The weapon he used differed from that used by Free's ("Sugartails'") Father; he (Free's Father) used a long stick with a bit of sythe {sic} on the end of it, but my ancestor used a short thick stick, and I am told he made lane where-ever he went. . . .

This spirited exchange of verbal blows with "The Man in the Swamp" and the reception given to "The Knob Dance" must have aroused Harris's literary ambitions. He and "The Man in the Swamp" evidently corresponded and made some plans together, for in an epistle entitled "Sayings and Doings in East Tennessee," over the pseudonym of "Roderick," the following appears:

> Have you heard anything of the "Smokey Mountain Panther?" a book to be published by "Sugartail" and "The Man in the Swamp?" It is now in the womb of the future, but I trust they will bring it forth ere long. It is to be illustrative of the manners and customs of East Tennessee—containing an account of Bear and Panther fights, Quarter racing, Card playing, anecdotes of the Rev. Anley, etc. etc., with illustrations.[50]

In the *Spirit* of November 22, 1845, in a column addressed "To Correspondents," Porter said: "G.W.H. Have your note of the 13th, and shall be glad to meet you at your earliest convenience." Evidently Harris contemplated a trip to New York at this time. Perhaps he hoped to make arrangements for the publication of the "Smokey Mountain Panther" or, perhaps, he had hopes of obtaining a soft berth at Washington through E. G. Eastman, who had been there since Polk's inauguration.[51] If Harris made this trip, he was unsuccessful in both of his endeavors. On January, 17, 1846, "The Snake-bit Irishman" appeared in the *Spirit* and almost immediately brought Harris more fame. In the column "To Correspondents," Porter wrote:

> "Sugartail"—(Phoebus! What a name!) has not an indefinite leave of absence. A gentleman who can write at heat such stories as "The Snake-bit Irishman," is just naturally "bound to shine," as was "Dandy Jim of Caroline."[52]

Harris's next literary effort appeared [in the *Spirit* on 12 September 1846] as "A Sleep Walking Incident," which opens with a nostalgic note. Perhaps an item that appeared in the Knoxville *Register* at about that time helps to explain this nostalgia: "Persons visiting *David L. Hope's place of business* . . . will find on the spot a certain Captain George W. Harris. . . ."[53] This indicates that Harris had lost the ownership of the shop. If true, this loss, combined with his failures at New York and Washington, certainly gave sufficient cause for a nostalgic outburst.

Harris's actions during the next year may be followed only by occasional notices in the newspapers. In May, 1847, an "Internal Improvement Meeting" was held at Knoxville for the purpose of "improving our rivers and constructing suitable roads for the accommodation of the trade and travel of the country" and to plan for "the assembling of a general Convention at Rogersville, on Thursday the 27th." Harris was appointed as one of the delegates to attend the convention.[54] In June a public meeting was held at Knoxville "in honor of soldiers who fought in the Mexican War." It was resolved that the citizens of Knox County "tender the volunteers of Tenn. a public entertainment on the 3d day of July, 1847" and Harris was appointed on the "Committee of Toasts."[55]

On March 16, 1847, the following significant item appeared in the Knoxville *Standard:*

> Capt. G. W. Harris called at our office on Saturday last, to take an impression of a head for "The Daily Union," and also one for the "National Union," which he has engraved for the publisher of the Union at Nashville.

E. G. Eastman had returned from Washington to assume the editorship of the Nashville *Union,* and had again befriended Harris by giving him this commission. In October, 1847, Harris's next story, "There's Danger in Old Chairs,"[56] appeared in Eastman's paper as written by "the Author of 'The Snake-bit Irishman.'" The story was reprinted in the *Spirit* [on 4 December 1847] and in the Knoxville *Standard* [on 19 October 1847].

For the next three years, arid ones in writings, Harris's life can be followed by Boswellian correspondents, "Dresback" and "Charlie," in the *Spirit*. For instance, only in an epistle by "Dresback" in the *Spirit* [on 16 October 1847] is there a hint that Harris was seeking a new vocation:

> . . . a company of jolly good fellows are going to the Chilhowee Mountains for *Bar* about the 25th inst. I shall be along, and so will "Sugartail," if he don't get elected; he has gone to Nashville now, to offer for a very important office in the gift of the Tennessee Senate. If he is along, look out for a rich report of *one grand Bar hunt.*

Harris was not even considered seriously for the office at Nashville. A letter from Miss Lutie C. Jones, assistant librarian, State of Tennessee, reads:

> I . . . have looked again in the Journals of 1847–48 and the only mention that I can find of George Washington Harris is in the election of a principal clerk. . . . Among those voted for—Mr. Rowles voted for George W. Harris. His name was not put in nomination as the others were, but in giving the vote. . . . This was for Clerk of the Senate, but I looked in the House Journal for the same period but did not find that he was a candidate for office.[57]

[On 5 March 1848] a note from Porter addressed to Harris appeared in "To Correspondents" of the *Spirit* offering "to send you such a Newfoundland dog as you describe for $50." Perhaps the incongruity of a small man wanting a Newfoundland dog aided the *Spirit* in securing a new correspondent, for on April 8th "Charlie" wrote in an epistle entitled "Stirring up an Old Correspondent":

> "What do you think?" said our friend "the Judge," last Saturday morning, meeting "S——l" and myself in the street. "What do you think?" with a quizzical puckering of his eyelids, so habitual with him. . . . "the Captain here, ('S——l') has written to Porter for a Newfoundland dog to cost *fifty cents!*" "What!" "Fact, sir; you may see it in the notice 'to correspondents,' and moreover, he is to pay Porter 5 per cent for purchasing." "S——l" va-*mosed* before I had sufficiently recovered to ask him, what in the world he needed with such an expensive dog!

"Charlie's" chief motive, however, was to stir up "S——l" again. He saw "S——l" daily but "spiritually S——l was missing," and it was in that light that "Charlie" wanted to see him again. What was to be done?

> This question has puzzled the brains of all your friends and his in these parts for some time past. We have repeatedly called upon him personally, to renew his correspondence—but to no purpose it seems, for he still

maintains a dogged silence although he is as usual, profuse in his promises. This, by the way, is a weak point in "S——l," (he will excuse me for saying so,) but like other men, he would be better off in the world had he the courage to say "no!" Not in matters of this kind, however—don't mistake me. As a general thing, I mean, you (S——l) are entirely too good natured.

"Charlie" was a doctor[58] and beneath the banter that he heaped upon Harris in this passage was a solid foundation of fact. He referred to Harris's fondness for many things—amusement, sport, drink—and, truly, Harris would have been better off "in the world" if he had had the courage to say "no!" to many things, perhaps even to writing stories.

It seems that at this time Harris was turning his creative instincts to things mechanical. "Charlie" said that "'S——l' . . . is preparing an account of {his} great discovery for Sillimon's Journal,[59] or some other scientific work. . . ."[60] "Charlie" then added that "you would scarcely have supposed our friend to have been engaged in abstruse studies, a day or two since, when he came charging down the street with a 'cock and bull' story . . . " which was very good, "particularly when you hear it told by 'S——l'" although it was "incompatible with the dignity of a philosopher!"

"Charlie's" epistle performed another valuable service when it stirred up "Dresback" by accusing him of devoting his Sundays to a perusal of the *Spirit*. "Dresback" emphatically stated that "is a fabrication of your ("Charlie's") own brain; for you know—like 'S——l,' I am a church going man."[61] "Charlie" replied [in the *Spirit* on 4 June 1848], reiterating the charge, and defended himself against another charge that involved "S——l":

The manner in which your printer murdered the story quoted from "S——l," in my last, brought that worthy "down upon me like a thousand bricks" (in his hat)[62]. . . I have expected to be "blown up" in print, by "S——l" before now, but have so far escaped—much to the disappointment of the b'hoys about here. I would submit with a good grace to a "rake down" if I could only succeed in starting again his "grey goose quill"—(When that is accomplished I am done—P.{orter} so you may rest easy.) I shall bore you no more, after that "consummation most devoutly to be wished."

Afraid that this taunt might not have the desired effect, "Charlie," with subtle skill and knowledge of his subject, added that "S——l's" failure to write was excusable

. . . for what with waterworks, steam engines, clocks, guns, watches, pistols, and every conceivable variety of machine or implement to repair and put in working order, his time is indeed well occupied and unless he should write on Sunday, (to do which he is too "square up an old Blue,") I don't know how the fellow could manage to scribble, at present.

"Charlie" also told an anecdote in this epistle that throws light on Harris both as a punster and as to his literary interests:

> A gentleman asked a druggist . . . his honest opinion of "Dalloy's Pain Extractor." "Why, sir," was the reply, "I believe it is one of the best things for *burns*, that I have ever seen." "S——l," who was present, immediately asked, "How is it for Byron?" and then "cut dirt" for home, with the druggist after him.

This correspondence finally brought Harris back "spiritually" into the arena. Over the pseudonym of "Zip" he replied in "Old Man Nincum's Horse,"[63] in which he thoroughly "blew" his taunters up in print and included himself as well. He also mentioned a very interesting organization:

> I presume to have one or two correspondents from this diminutive "burgh"—and from the signature, I should take one of these to be the ex-President of the "Axe-Handle Club," a society, alas, now defunct, but which only "kicked the bucket" after a combined attack from the Masons, Odd Fellows, two Brass Bands, and a division of the "Sons."

"Charlie" replied [in the *Spirit* on 2 September 1848]:

> I find, by an article in the "Spirit" of the 29th ult., that some *cowan* or *eavesdropper* has been disclosing certain secret transactions of a renowned association that once existed in this town, and rejoiced in the appellation of the "Axe-Handle Club." Your correspondent is correct in supposing that illustrious body has been smashed up by the introduction amongst us of several other *secret societies;* but it doubtless owed its final demolition to the establishment of the "Sons." I disclaim the honor assigned me by your *historian* as the President of the Club. I do not even insist upon any claim to membership, though my intimacy with several of its most efficient officers, *since its dissolution,* has afforded me frequent opportunities of learning some of its doings.

In this same epistle "Charlie" announced to Porter his intentions of coming to New York armed with an introduction in the form of a letter from "S——l," which he was not going to deliver "unless there should be something *good* in it." Evidently the letter contained something "too good" because after "Charlie's" return to Knoxville, he wrote Porter, "you have offended me, in that you have neither published nor made mention of the paper by 'S——l' which I left with you sometime last month." Porter replied [in the same issue,

23 December 1848] that "the communication of 'S——l' has been long under consideration. It is too highly seasoned to be published as it is, but we will try to 'fix it.'" However, the story did not appear in subsequent issues of the *Spirit*.

Porter in "To Correspondents" on March 3, 1849, begged: "'Vide lapis'—Do stir up 'S——l,' 'Charlie,' and other Knoxville correspondents." "Charlie" replied [in the *Spirit* on 26 May 1849]:

> I am not entirely heedless of such appeals, as, I am sorry to say, is your friend "S——l"—though the recent *glass* operations of this gentleman may have had some influence in making him so *slick* in avoiding you. The Captain, by the way, says he thinks the man who "built his house upon the *sand*," was a great ninny-hammer, that he did not, after the "floods came" and washed it away, proceed to the erection of a glass factory.

This indicates that Harris had changed his occupation, and further evidence bears this out. An advertisement in the Knoxville *Register* for September [29], 1849, shows that G. W. Harris of the Holston Glass Works desired the services of a washerwoman. Other notices of the Glass Works appeared in the newspapers, but none of them clears up Harris's exact connection with the business. However, one of these notices held forth bright promises for its success: "By the way, we are glad to learn that the Glass Works are doing a very good business. The fact that they sell glass as fast as they can manufacture it, is proof of the success that will attend the enterprise."[64]

Harris probably wrote another story late in 1849. Porter in "To Correspondents" for January 12, 1850, said: "W. A. S.—Will you send us another copy of the 'Courier' containing G. W. H.'s Christmas Story? Some one has 'boned' the first copy; blame him!" Unfortunately, the story was not reprinted at a later date in the *Spirit*, and a search of the extant issues of every possible "Courier" to which Porter might have referred has not uncovered it.

Harris must have been busy with the Glass Works because there is no evidence that he wrote again until 1854, nor is there any record that points to his activities during this time.

[On 18 February 1854], the Knoxville *American Statesman* stated that Harris was captain of "the new steamer Alida," which probably shows that he was no longer connected with the Glass Works. Later in the year [on 14 October 1854], Porter in "To Correspondents" said: "G. W. H.—Shall be gratified indeed to hear from the author of 'The Snake-bit Irishman,' and much more to shake hands with him." Perhaps Harris went to New York at this time. At any rate, a contribution over the pseudonym "S——l, of Tennessee" entitled "How to Marry" appeared in the *Spirit*. The setting of this story shows the influence of the Captain's second adventure in steamboating.[65]

In November, 1854, an important milestone was reached in Harris's life. On the fourth of that month "Sut Lovingood's Daddy, Acting Horse" appeared in the *Spirit*, Harris's first story under the pseudonym that was to bring him his greatest fame, and the last story that he wrote for the *Spirit*.

III. Sut Lovingood

The opening of the Virginia and East Tennessee Railroad brought to Knoxville a decade of growth from 1850 to 1860 exceeding that of any other previous period.[66] Of many manufacturing plants which were established, Harris's Glass Works, as has been seen, was one of the first. Though he had felt the pulse of the time, he had not been able to gauge his abilities to its tempo. In spite of his earlier failure, however, after his second trial at steamboating, he again turned to business. An item in the Knoxville *Standard* [on 30 August 1855] said:

> Capt. Harris is progressing finely with his Steam Saw Mill, on the site of the Churchwell Mills, and we hope soon to be able to announce that the Mill is completed and in successful operation, for there is nothing in greater demand in Knoxville than lumber for building purposes. The Capt. is the very man to push it through.

However, no further notices of the sawmill appeared in the papers, and an anecdote about Harris, recorded by Mr. E. Y. Chapin of Chattanooga, indicates that the mill may never have gone into successful operation:

> A prominent figure of Sut's (Harris's) time in Chattanooga was Col. John L. Divine. A Southern gentleman of the old school, his enterprise and his generosity led him into many undertakings which his easy good nature did not help to thrive. Sut and another—name unknown to the writer—beguiled Colonel Divine into furnishing the capital to equip a sawmill while they furnished the experience. We may doubt that Sut had much experience to start with, but he accumulated it rapidly, and so did Colonel Divine. The active partners notified him shortly that the mill needed a little more equipment, and they got the money for it; then they needed money to buy logs, and they got that; then they needed some more for working capital, reason given: the mill was doing a bigger business than they had anticipated. Col. Divine parted with his capital with growing reluctance. Finally, the requests for

money changed ends and began to come from him. Then he met the nameless partner on the street and asked for a statement of the Mill's affairs. "See Sut," he was told, "he keeps the books." He saw Sut; only to be referred to the other with the explanation, "he handles the sales."

Finally, the Colonel got them both in a room and locked the door. "You can't leave here," he said, "until I know what is the matter with the mill." "Tell him," said Sut. "No, you tell him," said the nameless partner, "You keep the books." "Colonel," said Sut, "I've given that question deep thought because I know how vital it is to all of us, and I've come to the conclusion that she sucks herself."[67]

If Harris had succeeded in his business endeavors, that success might have changed his social, economic, and political outlook. But he failed, and in his failure turned to politics again. In 1856 he was elected as alderman from the fourth ward in Knoxville.[68] Never afraid of action, he immediately became active on this job. The Knoxville *Register* reported [on 15 February 1856]:

Hog Law.—Our friend Harris, we perceive, has resuscitated the hog law, which has been, for some time, virtually laid on the shelf. On yesterday, he had about fifty porkers, which he did not consider exactly fit to "run at large," impounded and held up for sale, unless redeemed by the owners. The owners of hogs had better look out, for Harris is after them.

The ferment in national politics in 1856, with old party lines gone and new ones forming, stirred Harris to renewed activity. Shortly before the election, he published [on 18 October 1856, in the Nashville *Union and American*] a sketch entitled "Playing Old Sledge for the Presidency" in which, through a dream of "Sut Lovingood's"[69] he analyzed the political situation by picturing it as a game of old sledge (seven-up) between Fillmore, Fremont, and Buchanan. Thus, Harris clearly showed his allegiance to the remnant of the old Democratic party, from which he had never swerved. He pictured Seward as undecided, "peeping" at the cards held by both Fillmore and Fremont before making his decision on which way to jump. In the final analysis, Harris predicted that Buchanan would be elected President because he sat back and did nothing, while the other two candidates, motivated by a hesitant Seward, were at each other's throat.

Harris's analysis and prediction of the race proved surprisingly accurate. It is interesting that though he showed such mental acumen in a complicated problem of this sort he was unable to solve the much simpler puzzle of making a financial success of his endeavors.

In November, 1856, Harris went as a delegate to the Southern

Commercial Convention at Savannah, Georgia.[70] This visit was important for two reasons. In the first place since these "Commercial Conventions" had become hotbeds for the "secessionist" groups,[71] Harris's attending one showed the direction of his thinking about the slavery controversy. Secondly, William Tappan Thompson, author of *Major Jones's Courtship,* was editor of the Savannah *Morning News* at the time.[72] An indication that Harris met Thompson while in Savannah may be the fact that in the spring of 1857 Harris published his first story dealing with "Sicily Burns" in Thompson's paper.[73] It is not beyond reason to envision the two together sipping their "mint juleps," even chuckling over the "courtship" of "Major Jones." Perhaps, after several rounds of drinks, Thompson suggested to Harris the feasibility, desirability, or perhaps even "natural necessity," of allowing "Sut" to have a courtship. At any rate "Sut" told of his own peculiar courtship in the story called "Sut Lovengood [sic] Blown Up."

Early in 1857, Harris surveyed the Ducktown Copper Mines.[74] A sporting epistle in the *Spirit,* dated December 31, 1857 [and published 23 January 1858], states that "when camp was broken up we (a group of hunters) descended to the copper mines, where was seen the office of Geo. Harris, the present Postmaster at Knoxville." Since Harris became Postmaster on July 27, 1857,[75] the surveying must have been done before that date.

The Knoxville *Register* [on 17 September 1857] gave evidence of the way in which Harris handled his postmastership:

> THE KNOXVILLE POST OFFICE—Postmaster Harris has now completed the removal of the Post Office to the building formerly occupied for that purpose by Mr. Earnest. As we have said before we would very much prefer another locality, yet, the admirable manner in which Capt. Harris has fitted up his rooms will almost, if not quite, compensate our citizens for the additional length of walk. We do not think we have ever seen an office more nicely and systematically arranged. Even the order and regularity of outside appearances satisfies the visitor that all is right inside. Capt. Harris, by his strict attention to business, gentlemanly bearing and accommodating spirit, will soon become, we doubt not, one of the most popular public officers in the county.

However, Harris did not serve as postmaster long, relinquishing his position, willingly or unwillingly, February 10, 1858.[76]

During the time that Harris was postmaster he began one of the most productive literary periods of his life. A garbled version of "Sut Lovengood's [sic] Shirt" in the *Yankee Notions* for October, 1857, indicates that this story appeared in an exchange sometime during the summer. "Sut Lovingood's Lizards" was published [in the *Nashville Union and American* on 15 November 1857]; "Sut Lovingood's Dog" appeared January 8, 1858; and, April [15 and 22, respectively], 1858, both "Sut Lovingood at Sicily Burns's Wedding" and "Sut Lovingood's Version of Old Burns's Bull Ride" were [also published, again in Eastman's *Union and American*]. In addition, there is evidence that he produced at least one more story during this period. The New York *Picayune* for February 26, 1858, had a yarn entitled "The Cockney's Baggage" which was admittedly taken from an exchange as a product of Sut Lovingood.[77]

What Harris did for a living from February 10, 1858, until late in 1859 is not known. Perhaps Eastman paid him something as a correspondent for the *Union and American*. This might be borne out by his contributing a number of letters and anecdotes, in addition to his stories, to that paper beginning in the spring of 1858. This correspondence took Harris back to something like the "Free" letters, "The Man in the Swamp," and the "Charlie-Dresback" interchange. For example Harris told Eastman a fish story, Eastman printed it [on 10 June 1858] and denied the story in doing so; Harris came back [on 16 June] with additions and further insistence of its truth; then a "female" correspondent that Eastman insisted was not a "*she*" chirped in [on 17 June]—but this time it was "no go." The boisterous and lusty interchange of the 1840's was lacking, and with a final note of resignation "Sut" (Harris) expressed sorrow [in the 27 June issue] that he was "unable to throw more light on the fish business" and the matter dropped.[78]

Evidently Harris still harbored hopes for a collection of his stories in book form, for [on 30 June 1858], Eastman wrote in an editorial:

> Our readers will be glad to learn that . . . {Harris} intends to republish his Sut Lovengood [sic] and other sketches in a book, with illustrations by a first-rate artist. One of the largest publishing houses in the country has been negotiating for the copy-right and will probably undertake the publication of the volume. It will unquestionably have a very extensive sale and will increase the already wide spread fame of its author.

In the same issue as the above editorial "Sut Lovingood's Chest Story" appeared, the fourth and last yarn written around the Burns family. The author followed this [on 7 July 1858] with a letter containing several yarns about "Shell bark lawyers" and one [on 10 July

1858] entitled "The Doctor's Bill." In this last story he dropped the use of the pseudonym "S———l of Tennessee," and substituted for the first time "by the Author of Sut Lovengood [sic]."[79]

During the latter part of this summer Harris probably went to New York in the interest of his book. In August Eastman wrote:

> We have not received the first of this brilliant series of sketches which our friend Mr. Harris is writing for the New York Atlas. . . . We are truly glad that our old correspondent is receiving a just appreciation from the public and a proper remuneration from the publishers in the metropolis of the Union.

In this same issue Eastman copied the second installment of "Sut Lovingood's Adventures in New York."[80]

In this sketch Harris gave a hint as to his and the South's political veerings. When "Sut" had knocked down a policeman in a fight, that worthy, in attempting to escape, "made the 'no nothin' sign. . . ." "Sut" at this "mended his holt" and shook him again. The policeman thereupon shouted "Hurrar for Buckannon, sorter enquirin like. . . ." "Sut" released him and "Swung one of these yere laigs . . . arter him" and "hit landed rite where he forked. . . ." Again Harris was giving his own political opinions, using "Sut" as a mouthpiece. By 1858 Buchanan, befuddled and unable to act, was highly unpopular with the secessionist groups in the South. Harris stated in another story that Buchanan prided himself on sitting in the President's chair "more by a durn site nor them dus what set him thar."[81]

Although Harris is known to have published one more story, "Sut Lovingood at Bull's Gap" in the Atlas [28 November 1858], evidently his experience with New York newspapers and publishers did not solve his financial problems. The December 4, 1858, issue of the Nashville Union and American carried the following:

> The Chattanooga Advertiser says: "We are pleased to hear from reliable authority that the author of 'Sut Lovengood' [sic], the facetious George, is about perfecting arrangements to commence the publication of a Democratic paper at Knoxville, and already we have heard many say, 'if he does, you may put me, and me, and me down as a subscriber.' One thing is sure, that George Harris is an out and out Democrat, a good writer and a tip top clever fellow, and will make a sparkling editor." We vouch for that.

Again, however, Harris's plans did not materialize: the newspaper was not founded.

What he was doing for a living at this time, it is impossible to say. The only information about him is contained in the Knoxville City

Directory for 1859, the first published in that city, which shows that he lived on the east and south side of Gay Street, between Main and Hill (about where the Andrew Johnson Hotel is today), and that his father-in-law, Peter Nance, boarded with him. However, he must have devoted a considerable portion of his time to politics because the *Union and American* noted his presence in Nashville on March 17, 1859, as one of "our Democratic friends from different parts of the States" to attend a state Democratic convention. Harris was elected to the "Democratic State Central Committee" by this convention and his name was carried with the other members under the "masthead" of the Nashville *Union and American* until after the state elections in August.[82] While in Nashville Harris probably witnessed, from the outside, a meeting of the Opposition Party, for "Sut Lovingood's Love Feast ove Varmints, held at Nashville, March 28th and 29th.," began in the *Union and American* on April 19, 1859, and ran for four issues, [also on 21 and 30 April and 3 May].[83] Here [in the first installment] was Harris's concept of the new Opposition party as seen through the eyes of "Sut":

> You never hearn, George, how I got into a big meetin ove varmints to Nashville, and how durnd ni I cum gittin myself fixt for happiness and halelujah beyant the grave fur gwine amung 'em. Ketch me ever a mixin ove myself up again with pole cats, coons, groun-hogs, minks, house-cats, hoss-cats, hellcats, weazels, mus-rats, wharf-rats, bull-bats, owls, buzzards, water-dogs, wild boars, bell weathers, possums, moles, grub-worms, and tumble-bugs. . . .

Harris described certain "varmints" so that they must have been recognizable as specific individuals by the readers of his day. Then he classified them as a whole, since they had been out of office for ten years, as a very dangerous group that wanted to get back into control through any means, foul or fair. Certainly there was no doubt about Harris's being a Democrat, and that any one on the other side of the question was a "varmint."

On October 2, 1859, a notice appeared in the *Union and American* stating that "Col. G. W. Harris of Knoxville, author of the 'Sut Lovingood' sketches, has been appointed a conductor on the Nashville and Chattanooga Railroad." Whether he served in this capacity is not known. The *Nashville City and Business Directory, 1860–1861,* has the following: "G. W. Harris, down freight, N. & C. Railroad."[84]

Early in 1861 Harris published three sketches dealing with Lincoln in the Nashville *Union and American.* In the first sketch [28 February 1861] Sut Lovingood traveled with Old Abe as his

"Confidential Friend and Advisor"; in the second [2 March 1861], Sut accompanied "Old Abe on His Journey"; and, in the final sketch [5 March 1861], Sut landed "Old Abe Safe at Last" in Washington.[85] These sketches show definitely that Harris had a profound contempt for Lincoln, and he felt that with a man of Lincoln's ability and disposition as President the only hope of the South was in secession. [On 4 May 1861], the Savannah *Morning News* announced the results in due order:

> Rebels, Take Notice!
>
> Tomorrow, the 5th of May, is the day appointed by his Black Republican, Rail-Splitting High Mightiness, Abraham Lincoln, for rebels against his government to disperse and retire to their respective homes. Sut Lovengood [sic], having addressed an humble appeal to Abraham on behalf of his fellow-secessionists, begging an extension of the time, and as no answer has been vouchsafed by the said Abraham, it is to be feared that not even a "day of grace" will be granted. We, therefore, admonish all whom it may concern to be warned in time, and flee from the consuming wrath of Abraham, the Rail-splitter.

Exactly when Harris and his family started fleeing "from the consuming wrath of Abraham" is not known. However, it must have been very late in 1861 or early in 1862, as he was still in Nashville in November, 1861.[86] The family was on the move for four years, living successively in Chattanooga; Decatur, Alabama; Trenton, Georgia; and probably in other places.[87]

IV. War and Its Aftermath

It is difficult to understand how Harris kept from writing during the stirring days of the Civil War.[88] However, the sheer problem of moving his wife and five minor children from place to place, supplying them with shelter and food, must have been enormous. In spite of the difficulties, a reasonable guess is that he wrote for some of the peripatetic journals that struggled to keep up the Southern morale, but none of the few extant issues show any of his work under an identifiable pseudonym. Or, perhaps he wrote pamphlets, though none has been found. The difficulty of a search for his writings is intensified because it is not known where he lived. Mrs. Raymond remembers hearing the guns of the battle of Chickamauga booming in the distance while her mother paced the floor. She did not know until later that her oldest brother was in the battle. She also remembers living at Trenton, Georgia, but thinks that it was after the war. Mr. Ben T. Brock, an attorney at Trenton, supplied one definite bit of information about Harris during this time:

He {Harris} must have been here {Trenton} during the latter part of the Civil War, as I remember my mother telling me of a trip she made with other ladies from this section to Rome, Georgia, to procure salt under the permission of the Federal Authorities, granted the party, escorted by "Sut" riding an old tall, shanky, shaggy, grey mule. Arriving at Rome and handing their "Pass" to the Corporal of Guard, they were waiting for the proper officer to pass them through the lines. The "Sut" mule stretched and craned his neck and brayed. A "Yankee soldier" standing near, thinking to have a bit of merriment at the expense of "Sut" and his lady companions, brayed in imitation of the mule, when "Sut" {Harris} remarked—"kinfolks by God!"[89]

Soon after the war ended, Harris became connected with the Wills Valley Railroad and remained in its employ until his death.[90] Mrs. John G. Rawlings, daughter of William Crutchfield, who is mentioned in the "Dedicatory" of *Yarns,* stated that her father furnished most of the money to build this railroad and that "Mr. Harris procured most of the right-of-way."[91]

Harris became active again with his pen early in 1866 when, in "Sut Lovingood Come to Life" [published in the *Nashville Union and American* on 3 May], he replied to "Solomon Sunstruck," a Radical Republican commentator who had swung through the South on a hurried trip and had then prescribed for its Reconstruction. "Sut," as President Johnson's "Official Fool Killer," condemned "Solomon" to death and warned him to expect execution after breakfast the next day. [In the same newspaper on 10 August 1866], appeared "Sut Lovingood's Big Dinner Story," in which Harris castigated pedigree hunters who "ginerally has a pedigree wif one aind tied to thar sturn, an' tother one a-soakin' in Noah's flood." He also vented his spleen again on the "shell bark lawyers," concentrating on "Gripes . . . a legal fickshun . . . wif black frekils an' mink eyes." These were but "weeds" when compared to the "thirtytwo pound shot" that he hurled at the Radical Republicans in "Sut Lovingood's Dream" [published in the *Lynchburg Daily Virginian,* 23 January 1867], in which Harris left no doubt about his attitude, and the attitude of the South on the Reconstruction program engineered by the team of "Stevens, Sumner, Wade, Butler—surnamed the Beast— an' Wendell Phillips. . . ."[92]

In April, 1867, a collection of Harris's stories finally found its way into book form as *Sut Lovingood. Yarns Spun by a "Nat'ral Born Durn'd Fool."* The collection includes eight stories that have been found in newspapers in their original form, and sixteen stories that have not been found previously published outside the book. This ratio will be reduced no doubt, with the finding of the first printings of some of the sixteen. However, a review of the book in the [*Nashville*] *Union and Dispatch* [on 25 April 1867] states that the work contained both published and unpublished material. According to report, the book created a sensation in Knoxville,[93] but the reviewers generally over the country ignored it. Mark Twain, however, reviewed it on the Pacific Coast [in the San Francisco *Alta California*, 14 July 1967], and the New York *Times* [18 April 1867] gave it a sort of condescending yawn. Perhaps Harris frightened the reviewers away when he warned them in the "Preface" to leave his book alone. But a better guess is that they did not read the book.

The *Yarns* add little to the biographical information about Harris other than that he finally "hes made a book." However, a few indications are worth noting. In "Sut Lovingood's Sermon" Harris poured out his wrath on a "new kine of pisonus reptile" which the "shakin an' jumblin ove this year war ove ourn, hes fotch up tu the top ove the groun" and who "kin jis' beat the bes' cross atwix' a buzzard an' a wolf yu ever seed." This new "varmint" was none other than the "Perpryiter" of taverns. This man was

> . . . now perpar'd tu starve, 'sult, swindil, be-dirty, be-devil, an' turn inside out the puss, pockid, an' stumick ove every misfornit hungry tired devil, what am wayfarin on fun, bisness, ur frum a skeer. He an' she, ole an' young, citerzen, ur soger, he sucks em all out as dry as a spider dus a hossfly, an' turns em out tu thar wayfarin agin, while he looks zaminly arter em wif his fis' full ove thar shinplasters, than he wipes his horny bill ontu the door jam like ontu a hen arter she hes swaller'd a toad, an' waits fur the nex' hossfly! [*Yarns*, 174]

Clearly Harris was bemoaning the coming of industrialism—Northern ways—to his beloved South. He went on in this same sketch to make the tavern keeper symbolical of the "carpetbagger". . . .

Harris himself was tired and sorely needed rest because his heart had been "onder a mill-stone" since the death of his wife, about the same time the *Yarns* appeared.[94] The "Preface" to the *Yarns* gives a hint of the turmoil in Harris's own mind:

> Ef eny poor misfortinit devil hu's heart is onder a mill-stone, hu's raggid children am hungry, an' no bread in the dresser, hu is down in the mud, an' the lucky ones a-trippin him every time he struggils tu his all fours, hu hes fed the famishin an' is now hungry hissef, hu misfortins foller fas' an' foller faster, hu is so foot-sore an weak that he wishes he wer at the ferry—ef sich

a one kin fine a laugh, jis' one, sich a laugh as is remembered wif his keer-less boyhood, atwixt these yere kivers—then, I'll thank God that I *hes* made a book, an' feel that I hev got my pay in full. [*Yarns*, xi]

This consolation was for others and not for Harris. He turned bravely to the writing of more laugh-producing stories, but could not forget his own misery.

The Chattanooga *Daily American Union* published "Saul Spradlin's Ghost" [on 31 October 1867], "Sut Lovingood Reports What Bob Dawson Said, After Marrying a Substitute" [on 27 and 28 November 1867], and the "Big Music Box Story" [on 11 and 12 December 1867]. In the spring of 1868, the same paper published "Sut Lovingood's Hark from the Tomb Story," [17 March] and "Sut Lovingood, a Chapter from His Autobiography [31 March and 2 April].[95]

On April 30, 1868, the Knoxville *Press and Messenger* announced "The Early Life of Sut Lovingood, Written by his Dad." This newspaper was edited by John M. Fleming, who fiercely hated the radical element in the Republican party and who saw in the candidacy of General Ulysses S. Grant the perpetuation of that group in control of the Federal Government. It is not strange then that this "Early Life of Sut" was a bitter blast at Grant.[96]

With his hatred of Grant off his chest but not out of his heart, Harris wrote "A Story of the Old Times (1833) in East Tennessee," entitled "Bill Ainsworth's Quarter Race."[97] This story [published in the *Knoxville Press and Messenger*, 4 June 1868], has in it a haunting, lingering nostalgia—a softness almost—that may be explained by a letter which Harris wrote to his sister-in-law, Mrs. Fouche, on July 31, 1868, and which is quoted almost in its entirety:

> There is no one now in whose affection and sense I have so much confidence as yourself—I want the benefit of your advice and experience . . . in my perplexity. My daughter Mary is married. She married on yesterday. She has in my view made an excellent choice. . . . But her leaving me places me in a very awkward situation. We have had a young widow woman to do the work of the house ever since the spring of '66, a year before Dear Ema's death, until now. Now she leaves me also in consequence of no other woman being about the place, leaves regretfully, but gives a good reason—that she might be "talked about. . . ." What course to pursue now I cannot determine; I have no earthly desire to marry, and if I had and had even found a person suited to me, unless I was *absolutely* sure that she would be a kind mother to my poor motherless children, no consideration would induce me even to think of it. I only wish to live on account of the three little darlings yet helpless. . . . I never felt my fearful responsibility during her lifetime. I never felt

uneasiness even on their accounts for she, she, was my right hand, my all. Now, no tongue can tell my uneasiness, watchfulness and anxiety. . . . We are in a most *delightful* country but have fewer women in the right sense of that word than any place I ever saw: ignorant, rough, primitive—I don't know five in the valley whose hands I would trust Pillow's {Mrs. Raymond's} future—and they all have homes of their own. If I could get one (as a house-keeper) who has been measured by your experienced eye, I would feel al-most sure that I could raise my children right. . . . Suppose I were to marry some one and she proved unkind to them or unfit to raise them, why I risk all on one throw of the cards and *lose all*. But by *employing* them I can re-dress my children's wrongs by shipping her, which I would do in a moment, and hunting up some one else.

There is no evidence that Harris's sister-in-law secured a house-keeper for him, but "Sut Lovingood's Allegory," published in Sep-tember, indicated that his problems were not at all solved. Rather, nostalgia had settled in thickening clouds:

> Those of us who have not yet reached the ferry, so dreaded by many yet anxiously looked forward to by the footsore and weary ones, who have passed but few cool fountains, or hospitable shelters, along their bleak road, must well remember the good old days of camp meetings, battalion musters, tax gatherings, and shooting matches. Well! there was the house raisings too, and the quiltings, and the corn shuckins, where the darkey's happy song was heard for the last time. And then the moonlight dance in the yard. . . .

"Yas by geminey," Sut broke in upon "George" who had been speak-ing, "an' the ridin' home ahine the he fellers, on the same hoss, arter the dancin was done." The nostalgia was blacker as "George" added:

> I was just thinking, boys, while Sut was speaking, whether we are the gainer by the discoveries—inventions—innovations, and prayers, of the last forty years. Whether the railway—telegraph—chloroform—moral reform, and other advancements, as they are termed, have really advanced us any, in the right direction. . . .

Sut (inoculated with nostalgia himself) agreed that you may "take one person, a family, or a county, at a time" and you will find that they have not "gain'd a step on the right road an' if the fog would clear up we'd find heaven behine us, an' not strength enuff left to reach hit alone."[98] There was only one forgetfulness for both of them, one that Sut had appreciated from way back:

> I ken allways talk better, when I see a jug with a wet corn cob in hits mouth, leanin' up amung the saddles, an' hoss geer, like hit wer a listenin' to me. A

feller feels sorter like he has backin. Pour out a morsel for me, while yer han's in. Thar. Thar.[99]

With Grant's election to the Presidency in November 1868, Harris's world—politically, economically, and socially—was around him totally in a crumpled heap. Soon after the election, he wrote and published a story entitled "Well! Dad's Dead,"[100] which was pervaded with a sort of forlorn realization that the past was hopelessly gone as was "Dad," "strait out, an' for keep."

The shell of the man lived on, and from that shell emerged two more stories. In the first of these [published 13 May 1869 in the *Knoxville Daily Press and Herald*], entitled "Sut Lovingood on Young Gals and Old Ones," Harris commented on the difficulty of keeping up with the thinking of a young girl (probably Pillow), but showed also his interest in old ones when he concluded:

> Dad shave me, if I ain't sorter skeery ove the last one ove 'em, prim, trim, an proper, as they looks. Yea hoss, verily I watches 'em, a body don't know— you know.

In the second story [published in the *Knoxville Press and Messenger,* 29 September 1869], entitled "Sut Lovingood 'Sets up with a Gal— One Pop Baily,'" he again dealt with the subject of women and followed up his warning expressed in the first story by marrying Mrs. Jane E. Pride, a widow, at Decatur, Alabama, on October 19, 1869.[101]

Shortly after his marriage Harris wrote to the editor of the Knoxville *Press and Herald* [14 December 1869], stating that he had "married a wife and found happiness." His second wife was a tall, willowy blonde, and very beautiful. She was said to have been a marvelous conversationalist, and report has it that "they proved quite a match for each other at the dinner table."[102]

Perhaps this marriage might have brought momentary happiness to Harris and, had things been different, might even have bridged the gap into the new world. At any rate he busied himself with the editing of his stories, not published in the *Yarns,* to be published in a book entitled *High Times and Hard Times,* and in December, 1869, went to Lynchburg, Virginia, to transact business for the railroad and to attempt to arrange for publication of this book. During his return trip he became sick on the train, was taken off at Knoxville, and died on the night of December 11, 1869, without regaining consciousness. What became of the manuscript of his projected book has never been learned. . . .

Notes

1. Letter from Mrs. Amanda Pillow Harris Raymond, daughter of George W. Harris, hereinafter designated as Mrs. Raymond. Letter dated November 2, 1914.
2. George F. Mellen, "Samuel Bell," Knoxville *Sentinel*, October 12, 1916.
3. Goodspeed Publishing Company, *History of Tennessee... with an Historical and Biographical Sketch of the County of Knox and the City of Knoxville* (Nashville, 1887), 807. Cited hereinafter as Goodspeed, *History of Tennessee, Knox County*.
4. In 1851, when factional disputes and industrial development had come to Knoxville, Samuel Bell sold out and moved to San Antonio, Texas. See Mellen, "Samuel Bell."
5. Ibid.
6. Ibid.
7. Knoxville *Press and Herald*, December 14, 1869.
8. Samuel L. Clemens, *Life on the Mississippi* (New York: Harper and Row, 1917), 32–34.
9. Goodspeed, *History of Tennessee, Knox County*, 807.
10. Knoxville *Press and Herald*, December 14, 1869.
11. Ibid.
12. Goodspeed, *History of Tennessee, Knox County*, 843.
13. Information furnished by Mrs. Raymond.
14. Knoxville *Press and Herald*, December 14, 1869; George F. Mellen, "George W. Harris," Knoxville *Sentinel*, February 13, 1909; Franklin J. Meine, "George Washington Harris," *Dictionary of American Biography* (New York: Scribner, 1932), vol. 4, pt. 2, 309.
15. From a description by Mrs. Raymond.
16. Mellen, "George W. Harris."
17. This anecdote was told to the writer by Mrs. Raymond.
18. Related by Colonel Brownlow to J. Cleveland Harris of Knoxville, and written by Mr. Harris to Franklin J. Meine. The letter is not dated. J. Cleveland Harris is not related to George W. Harris.
19. Mellen, "George W. Harris." See also J. Thompson Brown, Jr., "George Washington Harris," *Library of Southern Literature*, 16 vols., ed. Edwin A. Alderman, Joel Chandler Harris, and Charles W. Kent (Atlanta: Martin and Hoyt Co., 1907–09), 5:2099–2100.

20. Letter from J. Cleveland Harris to Franklin J. Meine, March 12, 1931.
21. See Donald Day, "The Political Satires of George W. Harris," *Tennessee Historical Quarterly* 4 (1945): 320–338.
22. Records of Blount County, Maryville, Tennessee, September 5, 1839, Book "O," 207.
23. Ibid., December 23, 1840, Book "Q," 155.
24. Ibid., December 24, 1840, Book "Q," 157. This bill of sale actually amounted to a chattel mortgage.
25. Ibid., 173.
26. Ibid., 174.
27. A Letter from E. Y. Chapin to Franklin J. Meine, September 18, 1929, with an anecdote in Mr. Chapin's handwriting, beginning with this quotation. The anecdote deals with a later period of Harris's life.
28. Records, Blount County, Book "R," 247.
29. This same advertisement ran in the Knoxville *Register* and the Knoxville *Post* for several years.
30. Knoxville *Register,* June 26, 1846.
31. Knoxville *Standard,* March 16, 1847.
32. Knoxville *Register,* July 5, 1843.
33. *Acts of Tennessee,* 1843–1844, ch. 218.
34. Ibid., ch. 214.
35. See Franklin J. Meine, ed., *Tall Tales of the Southwest* (New York: Alfred A. Knopf, 1930), xxvii–xxix; Walter Blair, *Native American Humor, 1800–1900* (New York: Alfred A. Knopf, 1937), 82–101; Francis Brinley, *Life of William Porter* (New York, 1860).
36. Brinley, *Life of Porter,* 78–79.
37. Bernard DeVoto, *Mark Twain's America* (Boston: Little, Brown and Co., 1932), 95.
38. In addition to *Spirit of the Times,* Porter edited weekly and monthly journals devoted exclusively to racing. See *Spirit of the Times,* April 8, 1843; Brinley, *Life of Porter.*
39. *Spirit of the Times,* May 30, 1840.
40. Ibid., September 12, 1846. Harris's brother-in-law, Pryor Nance, owned the race track at Knoxville for years. See Knoxville *Argus,* February 16, 1841; Knoxville *Post,* April 20, 1842, ff.; *Spirit of the Times,* April 8, 1843.
41. Harris's obituary in the Knoxville *Press and Herald,* December 14, 1869, is the basis for assigning these sketches to his pen.

See also Donald Day, "The Life and Works of George Washington Harris" (Unpublished Ph.D. dissertation, University of Chicago, 1942), App. A.

42. "Sporting Epistle from East Tennessee," *Spirit of the Times,* February 11, 1843. [See M. Thomas Inge, ed., *High Times and Hard Times: Sketches and Tales by George Washington Harris* (Nashville: Vanderbilt University Press, 1967), 15–18.]

43. "Quarter Racing in Tennessee," *Spirit of the Times,* April 15, 1843. [See Inge, *High Times and Hard Times,* 19–22.]

44. "Sporting Epistle from East Tennessee," *Spirit of the Times,* June 17, 1843. [See Inge, *High Times and Hard Times,* 23–27.]

45. "Sporting Epistle from East Tennessee," *Spirit of the Times,* September 2, 1843. [See Inge, *High Times and Hard Times,* 28–31.]

46. Statement by Mrs. Raymond in personal interview.

47. Tippo Sahib was sultan of Mysore, India, 1749–1799.

48. Shown to writer by Mrs. Raymond, who kindly gave him permission to copy the memorandum.

49. Information given in a personal interview. ["Knob Dance" in Inge, *High Times and Hard Times,* 44–53.]

50. *Spirit of the Times,* November 15, 1845.

51. Mellen, "George W. Harris."

52. *Spirit of the Times,* September 19, 1846. ["The Snake-bit Irishman" in Inge, *High Times and Hard Times,* 54–58.]

53. The italics are mine. Knoxville *Register,* June 26, 1846. ["A Sleep Walking Incident" in Inge, *High Times and Hard Times,* 59–66.]

54. Knoxville *Standard,* May 18, 1847.

55. Knoxville *Tribune,* June 9, 1847. A report of this meeting was found, but no mention was made of a toast by Harris.

56. *Weekly Nashville Union,* October 6, 1847. ["There's Danger in Old Chairs" in Inge, *High Times and Hard Times,* 67–71.]

57. Letter to J. Cleveland Harris, July 18, 1928.

58. "Dresback" called him "Dr. S." See *Spirit of the Times,* April 29, 1848. Harris in "Sut Assisting at a Negro Night-Meeting," spoke of a Dr. Stone "hu wer fond uv seeing fun" [*Yarns,* 159]. It has not been determined whether this "Doctor Stone" is "Charlie" or whether a Doctor Stone actually lived in Knoxville at this time.

59. *American Journal of Science and Arts.*

60. *Spirit of the Times,* April 8, 1848. *Appleton's Cyclopaedia of American Biography* (New York, 1887), 3:91, says: "Capt. Harris made several inventions, which he described in the 'Scientific American.'" However, a search of this publication does not reveal these.

61. *Spirit of the Times,* April 29, 1848.

62. Refers to Harris's habit of wearing a "stovepipe" hat.

63. *Spirit of the Times,* July 29, 1848. The reason for assigning this to Harris may be found in Day, "The Life and Works of George Washington Harris," App. B. [This tale is not included in Inge, *High Times and Hard Times.*]

64. Knoxville *Register,* [29 December 1849. See also the *Register* for December] 1 and 8, 1849. Mrs. Raymond does not know of her father's connection with the Holston Glass Works.

65. *Spirit of the Times,* October 21, 1854. ["How to Marry" in Inge, *High Times and Hard Times,* 72–76.]

66. Goodspeed, *History of Tennessee, Knox County,* 845.

67. Letter from E. Y. Chapin to J. Franklin Meine, September 18, 1929.

68. Knoxville *Register,* January 10, 1856.

69. Spelled both as "Lovingood" and "Lovengood." ["Old Sledge" in Inge, *High Times and Hard Times,* 232–36.]

70. Knoxville *Register,* November 20, 1856.

71. R. R. Russell, *Economic Aspects of Southern Sectionalism* (Urbana: University of Illinois Studies in the Social Sciences, 1923), 179, ff.

72. Henry P. Miller, "Life and Works of William Tappan Thompson" (Unpublished Ph.D. dissertation, University of Chicago, 1941), 39–40.

73. The issue of the Savannah *Morning News* in which the story appeared is not extant. However, an editorial for August 31, 1857, said: "'Sut Lovengood [sic] Blown Up'—some two months or more since, we published a humorous sketch under this title, communicated to us by 'S.L., of Tennessee.'" This places the date of publication for the story sometime in June or July, 1857.

74. Mrs. Raymond confirmed the fact that her father surveyed these mines. She said that he knew every path in the Smokies and had a wide acquaintance with the people who lived there. [Milton Rickels, *George Washington Harris* (New York: Twayne Publishers, 1965), believes that Harris was in the Ducktown area in

1854, thus making a connection to the publication of the first Sut story (p. 28). A fuller discussion of this issue can be found in M. Thomas Inge, "Sut Lovingood: An Examination of the Nature of a 'Nat'ral Born Durn'd Fool,'" *Tennessee Historical Quarterly* 19 (1960): 233–34.]

75. Letter from the first assistant postmaster general to J. Cleveland Harris, April 19, 1928.

76. Letter from the first assistant postmaster to J. Cleveland Harris, April 10, 1928. The post office department does not have in its files the reason for Harris's quitting the office.

77. ["The Cockney's Baggage" in Inge, *High Times and Hard Times*, 77–78.]

78. [Harris's replies in Inge, *High Times and Hard Times*, 79–81, 88.]

79. [These stories in ibid., 89–91, 92–100.]

80. Nashville *Union and American*, August 15, 1858. A search for extant issues of the New York *Atlas* containing these stories has so far proved unsuccessful. The *Union and American* republished the second and succeeding sketches of this series. [All three *Atlas* stories are reprinted in Inge, *High Times and Hard Times*, 126–55. Three more *Atlas* stories have since been discovered. See McClary, 1983, in bibliography.]

81. "Sut Lovingood Travels with Old Abe as his Confidential Friend and Advisor," Nashville *Union and American*, February 28, 1861. [In Inge, *High Times and Hard Times*, 261–65.]

82. Nashville *Union and American*, March 19, 1859, ff.

83. [These stories in Inge, *High Times and Hard Times*, 237–60.]

84. A railroad man at Nashville told the writer that this meant that Harris had charge of the incoming freight.

85. These sketches have been collected by Edd Winfield Parks in *Sut Lovingood Travels with Old Abe Lincoln* (Chicago: Black Cat Press, 1937). A detailed discussion of these sketches is given by Donald Day in "The Political Satires of George W. Harris," 328–330. [See also Inge, *High Times and Hard Times*, 261–75.]

86. This is shown by a manuscript in the archives of the state of Tennessee, Box H-1, No. 22-H, with the following note in Harris's handwriting on the outside cover: "An account of the Battle of King's Mountain, supposed to have been written soon after the battle and found while tearing down an old house in Knoxville, Tenn., about the year 1840. From Mr. Geo. W. Harris, Nashville,

Nov. 6, 1861." It would seem probable that Harris may have been among those Southern sympathizers who fled Nashville when that city fell to the Union forces, February 23–24, 1862. For an account of this exodus, see Stanley F. Horn, "Nashville During the Civil War," *Tennessee Historical Quarterly* 4 (1945), 8–11; Horn, *The Army of Tennessee* (Norman: University of Oklahoma Press, 1941), 100–104.

87. Information furnished by Mrs. Raymond.

88. Nashville *Union and American,* July 17, 1861, has a story called "The Speaking at Fayettville" which may be by Harris. [This tale is not included in Inge, *High Times and Hard Times.*]

89. Letter from Ben T. Brock to J. Cleveland Harris, June 15, 1928.

90. Ibid.

91. Letter from Mrs. John G. Rawlings to Franklin J. Meine, November 18, 1932.

92. [See Inge, *High Times and Hard Times:* "Come to Life," 276–81; "Big Dinner," 164–74; "Dream," 288–92.]

93. Kate White, "Writers of Knoxville Famed in Literature," Knoxville *Sentinel,* undated clipping in George F. Mellen's scrapbooks, in my possession at time of writing but now on deposit in the Joint University Library, Nashville. [A search of Mellen's papers has not discovered this item.]

94. Letter from Harris to his sister-in-law, Mrs. Lucy Fouche, July 31, 1868; letter from Mrs. Raymond, November 2, 1941.

95. [See Inge, *High Times and Hard Times,* 175–97.]

96. See editorials in Knoxville *Press and Messenger,* and *Press and Herald* for this period; Oliver P. Temple, *Notable Men of Tennessee* (New York, 1912), 118–122. [There are three installments of Sut's biography by his Dad, all originally in the *Knoxville Press and Messenger.* See also Inge, *High Times and Hard Times,* 293–310, for all four pieces.]

97. Knoxville *Press and Messenger,* June 4, 1858. [See Inge, *High Times and Hard Times,* 198–202.]

98. ["Sut Lovingood's Allegory" was originally published in the *Knoxville Press and Messenger,* 17 September 1868. See also Inge, *High Times and Hard Times,* 311–16.]

99. "Bill Ainsworth's Quarter Race." [See Inge, *High Times and Hard Times,* 199.]

100. Knoxville *Press and Messenger,* November 19, 1868. [An earlier version appeared 15 November 1868 in the *Knoxville*

Daily Press and Herald. See also Inge, *High Times and Hard Times,* 207–11.]

101. Records of Morgan County, Decatur, Alabama, Marriage Record "C," 235, License No. 3500.
102. Undated letter from Mrs. Virginia Pride Binger to Franklin J. Meine.

Sudden and Mysterious Death

Anonymous

It is with no ordinary regret that we chronicle this morning, the death of Capt. George W. Harris, formerly of Knoxville, and more recently a resident of Decatur, Alabama.

Captain Harris, it appears, left Decatur about two weeks since, for Richmond, Va., on business connected with the North and South Alabama Railroad, now under construction from Montgomery to Decatur, with which road he was connected.

We recollect reading in a Lynchburg paper, of Thursday last, that Captain Harris was in that city, looking well and hearty, and in high spirits, having completed arrangements, during his stay in Richmond, for the publication of his later writings of the famous "Sut Lovengood" [*sic*] letters.

It was, therefore, with great surprise, that we learned on Saturday evening last that he was lying very ill, with no hope of recovery, at the Atkin House, in this city. On inquiry we learned the following facts regarding his illness:

As the passengers and freight on the Virginia and Tennessee train were being transferred to the cars of the East Tennessee and Virginia railroad, at Bristol, on Saturday morning, 11th inst., the conductor of the latter train was notified that a man, in an unconscious condition, had been transferred to the passenger car of his train from

Ben Harris McClary, ed., *The Sut Lovingood Papers, 1965* (Knoxville: University of Tennessee Press, 1967), 56–58. Originally in the *Knoxville Daily Press and Herald*, 14 December 1869.

the cars of the Virginia and Tennessee train. The conductor was also notified that the man had a "pass" over his road.

A few moments after the train had started for Knoxville, the conductor attempted to rouse the unconscious passenger and obtain his "pass." Failing in this he searched his pockets but found nothing in this with the exception of a gold watch in the vest pocket, which the conductor thought well to remove from his person, thinking in the imperfect and dim light of the grey dawn of morning, that the man was intoxicated.

We cannot learn that any attention was given to the poor fellow until a Mr. Cox, of the firm of H. T. Cox & Br., of Atlanta, got on the train at Strawberry Plains, who at once recognized the man as Capt. G. W. Harris. Attempts were then made to arouse him, but with the exception of an occasional vacant stare and low moans, they were unsuccessful.

As soon as the train arrived in Knoxville, at 1 o'clock P.M., he was kindly cared for by Col. P. H. Toomey, of the Atkin House, opposite the depot, who had the sufferer conveyed to a room in the hotel, and the aid of Dr. Kraus, who has an office in the hotel, was at once obtained.

Dr. Kraus believed the case one of apoplexy and treated Capt. Harris during the afternoon and evening. About 9 o'clock Dr. Fouche, a brother in law of Harris, was sent for, and soon after, accompanied by Dr. McIntosh, arrived at the hotel. They found the sufferer in critical condition, his eyes set in a glassy stare, and breathing heavily. Dr. Fouche was recognized a moment, and then Harris lost all consciousness. Drs. Boyd and Morton were then sent for. Harris rallied a little about 10 o'clock, recognized a few friends and replied, in answer to a question of one of the physicians, the word "poisoned." Nothing more could be obtained from the now dying man.

Toward midnight, he died.

On Saturday [this should read Sunday] morning, Squire Joroulman held an inquest over the body. The jury was composed of the following gentlemen: C. W. Park, M. A. Williams, Michael D. Sullivan, C. D. Munsey, J. L. Smith, Wm. Morrow, and A. L. Williams.

After hearing the evidence of Dr. Kraus, the conductor of the E.T. & Va. train, and of two gentlemen who were present during his illness at the hotel, the jury rendered a verdict that "the deceased came to his death by an unknown cause."

No *post mortem* examination of the body was made.

The wife of the deceased, who had been telegraphed for on Saturday afternoon, arrived on the morning train on Sunday, and accompanied the remains back to Chattanooga.

The cause of the death of Captain Harris is a mystery. Dr. Kraus thinks it was a case of apoplexy. The other physicians ascribe his death to *morphia*.

The Lynchburg press may shed some light on the mysterious cause of his death by publishing the particulars of Captain Harris' sojourn in their city, and gentlemen may be found in that city, who witnessed his departure on the train. In behalf of a community, who deeply deplore the death of Captain Harris, and who shudder to think of his horrible, lonely ride in a railway train, without one pitying glance or gentle hand to soothe his dying moments, we ask that whatever facts in the possession of any one, tending to explain this most mysterious death, be published, that the world may know, whether Capt. Geo. W. Harris, died by the stroke of God, or the poisoned chalice of a wicked man.

The Real Sut

Ben Harris McClary

George Washington Harris is known for his character Sut Lovingood, the prototype of the early East Tennessee mountaineer in literature. When Sut appeared in 1854 in the New York *Spirit of the
Times,* he and his escapades were the summation of Harris's vast and
varied experiences.[1] An obituary notice in the Athens (Tennessee)
Post, August 20, 1858, indicates that Harris's famous character was
in fact fashioned after a person with whom Harris probably had become acquainted in the early fifties[2] when he was working for the
Hiwassee Mining Company in the Ducktown area of Polk County,
Tennessee. The notice reads:

> "SUT LOVENGOOD." We learn that Sut Miller, the hero of the Lovengood
> [*sic*] papers, died suddenly in the neighborhood of Ducktown, a week or two
> since. Poor Sut! After having innumerable encounters and conflicts with
> man and beast—been shot several times, and consumed *bust-head* enough
> to run an over-shot mill for forty days and nights, he died ignobly at last from
> a blow inflicted with the fist of a fellow mortal.

The dependability of the *Post,* in this case, could hardly be questioned. Samuel P. Ivins, the editor, had been in Knoxville with his
paper in the forties and certainly had known Harris. The Knoxville
Post regularly carried an advertisement of Harris's metal-working
shop. After 1848, situated in Athens, roughly halfway between
Knoxville and Ducktown, Ivins was able to keep in contact with

American Literature 27 (1955): 105–06.

Knoxville and, as a study of his paper shows, to become thoroughly acquainted with Polk County. The familiarity with which he speaks of Sut Miller indicates that Ivins probably knew him personally. Knowing both George and Sut, Ivins would have been peculiarly qualified to appreciate the stories of Sut's life.[3]

Sut Miller was William S. Miller who had a little mountain farm on the western edge of the Ducktown District. His farm in 1850 was valued at $400, and his main crop was, significantly, corn![4] The real Sut was forgotten long ago by the people of his area, and the name of the "fellow-mortal" who struck him down is not known. Fortunately, George Washington Harris was able to capture Sut's spirit in his stories, and Sut can be seen in those audacious yarns today.

Notes

1. See Donald Day, "The Humorous Works of George W. Harris," *American Literature* 14 (1943): 391.
2. In a recent article, Mr. Day suggests that Harris had been a surveyor in Ducktown during the early part of 1857. His conclusion is based on a letter of December, 1857, to the *Spirit of the Times,* which shows that Harris had been at the copper mines sometime before he became Knoxville's postmaster in July, 1857 ("The Life of George Washington Harris," *Tennessee Historical Quarterly* 6 {March, 1947}: 26). In June, 1852, the newly organized Hiwassee Mining Company began the great productive prewar decade of the copper mines. See [Robert] E. Barclay, *Ducktown Back in Raht's Time* (Chapel Hill: University of North Carolina Press, 1946), 58–76. It is probable that Harris was in Ducktown in this early period when there was a real demand for surveyors. No records of Harris's activities between 12 January 1850, and February, 1854, are known (Day, "The Life of George Washington Harris," 23). [See the reprint of Day's biography in this volume.]
3. The Athens *Post,* in the fragmentary files preserved in the University of Tennessee Library, mentions Harris on one other occasion. On 27 December 1869, Ivins regretfully announced the death of "the author of the 'Lovengood [sic] Papers'" by "apoplexy."
4. United States Census, 1850, Unpublished Schedules: Agriculture, Tennessee, Polk County, p. 174.

Section Two

The Critical Tradition

New Publications

Anonymous

Sut Lovingood's Yarns [*sic*] had quite a popularity in their day, and Messr. *Dick & Fitzgerald* have undertaken to revive the interest in them by bringing out a new and handsomely printed edition. The wit, and their burlesque is exceedingly broad—at times, offensively so—but there are those who enjoy such reading, nevertheless.

Ben Harris McClary, ed., *The Sut Lovingood Papers, 1962* (Knoxville: University of Tennessee Press, 1962), 24. Originally in the *New York Times*, 8 April 1867.

New Books

Anonymous

This is a home book, though published abroad. A portion of its contents appeared originally in the *Union and American,* and it comes as an old friend, appearing after a long absence. We hail it as such, and as two old friends, meeting after a long separation, talk over the past, so we read with the greatest pleasure these returned "Suts." They are selected from the best and most popular of all the productions of the author, including a number never before given to the public. The genuine humor and exquisite touches of human nature which pervade these sketches, as well as the originality of style and subjects, stamp the author as one of the rarest of men, and makes his book a real treasure. Everybody in Tennessee should have a copy "apas'" him, not only as a just appreciation of the labors of a Tennessean, but as a specimen of funny literature inimitable in itself, and that cannot be counterfeited in a thousand years to come. That it will meet with a general reading there can be no doubt, and the publishers would study their interest by laying aside the "forms" of indefinite editions. The preface and dedication are alone worth twice the price of the book.

Ben Harris McClary, ed., *The Sut Lovingood Papers, 1965* (Knoxville: University of Tennessee Press, 1967), 56. Originally in the *Nashville Union and American,* 25 April 1867.

Sut Lovingood

Mark Twain

It was reported, years ago, that this writer was dead—accidentally shot in a Tennessee doggery before the war, but he has turned up again, and is a conductor on a railroad train that travels some where between Charleston, S.C. and Memphis. His real name is George Harris. I have before me his book, just forwarded by Dick & Fitzgerald, the publishers, New York. It contains all of his early sketches, that used to be so popular in the West, such as his story of his father "actin' hoss," the lizards in the camp-meeting, etc., together with many new ones. The book abounds in humor, and is said to represent the Tennessee dialect correctly. It will sell well in the West, but the Eastern people will call it coarse and possibly taboo it.

Ben Harris McClary, ed., *The Lovingood Papers, 1962* (Knoxville: University of Tennessee Press, 1962), 19. Originally in *San Francisco Daily Alta California*, 14 July 1867.

George Washington Harris

J. Thompson Brown, Jr.

In estimating the value of Sut Lovingood's humor, we must employ American standards, and bear in mind that our American school has alike the virtues and sins of unchastised youth. It is bubbling and irrepressible, and not infrequently lacking in dignity. Worse, perhaps, than aught else, three hundred years has not been a sufficient revolutionary cycle to induce an American to place courteous sympathy before his fun. In brief, American humor is boyish, crude, and boisterous, striking heedlessly, regardless of feelings, propriety, and often even of decency. Our country is large and free, our humor broad and unrestrained; there are none so high as to be immune from its stings. Within bounds these characteristics might be tolerated, but how easy it is for the truant school-boy to transgress the limits of noisy though innocent fun-making and become an untiring nuisance.

Not a few of our authors have invoked dialect, perverted spelling, and *patois*; but if they have succeeded, often it has been the triumph of art over artifice. Sut Lovingood has his own dialect, and along with it his homespun attire and unquenchable thirst for "moonshine," likewise his pride in uncivility. Good John Knox two hundred years ago invented the term, "a sinful carcuse." Sut would have thanked him for that word and laid it by for himself had he once got it. And still Sut is not without glory, nor has his day yet fully gone.

Edwin A. Alderman, Joel Chandler Harris, and Charles W. Kent, eds., *Library of Southern Literature,* 16 vols. (Atlanta: Martin and Hoyt, 1907–09), 5:2100–02.

The original was Harris's assistant, a long, lank, drawling East Tennessee mountaineer, a type worthy of preservation. His picture, though distorted and exaggerated, is none the less the record of a class, so he holds his place in the make-up of our composite nationality. Miss Murfree is far and away the better artist among these folk, but Sut has touches that in realism exceed the ordinary, so let him stand; but pity it is he is not fraught with a single virtue. Miss Murfree has clothed her characters in something of the nobility inherent in a race close to the rock-ribbed mountains, but Sut is *unclothed*, in perfect *unloveliness.* Unique, unrivaled, without a peer he stands alone, though unabashed, in the field of letters.

No recipe for American humor can omit the ingredient of exaggeration, but Sut too often makes exaggeration the lump, leaven, and all. The dough rises, and rightly it should, but it over-pushes all bounds and becomes unfit for either humorous or intellectual diet. Sicily Burns gives him two love powders dissolved in separate glasses of water. That the love prescription was made up of the white and blue of a seidlitz powder would have been delightful and even refined humor had Sut and the swallowed potions been left to the suggestion of the reader. In truth Sut's silence here would have placed him among the immortals. The details following the internal explosion are, however, over-much in the telling, and our hero loses the wreath within his easy grasp. But after all he may not have wanted it.

Again, to show where he just missed success. He "an' a few uther durn'd fools" were one day lounging around "ole man Rogers's" spring. Hen Baily rushes madly on the scene. In haste to get a good stolen pull at the ever-abundant, free-flowing corn-whiskey, he had snatched up the turpentine bottle and gulped down a large dose. Though horrible agony should the next minute take off the victim, what American is there with sympathies so over civilized as not to appreciate the delicate and delightful fitness of things and record in rib-bursting hilarity the writhings of his exquisitely tickled senses? The long-handled gourd, the frantic dip into the spring, the feverish haste with which Hen throws back his head and opens wide his mouth, the awakening of the lizard who was resting in the handle, the scurry for safety to the nearest haven of retreat, and that retreat Hen Baily's throat—these are details no true artist could possibly have survived and recorded; but Sut—yes, he lived to spoil the story with the most minute and disgusting details of the recovery of his friend and the lizard.

But sometimes the author forgets himself and gives a really good bit of description. This same Sicily Burns who played Sut such a sorry trick is painted with vigorous and artistic touches, though with probably too much realism. Sut thus defines her impression upon him:

"I'se hearn in the mountins a fust rate fourth proof smash ove thunder cum onexpected, an' shake the yeath, bringin along a string ove litenin es long es a quarter track, an' es bright es a weldin heat, a-racin down a big pine tree, tarin hit intu broom-splits, an' toof pickers, an' raisin a cloud ove dus', an' bark, an' a army ove lim's wif a smell sorter like the devil wer about, an' the long darnin needil leaves fallin roun wif a tif-tif—quiet sorter soun, an' then a-quiverin on the yeath es littil snakes die; an' I felt quar in my in'ards, sorter ha'f cumfurt, wif a littil glad an' rite smart ove sorry mix'd wif hit.

I'se seed the rattil-snake squar hissef tu cum at me, a-saying z-e-e-e-, wif that nisey tail ove his'n, an' I felt quar agin—mons'rous quar. I've seed the Oconee River jumpin mad frum rock tu rock wif hits clear, cool warter, white foam, an' music"—

"What, Sut?"

"Music; the rushin warter dus make music; so dus the wind, an' the fire in the mountin, an' hit gin me an oneasy queerness agin; but every time I look'd at that gal Sicily Burns, I hed all the feelins mix'd up, ove the litenin, the river, an' the snake, wif a totch ove the quicksilver sensashun a-huntin thru all my veins fur my ticklish place." [Yarns, 77–78]

The book now has little circulation. Three of its readers have expressed to me their opinion, and in justice to Sut the preponderating testimony must be given. From a master mechanic in Knoxville, and from a professor in the University of Chicago come, "It is the best thing ever done in American humor," and "Next to the Bible, it's the best book ever written."

Sut Lovingood's Yarns

George F. Mellen

"Have you a copy of George W. Harris' *Sut Lovingood's Yarns* [*sic*]?
The inquiry was put to the librarian of one of the two large libraries in the city which Harris made his home for the greater part of his life. It emanated from a professor of English in the institution which possessed the other large library.

The answer of the librarian was a negative. The seeker after Tennessee's most widely known book of humor doubtless thought it strange that his search should be so rewarded. Its author spent almost fifty years in Knoxville. The local color of his stories belonged to East Tennessee. The characters in the main were presented as types of the region.

It is true, the characters are grotesque in their exaggerations. In some of the passages, there are suggestions that offend. There is an indelicacy repulsive to those of squeamish tastes. One of the Puritanic mold would exclude the work as inimical to decency. The ultra orthodox would denounce it as hurtful to religious worship and sentiment. In the preface, Sut gives fair warning to such critics. Speaking to his interlocutor, "George," he says,

> "I wants tu put sumwhar atween the eyebrows ove our book, in big winnin-lookin letters, the sarchin, meanin words, what sum pusson writ ontu a 'oman's garter onst, long ago—"
> "*Evil be to him that evil thinks.*"

Knoxville Sentinel, 11 February 1909.

"Them's em, by jingo! . . . I want em fur a gineral skeer—speshully fur
the wimen." [*Yarns,* xi]

However, between the lids of *Yarns* there is many a hearty
laugh. There is much sound philosophy. Underneath the bald caricatures and the canny situations there is much rollicking humor.
Here and there are touches of pathos. In the sketch, "Trapping a
Sheriff," there is the fine passage which describes the sickly wife
of the faithless husband, Sheriff Doltin, calmly awaiting her end.
After picturing her wan cheeks, shrunken form, and hacking
cough, Sut says:

". . . yit in spite ove all this, a sweet smile kiver'd her feeters, like a patch ove
winter sunshine on the slope ove a mountin, an' hit staid thar es steddy an'
bright es the culler dus tu the rose. I 'speck that smile will go back up wif
her when she starts home, whar hit mus' a-cum frum. She must onst been
mons'us temtin tu men tu look at, an' now she's loved by the angils, fur the
seal ove thar king is stamp'd in gold on her forrid. Her shoulder blades, as
they show'd thru her dress, made me think they wer wings a-sproutin fur
her flight tu that cumfort and peace she desarves so well. She's a dealin wif
death now." [*Yarns,* 257]

As a touch of unadulterated philosophy, this is excellent:

". . . ef ever yu dus enything tu enybody wifout cause, yu hates em allers
arterwards, an' sorter wants tu hurt em agin. An' yere's anuther human nater:
ef enything happens [tu] sum feller, I don't keer ef he's yure bes' frien, an' I
don't keer how sorry yu is fur him, thar's a streak ove satisfackshun 'bout
like a sowin thread a-runnin all thru yer sorrer. Yu may be shamed ove hit,
but durn me ef hit ain't thar." [*Yarns,* 245]

While Harris spent most of his life in and about Knoxville, his last
years were passed in Chattanooga, Trenton, Ga., and Decatur, Ala.
When he died a sudden and mysterious death in Knoxville, December 11, 1869, his remains were taken to Chattanooga for inter-
ment. In this city he was intimate with William Crutchfield, who for
one term, 1873–1875, represented the Chattanooga district in Congress. Hesitating to whom he will dedicate his yarns, "George"
makes the suggestion to Sut that this dedication would be appropriate: "To William Crutchfield, of Chattanooga, my friend in storm
and sunshine, brave enough to be true, and true enough to be singular; one who says what he thinks, and very often thinks what he
says." To this Sut philosophically objects: "Ef ever yu is grateful *at
all,* show hit tu them what yu *expeck will* du yu a favor, *never* tu the
'tarnil fool what *hes dun hit*" [*Yarns,* xiv].

Harris was a versatile genius. Besides author, he was silversmith, engineer, steamboat captain, railroad constructor, and postmaster. He was captain of the steamboat "Knoxville," which plied between Knoxville and Chattanooga. When the latter was used in conveying the Cherokee Indians westward, the name "Indian Chief" was substituted. There is little local coloring discernible in the sketches. Here and there are mentioned Black Oak Ridge, Hiwassee Copper Mines, Frog Mountain, indicating the region other than Knoxville wherein he found some of his characters and scenes. One reading the quotations from *Yarns* should not regard the author lacking in ability to use choice English and to indulge in tender sentiment. A passage betraying these qualities and full of local color is in the sketch, "Eaves-dropping a Lodge of Free-masons." To those still living, the names of places and men will recall fond memories. Inasmuch as "George" was a participant, Sut insists that he tell the story, who begins:

"But even now, and here in the thickening twilight, I see gliding past in misty ranks, the forms of Jackson, Hu Lawson White, the Williamses, the Dunlaps, Haywood, Peck, Powell, McKinney, Pleasant Miller, the Andersons, Carrick White, and Mynott Scott. In my boyish eyes they seemed giants, and manhood's more discriminating gaze sees them undiminished. The quiet grave has long ago claimed the last of the band, but memory preserves their fame, and deeds of well-doing. There too, is 'College Hill,' with its clear cool spring at the foot. The 'Bluff,' with its triple echo, the 'Flag Pond,' and its sunny-sided inhabitants, Old Aunt Edy's cakes and beer, the White mill and its dripping dam, Scuffletown Crick, and its walnut trees, 'the Dardis lot with its forbidden grapes,' 'Witt's old field, and its forbidden blackberries,' the 'old church,' and its graveyards. 'Tis strange how faithfully memory paints the paths and places belonging to our boyhood—happy, ragged, thoughtless boyhood. The march of improvement first, then the march and crash of armies, have nearly swept away those, to me, almost sacred places. But they and those 'who were boys then,' still have a place in memory that time nor distance can take, nor the pressing, crowding, bloody events of now dim, nor sorrow obliterate with its tears."

Here Sut interrupts "George's" sentiment and memories, with an outburst, "Oh, komplikated durnashun! that haint hit . . . yu's drunk," and proceeds to tell it in his own vernacular [*Yarns*, 115].

"College Hill" is now the University of Tennessee, with its varied life and numerous buildings. Where the "Flag Pond" stood is now the seat of a busy commerce. The wholesale houses on Jackson Street, the railroad depot and yards of the Southern railway, and elevated thoroughfares tell little of the spreading bosom of the waters on which the village lads sailed their tiny crafts and into which they dashed and splashed. The "old church" was old Methodist Hill that stood with its graveyard across First creek. The forests on the neighboring hillside had been made resonant with the eloquence of Tennessee's most gifted and renowned orator, William T. Kaskell, whose name Harris calls up in the sketch, "Dad's Dog School."

Despite his coarseness here and there, in healthy minds the yarns of Sut Lovingood are provocative of merriment. They are in no sense intended to be faithful portrayals of the people among whom Harris dwelt and whom he loved. They are simply the outcome of a riotous imagination, which reveled in a keen sense of the ludicrous and the grotesque. They are far removed from delicate, delicious humor, taking on its boisterous and outlandish phases.

George Washington Harris

Walter Blair

The author who most consistently uses the framework narrative method to portray his chief character is George W. Harris. His book, *Sut Lovingood. Yarns Spun by a "Nat'ral Born Durn'd Fool"* (1867), the product of a man who himself was an adept at oral story-telling[1]—a book which is typical of Southwestern humor because it is full of local color, exuberant, masculine, "the nearest thing to the undiluted oral humor of the Middle West that has found its way into print"[2]—has never had the widespread appreciation it deserves, partly, perhaps, because its artistry has never been sufficiently appreciated, partly because its faults have been overemphasized by over-squeamish critics.[3] Nevertheless, this volume which, in a sense, may be thought of as a picaresque novel in the form of anecdotes within a framework, represents a highly artistic use of the formula employed by Thorpe in his masterpiece, ["The Big Bear of Arkansas"].

Harris's tales have all the qualities made possible by this technique. So artless do they seem that even such a discerning critic as Watterson takes for granted that any reader will observe that in Sut's yarns there is "little attempt at technical literary finish, either in description or proportion . . . ; the author is seemingly satisfied to aim merely at his point, and, this reached, to be satisfied to leave it work out its own moral and effect."[4] Yet a careful study will reveal that

Native American Humor (1937; reprint, with new material, New York: Harper and Row, 1960), 96–101.

there is sufficient artistry splendidly to reveal Sut's character and to underline various incongruities. In the framework, Sut is revealed by direct description—a "queer looking, long legged, short bodied, small headed, white haired, hog eyed"[5] youth, who comes into view at the beginning or the conclusion of various sketches—reining up his bow-necked sorrel in front of Pat Nash's grocery or Capehart's Doggery to tell a yarn to a crowd of loafing mountaineers, weaving along the street after a big drunk or a big fight, or stretching his skinny body at full length by a cool spring at noon. Indirectly, too, by showing the reactions of those who listen to Sut's tales, Harris reveals his hero's character. A rat-faced youth who is conquered by Sut's badinage (Yarns, 21), "George" (Harris), who claims that a part of a tale is not true (Yarns, 120) or who tolerantly encourages Sut's yarns, even when he is awakened to hear them (Yarns, 123), the book agent who is insulted and frightened by Sut's onslaught (Yarns, 244), others affected in various ways by Sut's talk, help us to understand the manner of person he is.

Sut's character is also revealed, moreover, by the tales he tells about himself, tales which display "his keen delight for Hallowe'en fun,—there is no ulterior motive (except occasionally Sut's desire to 'get even'), no rascality, no gambling, no sharping as in Simon Suggs . . . Sut is simply the genuine naive roughneck mountaineer riotously bent on raising hell."[6] They indicate his chief passions— telling stories, eating good food, drinking "cork-screw kill-devil whisky," hugging pretty girls, and "breedin skeers amung durned fools" by playing pranks. Just as revealing are his dislikes: Yankee peddlers, Yankee lawyers, Yankee scissor-grinders—any kind of Yankees, sheriffs, most preachers, learned men who use big words or flowery language, tavern keepers who serve bad food, and reformers. His idea of what is funny shows us what kind of person he is: a comic situation, according to this son of the soil, is usually one in which a character of the sort he hates, or preferably a large number of characters, get into highly uncomfortable circumstances.[7] Comic to him, too, are the procreative and bodily functions, the animal qualities in humans and the human qualities in animals.

The language he employs in his monologues helps reveal his character—a language polished little by book larnin', Rabelaisian, close to the soil, but withal poetic in an almost Elizabethan fashion.[8] The very figures of speech he employs have more than comedy to recommend them. They are conceits, comic because they are startlingly appropriate and inappropriate at the same time, devices for characterization because they arise with poetic directness from the life Sut knows. Consider these passages, redolent of Sut's knowledge of nature and of liquor groceries:

> Bake dwelt long ontu the crop ove dimes tu be gethered frum that field; that he'd make more than thar wer spots ontu forty fawns in July, not tu speak ove the big gobs ove repertashun he'd tote away, a shinin all over his close, like litnin bugs ontu a dorg fennil top. [*Yarns*, 62]

> her skin wer es white es the inside ove a frogstool, an' her cheeks an' lips es rosey es a pearch's gills in dorgwood blossom time—an' sich a smile! why, when hit struck yu far an' squar hit felt jis' like a big ho'n ove onrectifed ole Munongahaley, arter yu'd been sober fur a month, a-tendin ove a ten hoss prayer-meetin twist a day, an' mos' ove the nites. [*Yarns*, 76]

> Wirt hed changed his grocery range, an' the sperrits at the new lick-log hed more scrimmage seed an' raise-devil intu hit than the old biled drink he wer used tu, an' three ho'ns histed his tail, an' sot his bristils 'bout es stiff es eight ove the uther doggery juice wud. So when cort sot at nine o'clock, Wirt wer 'bout es fur ahead es cleaving [eleving],[9] ur half pas' that.
>
> The hollerin stage ove the disease now struck him, so he roar'd one good year-quiverin roar. [*Yarns*, 249]

> [Of a man howling in fear and pain:] The noise he made soundid jis' like a two-hoss mowin-mersheen, druv by chain-lightnin, a-cuttin thru a dry cane brake on a big bet. [*Yarns*, 268–69]

Recited in Sut's drawl, with far more touches of dialect than are here revealed, in fact, in "the wildest of East Tennessee jargon,"[10] these passages and others in Sut's stories contrast amusingly with the rhetorical framework language. Harris seemed to realize the possibilities of ludicrous antitheses in language, for he liked to put Sut's talk alongside of flowery passages or of learned language in which big words predominated. Humorous, too, is the contrast between the circumstances under which Sut tells his tale and the harrowing scenes he describes. Incidentally, most of the happenings about which Sut tells never could be amusing unless they were removed by several steps from reality.

But the great incongruity in the tales, only partly exploited by Harris, is that between the realistically depicted world of the framework and the fantastically comic world created by Sut in the highly colored, highly imaginative enclosed narrative. His is a world in which the religious life of the Smoky Mountains is grotesquely warped until all its comedy is emphasized, a cosmos wherein the squalor in which the Lovingoods live—squalor without alleviation,

without shame—somehow becomes very jolly. It is a world in
which the crowds at a camp meeting, a frolic or a quarter race[11] are
revealed in postures and garbs as amusing as those of the earthy and
lively figures that throng a canvas by Peter Breughel. Startlingly, it
is a world in which scent, sound, form, color, and motion are not
only vividly lifelike but also hilariously comic. Here is a mare in that
strange country, whose rider has just shouted "Get up!":

> Well she did "get up," rite then an' thar, an' staid up long enuf tu lite twenty
> foot further away, in a broad trimblin squat, her tail hid a-tween her thighs,
> an' her years a-dancin a-pas' each uther, like scissors a-cuttin. The jolt of the
> litnin sot the clock {which her rider was carrying and which prodded her
> unmercifully} tu striking. Bang-zee-bang-zee-whang-zee. She listined pow'-
> ful 'tentive tu the three fus' licks, an' they seem'd tu go thru her es quick es
> quick-silver wud git thru a sifter. She waited fur no more, but jis' gin her
> hole soul up tu the wun job ove runnin frum onder that infunel Yankee, an'
> his hive ove bumble bees, ratil snakes, an' other orful hurtin things, es she
> tuck hit tu be. [*Yarns*, 40]

Here is a bull on a rampage in the public market:

> . . . jis' a-tarin, a thuteen hunder' poun' black an' white bull, wif his tail es
> strait up in the air es a telegraf pole, an' a chesnut fence rail tied acrost his
> ho'ns wif hickory withes. He wer a-totin his hed low, an' every lick he made
> . . . he'd blow whoff, outen his snout. . . . He'd say whoff! an' a hunder' an'
> sixty poun' nigger wud fly up in the air like ontu a grasshopper, an' cum back
> spread like a frog. . . . Whoff! agin, an' a boy wud turn ten sumersets towards
> the river. Whoff! an' a Amherst 'oman lit a-straddil ove a old fat feller's neck,
> wif a jolt what jumped his terbacker outen his mouf an' scrunched *him,*
> while she went on down hill on all fours in a fox trot. . . . A littil bal'-heded
> man, dress'd in gole specks an' a gole-heded walkin stick, wer a-passin . . .
> he look'd like he wer a-cyferin out a sum . . . in his hed. Whoff! an' the specks
> lit on the ruff ove the market hous', an' the stick, gole aind fus', sot in a milk
> can sixty foot off. As tu ball hed hissef, I los' site ove 'im while the specks
> wer in the air; he jis' disappear'd frum mortul vishun sumhow, sorter like
> breff frum a lookin-glass. [*Yarns*, 126–27]

In such passages as these, in passages which use conceits even
more grotesque than those quoted above,[12] in passages of imaginative exaggeration,[13] of strangely linked entities,[14] the world of Sut's
stories, tremendously different from the world where Sut's whisky
flask flashes in the sun, takes its queer shape to delight the reader.
And from the passages about Sut, and from his imaginative tales
emerges a character, coarser and earthier, perhaps, than any other
in our literature during the nineteenth century, but at the same
time, understandably true to life, an ingratiating mischief-maker,

America's Till Eulenspiegel,[15] in his own right a poet and a great creator of comedy.

In *Sut Lovingood* the antebellum humor of the South reaches its highest level of achievement before Mark Twain. The author of this book, like his contemporaries, was a man of the world who became an author almost by accident. Like them, he wrote tales full of authentic local color, zestful yarns which blossomed from the rich subsoil of oral humor. Encouraged by the *Spirit of the Times* and other publications, he learned to employ the best method for telling a story developed by members of a highly artistic group, making the most of the framework technique for setting forth a mock oral tale, making the most, too, of the mock oral tale itself, with its colloquial richness, its disarming directness, its vivid comic detail. If his writings were better than the rest, they were better because he had more sense of incongruities, more exuberance, more imagination, and because he had greater genius than his contemporaries for transferring the unique artistry of the oral narrative to the printed page.

Notes

1. See Charlie's letter from "Out West," in which he tells how Harris came charging down the street to tell a "cock and bull story" about a steamboat explosion. "The story is very good," he concludes, "particularly when you hear it told by S——l [Harris's pen name] . . ."—*Spirit of the Times,* XVIII, 73 (April 8, 1848). [See the reprint of Day's biography in this volume.]
2. Napier Wilt, *Some American Humorists* (New York: T. Nelson and Sons, 1929), 130.
3. The book has three faults: 1) Sut employs a dialect which some readers think too hard to translate; 2) Sometimes the details about the plights of the victims or details incidental to the tales are coarse, in bad taste, and unfunny; 3) The repetition in his tales of the motif of physical discomfort is so frequent that it becomes monotonous. None of these faults, in my opinion, should damn the book. Sut's dialect is mastered after a little effort. Harris suggested that those who were troubled by the second fault would be those who had a wholesome fear of the devil, and ought to, and those who hadn't a great deal of faith that their reputation would stand much of a strain; and "fur a gineral skeer—speshully fur the wimen," quoted the words, "*Evil*

be to him that evil thinks" [*Yarns*, xi]. The point is well taken: the stories are no coarser than highly admired stories by some of the greatest writers. And the richness of the detail may well atone for the monotonous resemblances between situations.

4. Henry Watterson, *Oddities in Southern Life and Character* (Boston: Houghton Mifflin, 1882), 415.

5. [George Washington Harris, *"Sut Lovingood. Yarns"*: A Facsimile of the 1867 Dick and Fitzgerald Edition, ed. M. Thomas Inge (Memphis: Saint Lukes Press, 1987), 19. All references are to this edition and hereafter will be cited in the text.]

6. Franklin J. Meine, ed., *Tall Tales of the Southwest* (New York: Alfred A. Knopf, 1930), xxiv.

7. A host of wasps or bees which interfere with the business or social activities of various people, a wild bull on a rampage, lizards surreptitiously introduced into the pantaloons of a preacher, who thereupon disrupts a camp meeting—these and similar agencies are likely to be the inciting forces in Sut's little comedies.

8. In Sut's speech better than elsewhere, one may see what George H. McKnight meant when, in Chapter X of *Modern English in the Making* (New York: Appleton and Co., 1928), he spoke of Shakespeare's language being enriched by common speech. "The effect produced," he said, "is like that of the renewed metaphors to be heard in modern times in the speech of the frontier, where, free from the blighting influence of learning, forms of language are created afresh."

9. [See Hershel Parker's essay in this volume for a discussion about this word.]

10. Henry Watterson, *The Compromises of Life* (New York: Fox, Duffield and Co., 1903), 66.

11. Harris's masterpiece, among all the stories I have seen, a number of which have not appeared in book form, is "Bill Ainsworth's Quarter Race," in the Knoxville *Press and Messenger,* June 4, 1868. [See M. Thomas Inge, ed., *High Times and Hard Times: Sketches and Tales by George Washington Harris* (Nashville: Vanderbilt University Press, 1967), 198–206.]

12. For example, this description of a clever man: "Why he'd a hilt his own in a pond full ove eels, an' a swallerd the las durn one ove em, and then sot the pond tu turnin a shoe-paig mill" [*Yarns*, 38].

13. Sut's maw, for example, when frightened, "out-run her shadder thuty yards in cumin half a mile" [*Yarns*, 68], and of a man's big nose, Sut remarked that "The skin ofen hit wud a-kivered a saddil, an' wer jis' the rite culler fur the job, an' the holes looked like the bow-ports ove a gun-boat" [*Yarns*, 287]—and several lines of exaggeration of a similar sort follow.

14. The incongruous catalogue delights Sut. One example: a horse, running inefficiently, suggests this: "The gait . . . wer a 'sortmint made up ove dromedary gallop, shake slidin, side windin, an' ole Firginey jig, tetched off wif a sprinkil ove quadrille. . . " [*Yarns*, 291].

15. Eulenspiegel, too, liked to get people tangled up in conflicts, enjoyed particularly disrupting churchly gatherings by discomforting priests, and played tricks which were gross, coarse, and sometimes brutal. Sut's story, "Well! Dad's Dead"—in the Knoxville *Press and Messenger*, November 19, 1868 [an earlier version appeared 15 November 1868 in the *Knoxville Daily Press and Herald*; see Inge, *High Times*, 207–11], has the theme but none of the details of the anecdote about Eulenspiegel's burial: "He was strange in life, he wants to be so after his death"; like several of Sut's yarns, it poetically combines the macabre and the grotesque. Enid Welsford, in *The Fool: His Social and Literary History* (London: Faber and Faber, 1935), 47, summarizes Eulenspiegel's career in words which might apply equally well to Sut's career: he "indulges in an occasional wit-combat, but his main purpose is 'to live joyously for nothing,' he makes mischief for the fun of the thing, and slips away before he can be made to suffer the consequences. There is something elvish about him. . . ." Nevertheless, it is very improbable that Harris ever heard of Sut's medieval predecessor.

Man in the Open Air

F. O. Matthiessen

Harris took the by then traditional framework for the tall tale, and, because he possessed a keen eye and ear, could use it as a means to portray the frontier life with both realism and fantastic extravagance—the union of incongruities most natural to American humor. Sut, who tells all the stories to Harris, is not yet twenty but has a definite philosophy of life:

> "Men wer made a-purpus jis' tu eat, drink, an' fur stayin awake in the yearly part ove the nites: an' wimen wer made tu cook the vittils, mix the sperits, an' help the men du the stayin awake. That's all, an' nuthin more, onless hits fur the wimen tu raise the devil atwix meals, an' knit socks atwix drams, an' the men tu play short kerds, swap hosses wif fools, an' fite fur exersise, at odd spells."[1]

The world that is refracted through Sut's hard and knowing eyes is that of the practical joker who enjoys violence and cruelty, and often ends his situations in complete social disruption. He delights to put lizards in a parson's pants, or to turn loose a hornet's nest at a prayer meeting; and he strews unconscious bodies around the scene of a fight with as much gusto as Fielding. He is specially pleased with the result when the victims are the sheriff or the circuit-rider, who, with Yankee peddlers or anyone from Massachusetts, are the chief objects of Sut's lawless distaste. He can see no sense in preaching: "Oh, hits jis' no use in thar talkin, an' groanin, an' sweatin thar-

American Renaissance (New York: Oxford University Press, 1941), 642–45.

sefs about hit; they mus' jis' upset nater ontu her hed, an' keep her thar, ur shet up. Less taste this yere whisky" [*Yarns*, 77]. What Sut enjoys most are social gatherings, quilting parties and dances, and horse races, even though what he contributes to make a lively time livelier generally turns the occasion, as in the case of Sicily Burns' wedding, into the most misfortunate one "since ole Adam married that heifer, what wer so fon' ove talkin tu snaix."[2]

Sut's life at home with his folks was of a squalor unalleviated and unashamed, but he could admire a hero when he saw one, particularly Wirt Staples, the blacksmith's cousin. Even at the top of Wirt's boast of what he would do to the "ole false apostil" of the law, you couldn't think for the life of you that he had overbragged a single word:

> His britches wer buttoned tite roun his loins, an' stuffed 'bout half intu his boots, his shut bagg'd out abuv, an' wer es white es milk, his sleeves wer rolled up tu his arm-pits, an' his collar wer es wide open es a gate, the mussils on his arms moved about like rabbits onder the skin, an' ontu his hips an' thighs they play'd like the swell on the river, his skin wer clear red an' white, an' his eyes a deep, sparklin, wickid blue, while a smile fluttered like a hummin bird roun his mouf all the while. When the State-fair offers a premin fur *men* like they now dus fur jackasses, I means tu enter Wirt Staples, an' I'll git hit, ef thar's five thousand entrys. [*Yarns*, 253]

There is "the central man" of the Smoky Mountains to stand beside Emerson's. He is a blood brother to Bulkington, whose appearance so struck Ishmael at the Spouter Inn. That mariner

> "stood full six feet in height, with noble shoulders, and a chest like a cofferdam. I have seldom seen such brawn in a man. His face was deeply brown and burnt, making his white teeth dazzling by the contrast; while in the deep shadows of his eyes floated some reminiscences that did not seem to give him much joy. His voice at once announced that he was a Southerner, and from his fine stature, I thought he must be one of those tall mountaineers from the Alleghenian Ridge in Virginia." [*Moby Dick*, chap. 3]

When the *Pequod* sets sail, Melville dwells on the fact that Bulkington is at the helm. Though he had just landed in midwinter from a four years' dangerous voyage, he has unrestingly pushed off again. "Know ye, now, Bulkington?" Melville symbolizes in him the natural seeker for "the open independence" of truth's sea, and his last words to him are: "Bear thee grimly, demigod! Up from the spray of thy ocean-perishing—straight up, leaps thy apotheosis!" [*Moby Dick*, chap. 23].

Wirt Staples was troubled with no such tragic thoughts. His temper could be described in Rabelais' words: "a certain jollity of mind pickled in a scorn of fortune." Wirt is the common man in his full stature, but he is not quite what Jefferson had foreseen. Still less is he the representative of the race that Noah Webster had hoped to educate by his spelling book, a sober, dignified and well-trained folk, neither peasants on the one hand, nor corrupt aristocrats on the other, but developing the refinements of a wise culture. Wirt roars like a bull, or—in a shift of the animal imagery of which Harris was so fond since it brought man close to nature—when Wirt has had about eight drinks, he hoists his tail and sets his bristles ready for the sheriff, whom he presently knocks out with a leg of venison. The language Harris put in his mouth makes an epitome of what Mencken has found recorded in the American's speech: "his bold and somewhat grotesque imagination, his contempt for dignified authority, his lack of aesthetic sensitiveness, his extravagant humor."

Harris' gifts go beyond the difficult one of being able to translate to the printed page such tales as he had heard. Sut may say, "I ladles out my words at randum" [Yarns, 134], and he may repeat over and again the same comic-strip situations for his exploits; but his inventiveness is astonishing, particularly in the kind of similes that, irrelevant to his narrative, hand you gratis a compressed scene or character-sketch: "He watched fur openins tu work off sum kind ove devilment, jist es clost es a ole 'oman what wer wunst onsanctified hersef watches her darters when a suckus ur a camp meetin am in heat" [Yarns, 61]. Harris possesses on the comic level something of what Melville does on the tragic, the rare kind of dramatic imagination that can get movement directly into words. This brings a wonderfully kinetic quality to whole situations, to Bart Davis' dance or to the ructions caused in Lynchburg market by an escaped bull. The ability to use every possible verbal gesture of action alone could create this whirlwind description of a preacher attacked by hornets:

> "I seed him fotch hissef a lick . . . with both hans ontu the place whar they brands Freemasons an' mustangs, an' he shot his belly forwards an' his shoulders back'ards, like ontu a 'oman shettin the nex' tu the top drawer ove a beauro; an' he cum outen that pulpit back'ards a-tarin, his hans a-flyin' roun his hed like a par ove windin blades." [Yarns, 166]

The panorama of life that flashes by in Sut's yarns may well remind you of Josh Billings' definition of our humor: "Americans love caustick things: they would prefer turpentine to colone-water, if they had tew drink either. So with their relish of humor; they must have it on the half-shell with cayenne." But in many casual passages, without consciously intending it, Sut catches more surely the quality of homely existence. In his picture of Wirt's woman he completes his version of the heroic myth, as he celebrates the abundance he has glimpsed and so knows to be possible:

> "She aint one ove yure she-cat wimmin, allers spittin an' groanin, an' swellin thar tails 'bout thar vartu. She never talks a word about hit, no more nor if she didn't hev eny; an' she hes es true a heart es ever beat agin a shiff hem, ur a husban's shut. But she am full ove fun, an' I mout add es purty es a hen canary, an' I swar I don't b'l'eve the 'oman knows hit." [*Yarns*, 260]

This makes the prelude to his description of her cooking, for Sut understands the connection between good food and a husband's love, and gives his own kind of hymn to fertility:

> Wirt's wife got yearly supper, a rale suckit-rider's supper, whar the 'oman ove the hous' wer a rich b'lever. Thar wer chickens cut up, an' fried in butter, brown, white, flakey, light, hot biskit, made wif cream, scrambil'd aigs, yaller butter, fried ham, in slices es big es yure han, pickil'd beets, an' cowcumbers, roas'in ears, shaved down an' fried, sweet taters, baked, a stack ove buckwheat cakes, es full ove holes es a sifter, an' a bowl ove strained honey, tu fill the holes . . . I gets dorg hungry every time I sees Wirt's wife, ur even her side-saddil, ur her frocks a-hangin on the close-line. [*Yarns*, 261–62]

Notes

1. [George Washington Harris, *"Sut Lovingood. Yarns": A Facsimile of the 1867 Dick and Fitzgerald Edition*, ed. M. Thomas Inge (Memphis: Saint Lukes Press, 1987), 88.

2. [*Yarns*, 96.] Sut's recipe for a successful party is a pleasant one to remember, and also provides an instance of Harris' skill in building up rhetoric: "Hit wer the bigges' quiltin ever Missis Yardley hilt, an' she hed hilt hundreds; everybody wer thar, 'scept the constibil an' suckit-rider, two dam easily-spared pussons; the numbers ni ontu even too; jis' a few more boys nur gals; that made hit more exhitin, fur hit gin the gals a chance tu kick an' squeal a littil, wifout runnin eny risk ove not gittin kissed at all, an' hit gin reasonabil grouns fur a few scrimmages amung the he's. Now es kissin an' fitin am the pepper an' salt ove all soshul getherins, so hit wer more espishully wif this ove ours. Es I swung my eyes over the crowd,

George, I thought quiltins, managed in a morril an' sensibil way, truly am good things—good fur free drinkin, good fur free eatin, good fur free huggin, good fur free dancin, good fur free fitin, an' goodest ove all fur poperlatin a country fas'" [*Yarns*, 138–39].

Poisoned!

Edmund Wilson

The malignant Tennessee "cracker" had already been introduced
into literature by the Tennessee journalist George Washington Harris, who invented a comic character called Sut Lovingood and exploited him for fifteen years as a narrator of fantastic stories and as
a mouth-piece for political satire. These sketches, of which the first
appeared in 1854, were printed not only in the local press but also
in a New York sporting paper. Sidney Lanier may have known Harris: he was something of a public figure in Knoxville, which is only
fifteen miles from Montvale Springs, where Sidney Lanier's grand-
father Sterling Lanier, whose Christian name he had used for the
family name of his hero, possessed the impressive estate which is
also made to figure in *Tiger-Lilies;* and he must certainly have
known about the Lovingood stories. These stories were collected, in
1867, in a volume called *Sut Lovingood. Yarns Spun by a "Nat'ral
Born Durn'd Fool,"* which was reviewed by Mark Twain in a San
Francisco paper and to which he perhaps owed something; but Harris's work, after his death in 1869, seems to have been soon forgotten, and it was only in the thirties of the present century that—in
the course of the recent excavations in the field of American literature—such writers as Bernard DeVoto, Constance Rourke and F. O.
Matthiessen began to take an interest in Sut Lovingood.

Bernard DeVoto thought that it might be a good idea to have the

Patriotic Gore (New York: Oxford University Press, 1962), 507–19; originally in the *New
Yorker,* 7 May 1955, 138–46.

Lovingood stories "translated" out of the dense hillbilly dialect in which Harris had tried phonetically to write them, and this suggestion was taken up by Professor Brom Weber, who published in 1954 a selection of the Lovingood pieces slightly expurgated and transposed into a more readable language. This version was not, however, an entire success. In attempting to clean up Sut Lovingood and make him attractive to the ordinary reader—an ambition probably hopeless—Mr. Weber has produced something that is not of much value to the student of literature. He is correct in pointing out that Harris, in trying to render Sut's illiterate speech, has inconsistently mixed written misspelling, intended to look funny on the printed page—though Sut has never learned to write—with a phonetic transcription of the way he talks; but the writing does have a coarse texture as well as a rank flavor, and to turn it, as the editor has done, into something that is closer to conventional English, and to dilute it with paragraphs and strings of dots, is to deprive it of a good deal of this. By the time Mr. Weber gets done with him, Sut Lovingood hardly even sounds like a Southerner; it is fatal to the poor-white dialect to turn "naik" and "hit" into "neck" and "it." What is worse, from the scholarly point of view, is to comb out "words {that} are obsolete and others {that} are probably meaningless to all but a handful of contemporary readers." If the book was to be reprinted, the text should have been given intact, and the unfamiliar words as well as the topical allusions explained. Mr. Weber makes no effort to do this, nor—though Harris, at the time of his death, was preparing a second volume—does he add any new material except for three little lampoons on Lincoln. Sut himself is depicted on the jacket as a stalwart and bearded mountaineer, a portrayal that has nothing in common with the dreadful, half-bestial lout of the original illustrations.

One is also rather surprised at the editor's idea of deleting "three lines of an extremely offensive nature." One of the most striking things about *Sut Lovingood* is that it is all as offensive as possible. It takes a pretty strong stomach nowadays—when so much of the disgusting in our fiction is not rural but urban or suburban—to get through it in any version. I should say that, as far as my experience goes, it is by far the most repellent book of any real literary merit in American literature. This kind of crude and brutal humor was something of an American institution all through the nineteenth century. The tradition of the crippling practical joke was carried on almost to the end of the century with *Peck's Bad Boy*, and that of the nasty schoolboy by certain of the writings of Eugene Field, a professional sentimentalist, who, however, when working for the Denver *Tribune* betrayed a compulsive fondness for puerile and disgusting jokes: cockroaches and boarding-house hash and collywobbles from eating green peaches. But the deadpan murders and corpses of Mark Twain's early Far Western sketches are given an impressive grimness by the imperviousness to horror their tone implies, and the nihilistic butcheries of Ambrose Bierce derive a certain tragic accent from his background of the Civil War. The boorish or macabre joke, as exploited by these Western writers, does perform a kind of purgative function in rendering simply comic stark hardships and disastrous adventures. The exploits of Sut Lovingood, however, have not even this kind of dignity. He is neither a soldier nor a pioneer enduring a cruel ordeal; he is a peasant squatting in his own filth. He is not making a jest of his trials; he is avenging his inferiority by tormenting other people. His impulse is avowedly sadistic. The keynote is struck in the following passage (I give it in the original Tennessean):

"I hates ole Onsightly Peter {so called because he was selling encyclopedias}, jis' caze he didn't seem tu like tu hear me narrate las' night; that's human nater the yeath over, an' yere's more univarsal onregenerit human nater: ef ever yu dus enything tu enybody wifout cause, yu hates em allers arterwards, an' sorter wants tu hurt em agin. An' yere's anuther human nater: ef enything happens [tu] sum feller, I don't keer ef he's yure bes' frien, an' I don't keer how sorry yu is fur him, thar's a streak ove satisfackshun 'bout like a sowin thread a-runnin all thru yer sorrer. Yu may be shamed ove hit, but durn me ef hit ain't thar. Hit will show like the white cottin chain in mean cassinett; brushin hit onder only hides hit. An' yere's a littil more; no odds how good yu is tu yung things, ur how kine yu is in treatin em, when yu sees a littil long laiged lamb a-shakin hits tail, an' a-dancin staggerinly onder hits mam a-huntin fur the tit, ontu hits knees, yer fingers *will* itch tu seize that ar tail, an' fling the littil ankshus son ove a mutton over the fence amung the blackberry briars, not tu hurt hit, but jis' tu disapint hit. Ur say, a littil calf, a-buttin fas' under the cow's fore-laigs, an' then the hine, wif the pint ove hits tung stuck out, makin suckin moshuns, not yet old enuf tu know the bag aind ove hits mam frum the hookin aind, don't yu want tu kick hit on the snout, hard enough tu send hit backwards, say fifteen foot, jis' tu show hit that buttin won't allers fetch milk? Ur a baby even, rubbin hits heels apas' each uther, a-rootin an' a-snifflin arter the breas', an' the mam duin her bes' tu git hit out, over the hem ove her clothes, don't yu feel hungry tu gin hit jis' one 'cussion cap slap, rite ontu the place what sum day'll fit a saddil, ur a sowin cheer, tu show hit what's atwixt hit an' the grave; that hit stans a pow'ful chance not tu be fed every time hits hungry, ur in a hurry?"[1]

In view of this, the comments on Sut Lovingood by our recent academic critics are among the curiosities of American scholarship. We find Mr. J. Franklin Meine [sic], in *Tall Tales of the Southwest,* speaking of this hero's "keen delight for Hallowe'en *fun,* {italics the author's}—there is no ulterior motive (except occasionally Sut's desire to 'get even'), no rascality, no gambling, no sharping. . . . Sut is simply the genuine naive roughneck mountaineer riotously bent on raising hell," and again, "For vivid imagination, comic plot, Rabelaisian touch and sheer *fun,* the 'Sut Lovingood Yarns' surpass anything else in American humor." "Ultimately," asserts Mr. Weber, "the mythic universalities such as heroism, fertility, masculinity, and femininity emerge over a bedrock of elemental human values which Sut has carved out in the course of his adventures, values such as love, joy, truth, justice, etc. These are only some of the positive concepts which Sut has admired and championed, and it is no small feat that they emerge from behind a protagonist who has ironically been deprecated by his creator. This is humor on a grand scale."

Now, Sut Lovingood can be called "Rabelaisian" only in the sense that he is often indecent by nineteenth-century standards and that he runs to extravagant language and monstrously distorted descriptions. Unlike Rabelais, he is always malevolent and always excessively sordid. Here is an example of his caricature at its best:

"I seed a well appearin man onst, ax one ove em {the proprietors of taverns, evidently carpetbaggers} what lived ahine a las' year's crap ove red hot brass wire whiskers run tu seed, an' shingled wif har like ontu mildew'd flax, wet wif saffron warter, an' laid smoof wif a hot flat-iron, ef he cud spar him a scrimpshun ove soap? The 'perpryiter' anser'd in soun's es sof an' sweet es a poplar dulcimore, tchuned by a good nater'd she angel in butterfly wings an' cobweb shiff, that he never wer jis' so sorry in all his born'd days tu say no, but the fac' wer the soljers hed stole hit; 'a towil then,' 'the soljers hed stole hit'; 'a tumbler,' 'the soljers hed stole hit'; 'a lookin glass,' 'the soljers hed stole hit'; 'a pitcher ove warter,' 'the soljers hed stole hit'; 'then please give me a cleaner room.' Quick es light cum the same dam lie, 'the soljers hed stole hit too.' They buys scalded butter, caze hit crumbles an' yu can't tote much et a load on yer knife; they keeps hit four months so yu won't want to go arter a second load. They stops up the figgers an' flowers in the woffil irons fur hit takes butter tu fill the holes in the woffils. They makes soup outen dirty towils, an' jimson burrs; coffee outen niggers' ole wool socks, roasted; tea frum dorg fennil, an' toas' frum ole brogan insoles. They keeps bugs in yer bed tu make yu rise in time fur them tu get the sheet fur a tablecloth. They gins yu a inch ove candil tu go tu bed by, an' a littil nigger tu fetch back the stump tu make gravy in the mornin, fur the hunk ove bull naik yu will swaller fur brekfus, an' they puts the top sheaf ontu thar orful

merlignerty when they menshuns the size ove yer bill, an' lasly, while yu're
gwine thru yer close wif a sarch warrun arter fodder enuf tu pay hit, they re-
freshes yer memory ove other places, an' other times, by tellin yu ove the orful high price ove tuckeys, aigs, an' milk. When the devil takes a likin tu a
feller, an' wants tu make a sure thing ove gittin him, he jis' puts hit intu his
hed to open a cat-fish tavern, with a gran' rat attachmint, gong 'cumpan-
imint, bull's neck variashun, cockroach corus an' bed-bug refrain, an' dam
ef he don't git him es sure es he rattils the fust gong. An' durn thar onary
souls, they looks like they expected yu tu b'leve that they am pius, decent,
an' fit tu be 'sociated wif, by lookin down on yu like yu belonged tu the onregenerit, an' keepin a cussed ole spindel-shank, rattlin crazy, peaner, wif
mud daubers nestes onder the soundin board, a-bummin out 'Days ove Ab-
sins' ur 'the Devil's Dream,' bein druv thar too, by thar long-waisted, greasey
har'd darter, an' listen'd tu by jis' sich durn'd fools es I is." [*Yarns,* 176–78]

As for the "fun" of Sut Lovingood, it is true that Harris explained
his aim as merely to revive for the reader "sich a laugh es is remembered wif his keerless boyhood" [*Yarns,* xi], and that he liked
to express his nostalgia for the dances and quiltings of his youth,
but even in one of Harris's pre-Lovingood sketches that deal with
one of these, the fun seems mainly to consist of everybody's getting
beaten to a pulp, and in the Lovingood stories themselves, the fun
entirely consists of Sut's spoiling everybody else's fun. He loves to
break up such affairs. One of his milder devices is setting bees and
hornets on people. In this way, he ruins the wedding of a girl who
has refused his advances and dismissed him with an unpleasant
practical joke, and puts to rout a Negro revivalist rally—for he runs
true to poor-white tradition in despising and persecuting the Negroes. He rejoices when his father, naked, is set upon by "a ball
ho'nets nes' ni ontu es big es a hoss's hed" [*Yarns,* 24] and driven to
jump into the water. Sut gloats over "dad's bald hed fur all the yeath
like a peeled inyin, a bobbin up an' down an' aroun, an' the ho'nets
sailin roun tuckey buzzard fashun, an' every onst in a while one, an'
sum times ten, wud take a dip at dad's bald hed" [*Yarns,* 26]. This
leaves the old man "a pow'ful curious, vishus, skeery lookin cuss.
. . . His hed am es big es a wash pot, an' he hasent the fust durned
sign ove an eye—jist two black slits" [*Yarns,* 28]. Sut, who supposes
himself to be his mother's only legitimate child, has nothing but
contempt for his father as an even greater fool than himself, who has
bequeathed to him only misery, ignorance, and degradation. Most
of all, however, his hatred is directed against anybody who shows
any signs of gentility, idealism, or education. On such people, under the influence of bad whisky, to which he refers as "kill-devil" or

"bald face," he revenges himself by methods that range from humiliation to mayhem. His habit of denouncing his victims as hypocrites, adulterers, or pedants is evidently what has convinced Mr. Weber that Sut Lovingood cherishes "values such as love, joy, truth, justice, etc." But he is equally vicious with anyone who happens for any other reason to irritate him. In the case of an old lady who loves to make quilts, he rides into her quilting party with a horse he has driven frantic, ripping up all the quilts and trampling the hostess to death. This is Sut's only recorded human murder, but animals he has more at his mercy, and he loves to kill dogs, cats, and frogs. It is not in the least true, as another of Sut's encomiasts has said, that pain does not exist in Sut Lovingood's world. On the contrary, the sufferings of his victims are described with considerable realism, and the furtively snickering Sut enjoys every moment of them. It is good to be reminded by Mr. Meine that his hero is never shown as addicted to gambling or sharping.

Nor is it possible to imagine that Harris is aiming at Swiftian satire. It is plain that he identifies himself with Sut, and his contemporaries referred to him as Sut, just as Anatole France in his day was referred to as M. Bergeret. "Sumtimes, George, I wishes," says Sut, addressing his creator, "I cud read an' write jis' a littil" [Yarns, ix]. George Harris himself had had—apparently at intervals—but a year and a half of schooling, and it is obvious that he is able to express himself a good deal better as Sut than he can in his own character. He had been steamboat captain, farmer, metalworker, glassworker, surveyor, sawmill manager, postmaster and railroad man—none of them for very long and none with any great success. It is not known how Harris got along during the years of the Civil War. He seems to have dragged his family from pillar to post in Tennessee, Alabama and Georgia. His wife died in 1867, leaving him with three small children. He is evidently speaking of himself, in his preface to Yarns, when he makes his hero explain that he will feel he has got his pay in full if he can rouse to a laugh

> "Eny poor misfortinit devil hu's heart is onder a mill-stone, hu's raggid children am hungry, an' no bread in the dresser, hu is down in the mud, an' the lucky ones a-trippin him every time he struggils tu his all fours, hu hes fed the famishin an' is now hungry hissef, hu misfortins foller fas' an' foller faster, hu is so foot-sore an weak that he wishes he wer at the ferry." [Yarns, xi]

George Harris had anticipated both the protest and the plea of Helper's The Impending Crisis. He represented the same stratum as

Helper: that of the white "non-planter" who had got himself some education. We know nothing of Harris's early life except that he had once been a jeweller's apprentice; but his origins seem to have been humble—it is not known what his father did or what became of his parents—and he shared with what were called the "poor white trash" something of their consciousness of limitation and of their bitterness against those who did not want them to escape from it.

In Unionist eastern Tennessee, George Harris never wavered from his original allegiance to the Democratic party, which in the South represented the artisans and farmers as against the industrializing Whigs. But he failed in an attempt at farming as well as at his several industrial projects—his sawmill, his glass manufactory, his metal working shop—and it is plain that a sense of frustration—"flustratin" is one of Sut's favorite words—is at the root of the ferocious fantasies in which, in the character of Sut, he likes to indulge himself. Yet he also uses Sut as a spokesman for his own sometimes shrewd observations, and this rather throws the character out as a credible and coherent creation, since he is made to see the world from a level which in reality would be beyond him. The effect of it is more disconcerting than if Sut were simply a comic monster, for it makes one feel that Sut's monstrous doings really express, like his comments on the local life, George Harris's own mentality. It is embarrassing to find Caliban, at moments, thinking like a human being.

But the book is not without its power, the language is often imaginative, and Sut is a Southern type, the envious and mutinous underling, which it is well no doubt to have recorded, and which Harris could do better than Lanier. Mr. Weber says truly that Harris has something in common with Caldwell and Faulkner. He is thinking of the tradition of "folk humor"; but what is more fundamental is that these writers are all attempting to portray various species of the Southern poor white. Sut Lovingood is unmistakably an ancestor of Faulkner's Snopeses, that frightening low-class family (some of them stuck at Sut's level, others on their way up), who, whether in success or in crime or both, are all the more difficult to deal with because they have their own kind of pride—who are prepared, as Mr. Weber points out in connection with their predecessor, to "take on the whole world." All that was lowest in the lowest of the South found expression in Harris's book, and *Sut Lovingood. Yarns Spun by a "Nat'ral Born Durn'd Fool,"* like A. B. Longstreet's *Georgia Scenes,* with its grotesqueries of ear-chewing, eye-gouging fights and yokelish hunts and balls, is needed, perhaps, to counterbalance those idyls of the old regime by Kennedy, Caruthers, and Cooke and the chivalrous idealism of Sidney Lanier.

The dreamy nobility of a man like Lanier and the murderous clowning of Harris are products of the same society, and the two men have something in common. George Harris did not share Helper's politics: he was all in favor of secession. Nor was his Sut disaffected like Lanier's Gorm Smallin, who burned down his master's mansion. From the moment of Lincoln's nomination, George Harris turned Sut Lovingood loose on the Unionists. Here is a passage from one of his libels on Lincoln—to call them satires would be to give them too much dignity—of which still another infatuated editor, Mr. Edd Winfield Parks, has said that "though goodhumored, they reveal his {Harris's} feelings," and of which Mr. Weber, who includes them in his volume, has said that Lincoln "might not have enjoyed {them} as much as a secessionist would" but that "he would have laughed at the exaggeration of ugliness so customary in frontier humor." Sut Lovingood is supposed to be accompanying Lincoln on the latter's incognito journey through Baltimore on his way to the inauguration, and Lincoln is supposed to be terrified by the threats of the Maryland secessionists:

> I kotch a ole bull frog once an druv a nail through his lips inter a post, tied two rocks ta his hine toes an stuck a durnin needil inter his tail tu let out the misture, and lef him there tu dry. I seed him two weeks arter wurds, and when I seed ole ABE I thot hit were an orful retribution cum ontu me; an that hit were the same frog, only stretched a little longer, an had tuck tu warin ove close tu keep me from knowin him, an ketchin him an nailin him up agin, an nat'ral born durn'd fool es I is, I swar I seed the same watry, skeery look in the eyes, and the same sorter knots on the "backbone." I'm feared, GEORGE, sumthin's tu cum ove my nailin up that ar frog, I swar I am; ever since I seed ole ABE, same shape, same color, same feel (cold as ice) an I'm d—d ef hit aint the same smell.[2]

Sut's tirades after the defeat of the South are vituperative on a level that almost makes the passage above seem the work of a sensitive artist. A new rancor, a new crushing handicap have been added to his previous ones. He can only spew abuse at the Yankees. The election of Grant seems a deathblow. According to Professor Donald Day, the principal authority on Harris, one of the last of the Lovingood stories, called "Well! Dad's Dead," which appeared in a Tennessee paper on November 19, 1868, was inspired by this event.[3] I am not sure that I can accept Professor Day's idea that Sut

Lovingood's moronic father has here come to stand for the Old South. He passes, in any case, without lament: "Nara durn'd one ove 'em {the neighbors} ever come a nigh the old cuss, to fool 'im into believin' that he stood a chance to live, or even that they wanted him to stay a minit longer than he wer obleeged to. . . . That night {after they had buried him}, when we wer all hunker'd round the hearth, sayin' nothin', an' waitin for the taters to roast, mam, she spoke up—'oughtent we to a scratch'd in a little dirt on him, say?' 'No need, mam,' sed Sall, 'hits loose yeath, an' will soon cave in enuff.'" Sut has always claimed that his father sired him as "a nat'ral born durn'd fool," and his habitual falling back on this as an excuse for both his oafish inadequacies and his sly calculated crimes strikes the only touching note in these farces.

The creator of Sut himself did not long survive Sut's father. Returning from a trip to Lynchburg, where he had gone on railroad business and to try to arrange for the publication of a second Sut Lovingood book, he became very ill on the train, and so helpless that the conductor at first thought him drunk. He was carried off at Knoxville, and died there. His manuscript disappeared. The cause of his death is not known, but it is reported that just before he died, he whispered the word "Poisoned!"

Notes
[added for this volume]

1. George Washington Harris, "Sut Lovingood. Yarns": A Facsimile of the 1867 Dick and Fitzgerald Edition, ed. M. Thomas Inge (Memphis: Saint Lukes Press, 1987), 245–46. Subsequent references will be placed in the text.
2. M. Thomas Inge, ed., High Times and Hard Times: Sketches and Tales by George Washington Harris (Nashville: Vanderbilt University Press, 1967), 263.
3. An earlier printing of the story has subsequently been found: Knoxville Daily Press and Herald, 15 November 1868. See ibid., 207–11.

A Note on Edmund Wilson and George Washington Harris

Brom Weber

Edmund Wilson, one of our most distinguished American men-of-letters, has had an ambivalent relation with George Washington Harris since 1955. In that year Mr. Wilson reviewed the present writer's edition of *Sut Lovingood* (Grove, 1954) for the *New Yorker* (May 7, 1955). On the one hand Mr. Wilson granted Harris an acknowledgement of his "real literary merit"; on the other hand Harris' writing was mistakenly regarded as political literature. Recently, perhaps still wrestling with the nature of Harris' accomplishment, Mr. Wilson reprinted his review almost verbatim in *Patriotic Gore* (1962). The result has been to mar a book in many respects deeply felt and intellectually profound, for Mr. Wilson's essentially negative though still ambivalent attitude to Harris has not been made more persuasive or precise with age. In the context of *Patriotic Gore*, furthermore, it is easier to discover why Mr. Wilson was initially wrong about Harris and has remained so, for the book reveals a carelessness with focus and detail fatal for serious scholarship and criticism.

The *New Yorker* review lacked focus because it ranged haphazardly between Harris, the 1954 edition, and the book's editor, without making clear the identity of the review's subject. Additional confusion was created by Mr. Wilson's uncertainty about the pur-

Ben Harris McClary, ed., *The Lovingood Papers, 1962* (Knoxville: University of Tennessee Press, 1962), 47–53.

pose of the 1954 edition. On the one hand he granted that the book was a modern treatment designed for the "average reader"; on the other hand he persisted in discussing the book as though it were a scholarly edition published for the "serious student of literature."

The aura of confusion surrounding the review is now heightened by its inclusion in *Patriotic Gore,* ostensibly a study of American Civil War literature. The book's principle of selection is mystifying, for its pages discuss such non–Civil War writers as Adelaide Crapsey and Ezra Pound while overlooking the Civil War literature of the humorists whom Abraham Lincoln read and enjoyed to the day of his death: "Artemus Ward," "Orpheus C. Kerr," and "Petroleum V. Nasby." Additional mystification is created when *Patriotic Gore* devotes many of its pages to the character and editorial procedure of the 1954 edition—hardly a Civil War product—and goes so far afield as indiscriminately to include the 1954 dustjacket in its category of materials relating to Civil War literature.

Mr. Wilson's treatment of the dustjacket epitomizes the responsibility of his approach to Harris, for he has attempted to find both Harris and the contents of the 1954 edition guilty of association with the book's wrapper. Using a tactic familiar in some book-reviewing circles, Mr. Wilson asserts that Sut "is depicted on the jacket as a stalwart and bearded mountaineer, a portrayal that has nothing in common with the dreadful, half-bestial lout of the original illustrations" (509).[1] This is careless as well as petty. In one original illustration Sut stands bare-footed, wearing overalls; in a second illustration Sut is as respectably dressed and featured as a minister portrayed in another of the original illustrations; Mr. Wilson's adjectival outburst is unjustified by either of the illustrations. Worse yet, the 1954 dustjacket artist—certainly not Harris nor the editor of the 1954 edition—obviously portrayed the spirit of the Southwestern school of humor to which Harris belongs. It would have been equally trivial and extravagant for Wilson to have applauded Harris and his editor because the dustjacket, with a hearty wrenching, can be said to have offered a brilliant allegorical key to Sut's bestiality. After all, the dustjacket figure was printed in black ink (EVIL) and overprinted with yellow ink (COWARDICE, DEGENERACY, FASCISM) and red ink (MURDER or, rather, GORE).

The expansive range of Mr. Wilson's attention to Harris is not always fortified by a scrupulous concern for accuracy of fact and interpretation. In truth, *Patriotic Gore* is not as finished as it should be. In the area of verifiable facts, for example, the book gives us "Professor H. Foster" (p. vi) instead of Professor Charles H. Foster; "John Sherman . . . the candidate from Illinois" (p. 373) instead of John Sherman, the candidate from Ohio; "*Ode* by James Russell Lowell *Recited at the Harvard Commencement, July 21, 1865*" (472) instead of "Ode Recited at the Harvard Commemoration, July 21, 1865"; "J. Franklin Meine" (511) instead of Franklin J. Meine; and George Ade's "*Fables in Slavery*" (587) instead of *Fables in Slang*. Matters of interpretation are also handled in a cavalier fashion. It is flippant, I suggest, to write of Melville's *Billy Budd* as though it were a pill designed to combat insomnia, decrying its structure on the ground that "its huge units . . . make it one of the most inappropriate works for reading in bed at night, since it is easy to lose consciousness in the middle of one" (637).

But for our immediate concern the acid test of Mr. Wilson's literary acumen is his reading of Harris' text. How, with the best will in the world, can one defend this misreading of "Mrs. Yardley's Quilting"?

> In the case of an old lady who loves to make quilts, he {Sut} rides into her quilting party with a horse he has driven frantic, ripping up all the quilts and trampling the hostess to death. This is Sut's only recorded human murder . . . (514–15).

The sentimental progression from "old lady" to "murder" makes for touching rhetoric, but it has no basis in Harris' story. Neither the 1867 edition nor the 1954 edition justify the belief that Sut rode a horse into a quilting party or the belief that Sut or a horse trampled the old lady to death. The text clearly indicates that the old lady died of a broken heart because a nine-diamond quilt she valued had been torn. The point missed by Mr. Wilson is that in "Mrs. Yardley's Quilting" Harris ridiculed the conventions of nineteenth-century sentimental fiction in a manner that is one of his major achievements. There is no real need, of course, to defend Harris against reading as typically unreliable as the one quoted above from *Patriotic Gore*. They are not worth much as scholarship and are not too valuable even for intuitive criticism.

The truth is that Mr. Wilson embodies the best attributes of the genteel tradition modernized by exposure to the twentieth century, but that those attributes do not include a sensitive appreciation of American humor in its full range. He cannot comprehend the complexity of a humor which, like that of Harris, is frolicsome and serious all in one. I have elsewhere tried to demonstrate that this is the dominant characteristic of American humor at its best, and of most of our major American writers too, from the seventeenth century down to our own time. Nor is American humor unique in its combination of "low" and "high" elements, for parallels are plentiful in European literatures.[2]

The genteel tradition is dominated by the eighteenth-century view, developed in England and imported into American culture where it was nurtured by sentimentalists, that humor is wholly benevolent and compassionate. Credence was given to this misconception by adherents to Turner's frontier theory, who hypothesized that the violence and grimness of American humor—actually present since the seventeenth century—has been grafted onto humor by the American frontier experience. With the frontier officially buried in the 1890's, there was no longer any need to muddy American culture with frontier barbarities. Turned back on nineteenth-century "frontier" humorists such as Mark Twain, the modernized genteel tradition can only find aimless brutalities and vulgarities in writings which actually hold much more. Mr. Wilson writes that "all that was lowest in the lowest of the South found expression in Harris's book." True enough, but much that was also highest in the South was also given expression by Harris. My introduction to the 1954 edition, which made this point, is quoted in *Patriotic Gore,* so that it is more appropriate now to quote from another writer, one who has succinctly set forth the importance and quality of Harris' achievement which have eluded Mr. Wilson:

> It may well appear that Harris' imagery will bear close scrutiny, that it is art of no mean order. Sut appears to seek sheer fun, but the imagery associated with him enlarges his stature to a figure ambiguously comic and mythic, hopelessly desiring an impossible freedom, pursuing intensity of experience in the flesh, and an abandonment of the obsessive and irrational. Subtly communicated is the hint of large hopes of what man might be on the frontiers of the new world, and bitter disappointment in what he really was. Sut is hard and cruel because in the moral void of the American backcountry of his experience he can assert his individuality only through violence. The stories recount crude practical jokes; the imagery supplies the counterpoint, sounding a world only occasionally satisfying, but more often harsh, hypocritical, wicked, transitory, and meaningless.[3]

It is characteristic of Mr. Wilson's ambivalent approach to Harris that he does not find it inconsistent to balance his violation of Harris' substance with a deep concern for the purity of Harris' text in other respects. *Patriotic Gore* asserts, for example, that as editor of the 1954 edition I sought to "clean up" the text by my treatment of Harris' dialect. On this matter Carvel Collins has written: "Every critic and scholar I know of who has quoted brief illustrative passages from *Sut Lovingood's Yarns* [sic] has felt it not only proper but necessary to make Sut's speech more understandable: here Mr. Weber has changed the whole book, and has done it consistently and on sensible principles."[4] Mr. Wilson's handling of this matter is not as circumspect as Mr. Collins' nor can it do more than distract readers from Harris' significant achievements.

Mr. Wilson inaccurately guesses that my treatment of Harris' dialect was inspired by a "suggestion" put forth by Bernard DeVoto. Much more pertinent to the literary history antedating the 1954 edition is the fact that DeVoto himself, in *Mark Twain's America* (1932), provided a precedent for my treatment of the dialect. Furthermore, Walter Blair, in *Native American Humor* (1937), and F. O. Matthiessen, in *American Renaissance* (1941), also treated Harris in a manner similar to my own. The implication created by Mr. Wilson that there was a gap between DeVoto's "suggestion" and my procedure in the 1954 edition is misleading. Indeed, the full facts were available to Mr. Wilson in the introduction to the 1954 edition.

Modern textual scholars are not agreed upon the treatment to be accorded a text selected for reprinting. Much depends upon whether the reprinting is designed for scholars or for the general reader, or both, as well as upon individual characteristics of the primary document. In Perry Miller's *Major Writers of America* (1962), for example, Edward Taylor's poetry is reprinted in as verbatim a transcription of the original manuscripts as possible. But in *The American Puritans* (Anchor, 1956), not designed like *Major Writers of America* for students but for general readers instead, Mr. Miller felt it proper to follow the precedent set by Samuel Eliot Morison's edition of William Bradford and to prepare a modern text. Individual characteristics of a primary document which will affect the handling of its text for reprinting include printer's errors and the author's errors of spelling, punctuation, and paragraphing.

In my judgment, a modern edition of Harris' 1867 text was desirable. With all due respect to Harris' art, his dialect is one of his least valuable achievements. Its faults include inconsistent misspellings for humorous effect as well as the careless rendition of dialect terms in a confusing and unsystematic variety of form. A prime requisite for first-person narration, which Sut employs, is that the narrator use only one language—his own—rather than several languages interchangeably. To credit Harris with the scientific consistency of a philologist or a writer sufficiently concerned with dialect to have made *Sut Lovingood* an inviolable dialectal document is to violate the text by failing to read it with a responsive eye and ear. Under the circumstances as I saw them, I had to decide whether or not the best interests of Harris, American literature, and the reader would be served by verbatim reprinting of the flawed dialect and other flaws. I decided against verbatim reprinting because, like DeVoto, Blair, and Matthiessen before me, I believed that Harris' importance rested upon literary virtues other than his dialect and punctuation. Furthermore, I was preparing a text for the general reader. I was not interested in preserving Harris as an unreadable curio known to a handful of initiates, his condition prior to 1954 and one which, ironically, a fervent concern for his dialectual purity tends to foster.

Earlier in this note I commented upon Mr. Wilson's waving of a dustjacket before the eyes of his reader. That gratuitous gesture is matched in spirit by a reticence concerning scholars in the field of American humor whose names or contributions have been slighted by misprinting or omission in *Patriotic Gore*. Mr. Wilson cites the late Bernard DeVoto, Constance Rourke, and F. O. Matthiessen as those who "in the thirties of the present century . . . began to take an interest in Sut Lovingood." True, but not the whole truth. Franklin J. Meine's *Tall Tales of the Southwest* (1930) discussed Harris earlier than DeVoto, Rourke, and Matthiessen; the book also reprinted six Harris stories. Walter Blair's *Native American Humor* (1937) provides us with the first extensive critical and scholarly commentary on Harris as well as with four Harris stories. Both Meine and Blair are still alive and deserve credit for their efforts. The omission of Walter Blair's name from the pages of *Patriotic Gore* is especially puzzling, for this admirer of Harris is the most distinguished scholar in the field of American literary humor. Mr. Wilson cites Kenneth Lynn's *Mark Twain and Southwestern Humor* (1959) as having shown that Southwestern humorists used the frame device to establish their "cultural superiority" and their general distance from lower-class characters such as Sut. It just happens that Walter Blair had earlier set forth this theory with persuasive detail in *Native American Humor* (1937). One wonders why Mr. Wilson neglected either to praise or negate Mr. Blair's scholarship.

All notes end best when they end happily, and this one is no exception. It is pleasant to observe that Edmund Wilson's interest in George Washington Harris testifies to the latter's growing importance.

Notes

1. [See Wilson's review in this volume. Because some of Weber's remarks refer to other sections of *Patriotic Gore,* all page numbers to that book have been left in his text.]
2. Brom Weber, *An Anthology of American Humor* (New York: Crowell, 1962).
3. Milton Rickels, "The Imagery of George Washington Harris," *American Literature* 31 (1959): 187.
4. *New Mexico Quarterly Review* (Summer 1955): 263.

The Fool as Point of View

Milton Rickels

When William Faulkner, in the *Paris Review* interviews, was asked for his favorite fictional characters, he offered Dickens' Mrs. Gamp, Falstaff and Prince Hal, Don Quixote and Sancho, Huck and Jim, and a few others; he devoted his longest discussion to the least-known character in his list: "And then I like Sut Lovingood from a book written by George Harris about 1840 or '50 in the Tennessee mountains. He had no illusions about himself, did the best he could; at certain times he was a coward and knew it and wasn't ashamed; he never blamed his misfortunes on anyone and never cursed God for them."[1] The august company seems surprising, and Faulkner's point that Sut is an admirable literary creation invites examination.

The framework device of the earlier Southwestern humorists—A. B. Longstreet, T. B. Thorpe, and Johnson J. Hooper—always gave the gentleman observer superior comprehension and a moral system competent to understand and judge the native backwoodsmen whose oral stories he reproduced. Harris, by the time he prepared the *Yarns* for publication, had abandoned this framework except as the briefest convention and had endowed Sut with a vividness of language, expansiveness of spirit, and even a perceptive intelligence superior in vitality to those of gentleman George. Sut is a highly sophisticated point of view in the technical literary sense, a personality rich enough to evoke interest for itself and to perceive and

George Washington Harris (New York: Twayne Publishers, 1965), 95–106.

refract the world. With careful craftsmanship, Harris exploits Sut's point of view to destroy in his reader old habits of perception and to introduce a fresh and original vision of the world.[2]

In time and place Sut is to some degree a local type. He shares a language, a social condition, a set of traditions that define the outward form of his existence. From the first, however, he is detached both in life and in spirit from his community. Outwardly, he seems often to be one of the insulted and the injured—to have reason, as Faulkner felt, to curse God; but he is not one of Dostoievski's introspective underground men, or one of Dickens' victimized and terrified poor. Although mean-souled and often cruel, Sut is at the same time large-spirited, triumphant, and free. To achieve Sut's triumph over life, Harris has chosen one of man's ancient modes of existence within society; Harris defines his broadest intention for Sut in his subtitle by terming Sut a "nat'ral born durn'd fool."

The reader is early aware that Harris is not using the term in any loose, careless, or general way. Instead Sut is created in the literary tradition of the fool, a type which has since Classical antiquity been constantly reinvigorated by a parallel folk tradition.

Sut is always conscious of his mode of existence. In this sense, despite his constant disclaimers, his life is a free choice he has made for himself; his existence is the product of his own will. His choice frees him from the necessity of deceiving himself and thus provides him an authentic mode of being. His existence is not, like that of the average man, dead in the world of tradition, habit, and illusion.

In his preface, Sut calls himself an eternal fool. Writing prefaces, he tells George, "Smells tu me sorter like a durned humbug, the hole ove hit—a littil like cuttin ove the Ten Cummandmints intu the rine ove a warter-million; hits jist slashed open an' the inside et outen hit, the rine an' the cummandmints broke all tu pieces an' flung tu the hogs, an' never tho't ove onst—them, nur the 'tarnil fool what cut em thar."[3] Harris' conception of his fool, then, is not the antic simpleton but the wise fool; Sut is the ironic hero who perceives the human condition and knows he himself is a fool to communicate his perceptions, to cut his ten commandments in the rind of a watermelon.

In "Sut Lovingood's Daddy, Acting Horse," Harris provides one of the rare objective descriptions of Sut: a "queer looking, long legged, short bodied, small headed" [19] creature. He is five times the fool any other member of the family could claim to be, excepting his dad, of course. Sut's dad is called a damned fool and he calls his son a damned fool; and variously throughout the sketch the Lovingoods, father and son, are cursed as eternal fools. At the opening of the book, Harris defines Sut primarily in action. He is a demonically ebullient creature, commanding and free.

For the following sketch, Harris chose "Sut's New-Fangled Shirt," which is something of a falling-off from the opening; but Sut as fool is further developed by his telling a tale of his own ignorance. In Sut's authentic existence as fool, he always knows his own weakness and stupidity; and his expressions of comic despair are both recognition and acceptance of his life.

During 1858 Harris had begun considering more carefully how he might utilize the mode of Sut's existence to present a version of life. References in his sketches show that at the time he was reading Pope, Burns, Byron, and particularly Dickens and Shakespeare; from these sources he drew techniques and concepts to help him shape Sut's being. At the end of "Sicily Burns's Wedding" one of Sut's definitions introduces the element of irony possible to the point of view:

> Hit am an orful thing, George, tu be a nat'ral born durn'd fool. Yu'se never 'sperienced hit pussonally, hev yu? Hits made pow'fully agin our famerly, an' all owin tu dad. I orter bust my hed open agin a bluff ove rocks, an' jis' wud du hit, ef I warnt a cussed coward. All my yeathly 'pendence is in these yere laigs—d'ye see 'em? Ef they don't fail, I may turn human sum day, that is sorter human, enuf tu be a Squire, ur school cummisiner (97).

To become "sorter human" is not plaintive longing, but the ironic man's disdainful scorn for unrealized and, to Sut, unrealizable humanity. Sut has chosen not to try to become human.

After rejecting the human condition, Sut also rejects the religious life. In "Old Burns's Bull Ride" Sut repeats his comic fear, but what he fears is pain of the body. He has no fear of the hereafter, for he has no soul:

> I'se a goner I 'speck, an' I jis' don't keer a durn. I'm no count, no how. Jis' look at me! Did yu ever see sich a sampil ove a human afore? I feels like I'd be glad tu be dead, only I'se feard ove the dyin. I don't keer fur hearater, fur hits onpossibil fur me tu hev ara soul. Who ever seed a soul in jis' sich a rack heap ove bones an' rags es this? I's nuffin but sum new-fangil'd sort ove beas', a sorter cross atween a crazy ole monkey an' a durn'd wore-out hominy-mill. I is one ove dad's explites at makin cussed fool invenshuns, an' cum afore my time. I blames him fur all ove hit, allers a-tryin tu be king fool (106–07).

Within the *Yarns* the image of man as a worn-out kitchen machine and of dad as a lascivious beast is appropriate; behind the tale the mechanical inventiveness of Harris himself and of his foster father Samuel Bell provides possible psychological applications. But most important for the point of view he is constructing, Harris has freed him from any transcendental significance in making Sut soulless.

As has been argued in the discussion of "Rare Ripe Garden Seed" and "Dad's Dog School," Harris' work embodies expression of anti-authoritarian and anti-rational feelings. Sut as fool personifies this concept in another of his characteristics, his mindlessness. Sut says he talks, acts, and "thinks at random" because he has no "steering oar" to his brain. He then develops a comic biology to explain the imperfection of his mind:

> Well, I thinks peopil's brains what hev souls, am like ontu a chain made outen gristil, forkid at wun aind; wun fork goes tu the eyes, an' tuther tu the years, an' tuther aind am welded tu the marrer in the backbone. . . . idears start along the chain, an' every link is smarter nur the wun ahine hit, an' dergests em sorter like a paunch dus co'n, ur mash'd feed. . . . Now, in my case, thar's a hook in the chain, an' hits mos' ove the time onhook'd, an' then my idears stop thar half made. Rite thar's whar dad failed in his 'speriment; puttin in that durn'd fool hook's what made me a nat'ral born fool (210–11).

Planning and thinking, says Sut, are "ginerly no count" (67). One's fate is determined by how one conducts himself at the moment of action. Harris, like W. G. Simms, feared that thought and contemplation enfeebled life; both expressed a yearning to solve the problem of the conduct of life in moments of dramatic action.[4] Sut's conduct is uninfected by reason.

The elements of Sut's nature and his experience of life issue in a formulated philosophy. One of the primary elements of Sut's character is his search for joy. Such passages as "kissin an' fitin am the pepper an' salt ove all soshul getherins" (139) image his world and express his reason for being. His philosophy insists on the joy of sex: ". . . yere's my sentimints ontu folks: Men wer made a-purpus jis' tu eat, drink, an' fur stayin awake in the yearly part ove the nites: an' wimen wer made tu cook the vittils, mix the sperits, an' help the men du the stayin awake" (88). Sometimes the conflict between pleasure and the demands of social morality and religion are openly acknowledged, as in Sut's evaluation of Sicily Burns's function in the world:

George, this worl am all 'rong enyhow, more temtashun than perventitive; ef hit wer ekal, I'd stand hit. What kin the ole prechurs an' the ugly wimen 'spect ove us, 'sposed es we ar tu sich invenshuns es she am? Oh, hits jis' no use in thar talkin, an' groanin, an' sweatin tharsefs about hit; they mus' jis' upset nater ontu her hed, an' keep her thar, ur shet up (77).

Expressions of the joys, frustrations, and occasional horrors of sexual activity are possible to Sut because of his comic freedom as fool. The formal public man, George Washington Harris, abhorred, on a rational level, what he took to be Brigham Young's sexual license; and in his political satires he ridiculed the free-love utopias of nineteenth-century America. Harris found only the comic mode satisfactory to contain what he both abhorred and, at a deeper level, desired.

While Sut seeks joy, he also sees the harsh, bitter competition for existence. Harris' emphasis on the poverty and cruelty of the American backwoods implies a profound disappointment with life in the New World that was envisioned in his early Mr. Free essays. In "Rare Ripe Garden-Seed," which came late in Harris' career, Sut speculates on the social cannibalism of village America:

Well, es I wer sayin, mam wer feedin us brats ontu mush an' milk, wifout the milk, an' es I wer the baby then, she hilt me so es tu see that I got my sheer. Whar thar ain't enuf feed, big childer roots littil childer outen the troff, an' gobbils up thar part. Jis' so the yeath over: bishops eats elders, elders eats common peopil; they eats sich cattil es me, I eats possums, possums eats chickins, chickins swallers wums, an' wums am content tu eat dus, an' the dus am the aind ove hit all. Hit am all es regilur es the souns frum the tribil down tu the bull base ove a fiddil in good tchune, an' I speck hit am right, ur hit wudn't be 'lowed (228).

Harris' familiarity with Pope's *Essay on Man* assures his acquaintance with the "Vast chain of being! which from God began," vibrating in perfect, holy harmony. Sut's concluding ironic submission to a guiding divinity and his mock-faith that "whatever is, is right" reinforce the satiric tone of his version of the heavenly order of the universe.

It is a mistake to see in the vision of human wickedness the grasp of original sin. There can be no knowledge of original sin without knowledge of the will of God and without sacrifice to make that will be done on earth. For Christianity, the will of God is expressed centrally in the Sermon on the Mount. The *Yarns* are not concerned with the knowledge of God or with the will of God; on the contrary, they are a symbolic escape from the discipline of love, as well as the discipline of authority. Sut exists outside Christianity.

Some of Sut's vitality lies in his being conscious of the discipline of love but his choosing to be free of it, and thus he is free to express the reality of his primitive hatreds. His explanation of his hatred of an encyclopedia salesman who expressed boredom at one of his tales goes beyond revenge to embody the human impulse to inflict and to contemplate pain:

> I hates ole Onsightly Peter, jis' caze he didn't seem tu like tu hear me narrate las' night; that's human nater the yeath over, an' yere's more univarsal onregenerit human nater: ef ever yu dus enything tu enybody wifout cause, yu hates em allers arterwards, an' sorter wants tu hurt em agin. An' yere's anuther human nater: ef enything happens [tu] sum feller, I don't keer . . . how sorry yu is fur him, thar's a streak ove satisfackshun 'bout like a sowin thread a-runnin all thru yer sorrer. . . . An' yere's a littil more; no odds how good yu is tu yung things, ur how kine yu is in treatin em, when yu sees a littil long laiged lamb a-shakin hits tail, an' a-dancin staggerinly onder hits mam a-huntin fur the tit, ontu hits knees, yer fingers *will* itch tu seize that ar tail, an' fling the littil ankshus son ove a mutton over the fence amung the blackberry briars. . . . Ur a baby even, rubbin hits heels apas' each uther, a-rootin an' a-snifflin arter the breas', an' the mam duin her bes' tu git hit out, over the hem ove her clothes, don't yu feel hungry tu gin hits jis' one 'cussion cap slap, rite ontu the place what sum day'll fit a saddil, ur a sowin cheer, tu show hit what's atwixt hit an' the grave; that hit stans a pow'ful chance not tu be fed every time hits hungry, ur in a hurry? (245–46)

In spite of the rationalizations, the piece expresses primarily the impulse to give pain. Beneath is a strong sense that life is struggle and disappointment; man's natural response to the cruel urgency of the infant is not always kindness but often an equally selfish cruelty.

This passage not only expresses Sut's vision of life but also reveals his power to observe and to verbalize as a commanding storyteller. He is no simple poor white, and he goes considerably beyond Davy Crockett and the Big Bear of Arkansas in his grasp of his world. The movement of Harris' imagination toward myth is revealed in these presentations of Sut's vision of existence and in his numerous passages of advice to George about how to live. The impulse to give Sut supernatural characteristics is shown in the bird imagery associated with him. The farthest movement toward mythic birth does not appear in the *Yarns* but in "Sut Lovingood Lands Ole Abe Safe at Last," where Sut tells a newspaper reporter: ". . . we kep a pet sand hill crane, an mom an him hed a differculty, an he chased her onder the bed."[5] Our source of delight in the "mythy" Sut is not far to seek.

At his farthest symbolic meaning Sut escapes the Christian conception of man fulfilling himself by abandoning himself to Divine truth and goodness. Instead, he finds the significance of his existence within himself. He is the creator of his own being. His project is to identify himself and define himself to himself. Once he discovers his authentic desires, he wants to realize them in some condition of purity and permanence. By making Sut a self-conscious symbol of the essential poverty and mortality of human life, by restricting the meaning of his existence to the flesh's reality, by making comedy of the idea of resurrection (in "Well! Dad's Dead"), but by keeping undiminished in him the will of life to survive and enjoy itself, the fool Sut becomes the irrational comic figure who realizes the ancient yearning to escape death and to become God himself.[6]

By having Sut present his version of the world and the nature of his own being through self-analysis, Harris defines Sut's point of view as that of the fool as seer. He is outside the law, outside social morality, outside religion, even outside rational life. As fool, he can express the logically incompatible elements of comedy: cruelty and joy, logic and license, the knowledge of mortality and the insistence on permanence.[7] The summary reveals the parallels and affinities Sut has with the Fool of tradition.

Enid Welsford's *The Fool,* a study of the "historical origin and role of the Fool as comic entertainer," defines the fool's esthetic significance as he appears in the folk tradition, in society, and in the literary tradition. The fool, according to Welsford's definition, is the one who gets slapped, the ancient scapegoat of mankind; but also he is emotionally and spiritually tough, none the worse for his slapping:

> For the genius of the fool is manifested by his power of deluding us into the belief that he can draw the sting of pain; by his power of surrounding us with an atmosphere of make-believe, in which nothing is serious, nothing is solid, nothing has abiding consequences. Under the dissolvent influence of his personality the iron network of physical, social, and moral law which enmeshes us from the cradle to the grave, seems—for the moment—negligible as a web of gossamer.[8]

The fool, Miss Welsford argues, does not lead to revolt against the law; on the contrary, he acts as preserver of social life by exposing pretension, by providing a safety-valve for our own unruliness, and by nourishing the sense in us "of secret spiritual independence of that which would otherwise be the intolerable tyranny of circumstance."[9]

The illusion of freedom must be created by relief from pressures. In Sut's experience, his defiance of order and propriety, and his urge to revenge himself on Sicily are all outward symbols of inner pressures. His desires are real and at the same time impossible. It is less the pressure from without than the pressure from within that Sut symbolizes. As fool, he is creator not of order, not of beauty, but of freedom.[10] He is free to create his being and to be that self.

Harris' work and his literary associations contain many hints about possible sources for the fool Sut. The American folk tradition is rich in terms for fools and in anecdotes about simpletons, antic clowns, and clever rogues. Many of these tales found their way into the *Spirit of the Times* and *Yankee Notions* during the years Harris contributed to those periodicals. In 1845 and 1846—when "The Knob Dance" was printed in the *Spirit* and reprinted in Porter's anthology, *A Quarter Race in Kentucky*—Johnson J. Hooper's crafty rogue Simon Suggs was also appearing in the same journal and volume. The young Suggs cheats his father at cards and runs away from home, the grown Suggs swindles a camp meeting, the middle-aged Suggs deceives his neighbors into electing him to a military office. Harris never makes Sut a sharper, but he may have found in Suggs's freedom from morality and social ties hints for a type freer even than the rogue.

Harris was fond of Alexander Pope; he paraphrased for comedy a line from the *Essay on Criticism*[11] and quoted from the *Essay on Man,* which is full of references to fools. According to Pope, man cannot escape being a fool; he can only learn and then mourn his condition. From Robert Burns, whom Harris also read and quoted (*Yarns,* 158), he could have found, had he needed, precedent for Sut's caustic satire on social pretentions and religious hypocrisy. Somewhat more remotely, "Sut Lovingood's Adventures in New York"[12] echoes lines from Byron's *Don Juan,* Stanzas 128, and 132:

> This is the patent age of new inventions
> For killing bodies and for saving souls,
> All propagated with the best intentions.

A greater amount of evidence exists for the influence of Charles Dickens. Sut's victim in "Old Skissim's Middle Boy" is modeled,

Harris writes, on "Charley Dickins's son, the fat boy" (67), from *Pickwick Papers*. In a headnote to "Hen Baily's Reformation" Harris calls his mock temperance tract to the attention of Dickens' Reverend Mr. Stiggins, leader of the Grand Junction Ebenezer Temperance Association (198). Some of Dickens' most ebullient satire on religious cant and affectation is focused on the Reverend Mr. Stiggins. More significant for the creation of Sut's view of life may have been Harris' reading of *Hard Times* (1854). He intended to title his last manuscript *High Times and Hard Times*, which seems in the nature of a special tribute. Dickens' work may have been useful to Harris both in content and in the technique it manifested. Dr. F. R. Leavis has pointed out that the appropriateness of the vocabulary, rhythm, and imagery to the burden of meaning in *Hard Times* places Dickens among the greatest masters of the English language.[13] These three elements are strong qualities in Harris' work.

Hard Times is Dickens' most comprehensive version of the inhumanities of Victorian civilization, particularly in the way its harsh philosophy fostered and sanctioned "the aggressive formulation of an inhumane spirit."[14] These inhumanities reduce workers to "hands" in Bounderby's factory; children to numbers in Gradgrind's school, where only "facts" are allowed; and life itself to the measure of the "deadly statistical clock very hollow." Sut's objection to the excessive order of Squire Hanley's life, his complaint that "we know too much," his dissertation against planning might all have been reinforced by the reading of Dickens.

One of the ways in which Harris transmuted material from Dickens is indicated in what is at first glance one of Sut's more original flights of fancy. Discussing circuit riders in "Sicily Burns's Wedding," first published in 1858, Sut tells George: "Suckit-riders am surjestif things tu me. They preaches agin me, an' I hes no chance tu preach back at them. Ef I cud I'd make the institushun behave hitsef better nur hit dus. They hes sum wunderful pints, George. Thar am two things nobody never seed: wun am a dead muel, an' tuther is a suckit-rider's grave" (89). In *Pickwick Papers* the ingenious comic servant Sam Weller theorizes that postboys are immortal. He asks the medical student, Bob Sawyer:

"Never . . . see a dead postboy did you?" inquired Sam, pursuing his catechism.

"No," rejoined Bob, "I never did."

"No," rejoined Sam, triumphantly, "Nor never vill; and there's another thing that no man never see, and that's a dead donkey. . . ."[15]

In conceptualizing objections to the utilitarian society, in the techniques of rhythm, dialect, and imagery, even in items of comic fantasy, Harris is indebted to Dickens.

When Sut is considered in his generalized form, however, he seems to have most affinities with the Renaissance Fool of court and stage: he is a lean, ugly, creature; he leaps and runs; he has a rapid, commanding flow of talk; he is cruel or witty in repartee; he is sometimes privileged truthteller; he is sometimes the antic, diverting jester; he is sometimes the scapegoat; he is often the bitter seer. Harris could have learned most of this tradition of the fool from Shakespeare. *The Merchant of Venice,* from which Harris borrows twice in one sketch (67, 69), has a good traditional fool in Launcelot Gobbo. Launcelot tricks his father, can be both kind and cruel, and is the witty jester and privileged truthteller. Falstaff, Touchstone of *As You Like It,* and Feste of *Twelfth Night*—all represent the fool's flight from civilization, the freedom from law and order that many an American frontiersman yearned for.

The influence of one artist on another is never a simple matter, but Harris' utilization of material from other writers forms a significant pattern. His quotation from Pope reveals his interest in poetic techniques to control sound and speed of language. His utilization of material from Shakespeare and Dickens concentrates on the comic figures of Gobbo and Sam Weller, revealing his fascination with the clever, witty, free ironic character, and the capacity of such a point of view to refract a vision of life and evaluate a society. Byron and particularly Burns provide satiric elements. As one result, Sut becomes the most technically sophisticated point of view in Southwestern humor—one capable of exploring a variety of qualities of American and Southern life that lie obscurely along the fringes of perception.

Notes

1. Republished in Malcolm Cowley, ed., *Writers at Work* (New York: The Viking Press, 1958), 137.
2. For a useful definition of comic points of view see John Gerber, "Mark Twain's Use of the Comic Pose," *PMLA* 57 (June, 1962): 297–304.
3. [George Washington Harris, *"Sut Lovingood. Yarns": A Facsimile of the 1867 Dick and Fitzgerald Edition,* ed. M. Thomas Inge (Memphis: Saint Lukes Press, 1987), ix. All subsequent

references are to this edition and will hereafter appear in the text.]

4. William R. Taylor, *Cavalier and Yankee* (New York: G. Braziller, 1961), 294–96.
5. [M. Thomas Inge, ed., *High Times and Hard Times: Sketches and Tales by George Washington Harris* (Nashville: Vanderbilt University Press, 1967), 272.]
6. For a psychological study of this impulse, see Jean-Paul Sartre, *Being and Nothingness,* Hazel E. Barnes, trans. (New York: Philosophical Library, 1956), 566.
7. Wylie Sypher, "The Meanings of Comedy," in Sypher, ed., *Comedy* (New York: Doubleday, 1956), 218.
8. Enid Welsford, *The Fool: His Social and Literary History* (London: Faber and Faber, 1935), 321.
9. Ibid.
10. Ibid., 326.
11. In "Sut Lovingood Reports What Bob Dawson Said, After Marrying a Substitute." [See Inge, *High Times,* 171–83.] See also letter to Eastman, Nashville *Union and American,* June 16, 1858.
12. [See Inge, *High Times,* 134–43.]
13. F. R. Leavis, *The Great Tradition* (New York: Doubleday, 1954), 297.
14. Ibid., 274
15. Editions of Dickens' *Posthumous Papers of the Pickwick Club* exist in great variety. The quotation is from Chapter 51.

Sut and His Illustrators

M. Thomas Inge

A few great works of literature fortunately have fallen into the hands of artists and illustrators whose own creative talents were of such an order that their drawings have proved as immortal as the fictional figures they depicted. Thus Dickens' characters found memorable life in the sketches of George Cruikshank and "Phiz" (Hablot Knight Brown); Cervantes' *Don Quixote,* Dante's *Divine Comedy,* and Milton's *Paradise Lost* were depicted in epic proportions in the lavish, highly detailed etchings of the nineteenth-century French artist Paul Gustave Doré; and few editions of Lewis Carroll's children's classic *Alice in Wonderland* have appeared without the delightfully conceived original pictures by Sir John Tenniel. In America, Felix O. C. Darley helped boost the sales of many an edition of works by Irving, Poe, Simms, Cooper, or T. B. Thorpe with his dramatic, extremely original etchings; and subsequent depictions of Huckleberry Finn have rarely equalled those done for the first edition by E. W. Kemble.

For the author and illustrator to work hand in hand with any success, there should exist a common recognition of the nature and significance of their respective creations in word and picture. The more complex and unique the fictional characterization, the more difficult is the challenge to the artist to bring before the reader's vi-

Ben Harris McClary, ed., *The Lovingood Papers, 1965* (Knoxville: University of Tennessee Press, 1967), 26–35.

sion a believable portrayal. Over the past 107 years, only a handful of artists have attempted to capture a physical semblance of the spirited Sut Lovingood, whose creator gave him unrestrained life on the printed page but never bothered to provide a satisfactory prose portrait of him.

The nearest thing to a description of Sut by Harris is found on the first page of *Yarns:* ". . . a queer looking, long legged, short bodied, small headed, white haired, hog eyed, funny sort of a genius."[1] Such vagueness provides an artist with little to go on, and most would realize the futility of attempting to capture the metaphorically imaginative scenes of Sut's wildest escapades. It would be like trying to illustrate a metaphysical poem by Donne or Marvell.

One of the earliest illustrations for a Sut yarn demonstrates this. The artist is unknown. The cut appeared in the New York *Atlas* on August 8, 1858, accompanying the second installment of "Sut Lovingood's Adventures in New York." It is meant to depict Sut tearing down a New York street, with a captive Fifth Avenue dandy astraddle his shoulders, on his way to the Battery to throw his burden into the river. The distraught dandy has pulled down a pole-full of umbrellas, and a Jewish dealer—in an attempt to protect his goods—has come out only to be thrown into the gutter amid a tumult of open parasols. Apparently the editor of the Nashville *Union and American* thought it an admirable piece of art work. Upon reprinting the second installment of the story, he noted in the editorial columns,

> we copy . . . today the second of the series, which the *Atlas* has embellished with a first rate wood cut representing "the follower of Moses and old close" rolling into the gutter under the persuasive influence of his "umereller pole." The artist does full justice to Sut's beautiful features and elegant proportions as they exhibit themselves in his foot race with a dandy rider. (August 15, 1858)

Aside from the editor's irony, the fact of the matter is that the depiction is awkward, stilted, and inaccurate. Sut's legs are frozen in an unrealistic stance, and his features are barely discernible. The artist probably had no notion of how to dress a Tennessee mountaineer, as we find him wearing a claw-hammer coat. The only thing, in fact, that distinguishes Sut's dress from that of the dandy is his high boots—the artist's only concession to Sut's rural origin. But what artist could have matched the description Harris has Sut himself provide:

Him an' me looked jist like a travelin windmill in full blast, with a cord ove fence-rails tied tu the arms by thar middils, a swingin' about every way, ur a big crawfish totin' off a bunch ove grasshoppers an' long-laiged spiders ag'in thar will—laigs, arms, heads, coatails, an' watch-chains wer so mixed an' tangled that hit wer bewilderin' tu the eyes tu foller us.[2]

The similes make the action fairly leap from the page—what Matthiessen had in mind when he spoke of the "kinetic" quality in Harris's writing.[3]

In the same year that the *Atlas* illustration appeared, another artist tried his hand at Sut, this time for Samuel P. Avery's famous humor anthology *The Harp of a Thousand Strings,* in which several of Sut's yarns were printed for the first time between hard covers (called "Sut Lovegood's [*sic*] Yarns," "The Story of a Shirt," "How Sut Lovegood's [*sic*] Daddy Acted Hoss," and "Sut's Experience with S-o-d-y P-o-u-d-e-r-s").[4] The six sketches that accompany the four stories, although unsigned, were presumably done by the young W. J. Hennessy. Such is the conclusion of this writer, at any rate, after comparing the drawings with others signed by Hennessy on pages 29–35, 210–216, 263–272, and 350–362 (over thirteen artists

Sut's Experience with S-o-d-y P-o-u-d-e-r-s *by W. J. Hennessy*

Sut and Sicily Burns *by W. J. Hennessy*

contributed to the book and many of the engravings are un-signed).

William John Hennessy (1839–1917) came to America with his parents from Ireland at the age of ten and later studied at the school of the National Academy. After achieving fame with his landscape and genre paintings, his somewhat sentimental illustrations for the works of Tennyson, Longfellow, Whittier, and Bryant (he has been called the "graphic laureate" of the Victorian period), and a noted set of twelve studies of the actor Edwin Booth, Hennessy returned to Europe and finally settled in England in 1893.

The sketches of Sut must have been among Hennessy's earliest professional, commissioned works, and in view of his limited experience it is no surprise to find that his male figures look as much like Irishmen as Tennesseans. His conception of Sut as a lanky, long-nosed, wild-haired fellow is at least done with some verve and style (though a direct imitation, almost, of Darley's conception of Simon Suggs done for J. J. Hooper's *Some Adventures of Captain Simon Suggs* published in Philadelphia, in 1845, which in turn may have been intended as a caricature of Andrew Jackson); but again we see Sut improperly dressed in the riding habit and attire of a country gentleman. Perhaps the most interesting sketch in the group is that of Sut comfortably settled close beside a portly, heavy-bosomed Sicily Burns, a portrait which captures the corpulent vivacity if none of the beauty of the raven-haired belle. Hennessy's Sut, however, has little in common with the crude-mannered mountaineer of the yarns whose one and only starched shirt left him practically flayed.

When Dick & Fitzgerald agreed to bring out *Sut Lovingood. Yarns Spun by a "Nat'ral Born Durn'd Fool"* in 1867, they commissioned a comic illustrator who was active in New York during the 1850's and 1860's to do the drawings. Justin H. Howard was noted for his political caricatures and humorous cartoons contributed to such comic periodicals as *Yankee Notions* and *Punchinello,* and for his illustrations for such books as *Major Jack Downing's Letters* (New York, 1857) and *My Thirty Years Out of the Senate* (New York, 1859), *Josh Billings, His Book* (New York, 1865), and *Nonsense* by "Brick" Pomeroy (New York, 1868). A better artist might have been found for the task, but no one else has succeeded as fully as he did in bringing Sut to artistic life.

Out of the seven full-page illustrations for the book, at least three are artfully done—"Sut Lovingood's Daddy, Acting Horse," "Sut's

New-Fangled Shirt," and "Old Burns's Bull Ride." One of the three attracted the attention of William Murrell: " 'Sut's New-Fangled Shirt,' which has been carefully laundered by his hostess and which nearly took all the hide off his back when he tried to fall out of the agonizing thing through a loose board in his attic bedroom, is one of Howard's most successful efforts."[5]

Sut appears in four of the seven drawings, and in only one of these

Sut Lovingood's Daddy, Acting Horse *by Justin H. Howard*

("Sut Lovingood's Daddy, Acting Horse") do we find him *properly attired*—barefoot, in overalls, homespun shirt, and slouch hat. Sut's face appears in a sharp profile that is at least well in keeping with the sort of physiognomy we would expect him to have (and no one will deny that Howard did an excellent job in capturing the features of Sut's nether region in the drawing Murrell admired). Howard had no compunctions about displaying both Sut and his Daddy in complete nudity, quite in accord with Harris' ribaldry and frank treatment of aspects of life usually suppressed in his time.

Because he did a fairly suitable and competent job and because of their appearance in and identification with the first edition of the *Yarns,* Howard's depiction of Sut has come to be the accepted one—such at least was the assumption of Edmund Wilson when he criticized what he thought was a modern artist's attempt to depict Sut.

Several other artists subsequent to Howard have given Sut a try. In 1882, when Henry Watterson decided to include selections from Harris in his anthology of Southern humor, *Oddities in Southern Life and Character,* he had his illustrator, W. L. Sheppard, do a scene from "Parson John Bullen's Lizards."

William Ludlow Sheppard (1833–1912) of Richmond, Virginia, had largely failed as an effective watercolorist and depicter or army life during the Civil War. He finally experienced some degree of success in the North with his humorous sketches of Negroes for *Appleton's Journal* and *Punchinello* and his illustrations for John Esten Cooke's novels. In his sketch for Watterson, it is Parson Bullen who takes the central stage with a terror-stricken look on his face just as the first of the "Hell-sarpints," or lizards, have crawled up his pantsleg. Sut's back is to the reader, and there is a gleeful smile on his partly turned, youthful face; but he is so sketchily treated that there is little to distinguish him from the rest of the people in Bullen's congregation. Like the other sketches for the book, this is not an especially skillful performance.

Since Edward Windsor Kemble (1861–1933) had so greatly pleased Mark Twain with his interpretations of Huckleberry Finn, one would assume he might have been capable of doing an equally apt job with Sut. His chance to do so came when Twain commissioned him to illustrate the original edition of *Mark Twain's Library of Humor* (New York, 1888), in which "Sicily Burns's Wedding" was reprinted. In one of the two sketches Kemble did for the story, he produced an effective and lively portrayal of Old Burns atop his

"The Tarifick Shape of His Feeters" *by W. L. Sheppard*

rampaging, bee-infested bull.[6] But in the other sketch—meant to depict Sut in the opening scene of the story tearing down the mountain slopes "in a long kangeroo lope, holding his flask high above his head, and hat in hand" [*Yarns*, 86]—Sut seems to have more in common, in dress and appearance, with the Mississippi Valley frontiersman and settler of Huckleberry Finn's world than with the Tennessee mountaineer (compare Sut with any of the adults depicted in Kemble's drawings for the first edition of *Huckleberry Finn*, New York, 1885). His face is mostly shaded out, an unsubtle attempt to avoid drawing Sut's features; and unless our eyes deceive us, Sut

"Hey, Ge-orge!" *by E. W. Kemble*

seems to have a scraggly moustache. Of Kemble, we would have expected better.

A more stylized and modern attempt at the same scene that W. L.
Sheppard had tried for Watterson in 1882 is the drawing by Leo
Hershfield, done for James R. Aswell's 1947 anthology, *Native Amer-
ican Humor*. This sketch accompanied a thoroughly rewritten and

Parson John Bullen's Lizards *by Leo Hershfield*

Mountaineer *from a design by Roy Kuhlman*

modernized version of "Parson John Bullen's Lizards." In Hershfield's rendition Bullen appears at the point where he has completely stripped himself of clothing, while he shakes from his britches a whole roast chicken, biscuits, a bottle of "rot-gut," and other assorted belongings, as well as several lizards. Again, Sut is a smiling minor figure to the right, no more, actually, than the usual stereotyped mountaineer of American cartoonists.

The most controversial depiction of Sut has been that used as a part of the dustjacket design for the Brom Weber edition of *Sut Lovingood* published by Grove Press in 1954—a drawing which, as it turns out, was not intended to represent Sut at all. In his wholesale condemnation of Weber's editing technique, Edmund Wilson also took a swipe at the cover drawing: "Sut himself is depicted on the jacket as a stalwart and bearded mountaineer, a portrayal that has nothing in common with the dreadful, half-bestial lout of the original illustrations."

Aside from his strange interpretations of Howard's drawings of Sut (he hardly appears in them as a "dreadful, half-bestial lout"), Wilson failed to realize that the artist's intent, as Brom Weber has since pointed out, was obviously to portray "the spirit of the Southwestern school of humor to which Harris belongs."[7] The drawing, in fact, was simply adopted from an old print (presumably of an early frontiersman) by the jacket's designer, Roy Kuhlman, who has reported that he was not "trying to represent Sut Lovingood per se, but rather to make an attractive design which depicted the general mood of the book."[8] Most readers, of course, would assume with Wilson that the figure on the jacket was meant to represent Sut, and to those who know Sut there is little resemblance; but it is a rather petty point for a man of such grandiose notions as Wilson.

After a survey of the half-dozen attempts on the part of American artists to capture Sut, perhaps the only conclusion to be reached is that none has adequately met the challenge. If any comes near to a satisfactory depiction, it is Justin H. Howard in his illustrations for the *Yarns*. Unfortunately, Sut never met his Doré, Darley, or Kemble. On the other hand, it is a mark of Harris's technical virtuosity that he could bring to life a fictional character with such irrepressible vitality that no artist's pen has been able to capture him on paper.

Notes

[added for this volume]

1. George Washington Harris, *"Sut Lovingood. Yarns"*: *A Facsimile of the 1867 Dick and Fitzgerald Edition*, ed. M. Thomas Inge (Memphis: Saint Lukes Press, 1987), 19.
2. M. Thomas Inge, ed., *High Times and Hard Times: Sketches and Tales by George Washington Harris* (Nashville: Vanderbilt University Press, 1967), 137.
3. Matthiessen's comment is reprinted in this collection.
4. Samuel P. Avery, *The Harp of a Thousand Strings: Laughter for a Lifetime* (New York, 1858), 19–29.
5. William Murrell, *A History of American Graphic Humor* (New York: Macmillan, 1938), 2:12.
6. Walter Blair has reproduced the drawing in his *Mark Twain and Huck Finn* (Berkeley and Los Angeles: University of California Press, 1960), 251.
7. Edmund Wilson's review and Brom Weber's reply are both reprinted in this collection.
8. Letter from Marilynn Meeker, editor for Grove Press, dated 28 April 1965.

Timon in Tennessee

The Moral Fervor of George Washington Harris

Elmo Howell

George Washington Harris, antebellum humorist of East Tennessee, was the author of one book, *Sut Lovingood. Yarns Spun by a "Nat'ral Born Durn'd Fool,"* and a number of uncollected sketches, mostly in the local newspapers. He enjoyed some notoriety as the creator of Sut for a few years before the Civil War and after, but even his book, which appeared in 1867, could not project his image far into the new era. After almost a century of neglect, he was recalled to interest by passing remarks of Bernard DeVoto and Walter Blair, among others, and was later the subject of detailed studies by scholars like Donald Day and Franklin J. Meine. In 1954, Brom Weber published a collection of Sut's tales in simplified English, with some excisions, which made Harris's work more accessible to the public and, in spite of the objections of the purists, perhaps more palatable. Harris was already experiencing a "revival," and then came Edmund Wilson's review of Weber's edition in the *New Yorker,* which let loose a hornet's nest of criticism and created a stir amongst the Sutites which has brought to Harris an attention that he did not command in his own century.

Wilson did not like Harris in the first place, and still less Mr. Weber's version of him. The "rank flavor" of the original speech should have been retained, he said; but what disturbed him most was the current attention Sut Lovingood was arousing, this "dreadful, half-

Georgia Review 24 (1970): 311–19.

bestial 'Cracker,' " this "peasant squatting in his own filth."[1] He called Harris's book the most repellent in American literature. Without delving into moral implications he dismissed Sut, whom he identified with Harris, as "always malevolent and always excessively sordid," a view which recalls Thackeray's prim outrage over *Gulliver's Travels* and Sterne's "bad and wicked" pages.[2] Sut enthusiasts responded by organizing the Sut Society and founding their own publication, with all the bibliographical appurtenances of a major author.[3] A full-length biography of Harris appeared in 1965, a new edition of unexpurgated Sut in 1966, and in the following year a collection of Sut material garnered from various publications of the Civil War period.[4]

To what extent are the Lovingood sketches worthy of this attention? At best they are a frail body on which to establish a reputation. Like other works in this vein, they reflect a casual manner which at worst devolves into slipshod writing, and in subject matter they are tirelessly reiterative. The Harris formula is simple: some pompous ass needs to be brought down a buttonhole, the stage is set, and when Sut lifts the curtain all hell breaks loose. A Lovingood sketch is like the last few minutes of an old-time Western movie, when everyone joins in a chase. Harris does this sort of thing with great verve and with a ready command of word and image. One thinks immediately not so much of his contemporaries in the Southwest tradition as of the Elizabethan pamphleteers or eighteenth-century malcontents like Swift and Smollett. He is like Smollett in his salty prose and love of rude joke, but he has the trenchancy of the dark mind of Swift, who said his purpose was to vex the world rather than to divert it. Born into a period of political dissension and always partisan in his devotion to the cause of the South, Harris at best manages to rise above the topical. More than the "fanatical exponent of secession," as Kenneth Lynn calls him,[5] he is an idealist voicing his frustrations in a few spasmodic outpourings to the local papers. Sut Lovingood's tomfooleries pall after a time, but his view of life, which is the rustic version of Harris's own view, reflects an original mind that has something to say about the general human condition.

Sut Lovingood is an illiterate hill-country fellow of East Tennessee who, in spite of his calling himself a fool, has culled enough wisdom from experience to make him discriminate in his choice of men. He particularly enjoys a joke at the expense of Yankees, sheriffs, and ministers, and is not above having a little fun with Negroes, women of a certain kind, and even members of his own family. But in spite of his disaffection, he is basically an amiable fellow in that he is also able to laugh at himself. He says with typical exaggeration that he has no soul, only a "whiskey proof gizzard," and that he is "too durn'd a fool tu cum even onder millertary lor." He gets into "more durn'd misfortnit skeery scrapes, than enybody," and escapes only by virtue of his long "laigs," which are his special pride.[6]

Sut's self-appraisal has been taken at face value by some readers who conclude that he is morally degenerate. Edmund Wilson says that he represents all that is "lowest in the lowest of the South," concluding that he is the ancestor of William Faulkner's Snopeses.[7] "I orter bust my hed open agin a bluff ove rocks, an' jis' wud du hit, ef I warnt a cussed coward. All my yeathly 'pendence is in these yere laigs . . . " [*Yarns*, 97]. But on more than one occasion Sut proves that he is not a coward. His joke about the good use he makes of his long legs means only that to Sut—and to people of his kind in the South—self-depreciation is a form of good manners. If anything can be charged against him, it is an aggressiveness towards those who do not measure up to his ideals of behavior—the bullying sheriff, the meddling parson, the know-it-all Yankee, the snob, the hypocrite, and even a stranger who appears at the doggery and looks down at Sut across his drink, "like I mout smell bad" [*Yarns*, 247]. Sut is a humble fellow himself, and nothing moves him to wrath, and sometimes to violence, faster than a false notion of self-esteem.

The lines of his character were well developed in sketches Harris published on the eve of the Civil War. He first appeared in 1854, in one of his liveliest episodes—Mark Twain recalled it years later—"Sut Lovingood's Daddy, Acting Horse." In order to make the crop and provide for the family after the horse dies, the elder Lovingood has himself put into harness to pull the plow. His main purpose, however, is to cut the fool and have some fun: ". . . while mam wer a-tyin the belly ban', a-strainin hit pow'rful tite, he drapt ontu his hans, sed 'Whay-a-a' like a mad hoss wud, an' slung his hine laigs at mam's hed." Her dour observation is that he "plays hoss" better than he does husband. But the real fun comes when he plows through a sassafras bush and stirs up a nest of ball hornets. This tale at the expense of his father seems unconscionable on the part of Sut unless one remembers that the old man deserves what he gets: "he allers wer a mos' complikated durned ole fool," Sut says, "an' mam sed so when he warnt about" [*Yarns*, 23].

Three years later in 1857, Sut reappears, this time in a love adventure, "Blown up with Soda." He has fallen in love with a mountain girl, Sicily Burns, who leads him on and then plays a prank on him by feeding him soda powder—new to Sut, who thinks he is poisoned. In this sketch Harris introduces two important characters that indicate the direction his satire will take, the parson and the Yankee. Sut later turns the tables on Sicily and her circuit-riding husband, and in the same year he plays one of his liveliest jokes on another parson, old Bullen, who has meddled in one of Sut's love engagements. Pretending conversion, Sut goes to the service with a sack full of lizards and releases them, at a moment of eloquence, up the parson's breeches.

It was a Yankee peddler that sold the soda powder, supposedly a love potion, to Sicily Burns; and as the war drew on, the Yankee became a favorite target, most often as a salesman in the South, although Sut makes a few improbable trips to the North to observe him on home ground. In 1858, he goes to New York City, and again in 1861 at the outbreak of the war he goes North for a personal encounter with "ole Abe Link-Horn." Sut tells Lincoln that in Tennessee he is called a natural born durned fool, but as for the North, ". . . I think I ken averidge in these parts purty well."[8] After the war Harris continues the attack with greater virulence. In "Sut Lovingood, on the Puritan Yankee" [*High Times*, 284–87], in 1866, Sut in effect gives way to Harris himself in the indictment of a civilization.

The Yankee appears most often in Harris as some sort of peddler whose inventions and gadgets and ingenuity in making money have a dazzling effect on the simple Southern countryman, but which in retrospect strike Sut as an outrage to manhood. He is a deceitful fellow, oily and slippery, who could hold his own in "a pond full ove eels" [*Yarns*, 38]. In New York, Sut is amazed at the commercial activity of the natives, with little men chasing in every direction with papers in their hands, "like pissants afore a rain." ". . . when two ove 'em bumps together, they teches noses, jist like onto the ants, an' then they swops two ur three ove the papers, an' each pot-bellied, trottin', bacon-faced son ove a gun ove 'em is redy tu swar that he's made money by the swap. There's no nat'ral sence, ur corn, ur meat, ur honesty in the whole fixin'" [*High Times*, 128]. Their manners are offensive. In New York "they gin you sass enough tu make you fite" [*High Times*, 232]—that is in Tennessee, but not among a people who refuse to take offense.[9] Old Stilyards, the Yankee lawyer who ". . . cum tu this country, onst, a cussed sneakin lookin rep-tile" [*Yarns,* 37], tries to bribe Sut with a gill of whisky, generous by New England standards but not by Sut's. "Hit 'sulted me. Now, whu the devil ever hearn tell ove a gill ove whisky, in these parts afore? Why hit soundid sorter like a inch ove cord-wood, ur a ounce ove cornshucks" [*Yarns,* 39]. The Yankee is an arrogant fellow who knows all the answers, like the encyclopedia salesman, "ole On-sightly Peter," who stops Sut's narration to correct him in detail. "Yu go tu *hell,* mistofer; yu bothers me" [*Yarns,* 232]. But above all, he is deficient in what Sut considers a man ought to be. North Carolina is noted for pole cats, Georgia for groundhogs, and Tennessee for coons; but New York is noted "in the same line fur dandys," who are neither men nor women since they "can't talk good nor fight like wun, ur kiss ur scratch feelin'ly like t'uther" [*High Times,* 135].

Kenneth S. Lynn finds in Sut (whose name, he says, is "an ugly contraction of South") the "worst aspects of the slavocracy."[10] But Harris's antipathy to the North goes beyond the political and social issues of the Civil War. Long before Sut appeared, other Southern writers had questioned the New Englander's concept of character, which they found radically different from their own. The New Eng-land schoolmistresses who flooded the South in the first part of the nineteenth century amused Southerners with their grim concern for "dooty," but they were also a bundle of prejudices, says Joseph Glover Baldwin, "stiff, literal, positive, inquisitive, inquisitorial, and biliously pious." They salved their consciences with minor obser-vances and cant phrases, while they considered "the heart and the affections" a weakness.[11] A Yankee, says Davy Crockett in 1836 in his narrative of Job Snelling, the "gander-shanked" merchant, can "outwit old Nick himself."[12] In *Guy Rivers* (1834), the first of William Gilmore Simms's Border Romances, Jared Bunce, the ped-dler out of Meriden, Connecticut, is a swindler whom a group of Georgia settlers design for tar and feathers until he outwits them and gets away. Bunce is a major character in the novel, who in the course of time reforms under the tutelage of Southern manners and repudiates his New England heritage in the hope of becoming a Southern gentleman. A neglected comic character in a neglected novel, Jared Bunce shows how a generation before the war when slavery was not yet a burning issue Southerners regarded North-erners as deficient in what they thought a man should be. In *Border Beagles* (1840), another novel of the western South, a gentleman of

Raymond, Mississippi, is sued by a Yankee merchant for assault and battery. The defendant admits the charge; he thrashed the merchant for addressing his daughter uncivilly when she came to buy from him. But the defense attorney appeals to the jurors as Southerners, whose concept of character is under attack by this cunning foreigner.

> Gentlemen of the jury, it is now a new doctrine to be taught here—this meekness under blows. . . . This very patience under blows, I hold to be disgraceful to the manhood of the person, as it would be to the manhood of the nation that submitted to them tamely; and to pay him for thus submitting, will, gentlemen, be paying a bounty to the rankest cowardice that ever degraded man. Every dollar which you give to this mean creature for this affair, is neither more nor less than a bounty to the coward; the effect of which must be to raise a brood of cowards throughout the country. We want no cowards in this country.[13]

At the end of 1866, Harris published his sketch of the puritan Yankee, which, allowing for the extravagance of Sut's rhetoric, is a fair appraisal of sectional differences, as viewed by a Southerner after the Civil War. The puritan sings hymns and says long prayers; but his religion does not affect his personal relationships, where his sole aim is to strike a bargain and make money. He has "a winder in his breast" where his heart ought to be [*High Times,* 287]. To him a man's word is nothing, unless he has his note of hand also. Harris was particularly sensitive to the intellectual turmoil of New England in the nineteenth century, with the breakup of the puritan orthodoxy and the advent of esoteric religions and deviations in manners and morals represented by characters like Joseph Smith, Brigham Young, William Miller, Margaret Fox, and Amelia Bloomers.[14] What a pity, says Sut, that the Mayflower ever landed with "her pestiferus load of cantin cheats an' moril diseases" [*High Times,* 285]. Or if the Indians had only done their job and "carcumsized the head ove the las' durn'd one" as soon as they landed. "Oh! My grashus, hits too good to think about. Durn them leather injuns; they let the bes' chance slip ever injuns had to give everlastin comfort to a continent and to set hell back at leas' five hundred year. . . . GEORGE, pass the jug; the subjick is overpowerin me" [*High Times,* 286].

Harris was a violent partisan in politics, but the indignation that sweeps through his pages is fed by something more fundamental than political difference. After the victory of the North on the battlefield, Sut could do little but amuse himself with futile speculations about the Mayflower and the Indians. But before the war the type of manhood espoused by Harris and Simms was the pattern for half a nation, although from the beginning it was apparent that the Yankees, released from the old orthodoxy and obsessed by humanitarian dreams, were bent on reducing all manners, in the words of Joseph Glover Baldwin, to "the standards of New England insular habitudes."[15] And after the war, they were to follow up their victory on the field, says W. J. Cash, "with the satisfaction of the instinctive urge of men in the mass to put down whatever differs from themselves," by making over the South in their own image.[16]

Thus the attack on the Yankee is only Harris's most dramatic—most topically effective—way of getting at those qualities in human nature which he most dislikes. Too much has been made of the grotesqueries of Sut Lovingood, which are the distinguishing marks of region and class. In spite of his angularities, Sut is a fair approximation of Harris's ideal. His dislike for ministers and his knack for breaking up church meetings, says Milton Rickels, represent "an attack on institutionalized Christianity."[17] The Lovingood yarns, he says, are an escape from the discipline of love as well as the discipline of authority. But Sut's wrath is directed against perversions of Christian morality, not the thing itself. George Washington Harris was a devout Presbyterian, serving for a time as elder in the First Presbyterian Church in Knoxville, and noted throughout his life for his Sabbatarianism and "blue" orthodoxy.[18] Sut would not like the formality of Harris's church, but he does not, as Rickels says, "exist outside Christianity."[19] For all their violence and cantankerous ways, the country people of Sut's class are deeply pious and profoundly orthodox in their religious views—a fact which sets them apart from the New Englanders whom Sut attacks. In his long description of the invalid wife of Sheriff Doltin, Sut makes clear his own convictions. The dying woman bears her suffering and the long neglect of her husband with "a sweet smile" that goes to his heart.

I 'speck that smile will go back up wif her when she starts home, whar hit mus' a-cum frum. She must onst been mons'us temtin tu men tu look at, an' now she's loved by the angils, fur the seal ove thar king is stamp'd in gold on her forrid. . . . As I look fus' at him, an' then at her, I'd swore tu a here-arter. Yes, *two* herearters, by golly: one way up behint that ar black cloud wif the white bindin fur sich as her; the tuther herearter needs no wings nor laigs ither tu reach; when you soaks yerself in sin till yer gits heavy enuf, yu jes' draps in. [*Yarns*, 257–58]

Sut is not a rebel against institutions. Rather, he is a conservative, like his creator, lamenting the falling off from the standards of the past. When George, his gentleman friend, thinks back on the Knoxville of his South, Sut reprimands him for his sentiment. But Sut in his turn is also sentimental.

> That's what makes you compar the days ove the fiddle, loom an' cradle with the peaner, ball-room an' wetnurse, ove these days. In comparin' 'em, you may take one person, a family, or a county, at a time, an' you'll find that we haint gain'd a step on the right road, an' if the fog would clear up we'd find heaven behind us, an' not strength enuff left to reach hit alone, if we wer to turn back. No, boys, we aint as *good* as we wer forty years ago. [*High Times,* 312]

These rare pensive moments are the obverse side of Sut's wrath. Like Gulliver among the Houyhnhnms, he is inspired by the principle of right reason in human conduct and can never be satisfied again among the yahoo kind. Though inevitably associated with the altercation of the Civil War period, and with the boisterous mountaineer of his creation, George Washington Harris was the exponent of an ideal which lifts his sketches above the surface excitement of Sut's world and makes them unique among the writings of the Old Southwest.

Notes

1. Edmund Wilson, "Poisoned!" *New Yorker,* May 7, 1955, 138. [Reprinted in this volume.]
2. Ibid., 140.
3. *The Lovingood Papers,* edited by Ben Harris McClary, was issued annually from Tennessee Wesleyan College from 1962–1967.
4. Milton Rickels, *George Washington Harris* (New York: Twayne, 1965); M. Thomas Inge, ed., *Sut Lovingood's Yarns* (New Haven, Conn.: College and University Press, 1966); M. Thomas Inge, ed., *High Times and Hard Times: Sketches and Tales by George Washington Harris* (Nashville: Vanderbilt University Press, 1967).
5. Kenneth S. Lynn, *Mark Twain and Southwestern Humor* (Boston: Little, Brown and Co., 1959), 130.
6. [George Washington Harris, *"Sut Lovingood. Yarns": A Facsimile of the 1867 Dick and Fitzgerald Edition,* ed. M. Thomas

Inge (Memphis: Saint Lukes Press, 1987), 172. Subsequent references to this work will appear in the text.]

7. Wilson, "Poisoned!" 145.
8. *High Times and Hard Times,* 264. [Subsequent references to this work will appear in the text.]
9. *High Times and Hard Times,* 232. [Howell misreads this sentence. Sut is relating a dream about being in Washington, D.C.]
10. Lynn, *Mark Twain,* 136–137.
11. Joseph Glover Baldwin, *Flush Times of Alabama and Mississippi* (Americus, Ga., 1853), 292.
12. David Crockett, *Life of David Crockett: The Original Humorist and Irrepressible Backwoodsman* (Philadelphia, 1865), 244.
13. William Gilmore Simms, *Border Eagles* (1840; reprint, New York, 1865), 77–78.
14. In "The Conduct of Life," Ralph Waldo Emerson says: "A silent revolution has loosed the tension of the old religious sects, and, in place of the gravity and permanence of those societies of opinion, they run into freak and extravagance. In creeds never was such levity; witness the heathenisms in Christianity, the periodic 'revivals,' the Millennium mathematics, the peacock ritualism, the retrogression to Popery, the maundering of Mormons, the squalor of Mesmerism, the deliberation of rappings, the rat and mouse revelation, thumps in table-drawers and black art. The architecture, the music, the prayer, partake of the madness." *Nature, The Conduct of Life and Other Essays,* Everyman edition (New York: E. P. Dutton, 1963), 251.
15. Baldwin, *Flush Times,* 292.
16. W. J. Cash, *The Mind of the South* (New York: Random House, 1941), 103.
17. Milton Rickels, *George Washington Harris,* 51.
18. Ibid., 27.
19. Ibid., 100.

The Blind Bull, Human Nature

Sut Lovingood and the Damned Human Race

Noel Polk

For Ben Harris McClary,
Milton Rickels, and Tom Inge:
They were here first.

so that they are without excuse:

21 Because that, when they knew God, they glorified *him* not as God, neither were thankful; but became vain in their imaginations, and their foolish heart was darkened.

22 Professing themselves to be wise, they became fools,

23 And changed the glory of the uncorruptible God into an image made like to corruptible man, and to birds, and fourfooted beasts, and creeping things.

24 Wherefore God also gave them up to uncleanness through the lusts of their own hearts, to dishonour their own bodies between themselves:

25 Who changed the truth of God into a lie, and worshipped and served the creature more than the Creator, who is blessed for ever. Amen.
. . . .

28 And even as they did not like to retain God in *their* knowledge, God gave them over to a reprobate mind, to do those things which are not convenient;

29 Being filled with all unrighteousness, fornication, wickedness, covetousness, maliciousness; full of envy, murder, debate, deceit, malignity; whisperers,

30 Backbiters, haters of God, despiteful, proud, boasters, inventors of evil things, disobedient to parents,

31 Without understanding, covenant breakers, without natural affection, implacable, unmerciful;

32 Who knowing the judgment of God that they which commit such things are worthy of death, not only do the same, but have pleasure in them that do them.

—Romans I

Gyascutus: Studies in Antebellum Southern Humorous and Sporting Writing, ed. James L. W. West (Atlantic Highlands, N.J.: Humanities Press, 1978), 13–49. The author has revised his article for this reprinting.

I. Gadfly

In spite of the manifest difficulties of its language, the frequently savage and unpleasant nature of its humor, the intensity of its violence, and the vehemence of its author's hatred of so many of the agents of change in the mid-nineteenth century, George Washington Harris's *Sut Lovingood. Yarns Spun by a "Nat'ral Born Durn'd Fool"* has attracted a devoted readership for nearly 125 years.[1] The original edition of 1867 (Dick and Fitzgerald) stayed in print until well into the 1940s, and there have been as least six separate published editions of his works, including four of the *Yarns.* These editions, along with one published monograph-length study, at least three dissertations, and a spate of articles, form, quantitatively, a rather substantial body of scholarly materials on Sut Lovingood and his creator, most of which has emphasized the comedy of the *Yarns*[2]—and rightly so, for Harris's is possibly the most artistically complex sense of humor in American literature before Faulkner, saving perhaps only Melville—the brilliance of Harris's language, and the nature of Sut's numerous victims, as complete a catalog of stereotypical hypocrites and fools as can be found in any literary tradition. Here, however, I would like to focus on the book's supreme creation, Sut Lovingood himself. It is a mistake, I think, a serious underestimation of the *Yarns,* to see Sut as merely an irresponsible prankster who, like his literary forebears and peers in the southwestern humor "tradition," hates hypocrites, reformers, and Yankees and who plays his "pranks" just for revenge, and to assume that in his conflicts with authority Sut carries the moral force of Harris's approval because his victims are so manifestly deserving of Sut's vengeance.

In his book, Milton Rickels has stated that Harris "was always more interested in Sut as symbolic point of view than as a realistic construction,"[3] and, indeed, to the very large extent that Sut is a narrator, a storyteller, Rickels is absolutely correct. Sut is, of course, supremely, a storyteller. But he is not just a storyteller; Harris is careful to create a social context for him; he is in constant interaction with an assortment of cronies—including "George" and several intruders—and like any good raconteur, Sut is always mindful of his audience; much of the elaborated detail of his stories, including the tall-tale exaggeration, is his response to his auditors' laughter, calculated to create a desired effect—usually laughter, but frequently something else. In Sut's interaction with "George" and his other auditors Harris reveals a personality whose complexities are elaborated in Sut's wild tales.

In "Sut Lovingood's Daddy, Acting Horse," for example, Sut names the members of his family, calling his own five times in a wonderfully comic display of bumptiousness; when a "tomato-nosed" man falls into the trap Sut has set, and points out the repetition, Sut responds immediately: "Yas, ole Still-tub, that's jis the perporshun I bears in the famerly fur dam fool, leavin out Dad in course."[4]

Sut's description of himself as a "nat'ral born durn'd fool" here and throughout the *Yarns* has generated much discussion of his character. Again, Rickels reasonably suggests that "Harris' conception of his fool . . . is not the antic simpleton but the wise fool; Sut is the ironic hero who perceives the human condition and knows he himself is a fool to communicate his perceptions" (96). But it is a great deal more complicated than this description allows. At the end of "Sicily Burns's Wedding," for example, Sut opines that if his long legs do not fail him, he "may turn human sum day, that is sorter human, enuf tu be a Squire, ur school cummisiner" (97)—a remark that seems simple enough, one of many cheap shots Sut takes throughout the *Yarns* at various pomposities. It is of course not without its implications, but Rickels may be taking Sut a bit too literally and miss his comic irony: "To become 'sorter human,'" Rickels suggests, "is not plaintive longing, but the ironic man's disdainful scorn for unrealized and, to Sut, unrealizable humanity. *Sut has chosen not to try to become human*" (97, emphasis added). Rickels builds from this premise an argument about Sut's character: "After rejecting the human condition," Rickels continues, "Sut also rejects the religious life. . . . He has no fear of the hereafter, for he has no soul" (97). By making Sut soulless, Harris has "freed him from any transcendental significance" (98). Finally, Rickels contends that Sut, "in another of his characteristics, his mindlessness" (98), personifies the antiauthoritarian and antirational feelings Harris expresses in his work. From being a wise fool to being mindless is a long and contradictory progression; but it is necessary for Sut to be mindless, apparently, in order for him to be a backwoods anarchist, opposed to both order and reason: "For Sut," Rickels has earlier argued, "every practical joke is a delight because it is a conspiracy against all order" (84).

This argument gives Harris little credit as a thinker and even less as an artist. Simply, I would rather argue, Sut is not mindless, and *he is no fool*. His repeated description of himself as a "nat'ral born durn'd fool" is the ironic self-deprecation that is part and parcel of any humorist's equipment and that neither he nor Harris expects the reader to take literally: the few characters in the *Yarns* who do are scorned and ridiculed for their lack of comprehension. But more than that, his self-deprecation is the main thematic device by which Harris stresses the differences between Sut and his victims and emphasizes the moral nature of the *Yarns*.

Certainly Harris was aware of the literary tradition of the Fool, and certainly he was capitalizing upon it; but he was also using another aspect of that tradition, the one personified by Socrates. Sut is a kind of backwoods Socrates who pricks holes in ballooned egos, brings hypocrites and fools to their knees before their peers: indeed, Socrates encounters the self-assured and smug sophists, Sut the self-assured and smug preachers, sheriffs, lawyers, and Yankees. Both Sut and Socrates continually expose fools and frauds for what they are, and both are therefore continually in trouble with civic and religious authorities. And both, I would suggest, have the same purpose in life. Sut's goal in "Old Skissim's Middle Boy," for example— to awaken the fat, lethargic, and constantly sleeping boy—is, I propose, Harris's allegorical treatment of this famous passage in the *Apology:*

> the state is like a big thoroughbred horse, so big that he is a bit slow and heavy, and wants a gadfly to wake him up. I think the god put me on the state something like that, to wake you up and persuade you and reproach you every one, as I keep settling on you everywhere all day long. Such another will not easily be found by you, gentlemen, and if you will be persuaded, you will spare me. You will be vexed, perhaps, like sleepers being awaked, and if you listen to Anytos and give me a tap, you can easily kill me; then you can go on sleeping for the rest of your lives.[5]

Under the circumstances, it seems clear that the hornets that appear and reappear throughout the *Yarns* are Harris's own symbolic "gadflies."

Thus when Sut calls himself a "nat'ral born durn'd fool," it is not merely self-deprecation: by doing so he can subtly suggest how eagerly his victims, his neighbors and friends, and his family delude themselves into thinking that they are something they are not. All the characters in the *Yarns* act horse or fool in one way or another and do so while asserting their righteousness, their respectability, and their general superiority to all other creatures; they do not, Sut and Socrates would argue, "know themselves." Sut, however, like Socrates, does know himself, thoroughly, and is under no delusion about himself or society; he is, in short, wise precisely because he does not pretend to know anything he does not know or be anything he is not.

Sut, then, is not a fool, and he is by no means, as Edmund Wilson, Sut's harshest critic, would have it, a "peasant squatting in his own filth."[6] It is his lazy and worthless Dad who so squats, and it is one indication of Sut's strength of mind and character that he has been able, with no more of this world's goods than his Dad, to escape and overcome the poverty and filth, both real and metaphorical, upon which his Dad tried to rear him. Sut's wisdom is heired from an incredible background of poverty and deprivation; perhaps because of that background, certainly not in spite of it, he is a singularly perceptive student of human nature: and though his vision of the world is understandably dark, it is persistently realistic and tough-minded.

Sut's vision is summed up in two philosophical set pieces that express in no uncertain terms his profound pessimism about "univarsal onregenerit human nater." The first, Rickels describes as a kind of Great Chain of Being (100).

> Whar thar ain't enuf feed, big childer roots littil childer outen the troff, an' gobbils up thar part. Jis' so the yeath over: bishops eats elders, elders eats common peopil; they eats sich cattil es me, I eats possums, possums eats chickins, chickins swallers wums, an' wums am content tu eat dus, an' the dus am the aind ove hit all. Hit am all es regilur es the souns frum the tribil down tu the bull base ove a fiddil in good tchune, an' I speck hit am right, ur hit wudn't be 'lowed. (228)

The second expresses among other things an attitude toward Innocence, in any form, that out-Claggarts Claggart:

> I hates ole Onsightly Peter, jis' caze he didn't seem tu like tu hear me narrate las' night; that's human nater the yeath over, an' yere's more univarsal onregenerit human nater: ef ever yu dus enything tu enybody wifout cause, yu hates em allers arterwards, an' sorter wants tu hurt em agin. An' yere's anuther human nater: ef enything happens [tu] sum feller, I don't keer ef he's yure bes' frien, an' I don't keer how sorry yu is fur him, thar's a streak ove satisfackshun 'bout like a sowin thread a-runnin all thru yer sorrer. Yu may be shamed ove hit, but durn me ef hit ain't thar. Hit will show like the white cottin chain in mean cassinett; brushin hit onder only hides hit. An' yere's a littil more; no odds how good yu is tu yung things, ur how kine yu is in treatin em, when yu sees a littil long laiged lamb a-shakin hits tail, an' a-dancin staggerinly onder hits mam a-huntin fur the tit, ontu hits knees,

yer fingers *will* itch tu seize that ar tail, an' fling the littil ankshus son ove a mutton over the fence amung the blackberry briars, not tu hurt hit, but jis' tu disapint hit. Ur say, a littil calf, a-buttin fas' under the cow's fore-laigs, an' then the hine, wif the pint ove hits tung stuck out, makin suckin moshuns, not yet old enuf tu know the bag aind ove hits mam frum the hookin aind, don't yu want tu kick hit on the snout, hard enough tu send hit backwards, say fifteen foot, jis' tu show hit that buttin won't allers fetch milk? Ur a baby even, rubbin hits heels apas' each uther, a-rootin an' a-snifflin arter the breas', an' the mam duin her bes' tu git hit out, over the hem ove her clothes, don't yu feel hungry tu gin hit jis' one 'cussion cap slap, rite ontu the place what sum day'll fit a saddil, ur a sowin cheer, tu show hit what's atwixt hit an' the grave; that hit stans a pow'ful chance not tu be fed every time hits hungry, ur in a hurry? An' agin: ain't thar sum grown up babys what yu meets, that the moment yer eyes takes em in, yer toes itch tu tetch thar starns, jis' 'bout es saftly es a muel kicks in playin; a histin kine ove a tetch, fur the way they wares thar har, hat, ur watch-chain, the shape ove thar nose, the cut ove thar eye, ur sumthin ove a like littil natur. (245–47)

Nearly all commentators have noticed these superb passages, but no one has yet discussed them as the most direct statements of themes that in fact darkly underlie all of the exuberant comedy of the *Yarns* and that give thematic and structural unity to the collection. Though my comments could and should be extended to the fugitive pieces collected by Inge in *High Times and Hard Times,*[7] I am limiting my discussion in this paper to the twenty-four sketches that Harris himself brought together in the *Yarns,* for the reason that the *Yarns* is a deliberate book—not a random selection of things already published, but a collection of mostly new material, apparently written specifically for this volume (only seven of the twenty-four had received prior publication). I do not, however, intend to make this a brief for the structural integrity of the *Yarns,* for that would take a much longer essay. What I would like to do is discuss a few of the numerous patterns of recurring images and themes that give philosophical weight and complexity to the comedy, to try to come to terms with Sut Lovingood as a character in his own right, and, finally, to suggest that the *Yarns* is not merely a minor masterpiece but a major work of American fiction.

II. Bulls

It is difficult to disagree with those who hold, like Rickels, that Sut is "outside the law, outside social morality, outside religion, even outside rational life" (102) and that each of his "practical jokes" is a "delight" because it is a "conspiracy against all order"

(84). The actual sketches, however, suggest something considerably more complex: in the first place, no more than six of the twenty-four stories in the *Yarns* can even remotely be considered as having to do with "practical jokes" ("A Razor Grinder in a Thunder-Storm," "Sut Assisting at a Negro Night-Meeting," "Frustrating a Funeral," "Parson John Bullen's Lizards," "The Snake-bit Irishman," and "Mrs. Yardley's Quilting"). In the second place, Sut causes the chaos in only ten out of the twenty-four sketches; and of those ten, four depict Sut's righteous (indeed, perhaps self-righteous) revenge against persons who have done him or others injustice ("Parson John Bullen's Lizards," "Sicily Burns's Wedding," "The Snake-bit Irishman," and "The Widow McCloud's Mare"). Two are rather vicious jokes at the expense of Negroes ("Sut Assisting at a Negro Night-Meeting" and "Frustrating a Funeral"). Given the postwar social and political context in which these two were published, Sut's attitude toward the Negroes here is perhaps understandable: but even so, Harris is at pains to depict the Negroes as damn fools, with the same vices as their white owners. One story ("Old Burns's Bull Ride") is simply a happy but unlooked-for extension of Sut's actions in "Sicily Burns's Wedding." One ("Mrs. Yardley's Quilting") is a genuinely innocent practical joke. One ("Old Skissim's Middle Boy"), as I have suggested, is Sut's earnest, if metaphorical, attempt to do a good deed—to wake up the world. And only one, "Sut Lovingood's Dog," represents Sut's angry and irrational and totally unjustified attack upon a fellow human being—and it is told with a definite pedagogical purpose.

Moreover, the actual violence depicted in the *Yarns* is largely the product of Sut's narrative imagination. We are not actually expected to believe—are we?—that the mole in "Hen Baily's Reformation" actually, literally, crawls up Hen's pantsleg and through his anus, chasing that lizard out of Hen's stomach, into his esophagus, and then out his mouth? or that bulls and Wirt Staples actually kick Negro children so that they fly through the air like footballs, creating havoc and destruction when they land? or, for that matter, that the soda powders Sicily Burns administers to Sut actually, literally, produce all the foam that Sut describes?:

> Thar wer a road ove foam frum the hous' tu the hoss two foot wide an' shoe mouf deep—looked like hit hed been snowin—a-poppin an' a-hissin, an' a-bilin like a tub ove soapsuds wif a red hot mole-board in hit. (81–82)

This is not at all to say that violence is not a large part of Sut's world, or that he is unaware of it—indeed, he is all too aware of it, and the constant recurrence of astonishingly revolting images of violence is a conscious part of Sut's story-telling methods, a deliberate element of his attempt both to entertain and to teach. But to say that he *speaks* of violence is quite different from saying that he is an anarchist, a conspirator against all order.

Sut groups people into at least two classes, the wicked and the fools. There is plenty of overlapping, of course, but in general the wicked are those people who take advantage of other people, use them unfairly—economically, socially, legally, or sexually (e.g., Parson Bullen, Sheriff Doltin, Mary Mastin and her mother, Lawyer Stilyards, and Sicily Burns). The fools are characterized by a tendency to excess in whatever they do (Hen Baily's drunkenness, Mrs. Yardley's quilting, Skissim's boy's sleeping, and, of course, Dad's acting horse or bull or yearling): that is, the fools lose control of themselves. Sut is more often than not disgusted by the results of these excesses; he is certainly disgusted, even outraged, by Hen Baily's habitual drunkenness, as he is disgusted and shamed by Dad's excesses.

If it is possible to argue that Sut is opposed to excesses, and I think it is, it is then necessary to observe that he himself is not the Compleat Hedonist that he has been assumed to be. Critics generally describe him as a heavily excessive drinker, and he certainly is seldom without his flask. But we see him drunk only twice, in "Sut Lovingood's Dog" and "Contempt of Court—Almost," and in both cases he uses his probable drunkenness as reasons, but not excuses, for his own violent behavior. He drinks regularly throughout the sketches but seldom enough to lose control of himself.[8] Nor does he exclude himself from the category of Fools—as we will see later in discussions of "Sut Lovingood's Dog" and "Contempt of Court—Almost." He knows only too well that he must maintain a constant and sober vigil over the irrational part of himself, lest he too cause the chaos he abhors.

Sut, then, is a civilizing force and not a destructive one in the Tennessee backwoods. He wants nothing more earnestly than to tame the chaos in which he lives. Sheriffs, lawyers, and preachers are so frequently his victims precisely because they are violators of the order they are specifically sworn to uphold, the order Sut knows is essential if civilization is to survive.

Harris announces this as a theme immediately, in the first two pages of the book. In "Sut Lovingood's Daddy, Acting Horse," Sut is introduced in a vortex, astride the wildly bucking Tearpoke, who has apparently been "redpeppered" by some of Sut's friends as a practical joke:

> "Hole that ar hoss down tu the yeath." "He's a fixin fur the heavings." "He's a spreadin his tail feathers tu fly. Look out, Laigs, if you aint ready tu go up-'ards." "Wo, Shavetail." "Git a fiddil; he's tryin a jig." "Say, Long Laigs, rais'd a power ove co'n didn't yu?" "Taint co'n, hits redpepper." (19)

Before he can proceed with his tale about Tickeytail and Dad, however, Sut must, and does, bring Tearpoke under control, restore order:

> Sut's tongue or his spurs brought Tearpoke into something like passable quietude while he continued. (20)

The first paragraph, emphasizing the chaos, appears virtually unchanged in the story's first publication, in the *Spirit of the Times* (4 November 1854); the second was part of Harris's revision for the book version, an addition that argues that Sut is to be throughout the book an agent of order and not of chaos. The brief episode anticipates the situation in "Taurus in Lynchburg Market," in which Sut actually risks his life in order to bring a raging bull under control. So the basic conflict in the *Yarns* is not at all that between Sut and the hypocrites of the world, or even that between right and wrong, but that between chaos and order, with Sut strongly on the side of order.

At the metaphorical center of that conflict is the image of the bull, which is traditionally, and in the *Yarns* specifically, a symbol of masculine power and virility: not just sexuality, though the connection between masculine sexuality and chaos is very significant in terms of the number of sexual sins committed in the *Yarns*, and especially in terms of the characterization of Sut's Dad in such grossly sexual, animalistic terms. In general, then, bulls symbolize an uncontrolled subservience to physical appetites. The bull also symbolizes political and social aggrandizement: the pursuit of sexual, legal, religious, economic power. In "Sicily Burns's Wedding," for example, Sut gets his revenge on Sicily for her sexual humiliation of him. Thanks to Sut's "arrangements," the blinded bull Ole Sock backs through the house during Sicily's wedding dinner, his very phallic tail very erect, obviously displaying his genitals prominently, and frightening the entire wedding party with his brute sexuality: he passes through the bedroom first and destroys the bed (92), and moves on, wreaking havoc, through the house to the dining room, where Mrs. Clapshaw, the mother of the bridegroom, is hoisted by Ole Sock onto the dinner table. She so fears what she sees that she can only shout "rape, fire, an' murder" (93). Sut, then, uses the bull to desex, at least metaphorically, Sicily's marriage.[9] Sicily's feminine sexuality, which has so deceived, humiliated, and unmanned Sut, is simply overwhelmed by this unleashed masculine sexuality, which she cannot control as she can Sut's. In "Old Burns's Bull Ride," the follow-up story, however, the conflict moves beyond sexuality when Ole Sock, with Burns riding quite accidentally and unwillingly, moves out into the world and encounters not women and effeminate men, but one of his own kind, Ole Mills, another bull. With tails hoisted very high they proceed to thrash each other, and the relatively innocent Burns, a victim of the capricious circumstance that put him on top of Ole Sock, dangles helplessly from a tree, upside down, while the bulls, violent, anarchic forces, rage all around him. So well the bull symbolizes the chaotic forces set loose in the Tennessee backwoods, not to mention in the whole nation, during the Civil War, to destroy civilization.

But it is more complex than that, for the bull is not just a destructive force; properly harnessed and controlled he is a tame and useful creature. Ole Sock is in fact generally a very domesticated beast who is regularly saddled and ridden (90). It is only when they are allowed to get away from the confines of their own pastures (the bull in "Taurus") or are challenged on their own turf (Ole Mills), or are otherwise provoked that bulls lose control of themselves and go on destructive rampages. Thus in the *Yarns* bulls symbolize not just the abstract forces of chaos but the very concrete cause of much of it: onregenerit human nater. Harris is specific: "Now, George," Sut says, "ef yu knows the nater ove a cow brute, they is the durndes' fools amung all the beastes, ('scept the Lovingoods)" (90), and as epigraph to "Taurus," Sut sings of the "blind bull, Human nater" (123): and so it is structurally and thematically no accident that Sut provokes Ole Sock by covering his head with a feeding basket, blinding him. Ole Sock totally disrupts Sicily's wedding celebration with a blind, malevolent, and backwards rush through the house.

III. Dad

Of course what Sut sings is that "Daddy *kill'd* the blind bull, Human nater" (emphasis added), and in doing so suggests a relationship between "Hoss" Lovingood and the image of the blind bull that is to be more fully and more meaningfully developed in the book's final story. The man Sut describes as "dod-dratted mean, an' lazy, an' ugly, an' savidge, an' durn fool tu kill" (22)—Dad—quickly becomes the touchstone in the *Yarns* for all the foolish and irrational behavior, the onregenerit human nater, that Sut continually animadverts against. Dad appears in only two of the sketches, "Sut Lovingood's Daddy, Acting Horse," and "Dad's Dog School," but their placement at the beginning and the end of the collection provides an important frame for the other twenty-two yarns. If the bull is the book's central metaphor, Dad is its figurative and literal frame of reference. He is the human exemplum of all the things the bull comes to symbolize, the *reductio ad absurdum* of all the irrational behavior in the book. By placing him at both the beginning and the end of the collection, Harris casts his shadow over everything that Sut says and does.

The two stories in which Dad appears are very much alike. In both he acts damn fool and gets himself severely punished for it. In both he reduces himself quite deliberately to an animal level, and in both he is stripped naked. In both Mam offers her unasked-for running commentary on the proceedings, caustic commentary that centers on Dad's ability to play "hoss better nur yu dus husban'" (23). In both Sut "assists," and in both an outsider intrudes.

As Sut tells the first story, their plow-horse Tickeytail dies, leaving the Lovingoods without a way to plant their crops: "Well we waited, an' wished, an' rested, an' plan'd, an' wished, an' waited agin, ontil ni ontu strawberry time, hopin sum stray hoss mout cum along" (22). The lazy Dad, instead of trying to buy or even borrow or steal another horse, uses the lack of one as his excuse to do nothing at all. When he does decide that no "stray hoss" is going to come along and save the day, he determines that he will himself pull the plow, and Sut will drive. But Dad is not content just to pull the plow, he must *become* a horse; Sut sees him "a-studyin how tu play the kar-acter ove a hoss puffectly" (22). Dad demands a bridle and bit and then whinnies and kicks when he drops to his all fours. Dad sounds the order/disorder theme clearly when he insists that he wants the bridle bit made "kurb, es he hedn't work'd fur a good while, an' said he mout sorter feel his keepin, an' go tu ravin an' cavortin" (23). Rave and cavort, of course, he does. Dad keeps up his "kar-acter" as a horse throughout, and we watch him gradually though deliberately slough his humanity, a sloughing that is total when he finally divests himself of reason: instead of going around a "sassafrack" bush, as a sensible person would, he "buljed squar intu an' thru hit" like a horse (24) and inflicts upon himself a severe hornet attack. Chaos and destruction ensue; Dad goes completely out of control, pulls out of Sut's hands the gears, which symbolize the restraints of rationality. As he runs through a fence, he leaves his one garment behind on a snag and is completely naked, stripped of all vestige of civilization and exposed, as it were, for the fool he is. Sut watches him run over the bluff and into the creek, then taunts him cruelly as he keeps ducking to get away from the pestiferous hornets, his just recompense for not acting like a rational human being.

"Sut Lovingood's Daddy, Acting Horse," then, is an essentially comic fable about man's propensity to divest himself of his humanity; but it is not difficult to see, especially from the point of view of "Dad's Dog School," the seriousness underlying the comic action, the tragic potential in the characters of Dad and of Sut. This potential is realized in "Dad's Dog School," the book's masterful finale, in which all the important themes and images of the *Yarns* converge.

"Dad's Dog School" opens with Dad's determination to teach Sugar, the pup, to "hold fast"; school begins when Dad strips himself naked. In "Acting Horse," his clothes were pulled from him accidentally when they snagged on a rail of the fence; here, in an unmistakably symbolic act, he deliberately and consciously strips himself of his clothes and, as we shall see, of his humanity. He forces Sall to sew him up into the hide of a yearling bull. Snorting and pawing the ground, he orders Sut to sick Sugar on and unwisely threatens punitive action if Sut should restrain the dog before he is "made." Of course the plan backfires: Sugar manages to get a death hold on Dad's nose through the mouth of the hide, to Dad's infinite displeasure. Sut perversely refuses to pull Sugar off, and Dad comes very close to being killed—he does lose part of his nose and a finger—when Sall separates him and Sugar with a swing of the axe.

But it is much more complicated than this simple plot would suggest. Sugar is a "bull pup," Sut tells us, as "Ugly es a she ho'net"

(278), both of which images remind us of the other bulls and hornets in the book and which augur ill, very early in the story, for Dad. In the earlier story Dad "acted horse"; here he is just as intent on "acting bull." The hide, that of "a-tarin big black an' white yearlin bull beastes" (278) that they have killed some time before, suggests a specific association of Dad with the bull in "Taurus in Lynchburg Market," which is also black and white; Dad Lovingood thus symbolically and literally becomes the bull that he has killed. Later in the story the "snout ove the hide what wer tied back on the naik, worked sorter loose, an' the fold hung down on dad's an' Sugar's snouts"; the fold covers Dad's eyes and, as Sut puts it, "my onregenerit dad wer blinefolded" (293). Dad's transmogrification is complete: he has literally, at this point, *become* the blind bull—"the blind bull, human nater."

It is a wonderfully complex image, for Dad has been "acting bull" all of his life; he is a bestial, destructive man whose rampant sexuality (he has apparently fathered eighteen children on Mam {21}) is almost a parody of the bull as symbol of masculine virility. But it is precisely to the extent that he has "acted bull" all of his life that he has "killed" his own human nature. Harris shows this in "Dad's Dog School" with a series of details that depict the diminishment of Dad's sexual virility and his humanity: it is, in the first place, a "yearling" bull that Dad becomes, an adolescent, as it were, in contrast to the fully grown Ole Sock and Ole Mills and the bull in "Taurus." Further, while the obviously phallic tails of the other rampant bulls remain very erect throughout the sketches in which they appear, the tail Dad assumes as part of his animal nature is very flaccid indeed: it "trail'd arter him *sorter dead like*" (282, emphasis added), Sut tells us; it "trail'd limber an' lazy, an' tangled sumtimes amung dad's hine laigs" (283), making it difficult for him to walk, much less, in his state, to function as a human being. After Sugar bites him on the nose, the tail becomes "stiff strait out, way high up, an' sweepin the air clar ove insex, all roun the yard" (284), but this is centrifugal force, Dad being twirled around the yard by the dog's unvitiated strength.

The story becomes even more explicit: whenever the tail points toward Mam, in what can only be a grotesque parody of Dad's sexual excesses with her, Mam hits him with a bean-pole (294–95), repulsing his advances and punishing him for his bestiality and for the lifetime of misery and poverty he has made for them all. Dad's debilitation, his dehumanization, is almost complete: he tries "tu rise tu the human way ove standin" (294) at one point but is not able to, with Sugar still clamped to his nose. Later he does manage to stand momentarily, but it is by this time an unbearable burden to "act human"; Sut notes that Dad "begun to totter on his hine laigs" (296) and that "his tail {wer} a-trimblin, a mons'ous bad sign in ho'ned cattil" (297).

The tail, however, is only one of two phallic symbols in the story; the other, obviously, is Dad's nose, which receives the brunt of the punishment. And when Sister Sall "tuck a chunk ofen dad's snout" (297), the implications are pretty clear: Dad is, finally, completely, if symbolically, emasculated by the excessive exercise of the very virility that makes, or made, a "man" of him. He becomes a beast because he refuses to act rationally; he kills his own human nature by refusing to control his bestial impulses. Whereas in "Acting Horse" he is merely punished for his foolishness, slapped on the wrist, so to speak, and then more or less restored to human status, here he is shown in his ultimate degradation. He loses all of what is left of his tenuous hold upon humanness; his descent to animality is total and, with his symbolic castration, so is his dehumanization; there is no suggestion of a chance that he will, this time, be restored.

Thus Dad receives his just deserts for his actions here as well as in "Acting Horse." But Dad is essentially unchanged from one story to the other, his behavior basically no different, and so his punishment here is merely the logical extension, a thematic intensification, of his punishment in the earlier story. The different element here is Sut himself, or perhaps it is more accurate to say that the different element is Sut's changed relationship to the action. His reactions here reveal a different aspect of his character and help explain his views of himself, of Dad, and of human nature in general.

In "Dad's Dog School" Sut has complete *control* of the situation. In "Acting Horse" he is primarily a bystander after Dad wrenches the reins loose from his hands. There is nothing he can do to help Dad out of his predicament; he cannot, as it were, save Dad from himself by holding onto the reins. Perhaps he would not have even if he could have—certainly he takes a dim view of "acting horse"— but he cannot, and so he contents himself with taunting Dad from the top of the bluff and entreating him a moral: "Better say yu wish yu may never see anuther ball ho'net, ef yu ever play hoss agin" (27). But in "Dad's Dog School" he is in complete control, he *is* in a position to save Dad from himself and refuses to, even though he clearly knows how much pain Dad is undergoing: "The childer all yell'd, an' sed 'Sick 'im'; they tho't hit wer all gwine jis' es dad wanted, the durn'd littil fools" (285). He not only allows but encourages the episode to proceed, painful page after painful page, and Mam joins him in humiliating Dad.

Part of the reason Sut refuses to stop it is, apparently, the years of stored-up resentment that he understandably feels, but the immediate cause is the intrusion into the "famerly devarshun" (286), as Sut calls this Sunday morning activity, of an outsider, Squire Haney.[10] This too is foreshadowed by a parallel incident in "Acting Horse," when a stranger appears after all the excitement and sees only the aftermath of Dad's foolishness. He asks Sut to tell him "what ails" the man he has just seen back down the road, a "pow'ful curious, vishus, skeery lookin cuss. . . . His hed am es big es a wash pot, an' he hasent the fust durned sign ove an eye—jist two black slits" (28). Sut explains that the man is just "gittin over a vilent attack ove dam fool" (28), and the stranger asks, "Well, who is he eny how?" Sut bridles, expecting the man to say something derogatory about Dad or the rest of his family, "ris tu {his} feet, an' straiched out {his} arm" (28), preparatory to defending his family's honor, and says, defying him to criticize, "Strainger, that man is my dad" (28). But Sut has either misjudged or scared off the man; trouble is averted when the stranger looks at Sut's "laigs an' pussonel feeters" (28), recognizes the physical likenesses, especially the long legs, between Sut and Dad, and simply admits, "Yas, dam ef he aint" (28).

In "Dad's Dog School," however, the intruder is not a stranger but a man well known to Sut and Mam for his hypocritical piousness. Sut sees him approach, "a regular two hundred an' twenty-five poun retribushun, arter us, an' our famerly devarshun sure enuf, armed wif a hyme book, an' loaded tu the muzzil wif brimstone, bilin pitch, forkid flames, an' sich uther nicitys es makes up the devil's brekfus'" (285–86). Up to this point, this story is a pretty typical one, not that much different from the others in the *Yarns*. But with the entry of Squire Haney the tone changes considerably; Sut begins to feel shame:

> A appertite tu run began tu gnaw my stumick, an' I felt my face a-swellin wif shame. I wer shamed ove dad, shamed ove mam's bar laigs an' open collar, shamed ove mysef, an' dam, ef I minds right, ef I warn't a mossel shamed ove the pup. (286)

This is a convincing passage; Sut's shame at having an outsider witness the degradation of his family, even though the outsider be a hypocrite easily dealt with, is very real, and it is not, therefore, difficult to understand why Sut then sadistically allows Sugar to keep tormenting Dad, long after his point has been made. Harris's psychology is perfect. Sut turns from Squire Haney, the purveyor of his shame, to Dad, the cause of it; he lashes out, angrily and bitterly, with the only means he has at hand, by perversely following his orders not to pull Sugar off until he is "made." "Stan hit dad," he taunts, "stan hit like a man; hit may be a littil hurtin tu yu, but dam ef hit ain't the makin ove the pup" (296). Suddenly the story is not funny any more. Sut takes this opportunity, a gift, to flog Dad, to strike out at the one who is responsible for all of the misery and shame in his life; he works revenge against Dad and, by extension, against all the forces that make the world a difficult place in which to live. It is an opportunity not many have had, and Sut makes the most of it.

It is not a pretty picture: the worthless Dad, completely degenerated, his wife cursing and beating him with her every breath, and Sut, at this, the darkest point in an often dark book, unleashing all of his years of accumulated frustration and shame. And even though the story is told with the ironic rhetoric of the detached storyteller, it is clear that the episode, and his relations with Dad generally, have a profound effect upon Sut. Dad is for Sut a sort of foolish Everyman, in whose character are crystallized all of the faults of the human race, as Sut understands them, and his memory is a troubling one that hovers darkly over Sut's entire life: "I blames him fur all ove hit," he tells George earlier in the book, "allers a-tryin tu be king fool. He hes a heap tu count fur, George—a heap" (107).

IV. Sut

Profound as that effect is, though, Dad is not the only influence on Sut's vision. He is, of course, the dominant one, the one foremost in Sut's mind at all times, the standard of foolishness against which he measures all human behavior. He has seen nothing to make him alter the basic vision he has gleaned from his observations of his father; nearly everything has in fact tended to confirm it. In the world he knows, the Tennessee backwoods—and in the fugitive sketches collected in *High Times and Hard Times* the range is even further—

people are vain and selfish and mean and do not understand that their disregard of the laws of decency and kindness is as debilitating to themselves personally as their flouting of the laws of society is to civilization as a whole. Sut knows it, though, and it is part of the burden of the *Yarns* to preach that particular gospel.

This is not a lesson Sut has learned easily, however, even with Dad's pristine example before him; and at least part of what the other stories in the *Yarns* do is to help us trace Sut's education in the ways of the world. "Sut's New-Fangled Shirt," for example, the second story in the book, is among other things an allegorization of Sut's "birth" into the real world. In that story, Betts Carr, Sut's landlady, forces him to wear a heavily overstarched shirt, even though it is, to Sut, an "everlastin, infunel, new fangled sheet iron cuss ove a shut" (32) that makes him feel as though he's "crowded intu a ole bee-gum, an' hit all full ove pissants" (32). As he works and sweats, however, the shirt "quit hits hurtin, an' tuck tu feelin slippery" (33). Hot and tired, Sut climbs into his quarters in the loft and takes a nap. When he wakes, the shirt has dried again, this time cemented to his body, and is quite painful:

> "I now thort I wer ded, an' hed died ove rhumaticks ove the hurtines' kind. All the jints I cud muve wer my ankils, knees, an' wrists; cudn't even move my hed, an' scarsely wink my eyes; the cussed shut wer pasted fas' ontu me all over, frum the ainds ove the tails tu the pints ove the broad-axe collar over my years." (33)

He manages to get his pants off, so that he is naked save for the shirt. Removing a plank from the ceiling of the house, he nails the front and back tails of the shirt to the floor, and jumps through the opening; the shirt tears off, turning inside out as it does, and Sut hits the floor stark naked. It seems clearly a birth image, even to the shirt hanging there, to push the image as far as possible, as a grotesque parody of a placenta; it looks, Sut says, "adzactly like the skin ove sum wile beas' tore off alive, ur a bag what hed toted a laig ove fresh beef frum a shootin match" (35). It is, if birth it is, a violent, painful, and humiliating entrance into the world for Sut, who begins to learn about the world the moment he is born.

It is perhaps too much to say that Sut learns about life, in the course of the *Yarns,* in any systematic manner: it is neither possible or necessary to think that in each story he learns something different, or that from each person he encounters he learns a specific thing. But Sut is a keen observer of mankind, and over the years his initial observations, gleaned mostly from Dad, have been both confirmed and expanded. What Sut learns, and how he learns it, are very nicely summed up, condensed, into a superb story, "Taurus in Lynchburg Market," which stands directly, and significantly, at the center of the book, the twelfth of twenty-four stories.[11]

At the beginning of "Taurus" Sut sings the important quatrain referred to earlier, which suggests the allegorical significance of the story Sut is to tell:

> "Daddy kill'd the blind bull,
> Human nater, human nater!
> "Mammy fried a pan full,
> Sop an' tater, sop an' tater." (123)

Sut sings this in reaction against George's reading, and obviously approving, Henry Wadsworth Longfellow's very sentimental poem, "Excelsior," which is about, as Sut describes it, a "feller . . . what starts up a mountin, kiver'd wif snow an' ise, arter sundown, wif nuffin but a flag, an' no whisky, arter a purty gal hed offer'd her bussum fur a pillar, in a rume wif a big hath, kiver'd wif hot coals, an' vittils" (124)—flouting, it seems to Sut, the laws of reason and common sense. He is not, however, merely teasing George; indeed, he is considerably upset that George could be so duped by a view of human nature as sentimental and naive as that of the Longfellow poem. To make his point, Sut rises "to his tiptoes, and elevate[s] his clenched fists high above his head" (124); such a fellow, he says, "am a dod durn'd, complikated, full-blooded, plum nat'ral born durn'd fool" (124). This is apparently one of a series of heroes whom George has admired and spoken of, for Sut then alludes to "Lum Jack . . . darin the litenin" (124). George responds, obviously irritated at Sut's attack, "Ajax, I suppose you mean" (124), and Sut speaks contemptuously of Ajax's heroic dare by pointing out a couple of facts that George has overlooked:

> An' he wer a jack, ove the longes' year'd kine, fus', because eny fool mout know the litenin wudn't mine him no more nur a locomotum wud mine a tumble-bug. An' then, spose hit hed met his dar, why durn me ef thar'd been a scrimshun ove 'im lef big enuf tu bait a minner hook wif. (124–25)

Sut knows what George doesn't know, that no individual has any control over the real world, and so his contempt is both for the hollowness and stupidity of Ajax's meaningless gesture and for George's willingness to be impressed by it. Sut relates his experience

in Lynchburg, then, as a parable, to teach George a lesson about human nature and about the meaning of "heroism" and "sacrifice" in
the real world.

"Taurus" is, again, a simple story. Visiting in the mountain city
of Lynchburg, Virginia—and significantly it is a town, a center of
civilization, and not just the usual backwoods settlement, where the
episode takes place—Sut sees a "thuteen hunder' poun' black an'
white bull" (126) rampaging violently through the town, causing
destruction everywhere. His tail is "es strait up in the air es a telegraf
pole" (126). At issue in "Taurus," then, is the conflict between
chaos and order, between civilization and anarchy. Sut takes sides
in the conflict "agin the critter" (129), that is, against chaos. Seeing
his chance, Sut grabs the bull's tail and wraps it around a light
pole—which, like the "telegraf pole" to which Sut compares the
bull's erect tail, is both a symbol of civilization and one of its products, one of the things that, bringing light into the darkness, helps
make civilization possible. Sut's description of light poles as "mity
good things . . . fur a feller tu straiten up on, fur a fresh start"
(128–29), foreshadows Dad's inability, in "Dad's Dog School," to
stand up straight like a human being. Sut underscores the point that
civilization is the instrument whereby brute natural chaotic forces
can be tamed when he declares that the poles "can't be beat at stop-
pin bulls frum actin durn'd fool" (129). Sut steps in, puts himself at
extreme risk, hoping to halt the destruction of Lynchburg, hero-
ically taking sides "agin the critter."

What does he get for his trouble? The bull defecates on him, and
he is abandoned by the very people whose civilization he is trying
to save; one of the townspeople finds Sut's predicament funny and
taunts him from behind the safety of a door. Sut tells George, "Ef
hit hadn't been fur the cramp, skeer, an' that feller's bettin agin me,
I'd been thar yet, a monument ove enjurance, parsavarance, an' dam
fool, still holdin a dry bull's hide by the tail" (131). That is, he says,
if he had had some help or even some moral support from anybody
else, the fight would have been worth it, worth keeping up even in-
definitely; but he gets none. All he gets, literally and metaphorically,
is shat upon. All he can do alone is to put a couple of kinks in the
tail of chaos (132).

This is not at all to suggest that Sut is right to undervalue heroism or that two kinks in that metaphorical tail is not a magnificent
gesture in itself, perhaps the best that one can ultimately do. But it

is no wonder that Sut is so bitter and disillusioned about mankind or that he is so exercised about George's sentimentality.

What, then, does Sut learn? He learns about wickedness and foolishness, of course, that it is human nature to be unregenerate, to court violence and self-destruction. But the implications of "Taurus" suggest that he learns even more: not just that people are capable of and delight in doing evil in all of its manifest forms; not just that they are capable of destroying themselves and their civilization through wickedness and folly; not just that they are capable of these things and more, but that like Dad they do them deliberately, consciously, and will not lift a hand either to save themselves or to help somebody else save them. It is a profoundly pessimistic vision.

It is, of course, a vision that he shares with many others, but Sut does not make the self-righteous mistake that many of his "victims" do, of separating himself from the rest of mankind in this regard; he does not believe he is different. Indeed, he knows himself too well to deny, and is too honest to avoid confessing, his own tendencies to lose control, to act irrationally. As early as "Sut's New-Fangled Shirt," for example, he specifically associates himself with his Dad. The stiffened, starched shirt stands up against Betts Carr's cabin "like a dry hoss hide" (32), and Sut sweats "like a hoss" (32) when he wears it to work. Even more pointedly, Sut sleeping dreams that he has been "sowed up in a raw hide" and wakes to find the shirt pasted to him "es clost es a poor cow {is} tu her hide in March" (33).

Like all of his victims he is capable of meanness and violence, and two important episodes in the *Yarns* are in fact stories that Sut tells on himself. The lesser of the two is "Sut Lovingood's Dog," a story in which Sut's dog is mistreated by someone (we are not told by whom) while Sut is inside a doggery, "gittin on a hed ove steam" (151). Incensed and, significantly, probably drunk, Sut "got mad an' looked roun fur sum wun tu vent rath on, an' seed a long-legged cuss, sorter ove the Lovingood stripe" (152) riding down the street on his horse. Without knowing whether the man is guilty or innocent, Sut decides "yu'll do, ef yu *didn't* start my dog on that hellward experdition" (152). Sut tries unsuccessfully to provoke a quarrel, and so in a caveman-like rage hits the man with a rock: "I jist lent him a slatharin calamity, rite whar his nose commenced a sproutin from atween his eyes, wif a ruff rock about the size ove a goose aig. Hit fotch 'im!" (152). During the ensuing fight, Sut puts a blazing box of matches into one of the man's coat pockets—but this is before he knows that in the other pocket the man is carrying two pounds of gunpowder. Telling it, Sut recognizes that he could easily have gotten himself killed or seriously injured. If he had known, he says, "durn me, ef I hedn't let him beat me inter a poultis, afore I'd a-sot him on fire" (153).

"Sut Lovingood's Dog" is primarily comic, and its moral is lightly stated. The other episode is deadly serious, however, and much more sobering in its effect. It appears in "Contempt of Court—Almost" in the wake of Sut's frank admission that he "hates ole Onsightly Peter," the snobbish and unwelcome encyclopedia salesman who has invited himself to join their camp, and of his long monologue on "univarsal onregenerit human nater" (245–47). The anecdote is intended, Sut says, "Jis' tu show the idear" of "univarsal onregenerit human nater," and he himself is the onregenerit human.

A foppish fellow enters a doggery where Sut is, again significantly, busy drinking; he looks at Sut "like {he} mout smell bad" (247), and Sut is perhaps understandably irritated by the man's arrogance and general manner. "Baw-keepaw, ole Champaigne Brandy," the fop orders, "vintage ove thuty-eight, ef yu please, aw" (247). Sut's toes, he says, begin to tingle. He speaks to the stranger, again apparently trying to provoke a quarrel, but the man ignores him and turns to leave. Enraged and for no rational reason, Sut kicks the stranger as hard as he can. As the man flies out the door he turns, pulls a derringer, and fires twice. "I wer sorter fooled in the nater ove that feller," Sut confesses: "that's a fac'. The idear ove Derringers, an' the melt tu use em, bein mix't up wif es much durned finekey fool es he show'd, never struck me at all" (248–49). Sut of course "outruns" the bullets, but the point is lost on neither Sut nor the reader; like nearly everybody else in the book, Sut here loses control of his rational self and nearly destroys himself in the process. He knows, then, that he is no different from the rest of mankind, that he no less than anybody else will, upon the slightest provocation, act horse or bull or damned fool and so create the very chaos and destruction he abhors.

But the central episode of "Contempt of Court—Almost," of which Sut's brush with the fop is introductory, entails a situation that seems to contradict the case for Sut as a proponent of order and that provides an essential insight into Sut's character. The one person in the *Yarns* whom Sut admires is Wirt Staples, who assists in righting the wrongs done by Sheriff Doltin to his rather slow-witted and cuckolded cousin Wat Mastin. Sut introduces Wirt in terms with which we have been describing his typical villains: Wirt is drunken and violent; coming out of a doggery he "histed his tail" (249), stepped out into the street "short an' high, like ontu a bline hoss" (250), and looked up and down the street "like a bull looks fur tuther one, when he thinks he hearn a beller" (250). "Wirt wer bilin hot; nobody tu gainsay him {that is, nobody to control him}, hed made him piedied all over; he wer plum pizen" (252). Bragging loudly and looking for a fight, he throws a little Negro boy up in the air and kicks him as he comes down so that he flies like a football through a watch-tinker's window, wrecking the business and causing destruction generally. That is, even allowing for Sut's obvious exaggeration, clearly Wirt under the influence is very much like the bull of "Taurus in Lynchburg Market." And yet Sut sees him as the epitome of manhood:

> His britches wer buttoned tite roun his loins, an' stuffed 'bout half intu his boots, his shut bagg'd out abuv, an' wer es white es milk, his sleeves wer rolled up tu his armpits, an' his collar wer es wide open es a gate, the mussils on his arms moved about like rabbits onder the skin, an' ontu his hips an' thighs they play'd like the swell on the river, his skin wer clear red an' white, an' his eyes a deep, sparklin, wickid blue, while a smile fluttered like a hummin bird roun his mouf all the while. When the State-fair offers a premin fur *men* like they now dus fur jackasses, I means tu enter Wirt Staples, an' I'll git hit, ef thar's five thousand entrys. (253)

Why this contradiction? It is only apparent, I think. In the first place, Sut insists that Wirt's drunkenness, and therefore his "acting bull," is a freak chance, unusual for Wirt: he "hed changed his grocery range, an' the sperrits at the new lick-log hed more scrimmage seed an' raise-devil intu hit than the old biled drink he wer used tu" (249). In the second place, Sut understands the world, of course, but understanding it is not quite the same thing as having to live in it. For the fact that he understands it as capricious and violent does not necessarily make living in it any easier—it can in fact make it more difficult. He is constantly on the run, Sut keeps saying, from one person or another, trying to escape whatever doom is about to overtake him. He is a man with many fears and anxieties, weary of constantly contending with this world and yet afraid of confronting the next: "I feels like I'd be glad *tu be* dead, only I'se feard ove the dyin" (106–07), he tells George. Sut has a great deal of courage and a lot of spiritual toughness, but in the end he realizes that the preachers and lawyers and sheriffs have the upper hand and that to get on in the world he must either avoid them entirely, outsmart them, or outrun them: he runs. What Sut admires about Wirt Staples is not at all his capacity for violence but his competence, his ability to deal with the world on its own terms, in a way that Sut is not able to. Wirt is big enough and strong enough not to have to be afraid of anything—not even the sheriff or the judge.

Finally, and this is perhaps more important, there is nothing mean or vicious or selfish about Wirt; he is not out to use or misuse anyone, and his marriage is the only healthy, harmonious relationship in the book. So he and his wife stand in vivid contrast to the other characters—even, to a certain extent, to Sut himself. They are fine examples of what human beings can be if they want to be and are willing to make the effort to be. Wirt, and not Dad, is obviously what Sut would like to be, what he would like human beings to be.

V. Yarns

A final perspective on the meaning of the Yarns can be gained by a brief look, here, at the book's magnificent preface. No book was ever so introduced, and no preface I know of functions so brilliantly as a structural component of the book it prefaces. The preface to the Yarns does much more than merely introduce the book: it establishes character, conflict, and theme; and it states, clearly but indirectly, the serious moral tone and purpose of the entire book.

Sut initially objects, though not very strenuously, to the inclusion of a preface in "his" book, arguing that because most prefaces preachily try to sum up the moral content of the book, readers usually ignore them:

> Smells tu me sorter like a durned humbug, the hole ove hit—a littil like cuttin ove the Ten Cummandmints intu the rine ove a warter-million; hits jist slashed open an' the inside et outen hit, the rine an' the cummandmints broke all tu pieces an' flung tu the hogs, an' never tho't ove onst—them, nur the 'tarnil fool what cut em thar. (ix)

Prefaces, no matter how serious, are as often disregarded as the Ten, and Sut agrees to have one very reluctantly, with a highly ironical and even slightly cynical disdain of the whole business: "But ef a orthur *mus'* take off his shoes afore he goes intu the publick's parlor," he continues, metaphorically describing the moral disorder in the world as dirt, "I reckon I kin du hit wifout durtyin my feet, fur I hes socks on" (ix).

His preface, however, makes its moral point not by discussing the book, as most prefaces do, but by discussing his readers, whom he divides into two large and perhaps all-encompassing classes, the lucky and the unlucky. The latter he describes in a highly moving passage that almost certainly wells up out of Harris's own experiences during his years of wandering:

> Ef eny poor misfortinit devil hu's heart is onder a millstone, hu's raggid children am hungry, an' no bread in the dresser, hu is down in the mud, an' the lucky ones a-trippin him every time he struggils tu his all fours, hu hes fed the famishin an' is now hungry hissef, hu misfortins foller fas' an' foller faster, hu is so foot-sore an' weak that he wishes he wer at the ferry—ef sich a one kin fine a laugh, jis' one, sich a laugh es is remembered wif his keerless boyhood, atwixt these yere kivers—then, I'll thank God that I *hes* made a book, an' feel that I hev got my pay in full. (xi)

This sentiment is directly related in many and obvious ways to "Sut Lovingood's Sermon" and "Tripetown—Twenty Minutes for Breakfast" and the diatribe in those sketches against the many unscrupulous "Perpryiters" who out of simple mean greed make rest, surcease from wandering, prohibitively expensive for those "poor misfortinit devils" who need it most. Sut's sympathies are clearly for these "unlucky" ones, and his compassion is all the more heartbreaking for the implicit recognition in the passage of the fact that any comfort he can offer, any laughter, any relief, can be only a momentary stay, and that they must eventually face the struggle again. This melancholy note is gently but firmly sounded even as early as the book's title page, in the legend, which states with Shakespearean simplicity that the laughter in the *Yarns* is inextricably commingled with the portent, the actual foreknowledge, of doom:

> "A little nonsense, now and then,
> Is relished by the wisest men."
> "Suppose I am to hang the morrow, and
> *Can* laugh tonight, shall I not?"—OLD PLAY

The only comfort that Sut can offer the unlucky is the catharsis of laughter—the satisfaction of seeing their oppressors brought humiliatingly low by one of the unlucky. The *Yarns* are full of the lucky ones, the "perpryiters" and sheriffs and preachers who take advantage of or mistreat other people out of greed or simply because they have the power to do so. It is generally the lucky ones who become Sut's victims, and it is these that he advises to stay away from his book:

> "I dusn't 'speck this yere perduckshun will sit purfeckly quiet ontu the stumicks ove sum pussons—them hu hes a holesum fear ove the devil, an' orter hev hit, by geminey. Now, fur thar speshul well-bein herearter, I hes jis' this tu say: Ef yu ain't fond ove the smell ove cracklins, stay outen the kitchin; ef yu is fear'd ove smut, yu needn't climb the chimbley; an' ef the moon hurts yer eyes, don't yu ever look at a Dutch cheese. That's jis' all ove hit.
>
> "Then thar's sum hu haint much faith in thar repertashun standin much ove a strain; they'll be powerful keerful how an' whar they reads my words. Now, tu them I haint wun word tu say: they hes been preached tu, an' prayed fur, now ni ontu two thousand years an' I won't dart weeds whar thuty-two poun shot bounces back." (ix–x)

Finally, Sut tells George that he wants "tu put sumwhar atween the eyebrows ove our book, in big winnin-lookin letters, the sarchin, meanin words, what sum pusson writ ontu a 'oman's garter onst, long ago," and George supplies the words: "*Evil be to him that evil thinks*" (xi). These words are indeed writ large throughout the book, for most of Sut's victims do in fact *think evil*, if we can understand "evil" to mean not just wickedness but foolishness too— any of the things that cause misery and chaos and destruction. And Sut's "tremenjus gif . . . fur breedin skeers amung durned fools" (xi) is his genius at producing for his victims the very retribution they most fear. Time and time again in the *Yarns* the evil that people do simply turns around, sometimes with and sometimes without Sut's help, and consumes the evil-doer in the very deed: think of Sut's Dad, of course, and Parson Bullen; the Irishman who most fears snakes is run out of camp by what he thinks is a snake; Hen Baily is nearly destroyed by his love of liquor; Sheriff Doltin is frightened by a man he believes to be Wat Mastin, a man he has deliberately wronged; and in "Frustrating a Funeral" Sut arranges for the sins of the past to come back and haunt all the main characters. That is, Sut's victims know they are doing evil at the time they are doing it, and so they walk in fear of the retribution they know they deserve. In producing that retribution, or a figment of it, Sut breeds his "skeers."

There is not, of course, in the *Yarns* or in life, a simple division of mankind into the lucky and the unlucky. It is rather Harris's metaphor for describing human relationships: all are capable of rapacity and meanness, and given the chance all are capable of using their fortuitously gained power over others for their own aggran-dizement. At the whim of fate, common people become elders and elders become bishops, the worm becomes the chicken and the chicken becomes the possum (see 228); any may become, for the moment, a "lucky" one. And so it is with complete seriousness that Sut is able, finally, to dedicate his book "*tu the durndest fool* in the United States, an' Massachusets too, he or she"

DEDERCATED
WIF THE SYMPERTHYS OVE THE ORTHUR,
TU THE MAN UR 'OMAN, HUEVER THEY BE,
WHAT *DON'T* READ THIS YERE BOOK.

Obviously, the *durndest fool* is the man who persists in his own self-destruction, and Sut hopes that man will learn from his book not just how not, but *why* not, to destroy himself and his civilization.

But Sut is no optimist. He knows that nobody pays any attention to the Ten Commandments, or book prefaces, anyway, and Harris, in his warping and weaving of Sut's yarns, structures the book de-liberately to confirm the bleak world view: the *Yarns* ends not with the bright ameliorating picture of Wirt Staples and his wife and their happy healthy relationship but with the much darker portrait of Dad and Mam and *their* relationship. And in that contrast lies much of the ultimate meaning of the *Yarns:* people must learn to control their animal nature if the institutions of civilization, and therefore civilization itself, are to survive, and they are capable of doing so. But they simply will not do it.

Perhaps it is too early in the study of Harris to start making claims for him as an important American author, but it is difficult to escape the conclusion that the *Yarns* is among the most ambitious and complex achievements in nineteenth-century American fiction, one that deserves and will repay a serious and sustained effort to come to grips with it. Its artistry is highly sophisticated and original, and its articulation of the human condition, especially that of the mid-nineteenth-century South, is among the most profound and moving that I know. It is a dark, pessimistic book, among the darkest in nineteenth-century American literature, precisely because it does not end on a hopeful note; no life-in-the-midst-of-death coffin buoys up from the dark depths to sustain life or give hope to those with the courage or the luck to survive. It is a darkness punctuated and illuminated all the way through by Harris's unmatched sense of humor; but it is ultimately unrelieved by any suggestion that humanity will ever be saved. In Harris's vision people are not being destroyed by forces beyond themselves, though of course those forces do exist in Harris's world. They are rather hell-bent on destroying themselves; and that is dark indeed.

Notes

1. I would like to thank Jim West for permission to reprint this essay. I am grateful to Jim Caron and Tom Inge for the chance to republish it, with some revisions, in this collection. Those who have read the essay in its earlier avatar will know how deep my gratitude runs, especially to Tom Inge.
2. See the bibliography at the end of the collection.
3. Milton Rickels, *George Washington Harris* (New York: Twayne, 1965), 48.
4. George Washington Harris, *"Sut Lovingood. Yarns": A Facsimile of the 1867 Dick and Fitzgerald Edition*, ed. M. Thomas Inge (Memphis: Saint Lukes Press, 1987), 21. Subsequent citations will be to this edition.
5. W. H. D. Rouse, trans., *Great Dialogues of Plato,* ed. Eric H. Warmington and Philip G. Rouse (New York: New American Library, 1956), 436–37.
6. Edmund Wilson, "'Poisoned!'" *New Yorker,* 7 May 1955, 138. The review is reprinted in this collection.
7. M. Thomas Inge, ed., *High Times and Hard Times: Sketches and Tales by George Washington Harris* (Nashville: Vanderbilt University Press, 1967).
8. Sut definitely likes his whiskey, but he is not an indiscriminate drinker, like Hen Baily, and in "Sut Lovingood's Love-Feast Ove Varmints," one of the fugitive sketches collected in *High Times and Hard Times,* Sut advises George not to take unnecessary risks when he drinks, giving sound advice: "Why, durn yer little fool pictur, are you gwine tu take yer warter afore you licker? Dont ye no that licker's the lightest an ef ye take hit fust, hit cums up thru the warter an makes a ekel mixtry an spiles all chance ove being pisened by hit? Allers take yer whisky fust, fur you don't allers know what mout be in hit. I'se monsus keerful about everything fur all natur's agin me" (243).
9. Sut's initial intention was to "shave ole Clapshaw's hoss's tail, go tu the stabil an' shave Sicily's mare's tail, an' ketch ole Burns

out, an' shave his tail too" (90). Ormonde Plater, in "Narrative
Folklore in the Works of George Washington Harris" (Ph.D.
diss., Tulane University, 1969), 148, remarks that Sut intends
to "de-sex" the marriage by symbolically defoliating Sicily's
and Clapshaw's "pubes." But in light of what happens and in
light of the tremendous metaphorical importance of tails
throughout the *Yarns*, his comment seems a bit short of the
mark.

10.   Also called Squire Hanley the first two times his name is mentioned, *Yarns*, 285–86.

11.   And, had "Sut Lovingood's Chest Story" been published in the
Yarns following "Old Burns's Bull Ride," as the fourth story in
the Sicily Burns tetralogy, as apparently the original plan had
been, "Taurus" would have been squarely in the middle, the
thirteenth story of twenty-five.

George Washington Harris and Supernaturalism

Benjamin Franklin Fisher IV

Sut Lovingood and the supernatural? An unlikely topic, many might suppose. In a class on southern literature, long ago, when Arlin Turner introduced the name of George Washington Harris, he mentioned no aspects of the mysterious in the Lovingood yarns. Instead, the renowned authority on southern studies emphasized traits of southwestern humor and the realism inherent in these writings. Another influential source in times past for introducing the Lovingood pieces, Wallace Stegner's *American Prose: 1840–1900, The Realistic Movement,* also placed them among texts of literary realism. We need not belabor here the prominence ascribed to Harris as humorist-realist in other anthologies. Like Dickens and Twain, he performed at his best for most readers as a comic author, and to such audiences any theory that might take away from that image has been suspect.

Nevertheless, Harris did venture into territories where natural and supernatural draw close. In "Realism and Fantasy in Southern Humor," published before his remarks mentioned above—which were delivered in 1963—Arlin Turner had managed to move Sut almost, but not quite, into the camp of the otherworldy. Milton Rickels has suggested that in the Lovingood yarns "the impulse to give Sut supernatural characteristics is shown in the bird imagery asso-

Publications of the Mississippi Philological Association 1 (1982): 18–23. The author has revised his article for this reprinting.

ciated with him." Rickels's observation increased my own interest in the topic, and I offer forthwith my findings.[1]

I

Born in 1814, George Washington Harris wrote during the era of Dickens and Poe, themselves humorists and supernaturalists of no mean degree, as were surprising numbers of others among their contemporaries. Indeed, Kenneth S. Lynn once called attention to affinities between the comic impulses in the writings of Poe and Harris, but there has been little follow-up to his suggestions. We know how many tactics from terror tales in magazines and newspapers were adapted by Poe because of his familiarity with the journalistic world of the times; why not examine the methodology of supernaturalism in the fiction of Harris, who was also steeped in the newspaper and periodical world of the times?[2]

Internal evidence of Sut's supernatural bent is amply attested throughout the texts of the yarns proper. For example, in "Old Skissim's Middle Boy" the corpulent sluggard son of Skissim is overtly compared with the fat boy, Joe, from Dickens's *The Pickwick Papers*. The latter worthy terrifies his elderly mistress when he announces: "I wants to make your flesh creep." Instead of the anticipated account of blood-and-thunder or supernatural horrors, Joe agitates the old lady by informing her about the amorous intentions of her daughter and a man in the arbor.[3] Such reversals in a situation where supernaturalism might be expected are much a part of Harris's own procedures, although, like the fat boy, Sut Lovingood frequently conveys a "kind of dark and gloomy joy," creating through such tactics a genuine grotesquerie throughout the yarns. The ill-fated young man in "Old Skissim's Middle Boy" is actually made up by the vengeful Sut to resemble a being far more demon than human. Surely, through such methods, Harris grafted the twigs of sensational tales onto the hardy stock of native American humor and folklore. The resultant hybrids remain to this day a fresh subject for examination.

II

Sut's imaginative vision, and that of his friend "George" on at least one occasion, are positively morbid, running toward situations and, more restrictive and significant, dreams about the mysterious and ghostly. In the preface to *Sut Lovingood. Yarns Spun by a "Nat'ral Born Durn'd Fool"* appear solid examples of impulses toward death as well as attention to the figure of the devil in Sut's analogical imagination. He opens by comparing books without prefaces to coffin makers appearing in public without their customary black clothing. Sut continues in a manner adumbrating that of Huck Finn, whose fantasies consist largely of themes of illness, misfortunes, painful deaths, and wraiths. Educated fools, Sut adds, "breeds . . . devilment," and those who fear the devil—with good reason—will not enjoy the contents of this book. He emphasizes that it is rife with "sicknin skeers," created by his innate and "tremenjus gif . . . fur breedin skeers amung durned fools." As if these examples might have but insufficiently demonstrated Sut's predilection toward scenes overspread by anxiety, torment of a physical nature, and supernatural creatures (epitomized by Satan himself), he concludes by dubbing a married man a "poor misfortinit devil" and by reaffirming the primary purpose of the *Yarns:* to offer a "gineral skeer."[4]

If in so brief a compass as this preface, Sut's rhetoric, the articulated expression of his imagination, runs to frights and demons, what evil may lurk in the ensuing pages? Although Sut's language is accorded high esteem by those intent upon finding in American colloquialisms the stuff of great literature, that expression may as readily yield illustrative substance for those who discern significance in his repeated drawing upon supernatural undercurrents. Multiple connotations, if not absolute wordplay, may constitute a greater portion of the art in these sketches than many others have remarked.

Centering upon nineteenth-century evangelical, or fundamentalist, religious ethics, Sut hints at suffering (in this world and in eternal environs) and ghostliness as well as appearances by the Prince of Darkness himself—to great literary advantage. Sut frequently comments that he himself has "nara a soul," so perhaps vampire lore also figures into his background. Readers used to hell-fire from the pulpit encounter it in different guises under Sut's tutelage. Indeed, hell-firedness provides staples of fear, or "skeers," in many of his yarns.

To illustrate: when in "Eaves-dropping a Lodge of Free-masons" the unfortunate Lum crashes through the ceiling and hangs suspended above the gathering of puzzled brothers, some of them hastily conclude that the devil has penetrated their midst. How ap-

propriate that sentiment is: not long before this apocalyptic occur-
rence, Sut had described Lum and George as "little devils" and Lum,
later, as a "skeer'd divil." Author Harris may have recollected the
comic devil tales popular in *Blackwood's* and in that bible of con-
temporaneous American periodicals, William T. Porter's the *Spirit
of the Times,* or, maybe, those of Irving, Poe, and Thackeray; here,
instead of a genuine supernatural being experiencing defeat at the
hands of a wily potential victim who ultimately bests him, young
Lum suffers the ignominy of spanking at the hands of an unbefud-
dled lodge member.

As in numerous other burlesques of Gothic tradition, Lum's
predicament is described in terms calculated to disperse horrors by
means of intruding emphatic reality. Old Stack swings his piece of
ceiling plank, "an' jis' busted hit intu seventeen an' a 'alf pieces at
wun swollopin lick ontu the part ove Lum, what fits a saddil. Hit
crack'd sorter like a muskit a-bustin, an' the tetchin sensashun shot
Lum up thru the hole like a rocket" (*Yarns,* 119–20). Such rein-
statement of reality firmly ends any notions of the horrific, at least
that of otherworldly varieties, among the brotherhood and among
readers.

Like many older hands at literary Gothicism—Mrs. Radcliffe, say,
or nearer his own day, Poe—Harris undercuts exaggerated supernaturalism and the foolery of those who adulterate what should be
rational perceptions with overdoses of nonsensical but sensational
emotionalism. In this respect we must examine more closely the
rhetoric, direct from the graveyard school of an earlier day, albeit
still extant, vestigially at least, in the pages of sentimental magazines
and other kindred literature, with which "George" begins his portion of this narration. He centers upon the old Knoxville courthouse, noting particularly its "steep gable front . . . its gloomy walls
and ghostly echoes {as well as its} crime unveiled," all of which appropriately "belong to the past" (*Yarns,* 114). This sketching derives
from much the same vein as Harrison Ainsworth's in *Rookwood*
(1834), wherein the British novelist attempted a "romance in the
bygone style of Mrs. Radcliffe." A like accoutrement appears in the
"thickening twilight" accompanying and stimulating George's
memories, for without doubt this tale is a "twilight story" akin to
one offered by that old martinet of a lawyer, Mr. Tulkinghorn, in
Dickens's *Bleak House,* as he outlines the unsavory past of Lady Ded-
lock, or to those eerie narratives entitled *Twilight Stories* (1873) by

Rhoda Broughton. Gothic touches or not, George's memories quickly reveal the overly sentimental and lachrymose, especially when they take the form of reminiscences about the church and graveyard from childhood.

Sut can no longer tolerate his companion's sentimentality, so he takes over the thread of the story. He misses no opportunity to "skeer" or to create an atmosphere of anxiety and fearfulness during his outline of the boys' increasing foreboding while darkness descends upon their hiding place. They even suppose that it was "haunted": what a backdrop for their spying upon the secretive fraternity of Masons meeting below—because such groups were often suspected of diabolical pursuits. As if the youths had not sufficient "skeerin'," the Tyler of the lodge gives them sensational chase, threatening their lives, as they interpret his actions, when they attempt to escape. That bit of nightmare activity, verging very near the supernatural in its dreamlike aura, gives way as the boys flee the building, only to fall into what Harris euphemistically terms a "slush" hole, above which an outhouse had been removed, dash thence to the nearest creek for a wash, and, leaving all traces of that escapade behind, return naked to their homes. Persons they meet believe that they see "the cholery a-cumin" or frogs' ghosts, or spirits presaging an approaching famine (*Yarns*, 121). Sut leads into this conclusion by remarking sarcastically to George about the graveyard mentioned previously, as if Lovingood wishes to repeat his technique of taking over George's narrative materials but pruning them of sentimentality and irrational supernaturalism. The result is old-time Gothicism turned inside out with a vengeance.

In other ways Harris fashions his writing so that we find ourselves wondering what is and what is *not* of or in a world different from ours of the everyday stamp. "Well! Dad's Dead" gives us not merely the grotesque journey of the Lovingoods with old Hoss's corpse, which intermittently seems as lifelike and vital in death as ever he was in living days; the tale also affords a specimen of near supernaturalism in Mrs. Lovingood's harassed outburst: "I'd like to know when the devil *will* go out ove *him*."[5] Such an ejaculation combines with the high jinks of shoving the seemingly recalcitrant corpse into the hole dug for it to effect "graveyard" humor substantially different from the concept of graveyard used above. This tale has been, rightly, called Poe-like in its macabre cast; in its bordering on the grotesque, furthermore, it suggests the work of Bierce and Faulkner.

A similar manipulation of circumstances to achieve a supernatural aura (that is dispelled in the conclusion) occurs in an early, non-Lovingood sketch, "A Coon Hunt in Haunted Hollow." The narrator, Mr. Free, and his friend Tom D.—patterned upon Thomas Bangs Thorpe's famous Tom Owen, the Bee Hunter—believe that they have sighted a raccoon high in a tree, located calculatedly enough, on Harris's part, in "Haunted Hollow." After many shots to bring down the coon prove vain, Tom worriedly concludes that he has been encountering Satan himself in animal form. Returning in daylight, the hunters discover that a growth on the tree trunk was their opponent. They vow never to mention the truth of this hunt to any save the "spirit" and in so doing they provide a neat bit of wordplay: this sketch was published in the *Spirit of the Times* (11 February 1843). Tom's personal inclination to believe in otherworldly visitants, as expressed succinctly in a snatch of Burns's "Tam O'Shanter": "Where ghaists and owlets nightly cry," prepares the way for this "spirit" in the close of the sketch.[6]

"The Snake-bit Irishman," a like creation, revolves around the ambiguities in the appearance-reality theme that recurs in so much American literature, and particularly American comic literature, in which the Lovingood yarns stand out as a high peak. Sut contrives to fashion a "snake" from deer guts, attaches it to his victim, and enjoys the ensuing melee. Dashing through the campfire, the Irishman in his terror does not realize that he has ignited the bogus "snake" but believes that it is a fiery or supernatural serpent intent on accomplishing his downfall (*Yarns*, 112). The components of darkness, isolation, and a threatening "spirit" draw together several strands of Gothic import. As in a Radcliffe novel, the being from what seems to be another world, so long as suspense is essential, turns out to be far less fearsome than the victim has supposed.

An additional, potentially fruitful document in this context is the obviously titled "Saul Spradlin's Ghost," but because just the first of the two installments that appeared in a newspaper is available we can offer only surmises as to the outcome. From what is extant, we can conjecture that the "fat gourd" (*High Times*, 175) mentioned by Sut had in some way been mistaken for Saul's spirit. Sut's antagonism toward Parson Small, whose help is sought to lay the presumed spirit, seems certain to culminate in discomfiture for the sanctimonious clergyman, devolving from Sut's determination "*to help him lay Saul Spradlin's ghost*" (*High Times*, 176). In all probability, the parson's evident liking for widows would have been combined with Sut's ensuring that Small and perhaps one or (more likely) both widows, one old and one young, would have inflicted punishment or suffered it because the gourd might have been used to pound them. Or possibly the gourd's resemblance to Saul Spradlin in the flesh may have figured in some clandestine episode in bed if the ladies' attractions proved alluring to Mr. Small. This parson obviously delights in pleasures of the flesh, as we learn when Sut tempts him with visions of ample meals, and Sut is never behindhand at capitalizing on such impulses in others to victimize them. Because "George" knows about the ensuing "fright and stampede at Mrs. Hunter's" (perhaps one of the widows), we may lament the disappearance of part two of this tale, in which we would have discovered what Sut meant by remarking: "Instid ove layin {the ghost} as we aim'd tu do, we misfortinatly made a mistake in the cungerin an' raised the devil" (*High Times,* 175). We readers may rest assured, however, that raising the devil undoubtedly encompassed several implications of that colloquial phrase.

Another, more artistic production, wherein the seeming supernatural transcends the limitations of shoddy magazine-newspaper thrillers, is "Sut Lovingood's Chest Story." Here Sut finally gains revenge upon the philandering Sicily Burns, who had tricked him into ingesting too much soda and had taken wicked pleasure in his discomfiture when he tore away on horseback, looking like "a dreadful forewarning, ur a ghos', ur old Belzebub," according to the circuit rider Clapshaw, who encounters Sut in his misery (*Yarns,* 83).

The frequent recurrence of the word *devil* alerts one to Harris's careful modulations of elements that could originate in folk sources and in turn appeal to a folk, as well as a more sophisticated, mind. In other words, when Sut sets out to avenge his own emotional wounds, he also accomplishes the end of Sicily's adulterous propensities. In such a situation, where the governance of the wages of sin is but too obvious, the intrusive implications about nonhuman agencies of punishment would strike terror across the unsophisticated religious beliefs of the adulterers. Sut's opening remarks about strong-minded women becoming devils foreshadow the violence and torments that follow. Indeed, because Sicily seems ever to direct the situations within those tales featuring her high jinks or seems, at least, to control them sufficiently for setting in motion a chain of catastrophic events, her demonic attributes are but natural.

Intending initially to frighten only Gus Fabin's or "Gut Fatty's" great, black horse—itself an undeniable symbol of lustful human impulses—Sut decorates the "ole, black devil" with the phosphorescent fungus known as "fox fire," ties a charge of powder to the tail, and doses the animal with a sickening mixture of medicines (*Yarns*, d–e).[7] Seeing Sicily hurrying her illicit lover into a trunk (they supposing that a noise made by Sut might be that of her husband returning), Sut attaches the trunk to the horse. Next he torments the imprisoned Gus with visions of retribution consequent upon his adultery. The stroke of linking the sexually rampant man with the terrifying horse, which may symbolize a dominant animalism in the rutting relationship between Fabin and Sicily, is superb. The violent, erratic, and terrifying journey of the horse with its freight intensifies this theme. Once passion and violence gain sway, who can predict the outcome?

Following the horse and the battered Fabin, Sut encounters a North Carolinian, high in a tree whence he had scrambled, frightened by the spectacle of the apparently supernatural horse and rider. This man's thoughts are artistically fitting vehicles for the theme: "H——l's busted plumb open, an' this yere mountain's full ove the devils." He repeats, with variants: "we wus woke up by an arful yell, an' here cum the devil a-tarin es big es a corn crib, an' he had *hellfire harness on,* and a knot on the aind ove his tail es big es a turpintine still" (*Yarns,* g, h). To be sure, such visions as these, representative of chaos as they are, stem from reality, in this case the immoderate sexual passions of Sicily; and, "devil" that she is, no wonder ordinary mortals, in contrast to her own tempestuous but determined nature, grow literally and figuratively bewildered while confronting the results of her imposing presence and Sut's equally imposing handiwork in creating mixed displays of devilment.

Sut, of course, knows that there is no supernatural claptrap—of the sort so fascinating and delightful to unwitting readers. He sends off the woebegone Gus, remarking that folks in the region do not believe in "the devil what invented you," an observation wonderfully ambiguous in its ramifications. Sut's offhanded comments about Sicily's husband, who "believes in 'witches, an' warlocks, an' long nebbed {nosed} things' more than he does in Sicily," reveals additional psychological depths within this tale. Better, perhaps, to give credence to what we *know* are *false* ghosts than to the variety of deviltry Sicily manifests. Significantly, Sut adds that "she's warin

184 Benjamin Franklin Fisher IV

thin, her eyes am growin bigger, an' she has no roses on her cheeks. She *cant* laugh, an' she *wont* cry" (*Yarns*, j). These characteristics typify those who in folklore are bewitched; here they devolve from Sicily's frustrated, negative sexuality. Of such substance is the making of literary art, prompting us to question just where naturalism turns into supernaturalism. Through Sut's vision, in this yarn and with frequency elsewhere, Harris implies that there is no easy solution to this dualism.

Another form of such diabolism occurs in "Frustrating a Funeral," which in the table of contents for *Sut Lovingood. Yarns Spun by a "Nat'ral Born Durn'd Fool"* is subtitled "(never to be read by candle light)." This yarn is a veritable virtuoso's collection of horrifics, replete with a reworking of the popular nineteenth-century literary theme of live burials (shades of Poe!) and not just one but two devil figures to terrify beholders. An aura of drunkenness enlivens this story; early on "George" emphasizes Sut's easy access to whiskey, and, significantly, "kill-devil" whiskey is what brings about the death of one of the principals and the near burial of a living but intensely drunken man. Playing upon the heightened superstitions connected with funeral rites, Sut recounts his theft of the body of Caesar, or "Seize," presumably for a doctor's use in the laboratory. From his opening remark concerning premature burial, Sut goes on to apprise "George" of events surrounding the wake for the dead man, his own substitution of a drunken man for the corpse, and his making up both to resemble devils. First, Sut goes to work on Major, or "Maje," whom he has substituted for the corpse:

> I sot in an' painted red an' white stripes, time about, runnin out frum his eyes like ontu the spokes ove a wheel, an' cross-bar'd his upper lip wif white, ontil hit looked like boars' tushes, an' I fastened a cuppil ove yearlin's ho'ns ontu his hed, an' platted a ded black-snake roun the roots ove em, an' durn my laigs ef I didn't cum ni ontu takin a runnin skeer mysef, fur he wer a purfeck dogratype ove the devil, tuck while he wer smokin mad 'bout sum raskil what hed been sellin shanghis, an' a-pedlin matchless sanative all his life, then jinin meetin on his death-bed, an' 'scapin. (*Yarns*, 212–13)

As if to surpass this apparition, Sut turned to Seize:

> I'd got 'bout a tin cup full ove litning bugs, an' cut off the lantern ove the las' durn'd one; I smear'd em all over his face, har an' years, an' ontu the prongs ove a pitch-fork; I sot him up in the corner on aind, an' gin him the fork, prong aind up in his crossed arms. I then pried open his mouf, an' let his teef shet ontu the back ove a live bull-frog, an' I smeared hits paws an' belly wif sum ove my bug-mixtry, an' pinned a littil live garter-snake by hits middil

crosswise in his mouf, smeared like the frog plum tu the pint ove his tail. The pin kep him pow'ful bizzy makin suckils an' uther crooked shapes in the air. Now, rite thar boys, in that corner, stood the dolefulest skeer makin mersheen, mortal man ever seed outen a ghost camp. (*Yarns,* 213)

No wonder that episodes of terror and violence explode thereafter as various persons encounter this dreadful pair. Sut concludes this passage: "I tell yu now, I b'leves strong in ghosts, an' in forewarnins too." This comment is double edged; are we to interpret it as a straightforward admission, or, given Sut's fringe position in relation to the world about him, is this an ironic insinuation that means he disbelieves in otherworldly visitants? The devil-snake-horns motifs are redolent of rampant sexuality, of course, as they are in other Lovingood yarns.

Sut's ventriloquist's trickery materially assists in the emotional undoing of those who cross paths with these weird figures. Old Hunicutt comes into the death chamber first. Master of the dead slave Seize, he has evidently indulged an illicit passion for Mrs. Loftin. Aware of this affair, Sut, in the voice of the devil, threatens to take both of them to hell. In like manner he frightens the doctor, who had wanted Seize's body, out of his wits—and into a new line of work, that of a gristmill operator. This is a deft bit of comedy on Harris's part; doctors who experimented with cadavers were long thought to be in league with the devil. Later Sut goes to the funeral, informs the assembled group about several prominent persons' disappearances, and convinces them that he had seen Hunicutt and Mrs. Loftin on a burning ladder. The cook responds fittingly that she knew for three months previous that Mrs. Loftin would fetch the devil here before she was done—which persuasion led to an ironic kind of success.

En route to the burial ground, and with his wife sitting on top of his coffin, Maje begins to recover from his alcoholic stupor and, apropos of his hangover, mutters "Dis am the debil!" His words have the effect, naturally, of creating havoc among the mourners, as his speech puts his wife to flight and he pushes open the coffin lid, thus appearing in his full satanic glory before the others. Wright, who was the dispenser of "kill-devil" whiskey in his "doggery" (an unlicensed whiskey shop), supposed that his nefarious activities had marked him out as the devil's quarry, and Sut assists that mistake by speaking to him, again in an unearthly tone, about his time's being nearly up. Maje happens to see himself in a mirror and reacts as if he were facing off Satan. Again Sut's ventriloquism sends a sinner packing, although not before Maje meets the sheriff who, he thinks, can help him. We grow amused reading about yet another flight and pursuit that, to many who witnessed the spectacle, seemed unquestionably to be the devil intent on securing another victim.

This story ends with all of the customary pillars of the community gone and with Sut's notion, which preserves the context of his tale: "Why, the country's ruinated, an' hits haunted yet wif all sorts ove orful haunts; yu ken buy land thar fur a dime a acre, on tick at that" (*Yarns*, 226). The context is maintained equally well in his informing "George" that, after Wright's abandonment of the doggery, he had consumed all the remaining whiskey. Perhaps Sut's own "kill-devil" methods within his yarn were inspirited by that mammoth drinking feat, and if that is the case then "Frustating a Funeral" is exceptionally close in its methods to one of Poe's "Tales of the Folio Club," in which drunken narrators related incidents of drunken characters. Perhaps the reason that Sut's story should never be read by candlelight is twofold: it may cause hair-raising effects in its readers or, given its liquorishness, it might ignite them if a flame were too near. Just so, the "frustrating" aspects within this tale extend far beyond the mere funeral qua funeral. Instead, frustration is handled as one of the primary motivators in life; all of the chief characters experience thwartings of their uppermost goals. And Sut himself sustains frustration—in getting Seize's body to the doctor. Elsewhere in his yarns, he had been subjected to frustrated actor symptoms, for example, when he attempted to court Sicily Burns. In this story, however, his actor's abilities come to us via some superb role playing, which places him among the foremost confidence men in American literary history.

III

C. Hugh Holman writes that if the southwestern humorists had not given a comic edge to their productions those works would be Gothic.[8] I hope, in such context, that my observations may afford a fresh perspective on the Lovingood canon. There realism and fantasy mingle, taking the American colloquial style and realistic mode into compelling territories. These aims and methods raise new questions about the nature of realism. More extensively than any of the other frontier humorists, Harris employs these blendings of terror and comedy.

In such contexts, though, the name of Henry Clay Lewis and his "Louisiana Swamp Doctor" yarns also come to mind. In "The Day of Judgment" a group of roisterers break up a camp meeting by turpentining a mule, setting fire to the hapless animal, and, themselves clad in long white robes made from sheets and with horns and loud yells to increase the pandemonium, running him amid the assembly. To that group, the eerie intruders and their awesome companion resemble nothing so much as fiends straight out of hell: "The thousand echoes of the swamp took up the sound, and the wildwood, if filled with screaming devils, could not have given back a more hideous outcry."⁹ Ghost stories, including one in which a ghost-beset girl is found drowned in a churn of buttermilk, while away the time among the watchers over an ailing, elderly alcoholic in "My First Call in the Swamp." Elsewhere, "Dr. Tensas" tries in vain to conjure up the spirit of Major Subsequent in order that he might tell the story of his life himself ("The Man of Aristocratic Diseases"). In "A Struggle for Life," after combating a dwarfish slave who resembles an orangutan (and who seems to imbibe characteristics of both Poe's murderous ape in "The Murders in the Rue Morgue" and of the simian dwarf, Hop-Frog), the doctor passes through a period rather like those hypnagogic states recurrent within characters in Poe's writings. "Tensas's" sensations seem to be those of a dead person, although we ultimately learn that he has been stunned but not killed by his demonic assailant. This last is indeed an intensely Poesque piece, but in no way do Lewis's tales, taken collectively, offer the subtleties in handling conventions of the supernatural that we find in Harris's yarns. Lewis, in fact, excepting "A Struggle for Life" and, to a lesser extent, "The Day of Judgment," seems more inclined to smile away the otherworldly— about which he provides but few details—with an air of condescension, as if folklore and superstition were suitable for fleeting amusement and little else.

Conversely, the works of George Washington Harris demonstrate a more general functionalism in their supernatural substance, making Harris a transition figure between the grisly grotesque of Poe and the local-color vein of comic supernaturalism in Mary N. Murfree's stories or the diabolism in those of Virginia Frazer Boyle and Julia Peterkin (whose works bear no such stamp of hostile

racism as is found in Harris's fiction).[10] Actually, we might prof-
itably take note of similar techniques within the writings of a host
of southern writers (in addition to those mentioned by Holman)
well into this century, not the least of whom would be Ellen Glas-
gow—yet another whose name does not immediately come to mind
when supernaturalism is the subject—in *The Shadowy Third.*

Notes

1. Turner's comments appear in the *Georgia Review* 12 (1958):
   451–57; Rickels's are in *George Washington Harris* (New York:
   Twayne, 1965), 101.
2. Kenneth S. Lynn, *The Comic Tradition in America: An Anthology of American Humor* (Garden City: Doubleday, 1958), 193.
   See also Fred Madden, "A Descent into the Maelstrom: Suggestions of the Tall Tale," *Studies in the Humanities* {Indiana,
   Pa.} 14 (1987): 127–38; Harry M. Bayne, "Poe's 'Never Bet the
   Devil Your Head' and Southwest Humor," *American Renaissance Literary Report: An Annual* 3 (1989): 278–79; and Benjamin Franklin Fisher IV, "Devils and Devilishness in Comic
   Yarns of the Old Southwest," *ESQ: A Journal of the American
   Renaissance* 36 (1990): 39–60.
3. Charles Dickens, *The Pickwick Papers,* ed. Andrew Lang (London: Chapman and Hall; New York: Charles Scribner's Sons,
   1897), 1:459. The grotesque humor expands in the next chapter, 29, a tale in itself, "The Story of the Goblins Who Stole a
   Sexton."
4. George Washington Harris, *"Sut Lovingood. Yarns": A Facsimile of the 1867 Dick and Fitzgerald Edition,* ed. M. Thomas Inge
   (Memphis: Saint Luke's Press, 1987), x–xi. Further references
   will be cited in the text.
5. M. Thomas Inge, ed., *High Times and Hard Times: Sketches and
   Tales by George Washington Harris* (Nashville: Vanderbilt University Press, 1967), 210. Further references will be cited in
   the text.
6. The title of this sketch in *High Times* is "Sporting Epistle from
   East Tennessee," 15–18.
7. "Sut Lovingood's Chest Story" was added to Inge's facsimile
   edition of the yarns and is therefore paged with letters rather
   than numbers.

8. C. Hugh Holman, *Windows on the World: Essays on American Social Fiction* (Knoxville: University of Tennessee Press, 1979), 27–35. Holman demonstrates that the fine balance of humor with horror continues from southwestern humorists into recent writers like Faulkner, Caldwell, and O'Connor.

9. John Q. Anderson, ed., *Louisiana Swamp Doctor: The Writings of Henry Clay Lewis alias "Madison Tensas, M.D."* (Baton Rouge: Louisiana State University Press, 1962), 107. The pervasiveness of superstition in the Old Southwest is assessed by Everett Dick in *The Dixie Frontier: A Comprehensive Picture of Southern Frontier Life before the Civil War* (1948; reprint, New York: Capricorn Books, 1964), 30, 217–18, 220.

10. See Benjamin Franklin Fisher IV, "Mary Noailles Murfree's 'Special' Sense of Humor," *Studies in American Humor*, n.s., 4 (1985): 30–38; Fisher and Harry M. Bayne, "A Neglected Detective Novel: Henry Bellamann's *The Gray Man Walks*," *Mystery FANcier* 12 (1990): 3–19; Melissa Yow, "Virginia Frazer Boyle: An Annotated Bibliography," *University of Mississippi Studies in English*, n.s., 9 (1991): 205–34; and Irene Yates, "Conjures and Cures in the Novels of Julia Peterkin," *Southern Folklore Quarterly* 10 (1946): 137–49.

Sensuality, Revenge, and Freedom

Women in *Sut Lovingood.* *Yarns Spun by a* *"Nat'ral Born Durn'd Fool"*

William E. Lenz

Henry Adams mourned and yet questioned the absence in nineteenth-century American literature of what he called an "American Venus," a woman who would insist on the classic potentialities of her sex as a natural and direct inheritance from Eve.

> The monthly-magazine-made American female had not a feature that would have been recognized by Adam. The trait was notorious, and often humorous, but any one brought up among Puritans knew that sex was sin. In any previous age, sex was strength. . . . Adams began to ponder, asking himself whether he knew of any American artist who had ever insisted on the power of sex, as every classic had always done; but he could think only of Walt Whitman; Bret Harte, as far as the magazine would let him venture; and one or two painters, for the flesh-tones. All the rest had used sex for sentiment, never for force; to them, Eve was a tender flower, and Herodias an unfeminine horror. American art, like American language and American education, was as far as possible sexless.[1]

Despite the deliberate playfulness and ambiguity of Adams's tone, his insistent rhetoric suggests an underlying seriousness to his search that is decidedly contemporary. "Why was she unknown in America?" Were there no surviving visions of Eve in the American Eden? Had a dynamic force—and one-half the race—been disconcertedly covered with fig leaves?

Studies in American Humor, n.s., 1 (1983): 173–80 (under a differently worded title). The author has revised his article for this reprinting.

In the gentleman's magazines and Tennessee newspapers of the 1850s, however, George Washington Harris's Sut Lovingood vividly describes, in a stylized dialect both sexual and endemic, his numerous encounters with candidates for an American Eve.[2] Presenting Sut's pursuit in the tortured, self-consciously literary rhetoric of the conventional humorous frontier tale, Harris is able to insist, as the author of *Democracy* and *Esther* never could, on the cardinal power of sexuality. And although separated from Adams by much more than geography, Sut searches for an ideal woman possessing essential qualities—sensuality, vitality, and forcefulness—remarkably similar to those of Adams's elusive "American Venus." Seen in these terms, an examination of Harris's women, and of the themes governing their presentation, will result, it is hoped, in a greater appreciation of the *Yarns* and suggest avenues for further study.

In "Sicily Burns's Wedding," Sut Lovingood informs simple George that "every livin thing hes hits pint, a pint ove sum sort."[3] The following lesson makes quite clear Sut's views concerning the points of men and women.

> Men wer made a-purpus jis' tu eat, drink, an' fur stayin awake in the yearly part ove the nites: an' wimen wer made tu cook the vittils, mix the sperits, an' help the men du the stayin awake. That's all, an' nuthin more, onless hits fur the wimen tu raise the devil atwix meals, an' knit socks atwix drams, an' the men tu play short kerds, swap hosses wif fools, an' fite fur exersise, at odd spells. (88)

Women exist for the pleasures of men, to feed, fuel, and satisfy their physical appetites, and Sut's emphasis on sensuality is central. In "Parson John Bullen's Lizards," Sut divides women into eight categories according to their reactions to the parson's nude figure, and in "Mrs. Yardley's Quilting" he singles out widows as the most cooperative of women.

> Hits widders, by golly, what am the rale sensibil, steady-goin, never-skeerin, never-kickin, willin, sperrited, smoof pacers. They cum clost up tu the hoss-block, standin still wif thar purty silky years playin, an' the naik-veins a-throbbin, an' waits fur the word, which ove course yu gives, arter yu finds yer feet well in the stirrup, an' away they moves like a cradil on cushioned rockers, ur a spring buggy runnin in damp san'. A tetch ove the bridil, an' they knows yu wants em tu turn, an' they dus hit es willin es ef the idear wer thar own. I be dod rabbited ef a man can't 'propriate happiness by the skinful ef he is in contack wif sumbody's widder, an' is smart. Gin me a willin widder, the yeath over: what they don't know, haint worth larnin. (141)

Sensible in attitude and smooth in performance, widows are always willing in Sut's imagination to follow the lead of pleasure-seeking men. Sut's animal imagery emphasizes the earthiness of the women's desires and the type of skin-to-skin contact he anticipates. Yet the effect of Sut's language, which objectifies a class of women as spirited horses to be sexually ridden, is less descriptive than suggestive; the escalating accumulation of heated details—from their abject submission to their "naik-veins a-throbbin"—creates a critical, aesthetic distance between the narrator and the objects of his desire that suggests that these images are nothing more than the linguistic projections of Sut's pornographic fantasy. His stylistic stroking of these "smoof pacers" is surely the offspring of frustration rather than of consummation.

Sut's description of Sicily Burns may serve as an example of another version of his ideal female, at least in terms of external attributes and endowments. Her beauty marks her out as a possible "American Venus," almost a candidate for worship.

> She shows amung wimen like a sunflower amung dorg fennil, ur a hollyhawk in a patch ove smartweed. Sich a buzzim! Jis' think ove two snow balls wif a strawberry stuck but-ainded intu bof on em. . . . She kerried enuf devil about her tu run crazy a big settilment ove Job's children; her skin wer es white es the inside ove a frogstool, an' her cheeks an' lips es rosey es a pearch's gills in dorgwood blossom time—an' sich a smile! (75–76)[4]

Such sensuality seems to fit in well with Sut's philosophy, but distant worship cannot satisfy him for long: to be a candidate for his perfect woman, one must have the correct attitude and inclination; Sicily Burns is almost too classical (as Adams might say), existing "tu drive men folks plum crazy, an' then bring em too agin. Gin em a rale Orleans fever in five minits, an' then in five minits more, gin them a Floridy ager" (87). Unlike Sut's fantasized widows, who take direction at the touch of a bridle, Sicily manipulates Sut's fantasies and forcefully controls the reins of reality in "Blown up with Soda."

Sut's equivocating description of Sal Yardley reveals that he may have competing criteria for determining ideal womanhood. Beauty and sensuality are important, it is true, but neither is compelling unless the candidate possesses the right desires. As Sut struggles to judge Sal's qualities fairly, his clauses wind around like the tops of her stockings.

> Sal wer bilt at fust 'bout the laingth ove her mam, but wer never straiched eny by a par ove steers an' she wer fat enuf tu kill; she wer taller lyin down

than she wer a-standin up. . . . She wer the fairest-lookin gal I ever seed. She allers wore thick woolin stockins 'bout six inches too long fur her laig; they rolled down over her garters, lookin like a par ove life-presarvers up thar. I tell you she wer a tarin gal enyhow. Luved kissin, wrastlin, an' biled cabbige, an' hated tite clothes, hot weather, an' suckit-riders. (136–37)

In the end, Sal's enthusiasm outweighs her appearance. Twice Sut reminds us—as he reminds himself—of her value and utility. Her attitude, as he at last concludes, seems ideally suited to his needs and desires.

Yet throughout the *Yarns* women have quite different purposes from those imagined—needs and desires that often run contrary to Sut's simple equations. Sicily Burns, for example, after parading her pleasures before him, promising "a new sensashun," gives him soda powder as a love potion, curing rather than satisfying his immediate appetite. She is, like most spirited women in the *Yarns,* more serpent or siren than simply Eve. Even Sal, for all her willingness to be kissed, succeeds only in getting Sut kicked by her father.[5] In this rough-and-tumble, exaggerated, frontier world, wives do not long stay faithful to their loving husbands, the experienced widows do not experience Sut at all, the most respectable members of society are hypocrites, and even the proverbial nuptial bed is not what it once seemed.

Wat Mastin, because "at las' he jis cudn't stan the ticklin sensashuns anuther minnit" [230–31], marries widow McKildrin's daughter, Mary. Like many bridegrooms in the folklore tradition, Wat discovers that his bride is more than he bargained for; her sexual demands weaken him, make him physically thinner, and give him a backache. These unanticipated side effects encourage him to exchange her embrace for the grueling physical labor of a railroad factory.

Oh yas, he married Mary tight an' fas', an' nex day he wer abil tu be about. His coat tho', an' his trousis look'd jis' a skrimshun too big, loose like, an' heavy tu tote. . . . Purty soon arter he hed made the garden, he tuck a noshun tu work a spell down tu Ataylanty, in the railroad shop, es he sed he hed a sorter ailin in his back, an' he tho't weldin rail car-tire an' ingine axiltrees, wer lighter work. (232)

Nothing is sacred or secure, and between appearance and reality, between imagined intention and actual intent, grows a widening gap. Sicily Burns, who had seemed to promise love (or at least a variety of physical equivalents), uses her sexuality as a weapon against

Sut. Wat Mastin's "ticklin sensashuns" are irritated rather than relieved by marriage, and he eventually learns that his new bride, the previously and continuously unfaithful Mary, has lured him into matrimony so that her unborn child could have a legitimate father. Appropriately, they are married on April Fools' Day.

In Sut's world such attacks demand revenge. This forms a second theme in Harris's *Yarns,* one that seems to be a force of almost equal importance. Indeed, revenge is usually coupled with sensuality and functions as a form of confirmation: it can take a direct and immediate form, as in Sut's revenge on Parson Bullen, or it can be drawn out and intricate. In either case, however, return payment must be in kind.

The day Sicily marries the "suckit rider" Clapshaw, Sut manages to have the Burnses' bull, Sock, knock over their beehives and to lead "the bigges' an' the madest army ove bees in the world" [91] into the reception. The result is widespread damage, chaos, and sexual revenge.

> Sicily, she squatted in the cold spring, up tu her years, an' turn'd a milk crock over her head, while she wer a-drownin a mess ove bees onder her coats. I went tu her, an' sez I, "Yu hes got anuther new sensashun, haint yu?" Sez she—
> "Shet yer mouth, yu cussed fool!"
> Sez I, "Power'ful sarchin feelin bees gins a body, don't they?"
> "Oh, lordy, lordy, Sut, these yere 'bominabil insex is jis' burnin me up!"
> "Gin 'em a mess ove SODY," sez I, "that'll cool 'em off, an' skeer the las' durn'd one often the place. . . ."
> Ove all the durn'd misfortinit weddins ever since ole Adam married that heifer, what wer so fon' ove talkin tu snaix, an' eating appils, down ontil now . . . her an' him cudent sleep tugether fur ni ontu a week, on account ove the doins ove them ar hot-footed, 'vengeful, 'bominabil littil insex. (95, 96–97)

Not satisfied with this, however, Sut—or, noticing the less active role of simple George (he is only spoken to) and the verbal carnage created by such coinages as "suckit rider" and "insex,"[6] one is tempted to say Harris—completes his revenge in "Sut Lovingood's Chest Story." He discovers and drives off Sicily's lover, Gus, and leaves Sicily at the end "warin thin, her eyes am growin bigger, an she has no roses on her cheeks."[7] Sut destroys both her physical beauty and her sexual freedom—she will never tempt or taunt another man.

The revenge in the "Rare Ripe Garden Seed" trilogy takes a more complex form and brings to our attention almost by accident an-

other "American Venus." At its conclusion the conniving and meddlesome widow McKildrin disappears, the adulterous Sheriff Doltin
is humiliated and torn up by cats, Mary loses her lover and is frightened into fidelity and submission, and Sut, Wat, and Wirt are well
avenged. Yet "Rare Ripe" is too densely packed with actions, emotion, and impostors to be summarized; it deserves to be read, as it
is perhaps the finest story of revenge in the *Yarns*. I mention it first
as a further instance in which revenge and sexuality are intertwined,
and I will abstract from it a third variation of the Eve motif.

Wirt Staples's wife Susan appears briefly in "Trapping a Sheriff,"
the conclusion of the "Rare Ripe" story. She is an interesting version of the "American Venus," who appeals, unlike Sicily or Sal, to
Sut's stomach.

> Wirt's wife got yearly supper, a rale suckit-rider's supper, whar the 'oman
> ove the hous' wer a rich b'lever. Thar wer chickens cut up, an' fried in but-
> ter, brown, white, flakey, light, hot biskit, made wif cream, scrambil'd aigs,
> yaller butter, fried ham, in slices es big es yure han, pickil'd beets, an' cow-
> cumbers, roas'in ears, shaved down an' fried, sweet taters, baked, a stack ove
> buckwheat cakes, es full ove holes es a sifter, an' a bowl ove strained honey,
> tu fill the holes. . . . I kin tas'e em es low down es the bottim ove my trow-
> sis pokits. Fur drinks, she hed coffee, hot, clar an' brown, an' sweet milk es
> cold es a rich man's heart. Ontu the dresser sot a sorter lookin pot-bellied
> bottil, half full ove peach brandy, watchin a tumbler, a spoon, an' a sugar
> bowl. Oh! massy, massy, George! Fur the sake ove yure soul's 'tarnil well-
> far, don't yu es long es yu live ever be temtid by money, ur buty, ur smart-
> ness, ur sweet huggin, ur shockin mersheen kisses, tu marry ur cum *ni* mar-
> ryin eny gal a-top this livin green yeath, onless yu hes seed her yursef cook
> jis' sich feedin es that wer. Durnashun, I kin tas'e hit now, jis' es plain es I
> tas'e that ar festergut, in that ar jug, an' I swar I tasis *hit* plain. I gets dorg
> hongry every time I sees Wirt's wife, ur even her side-saddil, ur her frocks
> a-hangin on the close-line.
>
> Es we sot down, the las' glimmers ove the sun crep thru the histed
> winder, an' flutter'd on the white tabil cloth an' play'd a silver shine on her
> smoof black har, es she sot at the hed ove the tabil, a-pourin out the coffee,
> wif her sleeves push'd tight back on her white roun' arm, her full throbbin
> neck wer bar tu the swell ove her shoulders, an' the steam ove the coffee
> made a movin vail afore her face, es she slowly brush'd hit away wif hur lef
> han', a-smilin an' a-flashin her talkin eyes lovinly at her hansum husbun. I
> thot ef I wer a picter-maker, I cud jis' take that ar supper an' that ar 'oman
> down on clean white paper, an' make more men hongry, an' hot tu marry,
> a-lookin at hit in one week, nor ever ole Whitfield convarted in his hole life.
> (261–62)

I have quoted at length because Sut's description is lengthy, and
the image of this "rale suckit-rider's supper" is pivotal: Sicily Burns

may have a beautiful bosom, and Sal Yardley may be willing, but Susan Staples actually satisfies. She understands that "'Less a feller hes his belly stretched wif vittils, he can't luv tu much pupus, that's so. Vittils, whisky, an' the spring ove the year, is what *makes* luv" (123). But perhaps this is too strong. Mrs. Staples, after all, only satisfies his hunger, not his sexual desire. Food may be a reasonable substitute for sex, may even take on the tactile, visual, and olfactory sensuality of the sexual act itself, but it is still only supper that Susan Staples serves Sut. Notwithstanding her desires, Sal Yardley is essentially a child, still dominated by the force of a paternal boot. And when Sicily marries Clapshaw, she loses her freedom, her ability to compete with Sut on his own cruel and chaotic terms. For to be bound to an institution of authority, be it family, church, or state, is to limit oneself and surrender the personal mobility necessary to ultimate victory.[8]

Susan Staples, however, is able to transcend these limitations and has not, although she is married, lost her ability to function actively as an effective—and forceful—individual. Sut recognizes the wide range of her talents and pays her additional high tribute in the following passage from "Trapping A Sheriff."

> Wirt's wife did the planin, an' ef she aint smart fur an 'oman, I aint a nat'ral born durned fool. She aint one ove yure she-cat wimmin, allers spittin an' groanin, an' swellin thar tails 'bout thar vartu. She never talks a word about hit, no more nor if she didn't hev eny; an' she hes es true a heart es ever beat agin a shiff hem, ur a husban's shut. But she am full ove fun, an' I mout add es purty es a hen canary, an' I swar I don't b'l'eve the 'oman knows hit. She cum intu our boat jis' caze Wirt wer in hit, and she seed lots ove fun a-plantin, an' she wanted tu be at the reapin ove the crap. (260)

Wirt's wife is a powerful combination of thinker, looker, and doer, a credible "American Venus." And, of perhaps most importance, she is aligned with Sut. This is not to imply that either Sut or Susan Staples is an agent of morality or universal justice, as Brom Weber suggests.[9] Indeed, they are decidedly amoral, and what justice they desire is personal revenge. What they do form is a rather loose community in search of momentary pleasures, keen competition, and unlimited freedom: to compete is to assert one's individuality; to triumph is to secure it.

Susan Staples is undoubtedly the most successful woman in Sut's—and in Adams's—terms, and her appearance at the conclusion of the "Rare Ripe Garden Seed" trilogy forms a locus of meaning. Harris allows Sut to dwell lovingly upon her portrait, insisting by extended description on her integrity and importance. Her image—like her dinner—is obsessively detailed by Sut from her "full throbbin neck" to her "talkin eyes" (262), an image that insists self-reflexively upon its own iconographic power. A mere picture of Susan Staples and her supper would convert bachelors to the cause of marriage. Forceful and able, she is nevertheless "full ove fun," and while managing an ornery husband like Wirt, she still has the strength of will to maintain her identity as an individual. Like Sut, to whose character she is a key, Susan Staples celebrates the eternal joys of victory and survival and delights in the rejuvenating energy of vigorous action. If Sut can be seen as the prototypical Adam of the *Yarns,* she is certainly the most nearly Eve.

Yet Susan Staples is Wirt's wife, and her attractions, though great, must remain for Sut those of an unattainable ideal; for in spite of the spirited women he encounters, Sut is ultimately, like the conventional trickster or fool, bound by immutable laws to reveal what he cannot himself possess. As he so pointedly reminds us, he "gets dorg hongry" whenever he sees Susan Staples, or her sidesaddle (a reminder of her physical sexuality), or even most pathetically her dress on the clothesline (a symbol of her sexuality emptied of her physicality). But he has eaten at her table infrequently and, despite his elaborate description, recognizes that the fantasy of consumption must take the place of an impossible sexual consummation. Sut's fate consists of frustration, displacement, and denial. Full of "onregenerit pride," Sut shares with Natty Bumppo and Huckleberry Finn a clear if sobering perception of the price to be paid for independence: "Now ef a feller happens tu know what his pint am, he kin allers git along, sumhow, purvided he don't swar away his liberty tu a temprins s'ciety, live tu fur frum a still-'ous, an' too ni a chu'ch ur a jail" (88). The discovery of Adams's "American Venus" in a frontier landscape is all—and it is quite a lot—that he can accomplish.

Freedom can result in solitude, in escape, and the license it provides may go at first undetected. Wat Mastin must learn from Sut the benefits accompanying his newly earned liberty:

> "Sut, hell's tu pay at our hous'. Mary's been hid out sumwhar till this mornin. She cum up draggil'd an' hungry, an' won't say a durn'd word. An' ole Missis McKildrin's plum gone." Sez I—
> "Ain't yu glad?"

> He stretched his mouf intu the wides' smile yu ever seed, an' slappin me
> on the back, sez he—
> "I *is*, by golly!" (275)

It is this delight in and awareness of the moments of life, the re-assertion that humor can provide a meaning, that vigorous living can restore one's purpose in defeat and confirm the integrity of the individual in triumph, that informs *Sut Lovingood. Yarns Spun by a "Nat'ral Born Durn'd Fool."* Sensuality and revenge are major forces in this world, stark frontier humor is the modus operandi, and the goal, or rather, the final achievement, is an undeniable affirmation of freedom.

Sal, Sicily, and Susan Staples reveal that on the imaginative frontier of Harris's *Yarns,* American women existed who would have been recognized by Adam and applauded by Adams. Their awareness that sex is a power before which men are helpless suggests a tradition of American women characters who flaunt their inheritance in a popular, male-dominated genre, one that Harris had the good fortune to discover and exploit.

Notes

1. Henry Adams, *The Education of Henry Adams* (1918; reprint, Boston: Houghton Mifflin, 1961), 384, 385.
2. Adams, we suppose, dismissed or carefully overlooked the heroines of Hawthorne, Howells, and Henry James as sensual but unsuccessful, ultimately impotent to change men's lives; and, if he knew them, the fates of Maggie Johnson, Edna Pontellier, and Sister Carrie must have seemed clear illustrations of the tragic extremes to which an emerging "American Venus" might easily be reduced.
3. George Washington Harris, *"Sut Lovingood. Yarns": A Facsimile of the 1867 Dick and Fitzgerald Edition,* ed. M. Thomas Inge (Memphis: Saint Lukes Press, 1987), 87. All future quotations will be from this edition with page numbers incorporated into the text.
4. Sicily's breasts are, to my knowledge, the first revealed in American literature. Although they suffer some obvious domestication through misspelling and metaphor, Sut's admiring description seems anything but "sexless"; Harris's humor is always subversive.

5. Although Sut is caught "convarsin wif a frien'" named "Sall" in "Parson John Bullen's Lizards," I do not believe this constitutes sufficient evidence against my point that Sut is frustrated. In both "Sicily Burns's Wedding" and "Dad's Dog School" Sut refers to his sister as "Sall." And in "Lizards," it must be admitted, Sut receives only pain from Bullen's boot.

6. These orthographic gymnastics, although occasionally careless, reveal an energy primarily sexual in nature and, as opposed to Sicily's "buzzim" discussed in note 4 above, attract attention to themselves as deliberate obscene neologisms. The enthusiasm Sut displays is here more obvious, perhaps—as I suggest—because the distance between Sut and Harris has greatly decreased. The effect and intention are quite different from those observed in "Trapping a Sheriff," where Mrs. Staples "seed lots ove fun a-plantin, an' she wanted tu be at the reapin of the crap" (260).

7. Inge's facsimile edition includes "Sut Lovingood's Chest Story," pages a–j.

8. In "Blown up with Soda," Sicily thought nothing of using a cruel deception to trick Sut. Milton Rickels, in his invaluable study, *George Washington Harris* (New York: Twayne Publishers, 1965), notes: "Sut has matched cruelty with Sicily. As long as she is free, she wins. When she binds herself with the institutions, she becomes respectable and has a social place to lose" (54).

9. See Brom Weber's introduction to *Sut Lovingood* (New York: Grove Press, 1954), ix–xxix, esp. xxv–xxvi. I also strongly disagree with what Weber calls "the necessary task of simplifying the text" (xxvii), for in so doing much of the raw, untamed energy of the *Yarns* is reduced. As Sut warns in his preface to the 1867 edition, one should be very careful "afore yu takes eny ove my flesh ontu yer claws, ur my blood ontu yer bills" (x).

Sut Lovingood: A Nat'ral Born Durn'd Yarnspinner

Carolyn S. Brown

"Ef yu ain't fond ove the smell ove cracklins, stay outen the kitchin."
—Sut Lovingood

Certainly they warned us—Sut, the narrator, and George Washington Harris, the author—that the Lovingood *Yarns* would, like much folk humor, be too strong to please every taste. Indeed, it has been called "the most repellent book of any real literary merit in American literature."[1] And yet another critic has claimed that "for vivid imagination, comic plot, Rabelaisian touch, and sheer fun, the *Sut Lovingood. Yarns* surpass anything else in American humor."[2] While almost any literary work lends itself to a variety of interpretations, criticism of the *Yarns* is peculiarly split between hilarity and disgust. The main disagreement seems to be over whether Sut's actions are so morally reprehensible as to be ineligible for humor, or whether the sensitive modern reader for some reason can, in good conscience, laugh at the discomfort, pain, and degradation that Sut describes with such relish. It may be that the nineteenth-century male readers these tales were written for, having narrower sympathies and toughened by their own hardships, laughed at pain more easily than most of us do now. Certainly some of the incidents in Harris' stories are tasteless, others grotesque, by the standards of many modern readers. I contend, however, that the radical disagreement

The Tall Tale in American Folklore and Literature (Knoxville: University of Tennessee Press, 1987), 74–88.

over the value of the best of the Lovingood yarns is due more to dif-
fering perceptions of the stories' relation to the real world than to
our greater squeamishness. To be fully appreciated, the *Yarns* must
be understood as written versions of the tall tale.[3]

Our ability to laugh freely at discomfort generally depends upon
the degree of discomfort depicted, the level of our identification
with the victim, and the perceived distance between the unpleasant
event and our own real world. Nearly anyone can enjoy Mark
Twain's story of how William Wheeler was caught in a carpet machine and turned into fourteen yards of the best three-ply carpet.[4]
But what about Mrs. Yardley being trampled by a horse? The story
of Wheeler and his widow, as part of Jim Blaine's absurd monologue
in *Roughing It,* is clearly a fiction and a joke. The problem with Sut's
yarns is that they are not, at first glance, clearly told as fictions.
Modern readers tend to consider Sut's stories to be personal narratives (which, in folk culture, call for belief), and think of him more
as a practical joker than a storyteller. Yet when Harris collected the
stories, which had originally been published separately in periodicals, he called the book not *The Adventures of Sut Lovingood* but *Sut
Lovingood. Yarns Spun by a "Nat'ral Born Durn'd Fool."*[5] Sut is a storyteller, not simply a hell raiser who enthusiastically reports his escapades. Most of the yarns belong among the improbable tall tales:
they are realistic enough to be possible, but wild enough and filled
with enough ridiculous detail that the initiated listener knows not
to take them as factual accounts of the narrator's experiences. Harris intends for us to understand that Sut has played some kind of a
joke or gotten into a scrape; but, as with most fiction, we should
concern ourselves more with the manner of the telling than with the
suffering of fictional victims. The double distance established in fictional tales told by the fictional character Sut allows the reader to
concentrate on the craft and the implied or symbolic meanings of
the stories.

Beyond the title, our first clue to the fictionality of Sut's tales is in
the non-dialect sections that frame the narratives. Each of Sut's tales
is introduced by a brief non-dialect passage in which George, the
frame narrator, indicates how he happened to hear Sut's yarn.
Where many Southwest humorists used the framework device to
provide balance, control, and assurance of a morally superior guiding intelligence, Harris uses the frame to establish that Sut's wit and
verbal vitality are superior to those around him, and to indicate his

position in society as a popular joker and storyteller. In "Sut Lovin-good's Daddy, Acting Horse," listeners who presume to challenge his preeminence are quickly quieted by Sut's comebacks: "The rat-faced youth shut up his knife and subsided" and "a tomato-nosed man in ragged overcoat . . . went into the doggery" amidst the laugh-ter of the crowd (21). Throughout the book, Sut draws to himself the center of attention as groups of men gather inside or in front of the doggery, in camp, or beside a spring.

Sut's apparent popularity and the freedom with which he roams among groups of loafers and hunters seem to belie his frequent claims of outlawry. In "Sicily Burns's Wedding," for example, Sut ends with the claim that "they is huntin' me tu kill me, I is feared" (97). The severity of this statement, however, is undercut not only by Sut's own description of later encounters with wedding guests but also by the incidents in earlier stories. In "Parson John Bullen's Lizards," Parson Bullen's reward poster serves only as a vehicle and inspiration for Sut's wit—not as an inspiration for righteous bounty hunters. Finding copies of the poster "stuck up on every blacksmith shop, doggery, and store door in the Frog Mountain Range," George takes one down for preservation.

AIT ($8) DULLERS REW-ARD
TENSHUN BELEVERS AND KONSTABLES! KETCH 'IM! KETCH 'IM

This kash wil be pade in korn, ur uther projuce, tu be kolected at ur about nex camp-meetin, *ur thararter,* by eny wun that ketches him, fur the karkus ove a sartin wun SUT LOVINGOOD, dead ur alive, ur ailin, an' safely giv over tu the purtectin care ove Parson John Bullen, ur lef' well tied, at Squire Mackjunkins, fur the raisin ove the devil pussonely, an' permiskusly dis-cumfurtin the wimen very powerful, an' skeerin ove folks generly a heap, an' bustin up a promisin, big warm meetin, an' a-makin the wickid larf, an' wus, an' wus, insultin ove the passun orful.

Test, JEHU WETHERO
Sined by me,
JOHN BULLEN, the passun.

. . . In a few days I found Sut in a good crowd in front of Capehart's Doggery, and as he seemed to be about in good tune, I read it to him.

"Yas, George, that ar dockymint am in dead yearnist sartin. Them hard shells over thar dus want me the wus kine, powerful bad. *But,* I spect ait dullers won't fetch me, nither wud ait hundred, bekase thar's nun ove em fas' enuf tu ketch me, nither is thar hosses by the livin jingo! Say, George, much talk 'bout this fuss up whar yu're been?" For the sake of a joke I said yes, a great deal. (48–49)

Sut's claims of physical danger are clearly a part of his joke and in fact belong to a popular folk genre. In her studies of tall tales and other modes of "talking trash" in the Okefenokee Swamp Rim, Kay Cothran found that, while rough practical jokes ("nonverbal lies," she calls them) really are played by country men, "much of the fun is in the later narration of the victim's plight or of the biter's being bit." She also notes that the practical joke story typically ends with a statement that the victim carries a lasting grudge.[6] Most of Sut's stories end with such a claim, and he frequently explains that he escapes from revenge only through the exercise of his long legs. From the glimpses of Sut's life provided in the framing passages we can see that these tales must be taller than life and that they are told for the fun of the telling rather than for their mimetic value.

The frames of the stories also briefly demonstrate how this tale-telling game of Sut's is to be played. In folk culture, the tall tale challenges the listener to prove himself clever or dull, in or out of the group to which the tale belongs, through his ability to recognize and appreciate the fiction. Harris' frame narrator, George, the well-educated, city-bred outsider, has become a temporary insider through his responses to Sut's tales. We get from George nothing but straight-faced reactions, no matter how outrageous the tale. He never moralizes, he never laughs, and he seldom interrupts. Other outsiders—a stranger, a schoolmaster, an encyclopedia salesman— ask stupid or impertinent questions and seem confused or offended by the moral atmosphere of Sut's tales. These listeners evoke insults and threats from Sut and are ostracized from the group, while George's solemn appreciation is rewarded by further yarns. When the old schoolmaster first interrupts Sut's "Trapping a Sheriff," and then asks George, "Is not that person slightly deranged?" George replies:

> "Oh, no, not at all, he is only troubled at times with violent attacks of durn'd fool."
> "He is laboring under one *now,* is he not?"
> I nodded my head. "Go on, Sut." (264)

Only once does George crack. In "Eaves-dropping a Lodge of Free-masons" George begins, in somber, nostalgic tones, a story of his own boyhood adventures, only to be interrupted by Sut, who claims he will tell the tale himself, without any "durn'd nonsense, 'bout echo's, an' grapes, an' warnit trees" [115]. As Sut reaches the climax of the tale and his imagination begins to outrun history, George protests:

> "The ole man made a wicked cirklin lick at him wif his orful nakid wepun {a sword}. 'Voop,' hit went, an' cut the flat crown outen his cap, smoof es yu cud onkiver a huckleberry pie wif a case-knife."
> "That part's not true, Mr. Sut," said I.
> "Yes hit am, fur yu see he dun hit so slick that the crown whirl'd roun like a tin plate in the ar, six foot abuv yer hed, went faster nur yu did, an' lit afore yu, es yu flew down stars fas' es yu wer gwine. Oh, littil hoss, *he did du hit,* an' ef he'd lower'd his sites jis' a scrimpshun he'd a-saved a pow'ful site ove meat an' bread frum bein wasted, an' curius pepil wud a-been now a-readin ove yur vartu's frum a lyin stone newspaper stuck in the yeath ove the graveyard yu wer a-blatherin about jis' now. (120–21)

Having been interrupted, Sut switches from the third person to the second, directly addressing George in answer to the challenge. He also changes the tone of the tale, increasing the grotesquerie and the exaggeration:

> "An I haint told all, fur in yer skeer a-gwine away frum that orful place, yu run over the spot whar a fancy hous' 'bout five foot squar hed been up-sot, slunged in up to yur eyebrows, amungst the slush in the hole, broke fur the krick, lunged in, onbottoned yer shut collar, dove plum thru that ar crownless cap—hit cum ofen yer heels like a hoop—swum outen yer clothes, an' jis' let every durn'd rag float away, an' then went home es nakid es a well-scraped hog, but not half es clean. The pepil what yu passed on yer way tu the krick tho't yu wer the cholery a-cumin, an' burn't tar in thar yards an' stuff'd ole rags onder thar doors, an' into the keyholes; an' es yu sneaked back nakid frum the krick, they tho't yu wer the ghost ove a skin'd bullfrog, ur a forewarnin ove cumin famin." (121)

By the end of this passage the story sounds like the tales of Sut's own misadventures. What began as a humorous anecdote about his friend's boyhood has become a tall tale: not an outrageous impossibility, but a tall tale nonetheless. That some of it stretches the facts we know from George's interruptions; that it is intended not as a serious lie but as entertainment for "the crowd" in the bar we know from George's introductory statements and Sut's asides to the audience. As in all the stories, the framing sections emphasize that these are tales told rather that actions performed.

Harris further encourages us to view the *Yarns* as tall tales by his use of traditional materials. At the beginning of "Dad's Dog School," Sut interrupts George's narration of a traditional story, insisting that only he should tell it since the incident occurred in his own family.

By openly using the tall tale device of transforming traditional material into personal reminiscence, Harris and indeed Sut admit that Sut neither invented nor experienced the main events of the tale. Milton Rickels discovered that a version of this tale had been printed as an anecdote in *Yankee Notions* in 1857 on the page where "Sut Lovegood's {sic} Shirt" ended, and claims that the motif was still alive in oral tradition in the 1870s.[7] "Old Burns's Bull Ride," in which Sicily Burns's father takes a wild ride on a bull chased by angry bees, also uses traditional material that had previously appeared in print. A story in an 1851 edition of the *Spirit of the Times* tells how Mike Fink, the riverboatman who generally triumphs in any conflict and cares little for the people in the settlements, lost a tussle with an angry bull chased by hornets, and was dropped naked in front of the Deacon's house, much to his embarrassment and the astonishment of a group of worshippers. The tale's inappropriateness to the Fink character suggests that it was a free-floating oral tale which the writer adapted to Fink to take advantage of the riverman's popularity.[8] Another of Sut's yarns, "Taurus in Lynchburg Market," is reminiscent of the early part of Fink's bull story, for both Sut and Fink find themselves holding the tail of an angry bull. (A similar motif appears in Don Lewis' story about a young camper holding a skunk's tail down, wondering what to do next.) Of course a writer may use traditional material or may imitate other writers without intending his narrator to be conscious of those sources; but at least once, in "Dad's Dog School," Sut himself draws attention to the traditional nature of his materials.

Sut also frequently adopts the traditional tall tale structural technique of beginning with realistically described events that seem probable, as well as possible, and gradually expanding the tale into the realm of the incredible. In "Hen Baily's Reformation," even George conspires to give the story a mock air of factuality and solemnity by beginning with a tongue-in-cheek headnote:

> This truthful narrative is particularly recommended to the careful consideration of the Rev. Mr. Stiggins, and his disciples, of the Brick Lane Branch of the Grand Junction Ebenezer Temperance Association. This mode of treatment can be fully relied upon. (198)

Sut's story begins with a warning about drinking from gourds. The action of the tale then moves from Hen's mistakenly drinking turpentine to his swallowing an eight-inch lizard that had hidden in a drinking gourd, and on through his desperate acrobatics as he tries vainly to get the lizard up. Finally, when a mole sent up his trouser leg comes out his mouth on the tail of the scurrying lizard, we know we have been sold.

Once we are alert to them, tall tale characteristics abound in the *Yarns*. Sut maintains strictly his pose of truthfulness and plausibility when George attempts to catch him off guard. How did the quilting turn out? George asks, and Sut replies, "How the hell du yu 'speck me tu know? I warn't thar eny more" (148). When he can get away with it, however, Sut inserts the knowledge of an omniscient narrator into otherwise first-person accounts of his adventures. In "Sut Assisting at a Negro Night-Meeting," for example, Sut tells George what the preachers were thinking:

> The suckit rider tuk hit {a beef bladder filled with "carburated hydorgen"} tu be the breast ove a fat roas hen, an' the Baptis' thot hit wer the bulge ove a jug. (161)

And in "Old Burns's Bull Ride" Sut gives a detailed account of Burns's adventure without explaining how he happens to know the details when he had already "put the mountain atwixt" himself and the Burns's "plantashun" (96).

Mixed with this mock-historical accuracy is a good deal of tall tale exaggeration. Describing his mother's encounter with a sand-hill crane, Sut claims that she "out-run her shadder thuty yards in cumin half a mile" (68). In "Dad's Dog School," the pretended factuality of a folk tale is undercut by similar exaggeration. In an attempt to convey the grotesque proportions of the Squire's nose, Sut claims that once "a feller broke a dorg-wood hanspike ur a chesnut fence rail, I'se forgot which, acrost that nose, an' twenty-seven bats, an' three kingfishers flew outen hit" (287). Sut's uncertainty about the exact weapon used on the Squire's nose typifies a tall tale technique in which humor arises from the conjunction of gross exaggeration and a pretended concern for historical accuracy. Minute absurd details also characterize the tall tale, and Harris sprinkles these about the yarns as well:

> {Sut's dad} seem'd to run jis adzactly es fas' es a ho'net cud fly; hit were the titest race I ever seed, fur wun hoss tu git all the whipin. Down thru a saige field they all went, the ho'nets makin hit look like thar wer smoke roun' dad's bald hed, an' he wif nuffin on the green yeath in the way ove close about im, but the bridil, an' ni ontu a yard ove plow line sailin behine, wif a tir'd out ho'net ridin on the pint ove hit. (25)

Such precise detail simultaneously brings these exaggerations to life and points out that they are fictions.

While some of the tales contain only one or two clues to their tallness, many obvious tall tale characteristics appear in one of Harris' most popular tales—"Sicily Burns's Wedding." Perhaps it is because so many clues are given that most modern readers can recognize the story as a *story* and thus comfortably enjoy the humor. In this yarn, folkloric sources are suggested by the bull-ride motif. Harris also prepares the reader for a tall tale by first allowing Sut a straight-faced comic monologue on several topics having little to do with the story he eventually tells. Like the storytellers Mark Twain describes in "How to Tell a Story," Sut "strings incongruities and absurdities together" as if they were utterly serious and important.

> I'll jis' gin yu leave tu go tu the devil ha'f hamon, ef I didn't make fewer tracks tu the mile, an' more tu the minit, than wer ever made by eny human man body, since Bark Wilson beat the saw-log frum the top ove the Frog Mountain intu the Oconee River, an' dove, an' dodged hit at las'. I hes allers look'd ontu that performince of Bark's es onekel'd in histery, allers givin way tu dad's hon'et race, however.
>
> George, every livin thing hes hits pint, a pint ove sum sort. Ole Bullen's pint is a durn'd fust rate, three bladed, dubbil barril'd, warter proof hypockracy, an' a never-tirein appertite fur bal'face {liquor}. Sicily Burns's pint am tu drive men folks plum crazy, an' then bring em too agin. Gin em a rale Orleans fever in five minits, an' then in five minits more, gin them a Floridy ager. Durn her, she's down on her heels flat-footed now. Dad's pint is tu be king ove all durn'd fools, ever since the day ove that feller what cribb'd up so much co'n down in Yegipt, long time ago (he run outen his coat yu minds). The Bibil tells us hu wer the stronges' man—hu wer the bes' man—hu wer the meekis' man, an' hu wer the wises' man, but leaves yu tu guess hu wer the bigges' fool. . . . (87–88)

As the real action of the story begins, Sut liberally tosses in absurd details typical of the tall tale. The bee-covered bull, for example, backs into a tall Dutch clock, "bustin hits runnin geer outen hit, the little wheels a-trundlin over the floor, an' the bees even chasin them" (92). Sut also assigns to the bees the kind of exaggerated malice and intellect that most tall tale insects seem to possess: "They am pow'ful quick-tempered littil critters, enyhow. The air wer dark wif 'em, an' Sock wer kivered all over, from snout tu tail, so clost yu cudent a-sot down a grain ove wheat fur bees, an' they wer a-fiting one anuther in the air, fur a place on the bull" (91). Because the tall language draws attention to itself and away from the distress of bull and humans, the net effect is comic. Sut also employs understatements which are reminiscent of oral tall tales. After describing the wedding guests' frantic attempts to escape the bees, Sut remarks, "livelyest folks I ever did see" (95). In a more extended use of comic understatement, Sut praises old Burns' skill with a basket: "I swar old Burns kin beat eny man on top ove the yeath a-fiting bees wif a baskit. Jis' set 'im a-straddil ove a mad bull, an' let thar be bees enuf tu exhite the ole man, an' the man what beats him kin break me" (94).

The tall tale is also, of course, suggested by the near-impossibility of some of the story's main events: the bull piling all the tables on top of one another, with Mrs. Clapshaw perched on top of the pile; old Burns being thrown onto the bull's back and later (in the sequel, "Old Burns's Bull Ride") thrown off and caught in a tree, dangling by his heels. Quite possible but clearly a stretcher is Sut's claim that "they is huntin' me tu kill me, I is fear'd" (97).

At the end of the wedding story, Sut slips quickly into more general remarks and a lament on his foolishness:

> Hit am an orful thing, George, tu be a nat'ral born durn'd fool. Yu'se never 'sperienced hit pussonally, hev yu? Hits made pow'fully agin our famerly, an' all owin tu dad. . . . (97)

Like many tall tale narrators, in order to lend an air of credibility to his story and maintain a facade of seriousness, Sut ends not with a punch line but with a solemn statement about the significance of the action or with a transition to another topic of conversation.

Each of Sut's stories contains such tall tale elements, though the tallness is not equally obvious in all of the tales. In the collected *Yarns*, the better tales provide a guide for reading the lesser ones, and the book as a whole can be read as a collection of tall tales. Probably Sut is a rough joker; perhaps he does get into scrapes and live in an under-civilized world. But in his tales, these exaggerated or invented accounts of his escapades, the reader is intended to laugh not so much at the discomfiture of Sut's victims, but at his vivid comic language and at the outrageous, exaggerated relation between cause and effect, action and reaction. The initiated reader delights in seeing those exaggerated events illuminated by Sut's pyrotechnic language, and he feels liberated by the wild comic disorder at the same time that he admires Sut's imposition of artistic control on a disorderly world.

In creating this comic disorder, in flaunting and exaggerating his

defects of sense and morality, Sut plays the role of the professional
buffoon of literature and folklore, described by Enid Welsford as
"an absurd ne'er-do-well . . . who earns his living by an openly acknowledged failure to attain to the normal standard of human dignity."[9] Unlike the court fool, who is mentally deranged, often physically deformed, and utterly dependent upon his patrons, and
unlike the ordinary rogue (America's Confidence Man), who makes
his living by deceiving others, professional buffoons "have gained
some kind of recognition for themselves as men whose acknowledged defects are socially acceptable as a source of entertainment."[10] In folk society, this position may be filled by a local yarnspinner, as it was in the Okefenokee Swamp Rim society studied by
Kay Cothran.

> The storyteller is a source of pride for his locality. . . . But the man of words
> may also be a liability, because the social stratum from which he comes is an
> embarrassing one to the middle class. . . . Story tellers are headstrong men,
> deviant but clever or normal enough to stay out of jail and asylum, under-
> socialized but not unacceptably more than the common run of men, ac-
> complished fantasists from a moribund society of fantasy makers, anarchs
> in terms of middle class law-oriented society.[11]

While Sut's defects of sense and morality place him at the fringes of
what a man can do and still stay out of jail or asylum, his eccen-
tricity also makes him useful and entertaining to men more con-
forming than he. Scorned as a sinner by the righteous, cursed as a
troublemaker by the respectable, and rebuffed as a clown by the
beautiful Sicily Burns, Sut remains ever popular as a hunting and
drinking companion. Even his social superiors solicit his company
and encourage his tales and pranks, as he demonstrates in "The
Snake-bit Irishman." In that story, "some three ur four clever fellers
frum Knoxville" [109] invite Sut along on a hunting trip, and then
offer him a pair of new boots if he will scare off a vagabond Irishman who has joined them. Sut drives the man off by making him
believe he is being attacked by snakes. Within the tale, Sut's prank
satisfies his companions, while the telling of the tale amuses
George, who is of course the best example of the socially normal
man enjoying the company of the socially deviant buffoon. Unwill-
ing to deviate openly from cultural values and the normal standards
of human dignity, the socially normal characters and readers vicariously enjoy Sut's freedom. Enid Welsford's assessment of the appeal of Till Eulenspiegel applies equally to Sut Lovingood:

To identify oneself with Eulenspiegel is to feel for a moment invulnerable. True, one must regard other men as puppets of sawdust (in Sut's world, animals or machines), but then identification with Eulenspiegel does, for the time being, delude one into the intoxicating fancy that other men *are* made of sawdust, that sensation is not real, that fact is not inexorable, and that pain itself is comic. This momentary relief from the pressure of sympathy and fear is surely one of the secrets of comedy.[12]

We can enjoy Sut's crudeness, sensuality and vengeance at a safe distance—behind the facade of laughter and, furthermore, behind the buffer of fiction; for Sut, unlike Eulenspiegel, is not just a prankster but a storyteller.

Because he tells tall tales, Sut's pranks and social defects are not limited to the realm of the possible and the likely, and he uses this freedom deliberately to manipulate his audience. As he exaggerates the grotesqueness of his adventures and pushes on the limits of our credibility, he also approaches the limits of our ability to believe that other men are animals or machines and that pain is comic. Sut's yarns, then, offer the typical tall tale challenge: enjoy these tall tales and be, for the time at least, one of the boys (a society of free spirits) or be offended by them and be, like the schoolmaster and encyclopedia salesman, an outsider and an effete social conformist. The naive, overly squeamish listener (or reader) aligns himself with the victims of Sut's social aggression: Clapshaw, Sheriff Doltin, Parson Bullen, Mrs. Yardley. True, Sut sometimes victimizes the downtrodden and innocent as well as the socially smug. He disrupts a Negro camp meeting, terrorizes an Irish tramp, torments a turpentine-poisoned drunk, and kills or maims several animals. Nontheless, these are tall tales, and the listeners or readers who fail to recognize them as such and grant an undue amount of pity to the imaginary victims become victims themselves: first, because they have identified themselves with the squeamish middle-class hypocrites of Sut's tales; second, because they suffer the discomforts of being offended rather than being entertained or relieved of psychic pressures; and, finally, because they have been fooled into believing a fiction.

While giving Sut a kind of immediate power over his listeners and readers, his yarns also give him power over the world he lives in. The absurdity of that world, not entirely generated by Sut's pranks and not entirely imaginary, impinges on Sut as well as on the other characters. As a means of coping with the stupidity of his father, the temptations of Sicily Burns, the interferences of the clergy, the hypocrisy of the middle class, and the general disorder around him, Sut creates tales which accentuate these stresses. In tales like "Parson John Bullen's Lizards" and "Trapping a Sheriff," Sut's triumph is obvious. The prank brings pain and humiliation to the victim, the story's form and context allow Sut to exaggerate his success, and the comic tone brings further humiliation as the victim becomes the butt of a humorous tale. In tales where Sut himself is the victim ("Sut's New-Fangled Shirt," "Blown up with Soda," "Taurus in Lynchburg Market") and in the tales where Sut's primary function is merely to observe and report the workings of an unruly world ("Sut Lovingood's Daddy, Acting Horse," "A Razor-Grinder in a Thunder-Storm," "Bart Davis's Dance," "Dad's Dog School"), Sut masters his world by recreating it in his own image. Sut the tall tale artist controls his fictional world more surely than Sut the prankster could ever hope to control the real world. Even the affliction of Sut's own durn'd fooledness can be mitigated through storytelling:

> "Why, Sut, what's wrong now? you look sick."
>
> "Heaps wrong, durn my skin—no my haslets—ef I haint mos' ded, an' my looks don't lie when they hints that I'se sick. I is sick—I'se skin'd."
>
> "Who skinned you—old Bullen?"
>
> "No, hoss, a durnder fool nor Bullen did hit; I jis' skin'd mysef."
>
> "What in the name of common sense did you do it for?"
>
> "Didn't du hit in the name ove common sense, did hit in the name, an' wif the sperit, ove plum nat'ral born durn fool.
>
> "Lite ofen that ar hoss, an' take a ho'n; I wants two ove em, (shaking his constant companion, a whiskey flask, at me,) an' plant yersef ontu that ar log, an' I'll tell ef I kin, but hit's a'mos beyant tellin.
>
> "I'se a durnder fool nor enybody outside a Assalum, ur Kongriss, 'sceptin ove my own dad, fur he actid hoss, an' I haint tried that yet. (29–30)

Then follows the story of how Sut became stuck inside a freshly starched shirt and lost a good deal of his hide in getting out of it. He ends with this warning:

> "Now George, ef a red-heded 'oman wif a reel foot axes yu to marry her, yu *may* du hit; ef an 'oman wants yu tu kill her husban, yu *may* du hit; ef a gal axes yu tu rob the bank, an' take her tu Californy, yu *may* du hit; ef wun on em wants yu tu quit whisky, yu *mout* even du that. But ef ever an 'oman, ole ur yung, purty es a sunflower ur ugly es a skin'd hoss, offers yu a shut aninted wif paste tu put on, jis' yu kill her in her tracks, an' burn the cussed pisnus shut rite thar. Take a ho'n?" (36)

In orthodox tall tale style and spirit, Sut exaggerates life's difficulties and conquers them by laughing at them.

Behind the character Sut is George Washington Harris exaggerating, laughing, and conquering as he spins tall tales for his readers. In Sut Lovingood, Harris exaggerated the common notion of a poor white southern mountaineer much as, in oral lore, a farmer may exaggerate the poverty of his land, the appetite of the local insects, and the ferocity of the weather for the benefit of the tourist. Harris' use of Sut as a narrator for his anti-Lincoln pieces indicates just whom Harris was trying to offend, fool, and exclude, and whom he intended to amuse. He had begun writing political articles in 1839 and was active in secessionist politics through the fifties. The first of his Sut stories, "Sut Lovingood's Daddy, Acting Horse," appeared in the *Spirit of the Times* in 1854, but thereafter the yarns were published in Democratic newspapers of the South. Though the book *Sut Lovingood. Yarns Spun by a "Nat'ral Born Durn'd Fool"* was published in New York in 1867, the Lincoln pieces and other obvious satires were not included.

For Harris, Sut is a regional characteristic to be flaunted, a weapon to be wielded. Sut represents the lowest elements of southern culture—the white trash whose shiftlessness, sexual promiscuity, cruelty to the Negro, personal filth, and disrespect for the laws and values of Christian civilization would have chilled the very bones of any Yankee who met him. In the Sut Lovingood pieces, Harris the Southerner fought the battle against the North, industrial society, and the Republican party, not with the romantic agrarianism of a John Pendleton Kennedy or a John Esten Cooke, but with the aggressive humor of the tall tale. Even so, like all tall tales, these stories are primarily humorous, and Harris, like Sut, must have taken a great deal of delight in telling his *Yarns*.

Notes

1. Edmund Wilson, *Patriotic Gore: Studies in the Literature of the American Civil War* (New York: Oxford University Press, 1962), 509. [Wilson's review is reprinted in this collection.]
2. Franklin J. Meine, ed., *Tall Tales of the Southwest* (New York: Alfred A. Knopf, 1930), xxiv.
3. Two other critics have discussed Sut's stories as fiction. See Robert Micklus, "Sut's Travels with Dad," *Studies in American Humor*, n.s., 1 (1982): 89–101; and Noel Polk, "The Blind Bull,

Human Nature: Sut Lovingood and the Damned Human Race." [Polk is reprinted in this collection.]

4. Mark Twain, *Roughing It,* Chapter LIII. This story was also told many times on the lecture platform and retold in the *Autobiography*. See *Mark Twain in Eruption,* ed. Bernard DeVoto (1922; New York: Harper & Brothers, 1940), 217–24.

5. [The edition used here is George Washington Harris, *"Sut Lovingood. Yarns": A Facsimile of the 1867 Dick and Fitzgerald Edition,* ed. M. Thomas Inge (Memphis: Saint Lukes Press, 1987). All future references will appear in the text.] The first Sut story, "Sut Lovingood's Daddy, Acting Horse," appeared in the *Spirit of the Times* in November 1854. Until his death in 1869, Harris continued writing about Sut and planned a second collection of his works which was lost in manuscript at the time of his death. The uncollected works were finally edited by Thomas Inge and issued under the title *High Times and Hard Times: Sketches and Tales by George Washington Harris* (Nashville: Vanderbilt University Press, 1967). Selections from the *Yarns* have been reprinted in Meine's *Tall Tales of the Southwest* and in Walter Blair, *Native American Humor* (1937; reprint, with new material, New York: Harper and Row, 1960).

6. Kay L. Cothran, "Talking Trash in the Okefenokee Swamp Rim, Georgia," *Journal of American Folklore* 87 (1974): 348.

7. Milton Rickels, *George Washington Harris* (New York: Twayne, 1965), 80–81, 139.

8. Reprinted in Walter Blair and Franklin J. Meine, *Half Horse, Half Alligator* (Chicago: University of Chicago Press, 1956), 220–25; for the motif's history see Richard Dorson, "The Jonny-Cake Papers," *Journal of American Folklore* 58 (1945): 107, and D. M. McKeithan, "Bull Rides Described by 'Scroggins,' G. W. Harris, and Mark Twain," *Southern Folklore Quarterly* 17 (1953): 241–43.

9. Enid Welsford, *The Fool: His Social and Literary History* (London: Faber and Faber, 1935), 3.

10. Ibid., 55.

11. Kay L. Cothran, "Such Stuff as Dreams: A Folkloristic Sociology of Fantasy in the Okefenokee Swamp Rim" (Ph.D. diss., University of Pennsylvania, 1972), 198. In this particular

society, the storyteller's social deviance includes resistance to progress and upward mobility. In other places and other times, the middle and upper classes have their own yarnspinners.

12. Welsford, *The Fool*, 50–51. Walter Blair was perhaps the first to point out the similarity between Sut and Eulenspiegel as described by Enid Welsford. Milton Rickels, in "George Washington Harris" [reprinted in this volume], suggests that one of Sut's functions and part of his appeal consist in the fool's creation of the illusion of freedom.

Section Three

New Perspectives

A Tribute to Harris's Sheriff Doltin Sequence

Hershel Parker

On academic visits South I used to claim to be a Faulkner critic, according to my self-servingly stringent definition—anyone who had published at least three pages in an issue of *Mississippi Quarterly* edited by James B. Meriwether then had been argued with in print by Cleanth Brooks. My record as a George Washington Harris critic may look still more meager (the editing of a few Harris tales for the *Norton Anthology of American Literature*), but I have qualifications for writing on Harris shared by few of the contributors to this volume. My mother learned to talk in a part of Mississippi where one of the pronouns is "hit," and my father learned to talk in the part of Oklahoma where people get frogs in their "froat" in bad weather. When I was in the eighth grade, I discovered that the pronunciation charts for vowels in *Webster's Third Collegiate Dictionary* were all wrong—the start of my career as a textual scholar. If you pronounced according to those charts, you couldn't eat *aigs* for breakfast or run away on your *laigs,* much less drive a *tin pinny* nail straight. On the other hand, I have some disqualifications. Harris helped to "do in" a lot of my Cherokee kinfolks, and I do not enjoy hearing Sut Lovengood on "Injuns," "niggers," or the "Israelite" who "vash *not* Levi Shacobs." (I use "Lovengood" because that was the way the name appeared in early newspaper printings.)

But anyone with a sense of history must deal with such passages in Harris as they do with similar passages in Shakespeare, Milton, and Wordsworth, without roiling in self-righteousness. Moral superiority to great artists is not one of our more admirable stances. And in the face of political correctness, I take Harris to be one of the greatest American artists. In saying this, I assume that men and women become professors of American and British literature because they love to read literature and love most of all to read that literature which most challenges and offers the most intense rewards—usually, the literature that generations of readers, or at least some fine readers in different generations, have identified as extraordinary, great, in one way or another. I assume also that professors of American and British literature as a matter of course try to surmount their own limitations of background and experience so as to comprehend attitudes relating to race, class, gender, genre, and style as they vary over decades and centuries, determined to understand as fully as possible before judging. Those assumptions, I acknowledge, are not universally shared among professors, many of whom in recent years have repudiated the very idea of literary greatness. Such professors, and those professors who have transformed some English departments into cultural studies departments, have not yet shown much interest in reading George Washington Harris sympathetically, however significant the role he played in forming mass American culture.

Even undoctrinaire readers, those who try to listen sympathetically to diverse voices of the past, will have to overcome moral obstacles before enjoying the Sut Lovengood stories, as I do when I deal with Harris's behavior toward Cherokees in real life and Sut's attitude toward Injuns in Harris's fiction. I knew, in my youth, one Indian ancestor born to survivors of the Trail of Tears, and in 1994 I have a living half-Indian aunt, as old as the century, born in Indian Territory, whose mother was deprived of her tribal rights by white chicanery. Were I interested in feeling victimized, I could find grounds for not reading George Washington Harris. But by politically correct standards, no one in nineteenth-century American literature can escape whipping—not the sexist Hawthorne, sure that women should not try to think; not the bigoted Stowe, appalled at the immigration of Europeans who did not speak English; not anyone. If we decide to avoid reading and teaching once-popular or once-respected writers because we are morally superior to them, we quickly run out of people to read and teach. As we get older, most of us begin to accept our benighted parents, aunts and uncles, and grandparents (as long as their behavior stops shy of criminality) rather than shunning them because their social views are less enlightened than ours at any given moment. Any best-selling therapy book tells us that if we write off our families we cut ourselves off from our own histories and go through life as less than whole human beings. In similar ways, "writing off" our great writers diminishes us personally and very quickly diminishes us as teachers.

Of course even very competent writers can be so driven by bigotry, by sheer hatred, that any reader would want to avoid them, most of the time, the way a decent person may avoid any slasher movie, on principle, however cunning a reviewer says the camera angles are. Some of Harris's attacks on Lincoln, written in wartime (amid sufferings we cannot imagine), may be too rabid for us to read now with any aesthetic pleasure. Yet the pleasures of reading most of Harris are great indeed, and I deprive myself if I avoid Harris because of things he did to or said about some of my tribespeople. I reserve my outrage, just now, for anthologists who think they can enhance my self-esteem as a quarter-Indian by having me read a white man's homily packaged as if it were a speech delivered by "Chief Seattle," or a white racist's best-selling fake autobiography *The Education of Little Tree,* or a poem on "The Atlantic Cable" by John Rollin Ridge, an earnest Cherokee kinsman of mine who was just well educated enough to write conventional English verse. I would rather enhance my self-esteem, the Cherokee and Choctaw parts included, by reading something better, even if it is by a white man or white woman. As a son of a halfbreed, I resented being excluded from good things when I was young, and I am not about to exclude myself from them now.

Forty years ago, when I read Walt Whitman's announcement that his "Song of Myself" was the meal equally set, I knew he meant it, and I knew that my invitation was irrevocable, whoever I was. The Sut Lovengood stories are also a meal set for anyone to come to on equal terms, even—or especially—cultural materialists.

A problem beyond political correctness is that some people cannot easily decipher the invitation to read the Sut stories: the dialect looms as an intimidating barrier. Yet there is no need to feel left out. Even if you were not lucky enough to learn to talk from a mother who learned to talk in Mississippi (or, still better, Tennessee), all you have to do is read the stories aloud, learning pronunciation patterns as you go and pretending you are reading them the way

William Faulkner or Eudora Welty would, on an uninhibited evening in a circle of friends. The effort it takes to enter into Sut's world is repaid by bounteous rewards, heaped-up delights. In all of nineteenth-century American literature, there is no politically correct meal that remotely compares to the riches of Harris's banquet, and, to tell the truth, even a lot of the passages we all teach in Mark Twain look a little watery when judged against the bald-face whiskey of Harris's prose.

Having held forth on political and linguistic hurdles to reading Sut, I will focus my loving tribute to his creator George Washington Harris on three Sut Lovengood stories, "Rare Ripe Garden-Seed," "Contempt of Court—Almost," and "Trapping a Sheriff"— what I call for convenience the "Sheriff Doltin sequence." I will lead into my discussion by looking at some of the preliminary biographical-bibliographical problems any reader of *Sut Lovingood. Yarns Spun by a "Nat'ral Born Durn'd Fool"* (1867) confronts, then by talking generally about author and audience in Harris's tales, a tricky subject, and unusually tricky because of the state of scholarship.[1]

Despite the work of Franklin J. Meine, J. Cleveland Harris, John J. Heflin, Jr., Donald Day, Ben Harris McClary, M. Thomas Inge, my student Janet Casey, and others, we do not have all the Sut stories that Harris published, some of which probably are no longer extant. Some stories that were printed are known only by references to them in surviving stories and some stories are known only by quotations from them or references to them by early admirers. We do not know in any detail the sequence in which the known Sut stories in *Yarns* were composed, because we have to rely on only a little external evidence—the knowledge of when a handful of stories were printed in newspapers—and some internal evidence, such as cross-references to earlier stories in later-written ones (though some of these references could have been planted as Harris put together the book). We assume that the stories in the newspapers were written in something like the order of their publication, but we do not know for sure. Some of us assume that many, if not most, or even almost all, the stories in the 1867 volume were first printed in newspapers, but we do not know for sure. (We do not know, for instance, of any previous publication of the Sheriff Doltin sequence.) We know not to assume that either the order of the first printings in newspapers or the order of the stories in the book will necessarily correspond with the order of composition. "Blown up with Soda" starts off as if it should follow the starched shirt story more closely than it does in the book, yet Milton Rickels lists the first surviving text of "Sut Lovengood's Shirt" (*Yankee Notions*, October 1857) not earlier at all but *later* than the first known text of "Sut Lovengood Blown Up" (that of the *Nashville Daily Gazette*, 21 July 1857, reprinted from the *Savannah Morning News* of some unknown date). Janet Casey, one of the succession of students I sent down to the Library of Congress to solve such mysteries, found just what you would hope to find, an earlier printing of "Sut Lovengood's Shirt," in the *Nashville Union and American* (1 May 1857), as well as a reprint in the *Louisville Democrat* (7 May 1857). (I have been planning for years to make a systematic sweep for unknown Sut stories, as a gift for Nathalia Wright, and in the meantime have taken comfort from several reprintings of known stories that Janet Casey, and also Robin Gaither, have discovered.)

Many other matters that look anomalous to us may yet be explained, such as possible clues to the time of composition of the Sheriff Doltin sequence in relation to other stories. The Sheriff Doltin sequence in the 1867 book follows well after the story of "Bart Davis's Dance," which like the Doltin stories is not known prior to book publication. There is one clue to the date of the Bart Davis story: Sut's allusion to the famous wartime phrase "all quiet on the Potomac," which does not particularly help, because it could have been added in 1867 or before and because there is no such datable reference in the Doltin sequence. However, in "Contempt of Court—Almost" Harris has Sut use the word "horspitable" without playing upon it in any way, an odd lapse unless this story was written *before* "Bart Davis's Dance," where Sut creates chaos by persuading Davis that "ole Sock" the "hard-shell preacher" had insulted him by saying "'Yu is hosspitabil.'" There is, in short, a lot we do not know (even whether or not Harris wrote the Sheriff Doltin stories sequentially).

Ignorance, however, is not going to stop me from making some more guesses now. I would guess, for starters, that Harris was a remarkably privileged writer. That may sound like an odd thing to say about a man who was long frustrated in his efforts to publish a collection of the Sut stories, who faced censorship in the *Spirit of the Times* at least once, who made arrangements for a series of Sut stories to appear in the *New York Atlas* only to have the project fizzle out, who died on the way home after arranging to publish his second book, the manuscript of which disappeared (left on the train when Harris was carried off unconscious at Knoxville, as Professor Meriwether thinks possible, or kept and suppressed by his new second wife and her family, as some of Harris's children thought). Privileged indeed! But as far as we know there was a ready market for his stories in the newspapers once Harris had published "Sut Lovengood's Daddy, Acting Horse" in the *Spirit* (4 November 1854). In a backhanded way, it is a great privilege not to have to get paid for your stories but to publish them to the delight of your friends in Tennessee and strangers around the country. I would guess that the references in the stories to earlier Sut stories are not at all evidence of self-promotion for Harris or even a calculated attempt to establish a richly storied background for Sut. Knowing that his stories were reprinted enthusiastically all around the country—knowing of printings in some papers we have not yet searched—knowing of printings in many other papers no longer extant—Harris made these references as a convivial way of recalling and celebrating pleasures he and his readers had already shared.

And I would guess that once the "Acting Horse" story was published and widely reprinted and talked about, Harris did not have to worry about holding an audience. After a while, in any newspaper story (certainly in any story first printed in the *Yarns*), Harris could trust the reader to have confidence in Sut as a narrator, to know that Sut's self-deprecation of his ability as a storyteller was a surefire way of entrapping any unwary auditor around the camp or outside the doggery. In "Mrs. Yardley's Quilting," for instance, Sut claims to ladle out his words at random, "like a calf kicking at yaller-jackids" (135), but he turns that mock apology into a put-down of the man with a wen over his eye. In "Frustrating a Funeral," Sut says he thinks at random, just as he talks and does. He knows better, and we had better know better. In "Eaves-dropping a Lodge of Freemasons" Sut taunts George into trying to tell the story, but when George starts off in pompous formal style, Sut breaks in and decides to tell it his way, to "talk hit all off in English" (116). No contemporary reader could have doubted that Sut was in control in the narration. The modern reader, coming without preparation to one story or another, may have more trouble. A reader of the Cohen and Dillingham *Humor of the Old Southwest,* for instance, might well be confused about Harris's skill as a storyteller, inasmuch as that collection includes the first two stories in the Doltin sequence but not the final one, which resolves the plot lines.

Sure, Sut's way of telling a story may seem random enough to any new reader. In "Rare Ripe Garden-Seed" Sut bombards the reader, rapid-fire, with an anecdote about his "fust big skeer" from the sheriff who took away the bed and chairs when Sut was the baby of the family; a philosophical digression on the pecking order of the universe (better than anything in Dreiser); a little essay on sheriffs and their uneasy consciences; a mention of old John Doltin, a " 'spectabil sheriff" (a new one, we have to figure out, not the one who gave Sut his first scare); the introduction of Wat Mastin and the splendid evocation of what it is to be young, healthy, and in bad need of sex; an interruption by an officious encyclopedia salesman; the obscene but delicately euphemistic account of the devastating effects marriage has on Wat's health; and the rest of the wonderful fabliau about Wat, his wife Mary, her mother Mrs. McKildrin, and Little Rar Ripe, Mary's baby by Sheriff Doltin; and a final interruption by the salesman. In "Contempt of Court—Almost" Sut starts with an essay (better than Poe's) on human perversity, a subject suggested by the encyclopedia salesman (whom Sut, feigning to confuse the man's product with his name, refers to as Onsightly Peter), and leading into the illustrative anecdote of Sut and the dandy (which you think will have to do with Doltin but does not, and which itself is interrupted by a little disquisition on mustaches), followed by a one-sentence shift to Judge Smarty and a new shift to Wirt Staples (smoothed by Sut's promise to make it relevant to the Doltin story). Then comes Wirt's magnificent tall talk and Sut's tribute to Wirt as champion *man,* fit to be displayed at a fair, then the rampaging scene in which Wirt comes close to committing contempt of court by slamming the sheriff with his ham of venison then flinging it at the judge. In the concluding story, "Trapping a Sheriff," Sut has fun indulging in high Victorian sentimentality in describing Doltin's wife, then sabotages that style and moves on to a speculation on "hereafters," especially the part of hell where sheriffs go. After Sut's conversation with Doltin (who is nursing his head after Wirt's onslaught), there comes the conspiracy of Sut, Wirt, and Wirt's wife Susan that is broken by an enthusiastic, digressive tribute to Susan's cooking (capped by the great bit of deflected sexuality: "I gets dorg hongry every time I sees Wirt's wife, ur even her side-saddil, ur her frocks a-hangin on the close-line" [262]). Then comes more of the ironic sentimentalizing, a self-conscious "word-portrait" of Susan pouring coffee (the sort of portrait the grown-up Huck might have given of Mary Jane Wilks, if Mark Twain had been as good as Harris), then the story of the trapping of Doltin and his punishment—pages about as good as the best trickery in *Twelfth Night* mixed up with the most rambunctious pages of *Tom Jones*.

All this may seem to be a run-amok narrative extravaganza. Characters come in without being part of the present story, other characters come in looking as if they are part of another story but turn out to belong to this one, times shift without transition, from Sut's boyhood to the present, sheriff replaces sheriff, and literary styles change abruptly. But everything is in the control of one of the greatest characters in American literature, Sut—always peering (or peeping), absorbing, philosophizing on human nature and animal nature (making it clear they are the same), drinking, bullying, eating, inventing outrageous pranks, rampaging (by proxy), escaping serious punishment, and loving good (or well), entertaining us in his way, in his own good time, in words that are Shakespearean in plentitude and precision and felicitous combinations. The narration is not at all aimless, never like Mark Twain's Jim Blaine and the story of the old ram, where the point is not to get to the point. There is a character in Harris like Blaine, but it is not Sut—it is the late Mrs. Yardley, who in her prime talked in free association, nonstop. Sut's narration is headlong, pell-mell, but always controlled, always delighting us.

Sometimes our delight arises directly from our pride in following Sut's fancy turns, ambushes, leaps, shifts, digressions, and seeming irrelevancies. We know Sut, and we are up to the challenge. Sometimes Sut even cheats a little so as to set us up for special surprise, as in the great fabliau section of "Rare Ripe Garden-Seed," where he makes it look as if Mrs. McKildrin is going to persuade Wat Mastin, the April Fool bridegroom, that her daughter Mary conceived promptly after the wedding and bore his baby before the middle of August, all because of the "rar ripe garden-seed" Wat had bought from a Yankee peddler. Mrs. McKildrin serves Wat whiskey after he revives from his faint at the sight of Little Rar Ripe, and Sut reminds us of the power of alcohol: "*Wun* ho'n allers saftens a man, the yeath over" (234). Wat counts the months, and recounts, and says, "*Haint enuf, is hit mammy?*" (236). But she sweetly reminds him how active he had been about the place: "yu planted hit waseful . . ." (237).

And Sut comments on her strategy of patient waiting: "Widders allers wait, an' allers win" (237). Then Sut gives us a marvelous turn: obtuse Wat Mastin rises to the occasion at last with a retentive memory and a quite unexpected capacity for irony when he throws up to Mary her mother's description of her as a "pow'ful interprizin gal" (239): she ought to be good for twenty-six or maybe thirty children as opposed to the thirteen her mother had "the ole way." After this turn of events we have the delight of Sut's sudden, unaccounted-for presence, just in time to step on Doltin's note to Mary and pick it up when no one is looking so he can get Jim Dunkin to read it to him. You do not *want* to know why Sut is suddenly there, any more than you want to know why he is suddenly peeping out of the old doggery door at Wirt in "Contempt of Court—Almost." He is always around at just the right time.

In "Contempt of Court—Almost" the reader delighting in Sut's dazzling turns may well be thrown by two textual errors. In the 1867 edition Sut says that Wirt Staples "tuck a skeer in what's tu cum" of his "narashun about the consekinses ove foolin wif uther men's wives" (249), but that is a slip brought about, probably, by a compositor's memory of Sut's "furst big skeer"; the word has to be "sheer," the usual spelling of "share" in Sut's dialect. The first edition also contains a garbled passage describing how fast the spirits from the new doggery were working on Wirt: "So when cort sot at nine o'clock, Wirt wer 'bout es fur ahead es cleaving, ur half pas' that." As a native speaker of this dialect as well as a textual scholar, I figured out that what Harris wrote was "'bout es fur ahead es eleving, ur half pas' that" (249). The word has to be an hour of the day, and in Sut's dialect "seven" comes out "seving," so eleven should come out "eleving"—a form mysterious enough to baffle a compositor. What Harris meant was that when court went into session at nine in the morning, Wirt was as drunk as he would normally have been at eleven or eleven-thirty.

Quite aside from these unintended pitfalls, Harris set loose in his narrative a series of questions any good reader will have to hold suspended. What does all the opening of "Contempt of Court—Almost" have to do with Wat Mastin? Does the dandy, a new character, fit somehow into Doltin's punishment? Who is Judge Smarty? Who, for that matter, is Wirt Staples?—though Sut assures us that Wirt "tuck a sheer in what's tu cum" about Doltin. In listening to Wirt's tall talk we forget about Doltin, for it is not the sheriff but

Judge Smarty he is insulting so magnificently. After the heroic challenge has been followed by the wreck of the watch tinker's shop, Wirt gets a little more liquid kindling wood from Sut. That is when Doltin comes waddling out of the courthouse and when Sut says, "Now Wirt were Wat Mastin's cuzzin, *an' know'd all about the rar ripe bisness,* an tuck sides wif Wat strong" (253). Wonderful surprise, wonderful fun to have Wirt quote back to the sheriff his love note to Mary. It is even better—more coherent and more satisfying—than we thought it would be, for Wirt is on the rampage not only against Judge Smarty but also against Sheriff Doltin, as well as the assorted deputies who get laid low by the "buck's hine laig."

Here the reader holds a question in suspension until things turn out better than anything that could have been expected. Such rewards are joyous to encounter, but I think Harris gets stronger effects by having Sut leave us at times in a state of unresolved curiosity, or even uneasiness, which colors our response as we proceed through the tale. Sut does not acknowledge that he knows the cause of our uneasiness—a technique akin to his use of euphemism in order to be more suggestive than if he were direct, for euphemisms of this sort implicate the reader in the obscenity. The best example in the Sheriff Doltin sequence is at the start, the time the sheriff traumatizes little Sut. Things were going along fine because Sut was getting fed: "Mam hed me a-standin atwixt her knees. I kin feel the knobs ove her jints a-rattlin a-pas' my ribs yet. She didn't hev much petticoats tu speak ove, an' I hed but one, an' hit were calliker slit frum the nap ove my naik tu the tail, hilt tugether at the top wif a draw-string, an' at the bottom by the hem" (227). When the sheriff comes, Sut darts "on all fours onder mam's petticoatails" (229). Naturally, if you are solemncoly, you do not want to think about what little Sut might have seen there, especially if you remember how sharp-eyed he always is and if you recall a later story in which Sut watches his mother lose most of her clothes while fighting with Sall Simmons in the creek (after the fight is over, Sut says he "never seed a frock fit an 'oman as clost as hern did"—so close he could count her ribs through it). But naturally, if you are scholarly, you want to know when Sut gets out from under there. He does not. Well, he must have gotten out sometime, but you are not told when, and you worry about it, a little, in the back of your mind. If you are just a little prurient, you are bothered enough about it to be in a heightened state of awareness when you read about the manifestations of Wat

Mastin's interest in Mary McKildrin (his bellowing and pawing up the dust around Mrs. McKildrin, and so on). You might even worry about it through the whole Sheriff Doltin sequence, for you may be reminded by contrast when Doltin shows up with all that excessive yardage for Mary. For sure, you are reminded by the way the ferryman's wife exposes herself during Doltin's flight in "Trapping a Sheriff." She bounces out of bed and comes to the door in her "shif-tail." Then at the great spectacle of Doltin and the tomcats and the lighted, turpentine-soaked ball of tow, she forgets what she is wearing. As Sut says, she "pulled up what she tuck tu be her aprun, an' kivered her face, an' shet the door wif a snap, an' lef hersef *on the outside*. I holler'd 'Higher—yer forrid ain't kivered yet.' She run roun the chimley outen sight, still holdin up her aprun" (272).

Well, most of the narrative threads in the Sheriff Doltin sequence are tied up well enough. We know the "consekinses ove foolin wif uther men's wives," for instance. But maybe some of the best questions are left unresolved. Does Mrs. McKildrin ever return after she flees the accusing ghost of her husband? Mary comes back after her own flight, but does Wat keep her—and her and Doltin's Little Rar Ripe? When does Sut get out from under his mam's petticoats?—a question the more urgent because we know she was standing, the sheriff having taken away the chairs. These matters are not only unresolved but unresolvable; Sut is too far away to ask, working his long "laigs," his flask glinting in the sun, leaving us a little uneasy, and a little in awe. He would not have told us anyhow, and in the present academic climate it will be a long time before many professors ask such serious questions about either Sut or the man who created him, George Washington Harris, a man who could write about as good as anybody in our country.

Note

1. Page references to quotations from Harris's collection of stories are from George Washington Harris, *"Sut Lovingood. Yarns": A Facsimile of the 1867 Dick and Fitzgerald Edition*, ed. M. Thomas Inge (Memphis: Saint Luke's Press, 1987).

Seeing Sutly

Visual and Verbal Play in the Work of George Washington Harris

Shelley Armitage

George Washington Harris brings us closer than any other writer to the indigenous and undiluted resources of the American language. . . . Harris possesses on the comic level something of what Melville does on the tragic, the rare kind of dramatic imagination that can get movement directly into words.

F. O. Matthiessen, *American Renaissance*

As is the case with Matthiessen, Sut Lovingood and his yarns have invited high praise from a variety of critics. From Mark Twain to Walter Blair, William Faulkner to Edmund Wilson, Sut's coarse and cowardly yet honest and revealing tomfoolery has inspired, irritated, and rewarded generations of critics and laypersons alike. Scholars have argued a primary and lasting influence despite his slim output (newspaper sketches and tales numbering perhaps seventy-two; one book collection published two years before his death). Cited most frequently for his rendering of backwoods Tennessean vernacular and sophisticated brand of independence, George Washington Harris both as stylist and chronicler continues to appeal to the unbridled and celebratory within us, all the while admitting to the gullibility and corruption that violent nineteenth-century Tennessee engendered. Most lasting, perhaps, is the gift Matthiessen identifies: Harris's "dramatic imagination" gets "movement directly into words." When we consider in this ability the added psychological dimensions of Harris's work—the comic and ironic, the author as ear and dialogist, the writer's self residing between his projected public character and Sut—we may contemplate much more in Matthiessen's suggestive comment. For Harris's great genius and appeal are as much a result of the visual as the verbal. His periodic pieces stylistically mark the coemergence of the illustrated, visual text with the public fascination with picturing as changing forms of the visual text became technologically possible. Though the largely failed attempts of his illustrators are due to several factors, they mark a connection between the American vernacular, comic/narrative style, and popular expressive art. Further, because Harris lived in a time that perpetuated the popular illustrated press, his dramatic imagination influenced and was influenced by the developing visual culture.

While speculation on the relationship between word and picture is ongoing in current as well as historic scholarship, one must begin with the admission that for all practical purposes writers of Harris's era (the mid-nineteenth century until the 1920s) cared little what their illustrators made of their characters and scenes.[1] Scholarly documentation shows that authors like Mark Twain infrequently contemplated the final result of a collaboration that really took place between publisher and illustrator rather than author and illustrator. Most writers considered illustrations as a way of enhancing sales or, if not, at least as an embellishing activity aside and after the fact of the initial, primary creation.

However, as M. Thomas Inge has pointed out, the American book by its publishing nature was not a single-minded affair but rather collaborative in the sense of its cycles of writing, planning, and publishing.[2] As print media in general changed to accommodate illustrations, adding engravings to the already decorative pages, so the illustrated book involved not only the writer but the publisher, printer, binder—a host of contributors to the final product. As much as books of Harris's time were material possessions whose imaginative and entertaining appeal involved the very body of leather and pulp from which they came, for the reader, the writer and illustrator were pals of some desk that resulted in the finished object before them.

More, the pairing of writer with illustrator not only constituted an emerging form, convention, or publishing venture but resulted in a pictorial language. If one were to analyze the literary form Sut's vernacular speech takes, these action-related tomes speak to a reformative or experimental quality that invites seeing. While Sut's version of what Mark Twain would perfect as the frame tale often occurs in the telling of his adventures to a straight man (George, writer and character, himself a window to Sut's tales), the conventions of folk speech—understatement, metaphor, symbol, paradox, and imagery as well as alliteration—delivered in dialect, often sound out the action rather than philosophize about it. By comparison, earlier American writers used folk speech as conscious adornment, for example, in this sentence from Emerson's essays, in which he used conventions of folk speech in order to domesticate his intellectuality: "I expand like corn and melons." But Harris makes us experience rather than intellectualize his philosophy; as such, he dramatizes knowing. In describing his own moral or religious condition in regard to the hereafter, he has Sut remark to George: "Who ever seed a soul in jis' sich a rack heap ove bones an' rags es this? I's nuffin but sum new-fangil'd sort ove beas', a sorter cross atween a crazy ole monkey an' a durn'd wore-out hominy-mill."[3] Even in this conversational tone, Sut's description is more direct, closer, despite his more verbose rendering. Unlike Emerson, whose descriptions often turn on a simile, Sut's description is more than approximation. Language that attempts familiarity through literary reductionism may appear quaint, whereas Sut's, demanding more imaginative activity of the reader/listener, is not principally an idea but an idea in action.

This paper explores the relationship between Harris's means of picturing Sut's world for us and how that process has both derived from and challenged conventions of "seeing," most notably styles and traditions that also affected his illustrators. His collapsing of the assumptions about pictorialism and the picturesque demonstrates an artistic freedom that is matched by the narrative and psychological freedom of Sut's fabulations—freedom at odds with the categorical truths of technological and social conventions of the times. By vicariously challenging the limits of conventionality through Sut's escapades, Harris simultaneously inverted the frames of reference through which the reader typically "sees." Thus, the connection between Harris's ear and eye—between imaginative re-creations of Harris's own experiences as listener and viewer—contributes to imagistic and ideational interplay between subjectified and objectified experience.

I

Harris's ability to make language act, to give it not only muscle but a contortionist's surprise and even horror, adds to the pictorial quality of the Lovingood yarns. Yet the term *pictorial,* though a thoroughgoing nineteenth-century one, is inadequate and maybe inaccurate in the long run.[4] For what Sut does is conjure up images best depicted by the likes of the cartoonists for *Raw* magazine. His verbal gestures would not be lost on Art Speigelman's staff because they thrive on what we might call a quirky, even kinky, sense of humor. Just as Mark Twain predicted in an 1867 review of *Sut Lovingood. Yarns Spun by a "Nat'ral Born Durn'd Fool"* that the eastern people might call his dialect "coarse," might "taboo it," so Sut does not hesitate to make nouns verbs, wed the high with the low, abandon not only any conventions of written grammar but reconstitute a limp American literary language that was said later in the nineteenth century to have the drama of a broken teacup.[5] *Pictorial* suggests translation of still life characteristics in painting to illustration and later photography. What most illustrators of Harris's time sought to do was translate, describe, convey, rather than enhance. Thus, most standard illustrations are pictorial; they employ painterly traditions that often harken back to conventions from English periodicals.[6]

What Sut's language calls for, however, is either an abstract or a pithy realism that demands at least a series of related pictures or film. (It is not surprising that the adventures of Sut Lovingood informed the stereotypes of the backwoods Tenneseean—but most especially those in later cartoon strips—as *moving* pictures for the newspaper and magazine page.) Instead, the *Yarns* were illustrated by a series of often unidentified illustrators who chose high points, memorable moments from the prose, frozen adventures that suggest a residual inner image to which the reader may return. In the *Yarns* there are only seven illustrations in 299 pages of written text. In his essay, "Sut and His Illustrators," M. Thomas Inge attempts to identify many of Sut's illustrators, noting the limited success most of them have, their overall derivative quality, and lack of imagination.[7] But while each of these pictures is constrained by the general expectations of American book illustration at the time, despite the staid attitude of the drawings, a few are notable in their attempt to highlight Sut's most raucous tellings.

In "Sut Lovingood's Daddy, Acting Horse," the joke appears to turn on Sut getting his Daddy to play horse by pulling the plow. But of course Harris is a master of exaggerating the expectations of even his comic creation, and in this scene Sut's Daddy is stung by bees and runs off naked from Sut and the plow he was pulling. The illustration for this story dramatizes both Sut's Daddy's nakedness and Sut's surprise as he looks on. It further emphasizes the subtext of the story—that Sut has not only inverted parental control but totally humiliated it. In the picture, Sut is in the foreground, larger than his fleeing, helpless parent. The line from the Lovingood story that the picture seeks to illustrate is: "He seem'd to run jis adzactly es fas' es a ho'net cud fly; hit wer the titest race I ever seed, fur wun hoss tu git all the whipin" (*Yarns*, 25). In this case, pictorially as well as verbally, Sut generously reigns: the calculated naiveté of the race-horse/whipping horse comparison achieves through feigned gullibility the triumph of the son.

Without exception in the *Yarns*, all the illustrations involve attempted depiction of action within the single frame as with "Sut Lovingood's Daddy, Acting Horse." The result is a kind of iconographic effect, not really reducing the whole story to a line or action but attempting to suggest the spirit of the entire story in the single picture. The graphic quality of selectivity of each of these picture elements further relays this spirit, for nudity, compromising positions, power plays, implied violence, and scatological material constitute these choices. The virago female, the exposed male, the pompous and then embarrassed crowd each creates a scene of presumption subdued. These pictures demonstrate the extremes of physical nature in the conveyance of foibles of human nature. When taken together, they create a visual connection throughout the text.

Thus as the stories progress so do the illustrations provide a visual narrative collectively. But within this iconographic yet developing design, much of the flavor of the realistic aspect of Tennessee life is lost. Some of this is a result of the manner in which illustrators were chosen and illustrations employed within book texts in the nineteenth century. As Bill Blackbeard among others has shown, there was a common disaffinity among American illustrators of Harris's time for true depiction of American subjects. Inge himself notes how Sut, only briefly described by Harris ("a queer looking, long legged, short bodied, small headed, white haired, hog eyed, funny sort of a genius" {*Yarns*, 19}) is shown atypically and inauthentically, either in locale or Harris's own physical hints about his character. For example, Inge says of an unknown artist's attempt that appeared in the *New York Atlas* on 8 August 1858, accompanying the second of an installment called "Sut Lovingood's Adventures in New York": "The depiction is awkward, stilted, and inaccurate.

Sut's legs are frozen in an unrealistic stance, and his features are barely discernible. The artist probably had no notion of how to dress a Tennessee mountaineer, as we find him wearing a claw-hammer coat. The only thing . . . that distinguishes Sut's dress from that of the dandy is his high boots—the artist's only concession to Sut's rural origin."[8]

Blackbeard explains that because of the development in the 1860s of "artists' factories," many of the pictures supplied were certainly not drawn from firsthand experience or direct understanding of the work or the place and people to whom it refers.[9] That condition, along with the difficulty of American illustrators weaning themselves away from English-influenced imagery so familiar to an American public, makes the attitude of many of the Sut illustrations closer to British style and imagery than anything typical of regional America. This is certainly true of "Old Burns' Bull Ride" and "Blown up with Soda" in the *Yarns*. In fact, the artists are better when Sut loses his shirt (his father, his clothes) or when any form of nudity prevails. In such pictures, authentic clothing and accoutrements can reasonably be abandoned, leaving the artist the raw action as caricature or comedy.

While an argument may be made that Harris himself was influenced by the pictorial, hence his penchant for heightened scene and event, at his most creative he describes the undocumentable—sheer delightful fantasy that plays as comic overstatement or exaggeration. In the same poorly illustrated story about Sut in New York, for example, this is how Harris describes Sut in the midst of thrashing a dandy: "Him an' me looked jist like a travelin windmill in full blast, with a cord ove fence-rails tied tu the arms by thar middils, a swingin' about every way, ur a big crawfish totin' off a bunch ove grasshoppers an' long-laiged spiders ag'in thar will—laigs, arms, heads, coatails, an' watch-chains wer so mixed an' tangled that hit wer bewilderin' tu the eyes tu foller us."[10] Sut is bewildering to the eyes. Thus, as in all good literature, seeing Sut must result from hearing him.

II

The dimension of orality supersedes even the best pictorial conventions, such as the most adept illustration by E. W. Kemble in "Sicily Burns's Wedding." For when the fabulations of voice—

I mean inflection, accent, pace, as much as description words—prevail, the effect of painting/panel/pictorial is enhanced. Harris successfully weds the rise of the pictorial tradition before and after the American Civil War and the evocativeness of vernacular speech so that to work, his illustrators' drawings had to appear with cutlines from the text. In this way, they also serve as cartoons, complete with a derivative punch line. But the sheer, wonderful madness of laying extreme description upon extreme description, as in the quote given above, ensures an imaginative quality in the *Yarns* that verbally continues to pull our legs. Thus, no illustrator could possibly contain Harris's kinetic and fabulist language, let alone reduce it to a single drawing.

But Harris, understanding well the role of illustration, does use the pictorial device as a beginning place, which he then builds and augments through the verbalized and thus animated progression and embellishment in the tales. Reviewing his own creative periods, we may more clearly appreciate this process as a cycle of visual and verbal reciprocity.

When Harris first began writing, it was during the brief period, 1839 to 1843, during which he bought a 375-acre farm in the foothills of the Great Smoky Mountains east of Maryville, Tennessee. Most scholars believe his first work was a series of letters to the editor of the Democratic *Knoxville Argus,* a political newspaper dedicated to James K. Polk's support and politics. Possibly Harris's work consisted of the more regional accounts of frontier experiences in the South, though, because unidentified, now it is impossible to know. His first attributable work was signed "Mr. Free," letters describing quarter racing, hunting, and other activities in the east Tennessee mountains, appearing in William T. Porter's New York magazine, *Spirit of the Times: A Chronicle of the Turf, Agriculture, Field Sports, Literature and the Stage.* In both cases, Harris attempted to sketch backwoods and frontier life, recording the kind of local realism and rural folklore that contributed to the magazine's national and international appeal among male readers, despite its resemblance to English sporting journals. Likewise, the Free letters, modeled on dialect and folkways echoing Robert Burns, appear derivative, with allusions and quotations from Dickens, Thomas More, and Shakespeare. During this period, Harris, who likely had only eighteen months of formal schooling as a child, accumulated a library of seventy-five books and later, in Knoxville, as a member of the Young Men's Literary Society, helped build a library of standard works. Familiar as this would have made him with the British-illustrated volumes of Dickens and others, allusions in Porter's *Spirit of the Times* to sketches by Thomas Bangs Thorpe, motifs from Davy Crockett tales, and even popular songs would suggest Harris saw a number of popular illustrations, pictorial depictions of action-filled tales that appeared in book and periodical publications during this time.[11] With the invention of the daguerreotype and thus the further framing of experience that both illustration and photography ensured, Harris must have experienced along with the average American the proliferation of these popular pictorial forms.

In one of these early pieces, which anticipates the form and spirit of the Sut Lovingood sagas later on, Harris shows clearly the connection between subjective and objective experience, verbalization in the service of visualization, and the vicarious bodying out of experience the bawdy suggestions in his stories allowed his supposedly genteel readers. In "The Knob Dance," which appeared in 1845, the opening paragraph in standard English frames the tale, not only setting up the genteel narrator, Sugartail, but giving the illusion of his withdrawal to allow the folk narrator, Dick Harlan, full control of the story of the dance that is then told in dialect and comic images and relays a different set of values because of the varied speech. While we have always thought of this form as literary or oral, the effect suggests the combining of pictorial and verbal traditions. Sugartail frames the world of the knob dance, allowing his fellow (i.e., educated, higher class) readers to look intelligently if curiously upon it. Dick Harlan recreates his experience of the activity in a folk language at once literal and metaphorical. When he says, for example, that the girls come to the dance in abundance, "pourin out of the woods like pissants out of an old log when tother end's afire" (*High Times*, 47), he invites an exact picturing that ironically allows for imaginative enjoyment. As the audience reads the text, thus hearing as they are seeing, the subjective experience may be had safely, may even encourage feelings of superiority, due to the effect of the original frame. These devices further ensure the accomplishment of all great art: as in viewing a play upon a stage or entering a film within a movie house, or looking at a realistic painting or documentary photograph, the reader/viewer/listener willingly suspends his or her disbelief as in entering the truth of our own dreams. Harris, even in this early story, plays the ranges of this effect masterfully. His comic descriptions invite both graphic, precise viewing and the tease of suggestive language. He lists the men's arrival at the dance with money for the corn liquor and food: "sum a lick of meal, sum a middlin of bacon, sum a hen, sum a possum, sum a punkin, sum a grab of taters, or a pocket full of peas, or dried apples." More generalized, yet evocative: "and as to laffin, why they *invented* laffin, and the *last* laff will be hearn at a Nob dance about three in the morning!" Finally, more generalized, still: the attendants, particularly Spraggins, love "sin in eny shape" (*High Times*, 46). Thus, the language that shapes the reader's experience is pictorial in integrative and varying degrees.

Though critic Milton Rickels says that "Harris's sketches of backwoods characters and their adventures are not a history of his own life," they are a history of his seeing in which ear and eye finally imaginatively connect.[12] In 1854 when he served briefly as a captain of the steamboat *Alida*, he went to Ducktown, Tennessee, to oversee the survey of the newly opened copper mines. There he met Sut Miller, the model, according to Miller's obituary in 1858, for Sut Lovingood, and Patrick Nash, the keeper of a saloon later notorious in Sut-centered stories. Harris was a strict Presbyterian, an upstanding citizen, and a hard and trustworthy worker at the many jobs he had during his lifetime. Nevertheless, Harris was able to observe some of the characters and life-style he conjured in the Sut tales, though they were not his world. His ability both to objectify through his frame devices and to subjectify further suggests a psychological, vicarious, and voyeuristic ploy, possibly still so very appealing because it releases the "straight" reader, writer, and genteel narrator from social constraints by celebrating not only Sut's ribald independence but the absence of the psychological debilitations of naiveté or corruption. While Harris may well have trod the straight and narrow in his public life and in his conservative politics—antiunion, secessionist, and proslavery—in Sut he advocates the law of the self that seeks to deconstruct social, religious, and political limitations of human nature. When Harris has Sut say he is nothing but a cross between a monkey and a hominy grinder, the union of animal and mechanical argues for Sut not only as alterego but as a personality constantly seeking escape from George Washington Harris's own times. These themes abide throughout the Sut stories—machinery, tools, and implements alongside jackasses, pigs, bedbugs, cockroaches, lizards, snakes, and worms. In Sut's own take on the Great Chain of Being: "Jis' so the yeath over: bishops eats elders, elders eats common peopil; they eats sich cattil es me, I eats possums, possums eats chickins, chickins swallers wums, an' wums am content tu eat dus an' the dus am the aind ove hit all" (*Yarns*, 228). No wonder Sut's world view is full of ambiguities depicted by the shifting and fusing of material objects, human, animal, and plant worlds. In his universalizing scheme of things he creates backwoods versions of Hellenic and other highbrow narratives while referring to his own "invention": "we kep a pet sand hill crane, an mom an him hed a differculty, an he chased her onder the bed" (*High Times*, 272). If the reader recognized the adaption of the Leda and the swan story, he or she may further puzzle over Sut's origins. Such is his divinity, in sandhill crane rather than swan shape.

Harris's pictorialism is therefore also guided by a desire to create a new image of the self, one that admits to the contextual by celebrating the local and regional. Within the dialogues between George and Sut are conversations with himself. Such comic interfacing admits to more than just the stock delineation of narrators of different classes. Because Harris's own vision of his world and of himself was coming of age during a time in U.S. history when the religious, moral, and technological were codified in their effects on art and artists due to scientific innovations, rather than escape from such ambiguities, he embraced them. In one of his postwar tales, "Sut Lovingood Reports What Bob Dawson Said, After Marrying a Substitute," the theme of misogyny translates into a larger issue of humanness, sexuality, and technology (see *High Times*, 177–83). Dawson's tale of his experience on his wedding night functions stylistically by Harris's accretionary narrative. Building image upon image of "Julianner" removing false parts (glass eye, false teeth, wig, pads for her legs and bosom) raises the specter of what is left. Harris unites the theme of the castrating female with false, mechanized female parts, thus emphasizing the fear of emasculation due to mechanical and human means.

The false vagina motif metaphorically calls into question our own identities, so that Sut's comic grotesqueries are philosophical expressions of an absurd world—one in which appearances must be questioned. Sut's constant role as destroyer of the mask applies most interestingly, however, to himself. In "Parson John Bullen's Lizards," the motif of nakedness enforces the themes of the minister's hypocritical and presumptuous nature. Losing his clothes in front of his congregation occurs because Sut releases lizards into the crowd during the parson's hell-fire and slithering-demon sermon (*Yarns*, 53). But the act itself has more prescience than a mere prank. Like the instance in "Sut's New-Fangled Shirt," when Sut must himself slither out of a newfangled starched and scratchy shirt his landlady has tricked him into wearing (*Yarns*, 34), freeing oneself from uncomfortable entrapments often involves exposing oneself. By returning again and again to the unpremeditated or authentic behavior of the rural mountaineers, Harris attempts to remove shirt and mask. But rather than sentimentalize, advocate, or proselytize through such behavior, he exposes Sut's guilelessness in the process. Though a story such as "Sut Lovingood's Daddy, Acting Horse" is regularly read as a rebellion against parental authority, Sut's honest behavior, as in the later "Well! Dad's Dead" (see *High Times*, 207–11), strips away the veneer of external, socially conditioned behavior that Harris may have condoned but secretly longed to shed.

III

Throughout these tales, Harris thus challenges a pictorialism that might alternately convey a romantic, idealistic, boostering, or puritanical view of life. He also, like Sut, feared the apparent opposite: the absoluteness of a science that could posit an equally rigid definition of man and his world. Defying finiteness, that is, the philosophical restraints that denied humanity, Harris, like a rural Rabelais, retooled through Sut the country Tennessean many of the conventions of Cervantes' Don Quixote. Particularly, he redefined in regional terms the picaro in a pictorial United States. The inherently subversive action of the picaro thus propels the main character on his adventures, assuring that social conventions and assumptions may be challenged, even destroyed, in his wake. Harris obviously crafted these tales to express his own subversiveness, allowed vicariously through Sut. But added to this ironic plane is the fact that often Sut's "adventures" are retellings: his ability to relive his escapades through his willing listener, George (and hence the reader), makes for double action—the implied original experience and the secondary retold one. Thus language is itself a kind of action. In the active language of the subversive picaro, Harris perfected a foil for the tendency to the picturesque of his times.

Whereas Mark Twain would later burlesque or parody the late nineteenth-century tendency to romanticize "exotic" peoples and places, playing out a special brand of American naiveté and "preciousness," Harris's picaro's physical and narrative action—the shape of the tale itself—allows for the challenging of picturesque conventions not only of narrative but of visual art. While certainly described within the safety of the frame of George's genteel recording, Sut's verbal permutations, transporting us as they do through often growing exaggerations, form a bridge between the genteel world and the coarse, backwoods world, allowing our subversive natures to flower and, for Harris, returning us to the essentially human.[13]

By drawing further comparisons between Harris's illustrators and his verbal art in the context of the larger issues of shifting graphic perceptions during Harris's time, we may appreciate more how he revitalized the imagination beyond the sentimentality of the picturesque. If none of Sut's illustrators, not even the concentrated efforts of Justin H. Howard, fully capture the dramatic quality of Sut's stories, one reason may be that the "kinetic" language of Sut operates ironically, offering multiple perspectives for the reader.[14] Whereas humorous access and memorality exist in the iconographic moments Howard elected to depict, the nature of narration as conversation between the outsider, George, and the insider, Sut, allows the reader to eavesdrop through the mind's eye. Such doubletelling not only emphasizes the concrete and abstract or philosophical aspects of Sut's experiences but creates a disjunction, built on illogical juxtapositions and visual paradoxes. Howard's work does modestly attest to the principle of "survivals" that is at the heart of the vitality of the folk tale—the creation of a tableau of the highly memorable rituals or actions that rise to such peaks in the hands of verbal artists.[15] Folklore critics have theorized that survivals are like sculpture in the mind's eye: the lingering action of the narrative possesses a singular power through a single memorable image, etching itself in one's memory. If we look upon Howard's seven drawings for the *Yarns* as indications of this stilled yet sculptured memory, we do have an idea of what at least one reader "saw" from the narrative. As an iconographic referent to the entire tale, Howard's work prompts us not just to enter the local scene, even while jarred by the physicality of scene and language, but also to enter the more complex psychological planes of Harris's fabulation.

Howard's work, like much of his contemporary illustrators, demonstrates further the creative tension of a postdaguerreotype period in which painting and illustration were greatly influenced by the invention and evolution of the camera. Van Deren Coke argues convincingly in his *The Painter and the Photograph* that the period from 1839 through the remainder of the century was one in which human vision was challenged by camera optics. Though the use of the camera obscura had influenced from the Renaissance on the replication of figure and perspective and even lighting, the invention and development of the camera challenged not only what the artist believed he could see with the naked eye but the "truth" of what he saw, which was thought to be more accurately recorded in the photograph. Thus, philosophically, the human and artistic eye came to trust the truth of the "camera lucida," a revelatory tool that altered perspective. Many painters, such as Eugene Delacroix, began to depend heavily on the camera eye and to draw and paint from the photograph rather than their own direct vision. Likewise, illustrators, once dependent on the precedence of largely English imagery in the popular illustrated presses for their American subjects, could utilize the model of portraits and landscapes.[16]

While on the one hand the possible influence of this more "accurate" way of seeing is interesting to speculate on in regard to how writers perceived their subjects, in the case of Harris it offers yet another facet to his sometimes fantastic narratives. The thematic recurrence of Sut's vassalage to both the earthy/"nat'ral" and the mechanical/technological restates his ultimate drive. Freedom is Sut's greatest prize—physical, psychological, "spiritual." And while he bemoans that he may drown himself ("Sut's New-Fangled Shirt"), the reader must remember it is Sut who would do the drowning. Likewise, not only was Harris's personal decorum dictated by his region and class, but his creative freedom was challenged by the impingement of the stylistics of both the picturesque, on the one hand, and the new technology of the camera on the other. No wonder his Sut, while admitting he is part and parcel of animal and machine, fights tooth and nail, but mostly with his jaw, as storyteller, to free himself from these prescriptions. When viewed in this context, Harris's pictorialism, embracing as it does aspects of the picturesque, goes far beyond the merely descriptive.

In his early survey of Sut's illustrators, therefore, M. Thomas Inge is onto something when he remarks of the "futility of attempting to capture the metaphorically imaginative scenes of Sut's wildest escapades. It would be like trying to illustrate a metaphysical poem by Donne or Marvell," he says.[17] That quality in Harris's writing lifts it beyond the regional or folkloristic—or rather because of it the prose is finally allusive, accretionary, and fabulist. As commentary on metaphor has shown, even when Harris compares a regional event with another localized example, the effect is a bridge to the unknown. Critic Karsten Harries argues: "Metaphor joins dissimilars not so much to let us perceive in them some previously hidden similarity but to create something altogether new."[18] She thus echoes C. Day Lewis, who argues that poetry, and by extrapolation poetic language, turns on this tension of opposites: "We find poetic truth struck out by the collision rather than the collusion of images."[19] Thus, Sut's retold adventures are metaphysical, for they operate not simply on the internal metaphors and similes of "pissant" life but through the psychological disjunctions of Sut's action, his observation, his memory, his retelling, and through the final ear and mouthpiece, George, to the reader.

As we have mentioned, despite his centrality to the tales, Sut is vaguely described by Harris, yet another example of a pictorialism that relies on laminations rather than an absolute concreteness. A "funny sort of genius," he is perhaps best described by himself in his differentiation in the preface to the *Yarns* between a "Nat'ral Born Durn'd Fool" and an educated one. Sut relates genius to natural fooldom; after all, "the edicated wuns am the worst" of the fools, he declares. A natural fool, in Sut's case, is blessed with oral powers that are part of the physical: "I hes the longes' par ove laigs ever hung tu eny cackus, 'sceptin only ove a grandaddy spider, an' kin beat *him* a usen ove em jis' es bad es a skeer'd dorg kin beat a crippled mud turkil" (*Yarns*, 172). He reminds George of the measure of distortion that exists when an educated man like himself writes a "perduckshun," picking the brains of the illiterate taleteller. Thus, the collusion of writer and original narrator is also potentially a creative collision metaphorically conceived. Sut has got the goods, and George is left to "grease it good and let it slide down the hill hits own way" (*Yarns*, xi). "Seeing Sutly," though the process may seem anything but (subtly), in fact is the ongoing way in which word and image interact—the way in which imaginative language dissolves former frames of reference.

Notes

1. See especially Bill Blackbeard, "Humorous Book Illustration," in *American Humorists, 1800–1950,* vol. 11 of *Dictionary of Literary Biography,* ed. Stanley Trachtenberg (Detroit: Gale Research Co., 1982), 625–39. Also, Erving Goffman, *Frame Analysis, An Essay on the Organization of Experience* (New York: Harper and Row, 1974), still offers some interesting perspectives on signified behaviors.
2. M. Thomas Inge, unpublished paper delivered at the Popular Culture Association Meeting of the South, 1992.
3. George Washington Harris, *"Sut Lovingood. Yarns": A Facsimile of the 1867 Dick and Fitzgerald Edition,* ed. M. Thomas Inge (Memphis: Saint Luke's Press, 1987), 107. References will hereafter be cited in the text.
4. Though standard dictionaries define pictorialism as having to do with pictures ("Pertaining to, characterized by, or composed of pictures"; "Represented as if in a picture," *American Heritage Dictionary of the American Language*), the term has the lasting connotation of association with painterly conventions, sometimes, as in the case of the use of the term during the last half of the nineteenth century, even romantic or sentimentalized or nostalgic values. Therefore, the term does not always suggest fidelity, documentary, or so-called realism except in relative terms.
5. Mark Twain's remarks appeared in a review of the *Yarns* originally published in the *San Francisco Daily Alta California,* 14 July 1867. The review is reprinted in this collection.
6. See Blackbeard, "Humorous Book Illustration," 625–28. With the notable exceptions of Thomas Nast, Fred Opper, and Edward W. Kemble, Blackbeard demonstrates how "until well into the middle decades of the last century, talented Yankee cartoonists seriously interested in pursuing a creative career generally faced starvation." He emphasizes how livelihood depended frequently on plates for pirated British or European works left unillustrated; even with American works, the illustrator was expected "to imitate closely one or another of the popular London cartoonists in style; indeed, his handiest tool in obtaining such employment was a portfolio of prints of current English fashions, city locales, and domestic interiors,

which served to convince his American employers that his work would seem sufficiently authentic in even minor details that an American audience would feel comfortably certain that they were enjoying an English cartoonist's work."

7. See Inge, "Sut and His Illustrators," reprinted in this collection.

8. Ibid.

9. Blackbeard, "Humorous Book Illustration," 628–29.

10. "Sut Lovingood's Adventures in New York," in M. Thomas Inge, ed., *High Times and Hard Times: Sketches and Tales of George Washington Harris* (Nashville: Vanderbilt University Press, 1967), 137. References to stories not in *Yarns* will be to this edition and will hereafter be cited in the text.

11. In particular, the southwestern humorists seemed to have inspired in their roguery at least enlightened comic attempts at illustration, such as John McClenan's work for Joseph Baldwin's *The Flush Times of Alabama and Mississippi* (1853). Harris would have seen the equally distinguishable work of pictorial writers, such as Thorpe's "The Big Bear of Arkansas" (1841), a classic recreation of the tall tale. Biographical details are from Donald Day's "The Life of George Washington Harris," reprinted in this volume.

12. Milton Rickels, "The Imagery of George Washington Harris," *American Literature* 31 (1959): 173–87.

13. The older conventions of the pictorial and the picturesque became confused when, in the growing tradition of landscape painting and regional and travel essays, combined with the rise of realism during and after the Civil War, interpretations of "reality" encompassed almost any method of picturing that was not caricature. Even illustrations for articles, in magazines such as the *Atlantic Monthly* and *Scribner's,* proclaimed a fidelity to people and place by virtue of firsthand reportage coupled with the new technology of mechanical etching. Indeed, the more technology replicated the original drawing, the more it appeared to carry some indisputable scientific truth; this particularly was true with photographic images so newly and starkly conveyed in the work of in-field photographers such as Timothy O'Sullivan during the Civil War. Despite the fact that a number of the photographers working for Matthew Brady were trained as studio photographers, therefore in the

conventions of portrait photography, these war photographs were the first to be mass produced and distributed through newspapers and periodicals. By the time photographers at the close of the century applied the assumptions of realism in photography to soft-focused and manipulated subjects, pictorialism—the representation through pictures—had become associated with the romantic, artful, or picturesque, suggesting emotive and atmospheric themes. In a like manner, the picaro as narrative hero enacted in the parodic and comedic, as applied to travel and adventure, a truth in seeing connected to firsthand experience and the reconstruction of reality through verbal inversion and descriptive picturing. Thus many "new" conventions of picturing, whether through fiction or the verbal arts, were reactions to exhausted earlier forms or the author's truth-seeking through destruction, inversion, or conversion of formerly embraced forms. Therefore, the very different conventions of pictorialism, the picturesque, and the picaresque are related in artistic intent and cultural properties. See Susan Sontag, *On Photography* (New York: Dell, 1973), in particular the essays "In Plato's Cave," "America, Seen Through Photographs Darkly," and "The Image-World," for critical analysis of the provenance of photography in American cultural imaginings.

14. Inge comments extensively on the success of the Justin H. Howard illustrations. Active in New York in the 1850s and 1860s, Howard was commissioned by Dick and Fitzgerald in 1867 to illustrate *Yarns.* At that time Howard was noted for his political caricatures and humorous cartoons. He contributed to such comic periodicals as *Yankee Notions* and *Punchinello* and had illustrated such books as *Major Jack Downing's Letters* (New York, 1857), *My Thirty Years Out of the Senate* (New York, 1859), *Josh Billings, His Book* (New York, 1865), and *Nonsense* by "Brick" Pomeroy (New York, 1868). In Inge's opinion, "a better artist might have been found for the task, but Howard's depiction of Sut has come to be the accepted one." Indeed, Howard's seven full-page illustrations for the book represent a concentration of his imagery as well as an important contemporary style to the times of Harris. In particular, his depiction of Sut's risible state of nudity makes for a frank treatment of Harris's depiction of life usually suppressed during this period.

15. The term *survivals* has been used psychoanalytically to explain the residual motifs and symbols residing in the subconscious and resurfacing in subsequent retellings of tales. The term also has been expanded to attest to the lasting power of narrative imagery that, some theorists argue, becomes iconographic like a static piece of sculpture, thus manifesting a primary permanent image that reminds one of a scene, character, or prime event in the story. Folklorists using psychoanalytic theory believe that dreams contain the survivals of earlier folk culture, forms, and narratives so that by recalling and recording dreams a portion of the original folk experience may be recovered. But also in the act of recovering is the importance of the particular survival. Therefore, according to some critics, an image, a scene, a character, motifs, symbols, and the like are internal, subconscious but also historic keys, not only to cultural continuity but to what was most memorable in the initial cultural experience. For this reason, iconographic images are assumed to have this effect because a powerful image of the character—say, the hero—is, due to the crafting of the original story, powerfully recalled through the memorable image of the whole story. Survivals thus are important for what they show about the dream and dreamer but perhaps most for what they indicate about the art of the original folk piece. See in particular Ernest Jones, "Psychoanalysis and Folklore," in *The Study of Folklore,* ed. Alan Dundes (Englewood Cliffs, N.J.: Prentice-Hall, 1965), for a discussion of survivals in folk memory and dreams and how these relate to cultural events.

16. See Van Deren Coke, "Introduction," in *The Painter and the Photograph* (Albuquerque: University of New Mexico Press, 1964), 1–15, for a fuller explanation.

17. See Inge, "Sut and His Illustrators," in this volume.

18. See Karsten Harries, "The Many Uses of Metaphor," in *On Metaphor,* ed. Sheldon Sacks (Chicago: University of Chicago Press, 1978), 165–72.

19. Ibid., 166.

Propriety, Society, and Sut Lovingood

Vernacular Gentility in Action

Pascal Covici, Jr.

If propriety can be said to have its fictional antithesis, George Washington Harris's Sut Lovingood has the nomination, so far as his delightedly disgusted readers can tell. Edmund Wilson, the most prestigious critic to comment on poor old Sut and poor dead Harris, put the matter this way: "One of the most striking things about *Sut Lovingood* is that it is all as offensive as possible. It takes a pretty strong stomach nowadays—when so much of the disgusting in our fiction is not rural but urban or suburban—to get through it. . . . I should say that, as far as my experience goes, it is by far the most repellent book of any real literary merit in American literature."[1]

Sut's actions, thoughts, and language probably churn fewer stomachs than Wilson's overreaction suggests, but that Sut violates the proprieties in a really big way no reader can doubt. Whether he is putting lizards up the pants of a minister at one camp meeting or bedding young Sal in the bushes during another one, Sut's behavior tends toward the unambiguously vulgar. His thoughts have the same cast, too. His famous disquisition on the purposes of men and women suggests the very triumph of sexist vulgarity: "Men wer made a-purpus jis' tu eat, drink, an' fur stayin awake in the yearly part ove the nites: an' wimen wer made tu cook the vittils, mix the sperits, an' help the men du the stayin awake."[2] As for his language, after "George" has begun to tell "Eaves-dropping a Lodge of Freemasons" with a tear-stained imitation of sentimental literature, Sut interrupts in an explosion of vernacular contempt: "Oh, komp-likated durnashun! that haint hit," he rudely insists. George must either be "drunk, ur yure sham'd tu tell hit, an' so yu tries tu put us all asleep wif a mess ove durn'd nonsince. . . . I'll talk hit all off in English, an' yu jis' watch an' see ef I say, 'echo,' ur 'grapes,' ur 'grave-yard' onst" (115–16).

I shall be suggesting that Sut's attitudes, that Harris's presenta-tions of Sut, express more of the "proper" than at first seems obvi-ous. Meanwhile, however, I want to make clear just how gloriously improper Sut is in the context of his time and place. In contrast with the stories about Sut, those concerning Simon Suggs, Sut's main ver-nacular contemporary among the scalawags found in the humor of the Old Southwest, imply, and sometimes propound, a world view much closer to social norms than the world of Sut. And the same could be said of others. In the traditional story of a Johnson J. Hooper, a William C. Hall, an Augustus B. Longstreet—the list could go on and on—the authority of the speaker of standard Eng-lish usually establishes a moral and social distance between reader and vernacular character. In the wonderful episode in which Hooper has Simon Suggs attend a camp meeting, for example, the boorish boobies—hicks from the sticks, every one of them—get taken in by the equally boorish Simon, while the narrative voice emphasizes in a series of comments just how "low," how hopelessly far below the ideal of what true religion ought to be, he finds the whole sordid af-fair. No reader could doubt that such bumpkins as these deserve only contempt. Their language and their behavior all of a piece, the ideal is not in them. At the same time, even slightly educated read-ers could feel relatively elevated, relatively genteel, in measuring themselves against such louts. As I have shown at some length else-where, affectation, in Henry Fielding's eighteenth-century sense of the term, underlies a great deal of the humor coming out of the Old Southwest.[3] This region, geographically fluid over time, offered im-mense literary opportunities to the educated editors, lawyers, doc-tors, bankers, and other literate newcomers from the East as they re-ported on the odd behavior and ways of life suddenly before their eyes, under their feet, and in their ears. Nineteenth-century Ameri-cans though they were, they seem to have seen through eyes attuned to an eighteenth-century British way of looking.

At least three impulses run through the works often collected un-der the rubric of the region: the reportorial, the political or social, and the envious.[4] The reportorial seems self-evident: here is all this strange behavior going on, strange because it is different from what the writer has been accustomed to, along with equally "strange" scenes and situations. The impulse to share the newly encountered with the people back home—an impulse older than Xenophon and *The March of the Ten Thousand*—informs the pieces written from the new lands for publication in the East, most notably in William T. Porter's *Spirit of the Times* in New York City, 1831–61, but also in many other journals and collections. With this urge to share often came the urge to evaluate: the behaviors they witnessed often struck the observers as not only new but boorish as well. Sometimes with explicit political—that is to say, Whig as opposed to Democratic— leanings, sometimes with broader social concerns, the writers seem to have wanted their readers to understand just how much of an af- front to the feelings and expectations of decent human beings life in the backwoods could be. But one finds shocking only what one has buried deep within one's self, so it should be no surprise that a tone of wistful longing often creeps into the accounts of Simon Suggs's successful swindles, of Sut Lovingood's offenses against de- cency, of Huck Finn's idle and ungrammatical rafting-rapture.

When we laugh at affectation, "the only source of the true ridicu- lous" to Henry Fielding, we laugh not only because we know ex- actly what constitutes appropriate, socially approved behavior but also because we assume—however momentarily—the absoluteness of our standard. When people behave in an affected manner, when they are guilty of affectation and therefore have become legitimate targets for our laughter, they acknowledge that the standards against which we measure them are appropriate standards, correct standards, legitimate standards, the only standards that count. Oth- erwise, they would not bother to try to appear to be measuring up.

Without repeating a great deal that has already been said else- where, let me take as established the assertion that much of the hu- mor of the Old Southwest depended for its effect upon the reader's amusement at affected behavior. At the same time, important dis- tinctions need to be drawn when we look closely at the humor of particular writers; Sut Lovingood's adventures elicit deeper and more complex responses than those of Simon Suggs. Both adven- turers, however, show up the foibles of the affected: Harris's Parson Bullen and Hooper's Bugg (and anonymous others) pretend an ad- herence to approved patterns of behavior from which they are shown to deviate. Readers chuckle over their undoing and withhold sympathy.

Simon and Sut, however, cannot legitimately be seen as equivalent forces. Although Hooper gave Simon the unforgettable aphorism, "It's good to be shifty in a new country," Simon remains primarily (not exclusively) a mechanical creation, triggered into action usually by greed, on occasion by the desire to dominate. He suppresses, perhaps even represses, his bodily desires in the interests of money or power, although even these words suggest a more deeply imagined character than Hooper usually manages to convey. The reader's enjoyment of the stories lies not in reveling in Simon's successes or sympathizing with him in his occasional failure. Rather, because his victims seem even less attractive than he himself does, one somewhat smugly approves their downfall without exactly approving of Simon's triumph. Over and over, they show themselves—Hooper explicitly shows them—to be guilty of affectation. But Simon remains a scoundrel. In this connection, commentators note that Hooper objected to being referred to as "Simon Suggs."[5] Taking the form of a campaign biography—for the worthy Captain will most probably soon be a candidate for office, and Hooper feels "bound in *honor* to furnish the Suggs party with such information respecting himself, as will enable them to vindicate his character whenever and wherever it may be attacked by the ruthless and polluted tongues of Captain Simon Suggs' enemies"[6]—his book opens with unflattering reference to the "counterfeit presentiment" of two recent Democratic Party presidential candidates, Martin Van Buren of the "foxy smile" and "Major General Andrew Jackson," whose lithograph will be used to frighten "future generations of naughty children" into their beds, "their mammas" presenting it to them as "a faithful representation of the Evil One—an atrocious slander, by the bye, on the potent, and comparatively well-favoured, prince of the infernal world." Hooper's social sympathies seem in harmony with his politics: the roughnecks of the frontier, whether Simon's victims or Simon himself, represent behavior worth laughing at, worth keeping at an emotional distance, and worth condemning. No subversion that I can see lurks below the surface of the text.

Yet, by the mere act of writing vernacular humor, Hooper, as his biographer of 1872 made clear, forfeited "the respect of men" or, anyway, of some men whose respect he coveted.[7] We may take this evaluation with a reasonable amount of salted reservation, considering that, at the time of his death in 1862, Hooper was secretary to the Provisional Confederate Congress. Still, the general attitude of the leaders and representatives of mainstream American nineteenth-century culture, as demonstrated by its brutal effect on Mark Twain following his vernacular extravagance at the *Atlantic* dinner of 1877, saw in the vernacular nothing with which respectable people might care to identify themselves. Hooper's vernacular persistently provides a contrast between the qualities of the characters who use it and those of the educated, standard-writing narrator who reports, with repeatedly noted disapproval, the escapades in which those low characters find themselves.

George Washington Harris, on the other hand, seems to have had no objection to being called "Sut Lovingood." M. Thomas Inge notes that by 1858 Harris "had by now become identified with him to such an extent that he used the name as a pen name and was called 'Sut' by his friends."[8] Not that Harris was any less the representative of propriety in his own life than was Hooper: a recent biographer suggests that "a sense of social separation from the 'lower orders,' reinforced by strict Presbyterian upbringing, had already {1833, by the age of nineteen} produced a reserved, sedate, rather formal character," perfectly in keeping with Harris's self of three years later, who already "was making long-range plans for genteel living."[9] "George's" reaction to a hypothetical appearance in his sedate Presbyterian pew of Sut barely covered in a shift that is "slit frum the nap ove {his} naik tu the tail, hilt tugether at the top wif a drawstring, an' at the bottom by the hem" (227) seems close enough to what one might expect of the real George W. Harris to stand as autobiography. Harris expects his readers to enjoy the outrageous behavior of Sut Lovingood, but he also assumes that their sympathies will be with the affronted "George" when Sut asks, "What wud yu du in sich a margincy? say hoss?" and George answers, "I'd shoot you dead" (228). Unlike Hooper, however, Harris had the need, and developed the ability, to bring to life the gusto and vitality, the cynicism and shame, of the infantile facets of Sut. Because these characteristics lurk within all human beings, even readers who found Sut's yarns disgusting also found them fascinating.

We know a fair amount about George Washington Harris, but the psyche of the author must not sidetrack us from the works and their significance. Although readers of Harris fairly wallow in the underworld that Sut inhabits; and even though in at least one story—

"Eaves-dropping a Lodge of Free-masons," referred to above—Harris sets up the language of super-refined gentility to receive not only Sut's but the reader's scorn; and although in several places Harris presents with extremely plausible sympathy Sut's condemnation of the sentimental excesses of Longfellow's "Excelsior"; and despite the fact that a list of examples of an antigenteel perspective in Harris's work could be stretched to considerable length: still, even modern readers of Sut's adventures find his world repulsive. Certainly the delight that we today take in Sut's doings, and certainly the similar delight taken by Harris's contemporaries, suggests no seriously held wish to relinquish civilization, however constricting and demanding, for the libidinal jungle that is Sut's experience. But Harris did make vivid the fascination of that jungle. Harris further differs from Hooper in that he finally eliminated the voice of the educated speaker from his character's tales. By doing so, he gave weight to the vernacular, and to the vernacular world, to a far greater extent than had been done previously. But as if to counter this emphasis, his presentation of that world, especially in combination with his vernacular character's difficulties in coping with any world at all, can make the reader, however fascinated, extremely queasy.

Sut's stance certainly seems to lack the prime quality of gentility as explicated in the writings of Josiah Holland, whose repeated call for "reverence" reflects a genteel cringing at the increasing absence of that quality in the attitudes of the second half of the American nineteenth century. Let us consider, briefly, this most popular American lecturer of the 1860s—"the most successful man of letters in the United States, measured either by the number of his readers or by the solid pecuniary rewards that had come to him," said an early biographer[10] of the revered and respected Dr. Josiah Gilbert Holland, who in 1861 published a collection of his Lyceum lectures under the title of *Lessons in Life: A Series of Familiar Essays. By Timothy Titcomb.* (Timothy Titcomb was the wonderful penname that Holland, at that time an editor of the Springfield *Republican,* chose to use.)[11] Holland's main point comes down to the propriety, indeed the necessity, of working to retain our vision of the Ideal, no matter how inescapable the unfortunately "real" may appear to become. "Let us suppose," Holland suggests,

> that in a country journey we arrive at the summit of a hill, at whose foot lies a charming village imbosomed in trees from the midst of which rises the

white spire of the village church. If we are in a poetical mood, we say: "How beautiful is this retirement! This quiet retreat, away from the world's distractions and great temptations, must be the abode of domestic and social virtue—the home of contentment, of peace, and of unquestioning Christian faith. Fortunate are those whose lot it is to be born and to pass their days here, and to be buried at last in the little graveyard behind the Church." As we see the children playing upon the grass, and the tidy matrons sitting in their doorways, and the farmers at work in the fields, and the quiet inn, with its brooding piazzas like wings waiting for the shelter of its guests, the scene fills us with a rare poetic delight.

In the midst of our little rapture, however, a communicative villager comes along, and we question him. We are shocked to learn that the inn is a very bad place, with a drunken landlord, that there is a quarrel in the church which is about to drive the old pastor away, that there is not a man in the village who would not leave if he could sell his property, that the women give free rein to their propensity for scandal, and that half of the children of the place are down with the measles.

But these "facts" do not affect Holland's way of seeing, except to strengthen his determination to preserve his illusional vision: "The true poet," he goes on in the next paragraph, "sees things not always as they are, but as they ought to be. He insists upon congruity and consistency. Such a life in such a spot, under such circumstances; and no unwarped and unpolluted mind can fail to see that the poet's ideal is the embodiment of God's will."[12]

Intent on his vision of "rare poetic delight," committed to the Ideal, Holland fails to notice the undercutting anticlimax of those measles that, for any vernacular humorist of the time, would by themselves have invalidated all sense of the scene's ideality. The "poet's ideal," the purely imaginary structure in the poet's head, has a religiously based validity: the particulars of a viewer's experience—the facets of reality that, to use Howells's words, "can be perceived by the senses"—do not count. Josiah Holland's preference for, and definition of, unpolluted minds had considerable literary support, especially in the East. Understandably, responses differed elsewhere.

Holland's way of seeing and of saying found opposition in, among others, Mark Twain, as a little sketch from the *Territorial Enterprise* of 28 January 1866, will confirm. Twain entitled it "Sabbath Reflections," making his point by a clever use of parentheses, so that the first part of the article can be read as two quite separate "reflections," one consisting of the ideal mental expectation, the cultural and literary stereotype, while the parenthetical parts offer the irritating reality that disturbs the senses and distracts the attention of the struggling writer.[13] A very small portion of it will suffice:

> This is the Sabbath to-day. This is the day set apart by a benignant Creator for rest—for repose from the wearying toils of the week, and for calm and serious (Brown's dog has commenced to howl again—I wonder why Brown persists in keeping that dog chained up?) meditation upon those tremendous subjects pertaining to our future existence. How thankful we ought to be (There goes that rooster, now.) for this sweet respite.

And so on, through hens cackling, tomcats fighting, and street-hawkers crying their wares. Then, "Sunday reflections! A man might as well try to reflect in Bedlam as in San Francisco when her millions of livestock are in tune." The Ideal of the Sabbath can have no power over any sane person's perception of this reality. Twain concludes: "I have got to go now and report a sermon. I trust it will be pleasanter work than writing a letter on Sunday, while the dogs and cats and chickens are glorifying their Maker and raising the mischief." The power and the glorious humor of Twain's piece depend upon one's enjoying the juxtaposition. Instead of denying the dramatic conflict between perceptions of the material world and preconceptions of the Ideal, as Holland had done, Twain celebrates the difference.

The prose of Harris in the stories about Sut repeatedly takes into account this difference. The vernacular, as in Twain's 1866 "Reflections" and 1877 "Whittier Birthday Speech," reduces ideality, whether noble or sentimental, to crudely material experience. Love, that most tender emotion, becomes a matter of being "blown up" with soda. Or it is a question primarily of doing some of that notorious "stayin awake in the yearly part ove the nites." If we turn to a rustic from New England, we see that vernacular itself need not be the point: the contrast between Harris's Sut and James Russell Lowell's Zekle in "The Courtin'" more than highlights Sut's degraded nature. Instead of undermining the idealistic aura surrounding the matter of physical attraction between men and women in the rural New England nineteenth century, Lowell sentimentalizes, prettifies, and glorifies what must have been fairly crude rusticities. His ninety-six-line narrative poem (in *The Biglow Papers, Second Series* {1867}) has been frequently anthologized, but I do need to remind my reader of some of its details.

To begin at the beginning, Lowell's first stanza casts an aura of divine sanction over what is to follow:

> God made sech nights, all white an' still
> Fur'z you can look or listen,
> Moonshine an' snow on field an' hill,
> All silence and all glisten.

This, one must acknowledge from the start, is one of God's nights. The action will have an aura of the divine about it. As "Zekle" creeps up and peeps in the window, he sees "Huldy," sitting "all alone, / 'ith no one nigh to hender," paring away at a bowl of apples in a room toasty with a heaped-up fire in the fireplace, "chiny on the dresser," pots and pans, an old firearm from Concord against the chimney, and—most decorative of all—Huldy herself:

> 'T was kin' o' kingdom-come to look
> On sech a blessed cretur,
> A dogrose blushin' to a brook
> Ain't modester nor sweeter.

The contrast between Huldy and Sut's gal, Sal—or, for that matter, Sicily Burns—could not have been clearer had Lowell been deliberately trying to make it.

Like Sut, Zekle is a young man of some experience, although not of Sut's crudely explicit variety:

> He'd sparked it with full twenty gals,
> Hed squired 'em, danced 'em, druv 'em,
> Fust this one, an' then thet, by spells—
> All is, he could n't love 'em

In Huldy, however, he has found one whom he can truly love, one whose mere presence makes the blood in his veins "run / All crinkly like curled maple" syrup. And Huldy returns his feelings for her. In church—a place where, of course, they find themselves every Sunday for purposes of sincere worship, purposes different from those that drive Sut to camp meetings—Zekle sings in the choir, and "My! when he made Ole Hundred ring, / She *knowed* the Lord was nigher."

Most properly, however, Zekle is bashful in his approach, awkward and hesitant, with Huldy in full control.

> He stood a spell on one foot fust,
> Then stood a spell on t' other,
> An' on which one he felt the wust
> He could n't ha' told ye nuther.

Finally, her pretense that most probably he is there to see her "Ma" drives him to offer to call again some other time. "Says she, 'Think likely, Mister': / Thet last word pricked him like a pin, / An' . . . Wal, he up an' kist her." But no erotic orgy follows. When Ma finally does enter to give the pair her blessing, Huldy, "All kin' o' smily roun' the lips / An' teary roun' the lashes," blushes becomingly, and the poem concludes with the pleasant news that "they was cried / In meetin' come nex' Sunday," thereby ending on the religious note and the note of propriety that have been sounding gently all along.

Lowell's use of nineteenth-century vernacular, like that of his southwestern contemporaries, presents the uneducated but presents them as if they were as committed to properly genteel behavior as even the most exalted Brahman of Boston. But even the case of Sut Lovingood can confirm that George Santayana was correct in lamenting the inability of American humorists to offer something "solid" in place of the genteel tradition. Not only did Harris himself aspire to a solid gentility: his great creation exhibits on at least one occasion a kind of latent gentility that ought to be surprising but that, finally, seems to fit pretty well with the general drift of Harris's stories.

George Washington Harris expects his readers to enjoy the outrageous behavior of Sut Lovingood, but he also assumes that in general their sympathies will be with "George." The pleasure we are to take from Sut's vernacular telling of his stories is the pleasure of *carnival*, of vacation, of play; it has nothing to do with any suggestion that respectable society fails in a serious way to nurture adequately the totality of the human spirit. Even twentieth-century readers, with assumptions far less genteel than those of the readers who first met Sut, cannot mistake Harris's assumption of superiority to his "nat'ral born durn'd fool." About to relate one of his more outrageous escapades, Sut asks: " 'Say, George, much talk 'bout this fuss up whar yu're been?' For the sake of a joke I said yes, a great deal" (49). Condescendingly, "George" humors Sut in his delusions of importance, and we readers snuggle down for a titillating glimpse of raw impulses turned loose, impulses to which we ourselves, of course, share Harris's superiority. Our own sympathies may well be more involved with Harris's vernacular creation than Harris himself could have anticipated, but we cannot mistake Harris's own horrified fascination with, and ultimate (conscious) condemnation of, Sut's perverse sadism. Author and reader share a sense of what is right and proper.

The effect of Harris's work was to strengthen the grip upon readers' minds and hearts of the relatively safe, relatively known world that propriety offered. Although "reverence"—in Josiah Holland's sense of the term—seems an odd word to use in connection with the writings of any of the humorists of the Old Southwest, and perhaps especially so in thinking about Harris and his Sut, this humor often, even mostly, reinforces the claims of the conventionally suppressive and repressive society whose ways Sut and the others so pointedly flout. A quick look at one more of the tales in *Sut Lovingood. Yarns Spun by a "Nat'ral Born Durn'd Fool"* will show just how radically unsubversive Harris's fiction can be, despite its violence and apparent disrespect for law and order.

"Trapping a Sheriff" concerns a gruesome revenge taken against the adulterous Sheriff Doltin by the cuckolded Wat Mastin, his rip-roaring cousin, Wirt Staples, Wirt's wife, and Sut. The planning and execution of the terrible things that happen to Doltin form the framework of the story, and the descriptions of Doltin's sufferings constitute about half of its actual content. A surprisingly large portion of its language, however, celebrates three sorts of preoccupations close to the hearts of readers of the genteelly idealizing fiction of the day. First, Doltin's wife, dying of tuberculosis, elicits from Sut a most poetic description, including the angelic nature of her smile, which, Sut expects, "will go back up wif her when she starts home, whar hit mus' a-cum frum." Contemplating Mr. and Mrs. Doltin, Sut finds himself absolutely committed to the existence of a hereafter: "Yes, *two* herearters, by golly" (257). Sut's description of the hell that he wishes for Doltin has a vividness that most ministers could not have equaled, but the idea itself is precisely in keeping with George Washington Harris's reputation as "an old Blue," a kind of Presbyterian, Milton Rickels informs us, "notable for the strictness of his life at a time when the ordinary Presbyterian sabbath meant morning and afternoon church services—the prayers long; the sermons, dry and logical."[14] In addition to the sentimental portrayal of Mrs. Doltin, angelic forerunner of Emmeline Grangerford, so congruent with Sut's confirmation of traditional notions of heaven and hell, Harris presents both a rapturous celebration of true marriage and a traditional warning to sinners to mend their ways. The experience he has suffered drives Doltin into joining the church; part of Sut's share in the revenge includes pretending to be the voice of the devil for the edification and terrification of both Doltin and Mary Mastin. That they respond as they do does, to be sure, testify to their superstitious dread; in context, however, one sees Sut as using the rhetoric of belief not simply to add to his own fun but also to try to engineer (he succeeds only with Doltin) the reformation of people whose behavior has violated the sanctity of marriage.

Sut's appreciative description of the material and spiritual blessings evident in the home of Wirt and Susan Staples leads him to conclude that an accurate picture of Susan's devoted expression and the accompanying dinner table could "make more men hongry, an' hot tu marry, a-lookin at hit in one week, nor ever ole Whitfield convarted in his hole life; back-sliders, hippercrits, an' all, I don't keer a durn" [262]. Harris here, and over and over again, presents the odd-seeming circumstances of Sut's simultaneous rejection of civilized norms of behavior and support for some of the central ideals of genteel culture. It is, we notice, a painting, a work of art, that (to Sut's mind) can best represent the ideal that he finds embodied in the table and person of Susan. Harris has Sut almost literally gild the lily:

> Es we sot down, the las' glimmers ove the sun crep thru the histed winder, an' flutter'd on the white tabil cloth an' play'd a silver shine on her smoof black har, es she sot at the hed ove the tabil, a-pourin out the coffee, wif her sleeves push'd tight back on her white roun' arm, her full throbbin neck wer bar tu the swell ove her shoulders, an' the steam ove the coffee made a movin vail afore her face, es she slowy brush'd hit away wif hur lef han', a-smilin an' a-flashin her talkin eyes lovinly at her hansum husbun. (262)

Here Harris employs the vernacular for an effect very like that of Lowell's in "The Courtin'," making us smile condescendingly, as well as appreciatively, at the simple bliss of simple people. Notice that although Sut's appreciation of the coffee, and of the other drinkables and edibles, rings true, the Sut who appreciates that "white tabil cloth" is a Sut whom we really do not know. This self-indulgent sentimentality—gentility, really—reassures us that Sut shares with us a participation in the common humanity present in all social classes. Although nothing suggests that the thinker who coined the phrase, "the genteel tradition," did much reading around in the works of Harris, Hooper, and others of their relative obscurity, one of George Santayana's casual observations in his 1911 talk at Berkeley remains especially suggestive. Wondering about "any successful efforts to escape from the genteel tradition, and to express something worth expressing behind its back," he considers "the humorists, of whom you here in California have had your share." He concludes that they "only half escape": "They point to what contradicts it in the facts; but not in order to abandon the genteel tradition, for they have nothing solid to put in its place." Then he goes on to draw an analogy between the situation in the late nineteenth-century (and early twentieth-century) United States and the case of Italy during the Renaissance, considering the attitude of Italian humorists toward the Catholic tradition. He saw them as

> not intending to deny the theory of the church, but caring for it so little at heart, that they could find it infinitely amusing that it should be contradicted in men's lives, and that no harm should come of it. So when Mark Twain says, "I was born of poor but dishonest parents," the humor depends on the parody of the genteel Anglo-Saxon convention that it is disreputable to be poor; but to hint at the hollowness of it would not be amusing if it did not remain at bottom one's habitual conviction.[15]

So Harris's Sut voices the cynical truths that the tradition kept trying to hide, as in his observation that it's simply "univarsal onregenerit human nater" to feel "a streak ove satisfackshun" at the misfortunes of another, "I don't keer ef he's yure bes' frien, an' I don't keer how sorry yu is fur him" (245). This does have a lot more of Harris-the-Presbyterian in it than do most of Sut's *apercu*. A more obvious example of the appropriateness of Santayana's remark might well be in Sut's statement of his "sentimints ontu folks: Men wer made a-purpus jis' tu eat, drink, an' fur stayin awake in the yearly part ove the nites: an' wimen wer made tu cook the vittils, mix the sperits, an' help the men du the stayin awake" that I quoted earlier (88). This, surely, is one of the many places where Harris does absolutely confirm, as applied to his own case, Santayana's sense that "the humorists" do not succeeed in escaping from the genteel tradition because "they have nothing solid to put in its place."

The case of Harris may be more satisfyingly ambivalent than most—satisfying from the point of view of twentieth-century students of American culture, I mean—but not, surely, by very much. In case after case, readers of the actual humorists (as opposed to readers of commentators on their work) can see easily enough that the authors cling to the polite standards that some of their characters ignore, and that in many cases, the bedrock of gentility has no disguise at all. But we may find it surprising that crude, rude, unregenerate Sut himself, and not just George, has so well-bred an appreciation of the finer things of life. The "silver shine" that glows above Susan Staples's glorified head and the "movin vail afore her face," even though it consists of condensation from hot coffee, combine with that unlikely white tablecloth to locate Sut, however briefly, within the bounds of genteel propriety. And the sanctions of the Divine are not so very far away, either, whether in Susan's halo or in Sut's ruminations on the source of Mrs. Doltin's angelic smile. However repulsive Sut was to Edmund Wilson—"always malevolent and always excessively sordid . . . , a peasant squatting in his own filth"—however repugnant at most times to Harris and to his readers, Sut indirectly reveals how extensive were the boundaries of the respectable.[16] Just as Huck Finn will respect respectability, looking up to Tom Sawyer not only in his author's ironic condemnation of mainstream society but also in Twain's curious admiration for it, so, even though Harris can laugh at the ineffective pretentiousness of sentimentally genteel speech for telling a story, he allows Sut to evoke with yearning the very world from which Sut himself must be forever excluded. Even in the case of Harris and Sut, "vernacular gentility" turns out to be no oxymoron.

Notes

1. Edmund Wilson, *Patriotic Gore: Studies in the Literature of the American Civil War* (New York: Oxford University Press, 1962), 509. Wilson's review is reprinted in this volume.

2. George Washington Harris, *"Sut Lovingood. Yarns": A Facsimile of the 1867 Dick and Fitzgerald Edition,* ed. M. Thomas Inge (Memphis: Saint Luke's Press, 1987), 88. All subsequent quotations to Harris's collection will be to this edition and will be noted in the text.

3. Chap. 1 of Pascal Covici, Jr., *Mark Twain's Humor: The Image of a World* (Dallas: Southern Methodist University Press, 1962), reprinted in *The Frontier Humorists: Critical Views,* ed. M. Thomas Inge (Hamden, Conn.: Archon Books, 1975), 233–58, and in *Mark Twain's Humor: Critical Essays,* ed. David E. E. Sloane (New York: Garland, 1993), 51–83.

4. See inter alia, Hennig Cohen and William B. Dillingham, eds., *Humor of the Old Southwest,* rev. eds. (Athens: University of Georgia Press, 1975, 1994).

5. Stanley Hoole, *Alias Simon Suggs: The Life and Times of Johnson Jones Hooper* (University: University of Alabama Press,

1952), 102–03. And see the introduction to M. Thomas Inge, ed., *High Times and Hard Times: Sketches and Tales by George Washington Harris* (Nashville: Vanderbilt University Press, 1967).

6. Johnson J. Hooper, *Some Adventure of Captain Simon Suggs* (Philadelphia: T. B. Peterson, 1846), chap. 1.

7. Quoted by Henry Nash Smith, *Mark Twain: The Development of a Writer* (Cambridge: Harvard University Press, 1962), 106.

8. Inge, *High Times*, 41.

9. Milton Rickels, *George Washington Harris* (New York: Twayne, 1965), 21, 22.

10. Harriette M. Plunkett, *Josiah Gilbert Holland* (New York, 1894), 72.

11. Henry Nash Smith cites the following passage in his *Mark Twain: The Development of a Writer*, 6–7.

12. Josiah Gilbert Holland, *Lessons in Life: A Series of Familiar Essays. By Timothy Titcomb* (New York: Charles Scribner's Sons, 1893), 285–86 (from "The Poetic Test," 284–97, unchanged from the edition of 1861).

13. Reprinted in *Mark Twain's San Francisco*, ed. Bernard Taper (New York: McGraw-Hill, 1963), 199–200, 201; the last paragraph of the "Reflections" appears at the end of "Neodamode," also in the *Enterprise* for 28 January 1866. Henry Nash Smith makes this same juxtaposition and contrast in *Mark Twain: The Development of a Writer*.

14. Rickels, *George Washington Harris*, 27.

15. "The Genteel Tradition in American Philosophy," in *The Genteel Tradition: Nine Essays by George Santayana*, ed. Douglas L. Wilson (Cambridge: Harvard University Press, 1967), 38–64; extract is from 51–52.

16. See Wilson's review in this collection.

Sut and His Sisters

Vernacular Humor and Genteel Culture

Nancy A. Walker

George Washington Harris's character Sut Lovingood made his major appearance in *Sut Lovingood. Yarns Spun by a "Nat'ral Born Durn'd Fool"* in 1867, a publication bracketed historically by the publications of two women writers who also mined the possibilities of the vernacular tradition in American literature: Frances Whitcher, whose "Widow Bedott" sketches delighted readers of *Neal's Saturday Gazette* in the 1840s, and Marietta Holley, whose outspoken character Samantha Allen was launched in 1872 and who continued to deliver her homespun wisdom until 1914, well past the heyday of dialect humor. At first glance, this would seem company in which Sut would feel extremely uncomfortable. Whitcher, a minister's wife, wrote about the sewing circles of small towns from her vantage point of New York State, and Holley, also a New Yorker, created in Samantha Allen a dedicated advocate of women's rights; Harris's Sut seems as removed ideologically as he is geographically from them, practicing his lawless behavior in the hills of Tennessee. Sut's world is the outdoors, not the parlor or the kitchen, and his frank sexuality and crude life-style would seem to bar him from their polite company. His interlocutor "George" seems to sense this fact when Sut suggests that his *Yarns* be dedicated to "Anner Dickinson": "Oh, Sut, that would never do. What! dedicate such nonsense as yours to a woman?" Sut is far more apt to destroy quilts, as he does in "Mrs. Yardley's Quilting," than he is to describe their creation, and if he had ever met up with Holley's Samantha Allen, who is never shy about speaking her mind, it seems likely that he would characterize her as the "strong minded 'oman" he describes in "Sut Lovingood's Chest Story": "Ove all the varmints I ever seed Ise feardest of them. . . . you'd better cum in contact with a comit ur a coal porter than wun ove em any time."[1]

Yet despite their differences, Harris shares with Whitcher and Holley several essential values and attitudes that reflect the tension in the nineteenth-century United States between the virtues of rugged individualism and the Jacksonian "common man," on the one hand, and an increasing pressure toward conformity and middle-class gentility on the other.[2] Mark Twain, a great admirer of Sut, was later to produce the best-known indictment of the extremes of both unfettered freedom and genteel pretensions in *Huck Finn*, but well before its publication in 1885, American vernacular humorists had already discovered the rich material inherent in a society deeply conflicted about religion, politics, social class, and the "woman question." Like Whitcher and Holley, Harris used his comic persona to reveal hypocrisy, snobbishness, greed, and just plain foolishness.

Frances Whitcher (1814–52), in her humorous sketches for *Neal's Saturday Gazette* and later *Godey's Lady's Book*, reveals herself as a shrewd observer of small-town America during the transition from frontier to settled communities—a transition just beginning in Sut's east Tennessee in the 1850s. As the daughter of an innkeeper and the wife of a minister, Whitcher had ample opportunity to observe the conflicts engendered by aspirations to economic stability and social respectability in a society still largely agrarian. The churchwomen in her sketches may gather to sew for the poor and unfortunate of their community, but they spend their time in competition with one another regarding their talent for cooking and their taste in clothing; religious duty becomes subsumed under social striving. Whitcher's character Aunt Maguire, who functions as a voice of reason in some of the sketches, describes one ludicrous result of an effort at female gentility: "Her gintility seemed to consist in her wearin' more colors than I ever see on to once afore in all my born days. She had on a yaller bunnit, with a great pink artificial on it; a red shawl, and a green silk frock, and blue ribbon around her neck, and I forget what all; but 'twas enough to make a body's eyes ache to look at her."[3]

Whitcher's character the Widow Bedott derives from the stereo-

type of the husband-hunting widow; she is, for example, a garru-
lous woman for whom denominational affiliation has much to do
with which church has an eligible man as its pastor. Similarly, Aunt
Maguire tells of a social-climbing woman who "withdraw'd herself
from the Baptists because their Sewin' Society dident dew as she
wanted to have 'em."[4] Because Whitcher's female narrators inhabit
a largely female social world, the targets of her satire are primarily
women, but men are very much present as the objects for which
women compete, and their own economic opportunism merits
some commentary in the sketches. Aunt Maguire, speaking of Samson Savage, one of the town's wealthiest citizens, notes his dubious
beginnings as one of the "Varmounters" who "come over the Green
Mountains with a spellin'-book in one hand and a halter in t'other,
and if they can't git a school to teach, they can steal a hoss." Savage
has become wealthy, Aunt Maguire allows, "without actilly bein'
what you could call dishonest."[5]

Frances Whitcher ultimately despaired of being able to stem the
rising tide of pretense and materialism that so concerned her, and
by the time Marietta Holley began publishing her Samantha Allen
books two decades after Whitcher's death, the United States was set-
tling into what Mark Twain would call the Gilded Age. This fact did
not deter Holley from pursuing her own attack on hypocrisy and
pretense, but by the early 1870s, when Samantha made her debut in
My Opinions and Betsey Bobbet's, the "woman question" was a more
insistent issue than it had been in the 1840s, so that Holley's treatment of religion, politics, and social behavior has as its essence the
disparity between the actual and what she perceived as the ideal
places of women in society. As a hard-working farm wife, Samantha
would have understood well Sut's description of male and female
roles: "Men wer made a-purpus jis' tu eat, drink, an' fur stayin
awake in the yearly part ove the nites: an' wimen wer made tu cook
the vittils, mix the sperits, an' help the men du the stayin awake.
That's all, an' nuthin' more, onless hits fur the wimen tu raise the
devil atwix meals, an' knit socks atwix drams, an' the men tu play
short kerds, swap hosses wif fools, an' fite fur exersise, at odd spells"
(88).

A staunch advocate of temperance, Samantha would have had
nothing to do with the "sperits" and "drams" of Sut's depiction, but
she would have agreed that women do the work while men eat,
drink, play, swap, and fight, and this particular division of labor was

one she frequently protested, as she does implicitly in this description of her chores: "I had a fortnights washin' to do, the house to clean up, churnin' to do, and bakin': for Josiah had eat up everything slick and clean, the buttery shelves looked like the dessert of Sarah. Then I had a batch of maple sugar to do off, . . . and some preserves to make, . . . besides my common housework—and well doth the poet say—'That a woman never gets her work done up,' for she don't."[6]

Sensible, rational Samantha has no patience with the exclusionary practices of religious and political institutions, even though— or perhaps because—leaders of these institutions claim to be protecting the welfare of the "lady." When her husband, Josiah, echoes the antisuffrage argument that political involvement would be dangerously strenuous for women, she points out that he does not consider it too strenuous for her to pick bushels of hops on a hot day, and she wonders why putting a piece of paper in a ballot box in a shady room is supposed to be so threatening to her health. Holley is equally skeptical of the role that organized religion plays in defining women's "place" as outside the authority structure of the church. And like Whitcher, she can be especially scathing when it comes to women's attempts to be "fashionable." A trip to Sarasota in one of Holley's books provides a number of targets for Samantha's scorn, and she views with a mixture of pity and alarm the attempts of the spinster Betsey Bobbet to land a husband so that she can have the respectable status of married woman. Betsey's hair and teeth are artificial, her manner of speaking is pretentious, and her poetry is terrible; nonetheless, she clings to the notion that it is "woman's highest speah, her only mission to soothe, to cling, to smile, to coo."[7]

Even the "nat'ral born durn'd fool" Sut Lovingood would resist Betsey's clinging and cooing, and while both Frances Whitcher and Marietta Holley would have found Sut's lack of sobriety, his foul if colorful language, and his gratuitous practical jokes reprehensible, they would have found some of his "wise fool" sentiments quite congenial. For Sut is not merely a creature of his passions, however strong some of them (e.g., liquor, food, revenge) may be. He is a philosophical man who has studied the world from his corner of Tennessee and has come to some conclusions about it. Central to Sut's philosophy are a belief in a certain kind of order to the creation and a preference for reality over appearances. The latter point

Sut puts succinctly to George in "Sut Assisting at a Negro Night-Meeting" after he describes having put bladders full of foul-smelling gas under the seat of the pulpit in the Negro church. The circuit rider catches a glimpse of the bladders and fancies he sees roast chickens, while the Negro Baptist preacher believes the bladders to be whiskey jugs, and Sut intones, "*Shapes*, George, can't be 'pended upon, *taste* am the thing" (161). Everything in Sut's universe has its purpose, or "pint," however nefarious the "pint" might be, and it is the better part of valor to accept one's appointed place, as Sut accepts his role as "durn'd fool" a notch below his father, who is "king durn'd fool" (88). Sut's may be largely a world of predators, but it has an orderly chain of being: "bishops eats elders, elders eats common peopil; they eats sich cattil es me, I eats possums, possums eats chickins, chickins swallers wums, an' wums am content tu eat dus, an' the dus am the aind ove hit all. . . . I speck hit am right, ur hit wudn't be 'lowed" (228).

Sut is no fan of either civil or religious authority, and not only because such authority threatens his free-wheeling behavior. Sheriffs and circuit riders, who are the particular objects of his scorn, do more than attempt to arrest or reform Sut; they also attempt to impose a semblance of order and respectability on a culture that otherwise allows Sut whatever amount of autonomy a "durn'd fool" can manage. Further, Sut suspects these authority figures of hypocrisy and corruption, of operating from a desire for personal power rather than responsibility to others. In "Rare Ripe Garden-Seed," for example, Sut notes that sheriffs are "orful 'spectabil peopil; everybody looks up tu em"; but he doubts that they deserve this respect and is proud that he has never been elected to the position: "no country atwix yere an' Tophit kin ever 'lect me tu sell out widders' plunder, ur poor men's co'n, an' the tho'ts ove hit gins me a good feelin" (229). And at another point, musing on his "durn'd fool" status, he remarks that if the long legs that permit him to kick or run his way out of uncomfortable situations will hold out long enough, he "may turn human sum day, that is sorter human, enuf tu be a Squire, ur school cummisiner" (97).

Sut's suspicions about the integrity of such civil authorities is on one level that of the obstreperous backwoodsman who resents the intrusions of "civilization," but it also represents Harris's perception that those who claimed such power and influence were sometimes not deserving of it. In this respect, *Yarns* has much in common with

Caroline Kirkland's description of the settlement of frontier Michigan in *A New Home—Who'll Follow?* (1839); Kirkland's narrator, Mrs. Mary Clavers, is, unlike Sut, a member of the educated middle class, but they share an ability to discern duplicity and opportunism.

That Sut knows his Bible is clear from the many biblical allusions in the *Yarns,* but he regards men of the cloth as meddlesome hypocrites, and he does not miss a chance to trip them up either physically or verbally. Like Whitcher and Holley, he suggests that only when religion as an institution puts its own house in order will it be worthy of his respect. "Parson John Bullen's Lizards" is a case in point. When the parson catches Sut and a young woman in a compromising position in the bushes, Sut is angry enough that the parson has hit him on the head with a hickory stick, but he is angrier still that Parson Bullen has told the girl's mother about the incident after promising not to do so. Sut's verbal revenge is to call the parson a "durn'd infunel, hiperkritikal, pot-bellied, scaley-hided, whisky-wastin, stinkin ole groun'-hog" (51), and his physical revenge consists of releasing lizards into the parson's pants during a sermon, so that the parson must shed his pants and display his own nakedness to the assembled congregation. At the end of the sketch Sut tells George, "Now I wants yu tu tell ole Barbelly this fur me, if he'll let me an' Sall alone, I'll let him alone—awhile" (59). Like Holley's Samantha, Sut wants equality with religious leaders. In "Sicily Burns's Wedding," Sut makes this point explicit in regard to circuit riders: "Suckit-riders am surjestif things tu me. They preaches agin me, an' I hes no chance tu preach back at them. Ef I cud I'd make the institushun behave hitsef better nur hit dus" (89). It may be in the natural order of things for bishops to eat elders, but no mere circuit rider is going to preach "agin" Sut without consequences. Like the widows in Frances Whitcher's work, Sut's circuit riders want to marry, especially women with money, but those who "by sum orful mistake" marry women without money "jis' turns intu polertishuns, {and} sells 'ile well stock'" (89).

Anyone who puts on airs is fair game for Sut's scorn. He is equally suspicious of pretension in dress, education, and language. In "Rare Ripe Garden-Seed," the target is an encyclopedia salesman who has joined the camp "uninvited, and really unwanted." He wears "a square-tail coat, and cloth gaiters" and is "obtaining subscribers for some forthcoming Encyclopedia of Useful Knowledge" (231). He speaks pompously, affects not to understand Sut's language, and receives his comeuppance when he remarks at bedtime that he wants to "repose." "Yu mus' talk Inglish tu me," responds Sut, "ur not git yersef onderstood" (244). George himself is prone to rhetorical flights, as he is at the beginning of "Eaves-dropping a Lodge of Freemasons," but Sut interrupts him and proceeds to tell the story himself: "Yu's drunk, ur yure sham'd tu tell hit, an' so yu tries tu put us all asleep wif a mess ove durn'd nonsince, 'bout echo's, an' grapes, an' warnit trees" (115). Sut is more direct in dealing with the encyclopedia salesman, who points out that he has not quoted the marriage ceremony accurately: "Yu go tu *hell*, mistofer; yu bothers me" (232).

Sut's attitudes toward women are more complex than one might expect from this free-spirited backwoodsman. Both Jane Curry and William E. Lenz have pointed out the pervasive sensuality of the *Yarns,* and indeed the very presence of a number of female characters makes Harris's sketches unusual in the humor of the Old Southwest.[8] Curry points out that even women in "an advanced state of maidenhood" are assumed by Sut to have sexual desires (133), even though he characterizes their behavior at such times as "sorter like cats a-courtin" (*Yarns,* 140). Young widows are far more to Sut's liking than old maids, however, and he renders their sexual possibilities more graphically: "They hes all been tu Jamakey an' larnt how sugar's made, an' knows how tu sweeten wif hit; an' by golly, they is always ready tu use hit. All yu hes tu du is tu find the spoon, an' then drink cumfort till yer blind. . . . Widders am a speshul means, George, fur ripenin green men, killin off weak ones, and makin 'ternally happy the soun ones" (141–42). The very cult of gentility that Whitcher and Holley resisted would have prevented them, as women writers, from hinting at the sexual desires or prowess of any woman, much less an unmarried one. In the work of these female humorists, widows and old maids are after marriage, not sex, and their motives—accurately enough—are social respectability and economic security. Yet the emphasis on marriage and its implications of a settled, "respectable" way of life in the work of all three writers reflects the force of a growing middle-class ideology.

It would be out of character for Sut *not* to view women in somewhat stereotypical ways. The "wise fool" figure is, by his very nature, not a sophisticate, and Sut is bent on his own earthy pleasures in ways that would not have appealed to the primary audiences for Holley's and Whitcher's work. He is fond of categorizing women

according to their looks and behavior. When his lizard prank succeeds in running the pantless Parson Bullen out of the church, Sut observes and judges the reactions of the women in the congregation:

> sum wimen screamin—they wer the skeery ones; sum larfin—they wer the
> wicked ones; sum cryin—they wer the fool ones (sorter my stripe yu know);
> sum tryin tu git away wif thar faces red—they wer the modest ones; sum
> lookin arter ole Bullen—they wer the curious ones; sum hangin clost tu thar
> sweethearts—they wer the sweet ones; sum on thar knees wif thar eyes shot,
> but facin the way the ole mud turtil wer a-runnin—they wer the 'saitful ones;
> sum duin nuthin—they wer the waitin ones; an' the mos' dangerus ove all
> ove em by a durn'd long site. (57–58)

Not only does Sut sort women into groups but he also feels free
to offer advice based on his observations to George and anyone else
listening. Following, for example, his painful experience with the
overstarched shirt in "Sut's New-Fangled Shirt," Sut cautions his listeners never to take such a shirt from a woman whether she be "ole
ur yung, purty es a sunflower ur ugly es a skin'd hoss" (36). Listeners are also warned to beware of old women who wear glasses,
like Mrs. Yardley: "Whenever yu see a ole 'oman ahine a par ove
shiney specks, yu keep yer eye skinn'd; they am dang'rus in the extreme" (135).

Despite his categories and categorical statements, when we look
at the women whom Sut admires and the reasons for his admiration,
it becomes clear that his preferences have little to do with the ideal
of the genteel "lady" and much to do with the same sort of common
sense, reason, and strength that characterize Holley's Samantha and
Whitcher's Aunt Maguire. The widows whom Sut finds such good
candidates for intimate involvement, for example, are described in
Sut's colorful metaphor as fine horses who are "rale sensibil, steady-
goin, never-skeerin, never-kickin, willin, sperrited, smoof pacers"
(141). A woman who is sensible and spirited counters directly the
fragility of mind and body associated with the Victorian "lady," and
it is tempting to attribute Sut's preference in some measure to the
example of his mother. When Sut's father establishes his credentials
as the "king durn'd fool" in "Sut Lovingood's Daddy, Acting Horse,"
Sut's mother is neither skittish nor scolding but merely observes
that he "plays hoss better nur yu dus husban'," and suggests to Sut
that he "lead him off tu the field . . . afore he kicks ur bites sum-
body" (23). Just as Holley's Samantha Allen plays the commonsense
foil to Josiah's foolishness, so Sut's "Mam" expresses her exaspera-

tion with the antics of her "king fool" husband. In "Dad's Dog-School," for example, she attempts to head off his plan to train Sut's puppy: "Lovingood, yu'll keep on wif yer devilmint an' nonsense, ontil yu fetch the day ove jedgement ontu our bar heds sum night, kerthrash, afore hits time" (279–80).

Sut's infatuation with Sicily Burns has much to do with her physical appearance, which he describes in graphic terms, especially her breasts, which resemble "two snow balls wif a strawberry stuck but-ainded intu bof on em" (75). Yet he also admires her spunk, even though she eventually turns it against him. In the midst of extolling her white skin and black hair, he notes that "she cud cry an' larf et the same time, an' either lov'd ur hated yu all over. . . . She kerried enuf devil about her tu run crazy a big settlment ove Job's children" (76). In fact, it is the combination of physical attractiveness and strength of will that makes Sicily so compelling to Sut. "Oh durn sich wimen!" he concludes. "Why aint they all made on the hemp-break plan, like mam, ur Betts Carr, ur Suke Miller, so they wundn't bother a feller's thinker et all" (77). The fact that Sicily cures Sut's "puppy-luv" for her by making him drink soda water does not di-minish his admiration for her; as he summarizes it for George, "she wer gal all over, frum the pint ove her toe-nails tu the aind ove the longes' har on the highis knob on her head—gal all the time, every-whar, an' wun ove the exhitenis kine" (78). Sut also admires the woman in the black silk dress who pummels the sanctimonious and hypocritical parson in "Bart Davis's Dance." Observing her pull out the parson's hair "like hit wer flax," he reports admiringly to George that "that wer the fust spessamin ove a smokin mad gal I've seed in a hen's age; she kerried out my idear ove a fust-rate flax-puller" (189).

Some of Sut's highest praise for a woman is reserved for Wirt Sta-ples's wife, Susan, who combines such feminine qualities as mod-esty and outstanding culinary ability with courage and resourceful-ness. In "Trapping a Sheriff," which concludes the plot begun in "Rare Ripe Garden-Seed," Susan cooks a memorable supper for Wirt and Sut before playing a central role in the plot to take revenge on Sheriff Doltin. The image of Susan Staples—and in particular the memory of her meal of fried chicken, vegetables, and buckwheat pancakes—moves Sut to a positive contemplation of marriage, al-though it is clear that the way to Sut's heart is through his stomach, as he tells us that he "gets dorg hongry every time [he] sees Wirt's wife" (262). But he also places a high value on her intelligence and lack of pretension:

> Ef she aint smart fur an 'oman, I aint a nat'ral born durned fool. She aint one ove yure she-cat wimmin, allers spittin an' groanin, an' swellin thar tails 'bout thar vartu. She never talks a word about hit, no more nor if she didn't hev eny; an' she hes es true a heart es ever beat agin a shiff hem, ur a husban's shut. But she am full ove fun, an' I mout add es purty es a hen canary, an' I swar I don't b'l'eve the 'oman knows hit. (260)

Susan's modesty is genuine and natural, rather than being the product of a striving for middle-class respectability; thus it is worthy of Sut's respect.

It is in Sut's description of Sal Yardley, however, that we may see the clearest articulation of Sut's resistance to the ideal of womanhood promoted by genteel culture: "Luved kissin, wrastlin, an' biled cabbige, an' hated tite clothes, hot weather, an' suckit-riders. B'leved strong in married folk's ways, cradles, an' the remishun ove sins, an' didn't b'leve in corsets, fleas, peaners, nur the fashun plates" (137). In her love of kissing and wrestling, Sal meets Sut's standards for earthiness, strength, and sexuality. She has religious beliefs but shares Sut's hatred of circuit riders. And although she believes in marriage and "cradles" (implying children), her dislike of corsets and "fashun plates" marks her as a flesh-and-blood woman rather than a "lady."

It was a long way from New York State to Knoxville, and from *Godey's Lady's Book* to the *Spirit of the Times,* but Harris seems to have shared with some of the female practitioners of vernacular humor a deep distrust of social ideologies that encouraged conformity and venerated both secular and religious authority. Sut, with his strategically placed hornets' nests and other retaliatory measures, takes an active part in the fight against the forces of gentility, while his eastern "sisters" had to be content with raising their voices instead of raising hell against what they perceived as the excesses of "civilization," but all three are effective reminders that the values of middle-class culture were not easily or uniformly embraced by nineteenth-century Americans.

Notes

1.   George Washington Harris, *"Sut Lovingood. Yarns": A Facsimile of the 1867 Dick and Fitzgerald Edition,* ed. M. Thomas Inge (Memphis: Saint Luke's Press, 1987), b. "Sut Lovingood's

Chest Story" was added to this facsimile edition of the yarns and therefore is paged with letters rather than with numbers. All page references to the *Yarns* will be to this edition.

2. For an early nineteenth-century account of these tensions, see Caroline Kirkland's *A New Home—Who'll Follow? Or, Glimpses of Western Life,* ed. Sandra A. Zagarell (1839; reprint, New Brunswick: Rutgers University Press, 1990). Kirkland describes the encounter in Michigan in the 1830s between early settlers who valued, like Sut, their individual freedom and the newer, middle-class settlers from the East. The biographies of Whitcher and Holley offer insights as well. See Linda A. Morris, *Women's Humor in the Age of Gentility: The Life and Works of Frances Miriam Whitcher* (Syracuse: Syracuse University Press, 1992), and Kate H. Winter, *Marietta Holley: Life with "Josiah Allen's Wife"* (Syracuse: Syracuse University Press, 1984). See also Ann Douglas, *The Feminization of American Culture* (New York: Knopf, 1977); Glenna Matthews, *"Just a Housewife": The Rise and Fall of Domesticity in America* (New York: Oxford University Press, 1987); Kathryn Kish Sklar, *Catharine Beecher: A Study in American Domesticity* (New Haven: Yale University Press, 1973).

3. Frances M. Whitcher, *The Widow Bedott Papers,* ed. Alice B. Neal (New York: J. C. Derby, 1856), 316.

4. Ibid., 301.

5. Ibid., 302.

6. Marietta Holley, *My Opinions and Betsey Bobbet's* (Hartford: American Publishing Co., 1872), 58–59.

7. Ibid., 62.

8. Jane Curry, "The Ring-Tailed Roarers Rarely Sang Soprano," *Frontiers* 11 (1977): 129–40; William E. Lenz, "Sensuality, Revenge, and Freedom: Women in *Sut Lovingood. Yarns Spun by a "Nat'ral Born Durn'd Fool,"* reprinted in this volume.

Playin' Hell

Sut Lovingood
as Durn'd Fool Preacher

James E. Caron

"Suckit-riders am surjestif things tu me. They preaches agin me, an' I hes no chance tu preach back at them. Ef I cud I'd make the institushun behave hitsef better nur hit dus."
—"Sicily Burns's Wedding"

Since Milton Rickels explored the idea at some length, a central point of commentary on the artistry of George Washington Harris is his use of long-standing conventions about the figure of the fool. Sut as fool allows Harris to depict behavior and express sentiments usually forbidden to writers in the antebellum United States. Rickels, however, draws a stark conclusion from his thesis. In his view Sut is hell-raising, whiskey-drinking, poor white trash—beyond the pale, detached both in life and spirit from his community and always threatening to overthrow authority. While his insight about Sut as fool remains valuable, Rickels, I will argue, veers from its truth when discussing the relationship between Sut and his community. Precisely because Sut enacts the role of fool and thus represents the fringe of society, he has the potential of representing the mainstream values of his east Tennessee, antebellum community.[1]

The paradox of the fool—on the margin yet potentially in the center—can be expressed as a structural relation with a community's ruler. Especially helpful for demonstrating that relationship is the trickster figure, a mythological form of the fool who is an enemy of order and boundaries: "since the disorder of which {the trickster} is the spirit is largely contained within his show {of foolishness}, he serves the boundary of which he is the enemy; and in doing this, he sometimes even demonstrates an authority proper to the central figure of established order . . . such as the king."[2] Late medieval and Renaissance European courts illustrate this photographic-negative relationship: the licensed fool embodied disorder while the king or prince or duke embodied order. Yet, as King Lear's fool suggests, the fool's position endows him with the freedom to speak most forcefully for reason and order.

During ancient times, when kingship entailed a magical as well as political dimension, the king was not only the guarantor by force of arms of the kingdom's geographical boundaries but also the mediator between his people and the realm of the supernatural. He was the center of political and social life *and* the symbolic conduit through which divine life passed to ensure an abundant harvest. Within this aura of magic the doctrine of the divine right of kings assumed its full power. And with so much contingent upon the king, a hedge against failure became a necessary corollary: "the king came very early to have a double, who embodied the threat of natural catastrophe and was deliberately mocked by the people. . . . The mock king was not always a fool, but by the nature of his office the fool as court jester became a kind of mock king."[3] The roles of fool and king, then, ultimately functioned to preserve the community. Much the same way as ritual scapegoats provided a formal means whereby a community could rid itself of unwanted and unlucky elements, thus strengthening the group by reaffirming its proper members and by soliciting the goodwill of the gods, the fool, as mascot and scapegoat, either warded off antithetical powers or introduced them in order to ensure their defeat. While the fool generally evokes boundaries because of its marginal status yet has the potential to fulfill a central role, the king's central role is overlayed, at special times, by an evocation of the boundary between this world and the next. The king and fool thus were the symbolic center and margin of community, mapping by their dynamic the space wherein all other legitimate members resided.

If Milton Rickels's point about Sut as a fool makes sense, then the relation of fool and king as types that define a community argues for Sut's inclusion in his own historical community, Ducktown. Sut's wild behavior, however, runs counter to the order of a settled community, suggesting the ambiguity of a trickster fool. Indeed, Sut's liminality is also indicated by his status as a mountaineer who has moved into town.[4] Sut himself remains a candidate for purging yet explicitly performs the task of expelling the undesirable outsider— like a Yankee or an Irishman—and thus maintains the integrity of the town. Sut, then, is both potential scapegoat and the representative of the communal authority that performs the cleansing action of scapegoating. Sut is both Fool and Fool Killer.[5]

An objection to my point about the fool's relation to king and community might be that the European analogy applies only on the mythic or literary level and not on a social or political one. After all, where is the authority in frontier America's southern communities comparable to a king? In fact, one institution did exercise an influence pervasive enough and did create a cohesiveness strong enough to function as such a powerful center of community: evangelical Christianity.[6]

This essay will explore how Sut's foolishness playfully evokes and revokes this authoritative center of his specific community. Although Sut's role as fool inevitably contains elements of the scapegoat and the trickster, the essay's argument does not insist on a sense of magic in the yarns; there is, however, a permeating sense of the supernatural.[7] Indeed, Sut *must* commit his narratives to a running engagement with the other world. Just as the court jester clowned in front of his lord, taking license with the sacred and secular principles of order represented by the office of king, Sut's antics can be read as clownish presentations of evangelical Christianity, the center of his community. Sut is a mock preacher. As a fool who acts in the historical context of the antebellum United States, Sut cannot fulfill the role of mock king, but his particular manifestation as a fool nevertheless functions similarly within his community.[8]

Sut carries on his foolishness by appropriating religious discourse. Whether he mocks church or state, Sut as comic preacher delivers "sermons," the abiding text of which is human nature as he finds it both in himself and in his neighbors. Of course, Sut expounds anything but orthodox doctrine. His basic premise, however, echoes the Calvinistic view of human depravity: the hell-deserving nature of people. And he does acknowledge a basic division of sinners and saints, the unregenerate and the sanctified. Yet Sut himself is not a believer in the sense that he has experienced God's grace. His parodic fool's religion is as much folkish superstition as Christian tenet. Moreover, Sut's "preaching" does not represent a definable moral order inasmuch as a pursuit of play and freedom motivates everything Sut does. For Sut, license is always better than law. Yet, as we will see, woven into his pleasure principle is Sut's notion of proper behavior, a notion that, while falling short of a true ethic, establishes a right and a wrong way to act. I will not claim that all of Sut's behavior can be explained within a framework of religion. However, all the tales in *Sut Lovingood. Yarns Spun by a "Nat'ral Born Durn'd Fool"* are about the creation or maintenance of community according to his foolish notion of proper conduct, a notion that can be discussed by focusing on two other religious terms besides unregeneracy—tribulation and retribution. We will see that for all of the wildness of Sut's yarns, there is nevertheless a conservative element in the tales.

I

One example of how Sut mimics sermonizing comes in "Eavesdropping a Lodge of Free-masons," after Sut has interrupted George's nostalgic way of beginning the tale. Sut starts his version saying, "Ahem! I takes fur my tex, the fac' that eaves-drappin am a durn'd mean sorter way tu make a livin . . . an' hit hes hits retribushun, a orful wun" (116). An equally obvious example of Sut as comic preacher is in "Sut Lovingood's Sermon—'Ye Cat Fishe Tavern,'" a tale completed by "Tripetown—Twenty Minutes for Breakfast." The message of these stories has been repeated since antiquity: innkeepers are a herd of rascals. But Sut frames his diatribe with the conventions of a church sermon, again by announcing his text and by repeating part of that text at regular intervals as a refrain. Very much aware he is acting the role of preacher, Sut jokes about his credentials for preaching by noting five "facts": he has no soul, he is a lawless fool, he has the longest pair of legs of any creature, he can drink more whiskey without falling over than anyone else, and he can get into and out of more scary scrapes faster than anyone else. While this list bears a resemblance of form to the boast of the backwoods roarer, Sut is also making fun of the lack of formal training that usually characterized Methodist and Baptist preachers of the antebellum period: "ef these . . . pints ove karactar don't gin me the right tu preach ef I wants tu I wud like tu know whar sum preachers got *thar* papers frum" (172–73). Sut's negative credentials comically comment on an age when virtually any man with a religious turn of mind who felt the "call" could claim a right to preach.[9]

That Sut himself possesses the requisite religious mind-set can be illustrated by a comment he makes that shows how he conceptualizes his own self in religious terms: "I hes a trustin reliance ontu the fidelity, injurance, an' speed ove these yere laigs ove mine tu tote me *an' my sins* away beyant all human retribushuns ur revenge" (xi, emphasis added). Moreover, there is Sut's readiness with biblical phrasing and his more direct references to the Holy Book, as he calls it (35). Appropriate to the tendency of evangelical Christianity, the allusions nearly all refer to the Old Testament.[10] Harris also has Sut close "Dad's Dog School," the last of the *Yarns*, in a way that underscores Sut's mock religious orientation. Just before all who have been listening retire, Sut wishes them pleasant dreams. In particular he wishes George will "dream ove ownin three never-failin springs, so clost tugether yu kin lay on yure belly an' reach em all—the bigges wun runnin ole whiskey, the middil one strained honey, an' the leas' an' las'—cold warter" (298). This mountaineer's version of the biblical land of milk and honey is complemented by Sut's wish for himself: "Es tu me, ef I kin jis' miss dreamin ove hell ur {the circuit rider} ole Bullen's all I ax" (299). Sut's comic picture of paradise fits with his biblical allusions and phrasing, indicating the most basic credential for preaching: a mind shaped by the Good Book. Sut even mentions one of the most famous of the early evangelical preachers, Whitefield (262), showing a sense of history about the typical style of Christianity in antebellum east Tennessee.

For all of his apparent religious background, however, Sut has not "joined meeting." Sut is not part of the community of saints, nor is he even a believer in any usual sense of that word. His status in the community at large is summed up by the wanted poster Parson Bullen posts after Sut had interrupted his preaching by releasing lizards up his pant leg: "fur the raisin ove the devil pussonely, . . . an' a-makin the wickid larf" (48). Sut primarily acts as an agent of the pleasure principle, a trickster who disrupts community order. His willingness to mock, parody, and otherwise abuse religious discourse for unorthodox purposes illustrates the nature of his belief in Christian doctrine. Sut believes as the blasphemer believes, negatively.

The fundamental tenet of Sut's belief, however, is identical with his community's orthodox Christianity: "univarsal onregenerit human nater" (245). When, in "Contempt of Court—Almost," Sut lists a number of concrete examples to show what he means by "onregenerit human nater," the thread running through them all is people's arbitrary and mean-spirited enmity for each other. The example par excellence of this enmity is Dad: "{the bulldog pup} wer the only critter I ever know'd dad tu be good tu, an' narra pusson yet" (278). This enmity is antithetical to community and thus represents the basic transgression against Sut's idea of proper behavior. Against this manifestation of unregeneracy Sut directs the force of his comic sermons, which usually consist of practical jokes.

Such scapegoating, however, does not constitute a morality, for Sut does not believe people will change. Rather, his motivation is an impulsive desire to expose someone's pretense of being outside the basic fact of unregeneracy, for the postulate about human nature most emphatically includes Sut and is part of the meaning of his constant reference to himself as a "nat'ral born durn'd fool."[11] When Parson Bullen says that Sut is "a livin proof ove the hell-desarvin natur ove man" (59), no one understands that better than Sut himself. What galls Sut is when people like Bullen act as though they are clearly exempt from the same statement. "Well, durn my rags ef gittin ove religun ain't the city ove rayfuge now-a-days; yu jis' let a raskil git hissef cotch, an' maul'd, *fur his dam meanness,* an' he jines chuch jis' es soon es he kin straitch his face long enuf tu fill the pius standurd" (274, emphasis added). Thus Bullen is guilty of the sin of pride, a fault that hollows out Bullen's claim of respectability and, like Dad's meanness, raises a threat to community. Yet Sut's "sermons" against meanness do not erase his own obviously mean acts; together they illustrate the complexity of his role as fool, both threatening and maintaining the amity fundamental to any community.

A corollary of human nature's unregenerate quality is the propensity to indulge one's appetite. The figure for such "sins of the flesh" is, again, Hoss Lovingood. When Sut's father discards the sign of his humanity, clothes, and behaves like both a horse and a steer, he reveals everyone's link to the animal world of mere appetite, body. Denial of that link by sheriffs and parsons constitutes part of the claim to respectability by such folks, and exposure of that link—entailing a diminution of respectability—is a standard outcome of *Yarns.* Sheriff Doltin, for example, is exposed as an adulterer. Moreover, all the preachers in the stories are exposed as worldly because they succumb to the desires of the body. Thus, a black Baptist preacher and a white, Hardshell Baptist preacher both are fond of whiskey (161,

184), a Methodist preacher is fond of food (161), and Sut's archenemy, the Methodist Parson Bullen, is fond of both, for among the items that fly out of Bullen's clothes as he tries to shake the lizards Sut has released up his pant leg are "fifteen shorten'd biskits, a boiled chicken, . . . a hunk ove terbacker, {and} a sprinkil ove whisky" (55). Parson Clapshaw is the apex of this enslavement to creature comfort, for he retires from circuit riding to marry the well-endowed Sicily Burns, possessed not only of good looks but a dowry substantial enough to set him up as storekeeper.[12]

Sut is most acutely aware of the weakness of the flesh in his dealings with Sicily Burns, whose charms he describes vividly and to whom he reacts like a comic version of the traditional lovesick swain. An Aristophanic embodiment of comic principle, Sut is all for food and drink and sex. His animus against respectable folks, moreover, goes beyond a pretense to be above those desires: "George, this worl am all 'rong enyhow, more temtashun than perventitive; ef hit wer ekal, I'd stand hit. What kin the ole prechurs an' the ugly wimen 'spect ove us, 'sposed es we ar tu sich invenshuns es {Sicily} am? Oh, hits jis' no use in thar talkin, an' groanin, an' sweatin tharsefs about hit; they mus' jis' upset nater ontu her hed, an keep her thar, ur shet up" (77). Sut does not frame his problem in moral terms. More fundamental than hypocrisy or other social forms of controlling desire, the problem is human nature itself. Because desire is temptation *and* is built into human nature, prevention could exist only if human nature were changed. In reality, desires can neither be always satisfied nor always controlled. From the viewpoint of the durn'd fool preacher, "univarsal onregenerit human nater" is a problem without a solution—something to be ridiculed, not rectified.

II

Giving Sut the habit of expressing himself with biblical allusions and making the concept of universal unregeneracy a theme of several tales signal the commitment by Harris to representing Sut-as-fool through the role of comic preacher. Two other concepts depend upon the idea of unregeneracy and round out Sut's "religion": tribulation on earth and retribution in the hereafter.

In his enumeration of examples of universal unregeneracy Sut points out that pain and disappointment—tribulations—are what stand between an individual and the grave (246). In another instance, when Sut imitates the voice of Sicily Burns as part of a scheme to scare her lover, Gus Fabin, he refers to signs and wonders in the air that signify their sin and then exhorts Fabin to begin a "rale strong devil skurin prayr, . . . fur thars vexashun ove sperit an' bodily tribulashun ahead fur us bof."[13] Sut's speech wonderfully parodies the sinner who has seen the error of her ways. While Sut is aware that tribulations are spiritual as well as physical in nature (71) and that the ultimate tribulation is hell (176), the comic perspective of Yarns emphasizes bodily pain, even for animals. When his howling dog runs past him in the street, a victim of some town prankster, Sut thinks of "Dad's ho'net tribulashun, an' felt that thar wur such a thing as a tribulashun at las'" (151–52). Of course, someone always looks as though he or she has been soundly thrashed by the end of a tale. When Sut begins to peel away his starched shirt from his body ("Sut's New-Fangled Shirt"), he calls the awful pain a "quick-stingin trebulashun" (33).

Such representations of physical pain, usually the direct result of Sut's machinations, are the standard fare of Yarns. Equally ubiquitous is the fright that accompanies the pain. This combination of fright and pain is roughly equivalent to the religious notion that people must suffer. One of the foolish traits qualifying Sut as mock preacher is his ability to "git intu more durn'd misfortnit skeery scrapes, than enybody, an' then run outen them faster, by golly, nor enybody" (172). Scares or scrapes are the colloquial version of tribulations. It is not surprising to point out that the plots of all the tales in Sut Lovingood. Yarns Spun by a "Nat'ral Born Durn'd Fool" are structured by someone's involvement in a scary scrape. Less apparent is the way in which such scares and scrapes are sometimes directly presented as tribulations that function as a purification of the sufferer. Examples are the pain Sut endures from his shirt, the scare Gus Fabin receives, and, as we shall see, the series of scares Sut doles out in "Frustrating a Funeral." Even in the stories where religious discourse is not directly employed, the basically religious idea of purification remains a motive, for Sut either consciously wishes to purify his community of meanness of spirit or unconsciously wishes to purify himself of such a spirit. Perhaps Sut's unconscious desire to purify himself can be more properly described as a thoughtless want, like scratching an itch. Such a trope is more consonant with the comic tone of Yarns.

However much tribuation is presented as purifying, at times Sut's tales question the religious idea that tribulations lead to purification. Such contradiction should be seen as commensurate with Sut's role as trickster, by definition the playful enemy of boundaries. Scares may therefore cause someone's faith to weaken. Such is the case with Clapshaw the circuit rider when he sees Sut riding toward him at the height of Sut's tribulation with the soda powder he has drunk, thinking it was a love potion: "As I cum tarin along, [Clapshaw] hilt up his hans like he wanted tu pray fur me; but es I wanted sumthin tu reach furder, an' take a ranker holt nur his prars cud, I jis' rambled ahead. I wer hot arter a ten-hoss dubbil-actin steam paunch-pump, wif wun aind sock'd deep intu my soda lake, an' a strong manbody doctur at tuther; hit wer my *big want* jis' then. *He* tuck a skeer, es I wer cumin strait fur him; his faith gin out" (82–83). The circuit rider's fear of physical harm is matched by Sut's desire for physical aid that reaches further and has an ability to "scratch" more vigorously than does prayer. Sut's practical response to his situation is, in fact, his fundamental reaction to tribulation. "When I'se in trubbil, skeer, ur tormint, I dus but wun thing, an' that's onresistabil, onekeled, an' durn'd fas' runnin, an' I jis' keeps at hit till I gits cumfort" (71). Such a response emphasizes the foolish presentation of religious discourse, not its morality. While Sut can unleash tribulation designed to purify the soul and can speak in biblical phrasing about manyfold tribulations this side of hell (176), he remains a *comic* preacher, one whose wish for fun is as least as strong as his wish for chastisement. While Sut can be earnest in his use of religious discourse to speak of the failings of people (himself included), he never loses his basic parodic function, to reduce spiritual values to material ones. Thus the comfort of spirituality will always lose out to the comfort gained from physically running from trouble because for Sut running is so immediate and instinctual.

I have been arguing that notions about what constitutes right and wrong behavior lie at the core of Sut's role as fool preacher. Such notions, of course, imply a system of justice. In Calvinistic terms, this system of justice becomes the idea of "divine retribution," God's punishment for transgressing sacred law. God's retribution is often represented by the threat of the devil and hell. That Sut maintains a belief in the idea of divine retribution is clear when we examine in some detail the stories "Sut Lovingood's Daddy, Acting Horse" and "Sut's New-Fangled Shirt," which begin *Yarns*, as well as "Dad's Dog School," which ends it. All are concerned with Sut's relationship to his family.

The opening stories should be read as complements of each other, Sut's mishap with a new, freshly starched shirt commenting upon Hoss Lovingood's encounter with a swarm of hornets while "acting horse." Though Sut does nothing to put his father into the role of victim, once Hoss Lovingood has jumped into the creek to avoid the hornets, Sut taunts his father, prompting vows of revenge and the necessity for Sut's departure. "Them words . . . mus' be my las, knowin dad's onmollified nater. I broke frum them parts, an' sorter cum over yere tu the copper mines" (27). Harris thus provides the rationale for Sut's career as fool, inasmuch as his departure is triggered by laughter, as well as the rationale for his presence in Ducktown. Harris's representation of Sut's break with his family follows the historical pattern for many actual antebellum men, the son breaking with the father by leaving home to seek a new fortune, in this case a piece of the economic boom associated with the copper mines near the Hiwasee River in Polk County.[14] In effect, the next story, "Sut's New-Fangled Shirt," reveals the guilt Sut feels about that break. Summing up his misadventure for his favorite interlocuter, George, Sut says:

> Hits a retribushun sartin, the biggest kine ove a preacher's regular retribushun, what am to be foun' in the Holy Book.
> Dus yu mine my racin dad, wif sum ho'nets, an' so forth, intu the krick?
> Well, this am what cums ove hit. I'll drownd mysef, see ef I don't, that is ef I don't die frum that hellfired shut. (35–36)

Sut's familiarity with the fundamentalist emphasis on the ultimate retribution of hell-fire is apparently a long-standing one, as the last story in *Yarns*, "Dad's Dog School," makes clear. Like the lead tale about dad "acting horse," this narrative recounts events from Sut's background, in this case when he was "'bout sixteen" (278). Also like the lead tale, this story partly functions as Sut's explanation for his own chronically foolish behavior: he is his father's child. But Sut sees the ridiculous attempt to train their dog, which takes place on a Sunday, as a parody of Sabbath solemnity too. He describes as a family devotion (286) his father's crawling inside the hide of a freshly skinned steer in order to teach their bulldog pup to grab its opponent and not let go. The joke has the fearful piquancy for Sut of any well-delivered blasphemy because he is quite aware that his family's behavior profanes the Lord's day: "I hearn a new soun in the thicket, an' hit bein Sunday, I wer sorter 'spectin a retribushun ove sum nater" (285).

But the sound of retribution Sut hears is only Squire Haney going to meeting on his horse.[15] Haney is one of the local gentry—money lender, landowner, and elder in the church. His piety is comically revealed through the actions of his livestock, for his horse is of a pious turn of mind (it does not kick, gallop, or chew its bridle) and his hens never lay on Sunday. The squire gives the whole of Sunday to the Lord, controls the purse strings of the church, and chastises backsliders. "He wer secon enjineer ove a mersheen, made outen . . . thin minded pussons, fur the pupus, es they sed, ove squelchin sin in the neighborhood, amung sich domestic heathins es us" (287). Squire Haney also represents the prototype for all the hypocrites that Sut will attack in his career at Ducktown. The Squire is known not only for his activities with the local church but also for "shaving notes of hand," that is, purchasing personal IOUs at a price reduced below the legal or customary rate in order to turn a quick profit. As if this kind of financial manipulation were not enough, Haney supplements the action by giving his victims religious tracts warning against the vanity of storing up earthly goods. Moreover, Sut's mother suggests Haney's sexual impropriety when she says that the squire should leave or he will be "late fur meetin, speshully ef he stops at *Missis Givinses*" (289).

That sarcastic remark from Mam is hardly an offhand one. When Squire Haney comes out from the woods on his horse and interrupts the Lovingoods' family devotion, he chastises them for tormenting animals and breaking the Sabbath, calling them "onregenerits" and demanding to know the whereabouts of the "patriark ove this depraved famerly" (288). The joke is that the patriarch is right in front of him, sewn into the hide of a steer and bellowing with pain because the bulldog pup now has a lockjaw hold on his nose. Yet Sut's reaction to the squire's sudden appearance is not a religious fear of Sabbath breaking but a social shame for the family's way of living, encompassed both by his dad's obvious folly and by Mam's "bar laigs an' open collar." Sut feels an overpowering urge to run from the scene but does not because he notices "the squar, blazin look mam met [the Squire] wif" (286). If she could stand the storm, Sut decides he can too. Mam's answer to the squire's question matches her look: "Look a-yere, Squire Haney . . . I'se {the} patriark jis' now; . . . yu'd bes' trot along tu yer meetin. This am a *privit soshul famerly* '*musement* an' hit needs no wallin up ove eyes, nur groanin, nur second han low-quartered pray'rs tu make hit purfeck, 'sides, we's got no notes tu shave, nur gals ole enuf tu convart, so yu' better jis' go way wif yer four-laig'd, bal-faced pulpit, an' preach tu sich es yersef, sumwhat else; go 'long Squire, that's a good feller" (288–89).

Mam's answer reveals several things. First, she demonstrates the fierce southern pride that resents even the slightest aspersion against one's behavior and the equally fierce independence that resents any intrusion into one's privacy. But more to the point is Mam's translation of these qualities, which characterized all classes of the southern white population, into a blistering attack on the morality of one who sets himself up as a paragon of virtue in the community. Though my argument about Sut's foolish use of religious discourse downplays any consistent intent to use that discourse for moral purposes, clearly Mam's awareness of Squire Haney's worldliness (his financial dealings) and sensuality (Mrs. Givins and the reference to girls old enough to convert) provides Sut with a model for detecting hypocrisy. Moreover, Mam's response to Haney's righteousness illustrates the relationship Sut will maintain toward religion: a nonmeeting, quasibelief in evangelical Christianity laced, however, with comic, folkish attitudes. We have a sense of this mixture even before Squire Haney arrives when Mam reacts to her husband's plan for training the pup: "Lovingood, yu'll keep on wif yer devilmint an' nonsense, ontil yu fetch the day ove jedgement ontu our bar heds sum night, kerthrash, afore hits time, ur some uther ailment—collery—measils—pollygamy, ur sum sich like, jis' see ef yu don't" (279–80). The incident with Squire Haney, then, reveals Mam as the probable source of Sut's inchoate morality and considerable familiarity with the Bible and Christian tenets. Dad as the model for foolishness, Mam for perspicacity—both parents contribute to Sut as comic preacher.

If Mam should be thought of as Sut's role model for his preaching ways, her behavior in "Dad's Dog School" toward her husband provides a model for the comic manifestation of those preaching ways too: she beats Hoss Lovingood, still in the steer's hide on all fours and still trying to break the dog's hold, with a wooden beanpole. This penultimate scene of the tale emblemizes the usual physical retribution of Sut's comic sermons. In addition, the scene creates an allegory basic to *Sut Lovingood. Yarns Spun by a "Nat'ral Born Durn'd Fool."* Mam represents conscience, not religiously orthodox but sincere. Dad is *the* symbol of original sin and the unregenerate, representing "the blind bull, Human nater" (123), that deserves to be punished, needs to be chastised, to achieve salvation. This allegory suggests the historical fact that most men in the antebellum South did not join churches while most women did and then tried to convert their stubborn husbands.[16] The allegory also represents what comes closest to morality in Sut's behavior: he is all too aware of his replication of Dad's unregenerate fool nature while, like Mam, he maintains his antipathy against those, like Dad or Haney, who refuse to acknowledge their foolish or hypocritical natures.

In *Yarns*, retribution from God often means evoking the devil. For Sut personally, Satan is never far away, and when he dreams of things that frighten him, the list includes the devil and hell (69, 299). This sense of the devil's presence is partly attributable to folk belief in supernatural powers, an attitude exemplified even by Clapshaw, the circuit rider married to Sicily Burns who "believes in 'witches, an' warlocks, an' long nebbed things'" (j). Sut "b'leves strong in ghosts, an' in forewarnins too" (213). For most of the folk, the devil was a constant presence. Thus, when a man from North Carolina is caught up in a trick perpetrated by Sut, he says, "H——l's busted plumb open, an' this yere mountain's full ove the devils" (g), and one woman, fortunate to be only a spectator of another trick, says that what she saw must be "the Devil arter a tax collector" (47). Sut's profound belief in the nearby presence of the devil matches the evangelical emphasis on the necessary justice of God. His attitude toward the devil, however, is more complicated than most. When Sheriff Doltin says Sut has "'play'd hell,'" and Sut replies, "'Folks generlly sez that's my trade'" (259), clearly all concerned believe Sut to be a first-rate troublemaker of the sort usually referred to as a hell-raiser.

But, if Sut usually plays hell in the sense of behaving wildly and unsociably, at other times he can sound so much like a true preacher using hell-fire and brimstone that he seems to lose his parodic function and occupy the figurative center of his community. Sut "preaching" against a tavern, for example, says it is the worst place this side of hell, with a "brimstone retribushun . . . a-follerin clost arter hit" (179). Doggery owners are said to help the devil catch sinners (221), but being a tavern owner means losing one's soul: "When the devil takes a likin tu a feller, an' wants tu make a sure thing ove gittin him, he jis' puts hit intu his hed to open a cat-fish tavern" (177–78).

In "Frustrating a Funeral" Sut demonstrates more completely his ability to play hell and uphold traditional values, as a preacher would invoke demons in a sermon to bring sinners to an awareness of their ways. Sut finds himself an uninvited mourner at the wake of a slave because one of the town doctors wants the cadavar for dis-section. Sut wants to avoid digging up the grave, so his plan is to substitute a drunk mourner for the corpse, but he is not satisfied with a simple swap. Major, the drunken slave, is made to look like "a purfeck dogratype ove the devil, tuck while he wer smokin mad 'bout sum raskil . . . jinin meetin on his death-bed, an' 'scapin" (212–13), while the mortal remains of Seize also resemble the Evil One, complete with snakes and a pitchfork. With Major installed in the coffin, Sut commences his exhortation of sinners, using Seize.

His first victim is Simon, known for preaching among his fellow slaves. At the moment Simon sees the "skeer makin mersheen" (213) Sut has made of Seize, Sut "imitates" the devil's voice, accus-ing Simon of stealing corn, which in fact Sut had seen him do. In a panic, Simon falls out the door, faints, and then runs off. More vic-tims follow, including Mr. Hunnicut and Mrs. Loftin, symbolically accused of adultery by Sut when he tells Mrs. Hunnicut he saw the two "way up in the air, ridin a-straddil ove a burnin ladder" (218). Both Mrs. Hunnicut and her black cook believe the sign, the cook saying that she "know dis tree munf Missis Loftin fotch de debil heah" (219). When Major wakes up in the coffin as it is on its way to the cemetery, he frightens not only all those in the procession but also (with the help of Sut's voice) the doggery keeper and the sher-iff. The doctor Sut was supposed to help is especially included in Sut's list of sinners because, Sut says, a look at Seize "wud take away {the doctor's} appertite fur grave-yards . . . an' mout even make him jine meetins. I cudn't tell how much good hit mout du the on-b'lever" (214). Perhaps more than any other tale except "Sut's Ser-mon," "Frustrating a Funeral" reads like a deliberate effort on Sut's part to "preach a sermon," in this case using artful representations of hell-fire to chastise sinners. Nevertheless, Sut does not lose an es-sentially playful attitude about his own behavior. Finishing up the grotesquely comic tale, Sut says he performed two Christian duties: one, he buried Seize; two, he "minister'd ontu Wright's doggery, an' run hit till . . . hit went dry" (226). This presentation of religious discourse typifies Sut as mock preacher, for any sense of moral intent is undercut by the joke enwrapping the pious sentiment. Sut is not a parson *manque* but a parson *malgré lui*.

III

As comic fool, Sut has a license to flaunt order, and his antics target secular as well as sacred law. Throughout *Yarns* this flaunting produces ironic results because Sut's role as comic preacher functions to maintain community values. However, such improper maintenance would not be necessary if officials, such as preachers and sheriffs, behaved properly. In Sut's mind, phony sheriffs are indistinguishable from phony parsons, a basic attitude suggested in an insult directed against a judge by Wirt Staples, a good friend of Sut's: "yu ole false apostil ove lor" (251).

The intertwining of sacred and secular law is made clear in a number of places in *Yarns*. A particularly good example comes at the beginning of "Rare Ripe Garden-Seed," which leads off a trio of stories ("Contempt of Court—Almost" and "Trapping a Sheriff" follow) that collectively tells of the downfall of the local sheriff, John Doltin, who is exposed as an adulterer by Sut, his friend Wirt Staples, and Wirt's wife Susan. At the outset, Sut speaks of his first scare. He is just a child, dressed in nothing but a shift that is split from neck to tail and held together with a drawstring and a hem. The scare will come from a sheriff's sudden appearance to confiscate the family's furniture, presumably for debts owed, but describing his attire causes Sut to digress, asking George what he would do if Sut came to George's city church dressed the same and sat in George's pew. This image of license in sacred precincts is followed by a comic food chain, bishops at the top, that parodies the Great Chain of Being, implying that high church officials always get to the trough first. The flaunting of church-going decorum and the reducing of spiritual leadership to gluttony prefaces the tales about the sheriff because in them Sut and his accomplices will flaunt an official of secular law, revealing him to be like the bishops—nothing more than appetite. At bottom, the issue is hypocrisy or the *appearance* of respectability. The stories about preachers and sheriffs emphasize their hollow respectability and undeserved pride. Pride is dangerous to a democratic community because it stresses a better-than-thou attitude. This "sin" is doubly threatening when parsons and sheriffs act as though they are above the laws they preach or enforce.

I place "sin" in quotes because Sut's homespun backwoods dialect rewrites the religious discourse of *Yarns*. Thus tribulations become "skeers," while original sin and the consequent unregeneracy of human nature become "dam meanness." Because the enmity represented by meanness and pride is virtually a universal condition that threatens community by emphasizing separateness and strife, it would seem that *Yarns* argues against the existence of "grace," which might be defined as the neighborly amity that forms the bedrock of any community. This gloomy conclusion seems justified by the numerous examples of adulterous couples in the tales. How authentic can a community be when its backbone—the family—is represented by so many shams? Historically, Ducktown, like any antebellum southern community, no doubt had its share of worthy families, parsons, and sheriffs. And while *Yarns* may emphasize negative behavior for comic purposes, an example of an admirable family does exist in the persons of Susan and Wirt Staples. In effect, the Stapleses represent grace and salvation, the possibility of people who transcend mean-spirited behavior and unneighborly pride.

My use of theological vocabulary, especially transcendence, seems to make Susan and Wirt saints. They of course are as unorthodox an example of a worthy family as Sut is a preacher. Indeed, a whiskey-soaked boast by Wirt makes clear that he is a backwoods roarer (250–51).[17] And Susan is certainly as fun-loving and eager to unmask damn meanness as Sut, given her role as the architect of Sheriff Doltin's punishment. As comic versions of saints, Wirt and Susan do not stretch their faces to fit the dour mold of what passes for piety, nor do they pretend to abjure the body while in fact indulging it illicitly. Instead, descriptions of them suggest their physical beauty, Wirt with the strength typical of the roarer (253) and Susan "es purty es a hen canary" (260). Significantly, Susan's good looks are accompanied by a good nature that contrasts with the other beautiful woman of *Yarns*, Sicily Burns, a good nature manifested in Susan's demeanor, especially toward Wirt: "She aint one ove yure she-cat wimmin, allers spittin an' groanin, an' swellin thar tails 'bout thar vartu. She never talks a word about hit, no more nor if she didn't hev eny; an' she hes es true a heart es ever beat agin a shiff hem, . . . a-smilin an' a-flashin her talkin eyes lovinly at her hansum husbun" (260, 262).

Susan and Wirt's love represents the ties that bind not just family life but the neighborly life of a true community. Doltin's adulterous behavior cuts those ties, for he only pretends to live as a neighbor, a pretense dramatized by his answer when Wirt asks what Doltin is doing trying to kiss Susan: "'Yer—yer wife got her coatail tangled in the briars, an' I wer jis' in a neighborly way *ontanglin her*'" (264–65). Doltin's revises the rule "love thy neighbor" to "love thy neighbor till her husband comes home."

When parsons and sheriffs, pillars of communal law and order, actually enact disorder, the chaotic punishment that Sut constructs for them represents just deserts. The license of the fool is especially effective at revealing licentious behavior, and as self-proclaimed fool, Sut comically inverts what is already inverted when he appropriates the role of these so-called upholders of the law by righteously doling out justice for their transgressions. This inversion is obvious in Sut's use of comic deadpan to mimic piety, as when Sut fools Parson Bullen at the camp meeting by appearing with a face indicative of sorrow for sins (51) or when he mocks the rhetoric and manner of a "hard-shell" preacher (185). Another good example is Sut's retort to Mrs. Rogers, who implicitly accuses Sut and his friends of stealing her eggs and butter by sarcastically noting that their presence near her springhouse is not the holding of meeting. In a mock-pious fashion Sut claims that Hen Baily has been poisoned by Mrs. Rogers's dairy products (thus confirming her worst fears) when in fact he has swallowed turpentine and a live lizard: "Sez I, mouns'us solimn, straitenin mysef up wif foldid arms, 'Missis Rogers, . . . take a look at sum ove yu're work. That ar a-dyin feller bein; let jis' a few ove yer bowils melt, an' pour out rite yere in pity an' rey-morse'" (205). Sut not only uses deadpan to counter her reference to the crowd's unsanctified status but he also implies a rebuke for her notorious habit of feeding her workhands with buttermilk so sour "hit wud eat hits way outen a yeathen crock in wun nite" (206). Sut's consciousness of such mean-spirited acts and his readiness to chastise for them might have us agree with Sicily Burns's mother when she claims that Sut is not "one half es durn'd a fool es ole Burns, an' ten times more ove a Cristshun than Clapshaw" (105).

When Susan prepares a supper for Wirt and Sut after they have planned how to trap Doltin, the three at table constitute a community of comic saints. Sut refers to the meal as "a rale suckit-rider's supper, whar the 'oman ove the hous' wer a rich b'lever" (261), and in laughable fashion that is exactly what the scene represents. Sut is the preacher being served a lavish repast by a household that believes in his comic dogma, which extols generosity and states that the mean-spirited and hypocritical shall be punished or, as Sut puts it, initiated "intu the seekrit ove home-made durnashun" (263). The supper, lovingly recounted by Sut in copious detail, constitutes meeting for the "saints" Susan and Wirt and Sut. In keeping with the comic principle of reducing spiritual and moral values to a material plane, a principle about to be prosecuted upon the body of Sheriff Doltin, the supper is a parodic communion supper, celebrating not what bread and wine might symbolize but celebrating instead the material symbols themselves, food and drink. However, for all the amusement this inversion is designed to create, the supper also functions to bind people to a common purpose, just as Sut's role of fool places him at the margin yet allows him to mock the center in such a way as to usurp its power. The supper establishes a comic community marked by a spirit of generosity.

IV

Exemplified by an exalted notion of hospitality, a generous spirit was an important feature of southern culture before the Civil War. The supper taken by Sut with Susan and Wirt Staples presents a comic embodiment of that ideal. Such a presentation underscores the ambiguity of Sut playing the fool. On the one hand, he seems a champion of a core southern value; on the other, he remains a comic figure on the margin. As a self-proclaimed nat'ral born durn'd fool, Sut in effect represents an exaggeration of the fringe status of the mountaineer; that is, even in the mountains of east Tennessee, Sut the fool would be on the edge of his community, and that sense of being on the outside is doubled when he moves to Ducktown. I have argued, however, that by virtue of his homespun religious rhetoric Sut assumes a central role in the maintenance of an idea of community that could characterize a place like Ducktown. I now want to raise the stakes and claim that he is even more important. Sut is not only potentially the center of a particular southern community; he should also be seen as the comic bard of the Old South. Kenneth Lynn once said that "Sut" is an ugly contraction of "South." He was right. After all, the comic is a species of the ugly.

Sut, as a yarnspinning, whiskey-drinking pleasure seeker, represents, in his own comic and not-so-pretty way, values besides generosity that were important to the antebellum South's sense of identity: leisure, liberty, and the communal function of talking.[18]

Leisure was probably as crucial as generosity to a sense of southern identity. I do not mean that no one in the antebellum South valued hard work or that hard work, and plenty of it, did not happen. However, hard work was not raised to an ideal in the South the way it was in New England. Undoubtedly this difference owed some of its existence to the slave system, which encouraged southerners to lead or aspire to an aristocratic life of ease. But it also stemmed from preexisting facts of climate and soil conditions as well as the Old World culture of many immigrants to the southern portions of North America. For very specific material reasons the southern white, whether high or low on the economic scale, attempted to create a life-style that did not emphasize personal hard labor.[19]

Though Sut seems to be that most notorious of stereotypes about the leisured life of a southerner, poor white trash, *Yarns* does sometimes show him capable of work. For example, he builds Betts Carr an ash hopper (30, 32). And Sut apparently earns money from a still, if his routine walk through town can be taken as a round of deliveries (158).[20] Nevertheless, work in the usual sense does not occupy much of Sut's life. His true avocations are *drinking* whiskey and telling stories. For Sut, these activities are virtually the same. When he narrates, Sut distills raw experience into something as pleasurable as whiskey—and as ubiquitous to the social scene. In a community where leisure time is highly valued, whiskey is very often the complement to yarns: one is poured into the mouth and the other pours from the mouth. Whiskey facilitates the yarn pouring forth, which in turn necessitates more whiskey pouring. In the comic, backwoods stories of the antebellum South, a tipping of a flask or bottle can precede a tale as surely as a throat-clearing call begins a bardic singer's epic song. As a yarnspinner who sounds like a comic preacher and makes whiskey, Sut unofficially challenges Parson Bullen, who is known for selling adulterated whiskey (86). Bullen as Sut's chief rival thus epitomizes those people against whom Sut always directs his comic sermons, the mean-spirited. In effect, Sut's impromptu campaigns are always against bad spirits.

If the South valued generosity and leisure, it also placed a premium on liberty, and boyhood in *Yarns* represents the comic version of liberty: freedom from responsibility. His intention for making the book, Sut tells us in his preface, is to raise "sich a laugh es is remembered [in] keerless boyhood" (xi). Sut, whose age one can never be sure of but who has white hair and is apparently old enough to remember what George and Lum did thirty-five years ago, never acts his age. His freedom from responsibility—manifested by his whiskey drinking, story telling, and wild pranks—makes him seem to deserve the epithet "yung man" a preacher gives him (184). Indeed, Sut's pranks are essentially boyish, designed to disrupt the serious business of society. When a number of Knoxvillians plot against a Yankee razor grinder who sets himself up to lecture to that southern community, Sut says that the Yankee's lecture should not have included a comment about the depravity of man in boyhood, "fur hit wer boys what he wer dealin wif jis' then" (63). Sut's story about George and Lum Jones when they are thirteen, a story of eavesdropping on a meeting of Masons to learn their secrets, refers to the boys as "the durndest littil back-slidin devils outen jail" (116). At bottom, all the "devilment" that goes on in *Yarns* consists of boyish pranks.[21]

In this vein, *Sut Lovingood. Yarns Spun by a "Nat'ral Born Durn'd Fool"* resembles *The Adventures of Tom Sawyer;* both underline the liberty of youth. Despite Sut's interrupting George's eulogy to boyhood that is sentimental even by the standards of *Tom Sawyer,* Sut would agree when George speaks of a "happy, ragged, thoughtless" (115) quality of boyhood, for Sut embodies what George describes, a pleasurable freedom from rational thought. Yet, if *Tom Sawyer* is a hymn to boyhood, *Yarns* is a drinking song that comically emphasizes the continued presence of the boy in the man instead of a nostalgia for a boy forever gone. Moreover, Tom Sawyer's world does not contain the elemental level of fear and desire and gratification that Sut's world represents. Finally, Tom never remains for long outside his community; Sut never remains for long inside his. Like a natural fool, like a child, Sut seems to be excused from the censure of rational, responsible behavior.

The last aspect of Sut's character that suggests his role as comic bard involves the communal function of talking in the Old South. In a culture that valued oratory, both political and religious, as its highest form of literature, narrating, whether for information or for entertainment, assumed a vital role, binding together its participants with a sharing of events that established and reinforced the

values of the social group. In this role, Sut as champion yarnspinner assumes a larger-than-life status. Yet Sut's talk, mirroring his
role as fool, operates ambiguously in his community, whether at a
particular or at a general level. His wild tales, reeking of whiskey
and a careless freedom, partly function as the antics of sacred
clowns do for Zuni Indians—as encouragement for a mass return of
repressed impulses. For a brief interval, the audience is allowed to
laugh at accounts or displays of how not to behave. It is this beyond-
the-pale quality that is so celebrated or lamented in discussions of
Sut's stories. My argument, however, suggests that a conservative
thread also runs through *Yarns* and that Sut upholds values that
were central to the Old South, even going so far as to mimic the religious rhetoric of evangelical Christianity. Perhaps narrating itself
constitutes Sut's most conservative act. By plotting a story out of his
wild, nonsensical actions, in effect Sut makes a bid to be taken as a
rational, adult member of a community. There is truth in that last
assertion if we also do not forget how the fool always undermines
such effects as he apparently achieves them. Sut's power comes not
from being the bard of the Old South who speaks as a preacher but
from playing hell with that role.

"He who would become wise must persist in his folly." William
Blake's proverb of hell seems particularly apt for Sut Lovingood,
who dispenses his own kind of perverse wisdom when he reminds
us that he is a natural born durned fool. The notion that there is a
wisdom in foolishness looks back to a favored figure of the Renaissance, the wise fool. My argument that Sut is a mock preacher insists on the similarity extending to the Christian background in
which the tradition of the fool arose. As Blake in *The Marriage of
Heaven and Hell* sought to overturn conventional wisdom about
how to lead a religious life, Harris uses *Sut Lovingood. Yarns Spun by
a "Nat'ral Born Durn'd Fool"* to challenge those who are complacent
about their rectitude. That is the wisdom that may be extracted from
the tales. But their comic power comes from the marvelous ex-
ploitation of the inherent ambiguity of the role of the fool. Licensed
to do what ought not be done and thus to draw ridicule, the fool disrupts in order to remind a community of its self in two ways: that it
too is ridiculous and that it should be better. Like the licensed fools
in medieval and Renaissance European cultures or Amerindian cultures such as the Zuni, Sut is meant to entertain the audience with
his presentations of chaos, but he is also meant to warn the audi-

ence against its own brands of foolishness. Like all fools, Sut helps willy-nilly to define community. Of course, Sut carries out this function in his own way. If *Yarns* argues for a proper way to behave in a community, that argument is not so much a moral imperative as an impulsive lashing out against those who threaten the community, a tongue-lashing that presents literal lashings of such undesirables. Those lashings are Sut's own style of comic wisdom.

Notes

1. Milton Rickels, *George Washington Harris* (New York: Twayne, 1965), 78, 83, 86, 96. Some of Rickels's comments appear in the selection reprinted for this collection. Kenneth S. Lynn, *Mark Twain and Southwestern Humor* (Boston: Little, Brown, 1959), 135–36, expresses a similar view on community and authority. For a view much closer to mine, see David C. Estes, "Sut Lovingood at the Camp Meeting: A Practical Joker Among the Backwoods Believers," *Southern Quarterly* 25 (1987): 53–65. Estes not only sees Sut as part of his community but also sees him as a "true pastor" (64). And for a discussion of Sut's public role that uses the notion of playing hell in a very different context, see John Wenke, "*Sut Lovingood's Yarns* {sic} and the Politics of Performance," *Studies in American Fiction* 15 (1987): 199–210. I have based my argument solely on Harris's book. The edition used is "*Sut Lovingood Yarns*": *A Facsimile of the 1867 Dick and Fitzgerald Edition*, ed. M. Thomas Inge (Memphis: Saint Lukes Press, 1987), and all parenthetical page insertions refer to this edition. Despite being published in 1867 and having one or two references to the Civil War, *Yarns* gives the feeling of taking place before the war and I will refer to the community represented in it as antebellum.

2. William Willeford, *The Fool and His Scepter: A Study in Clowns and Jesters and Their Audiences* (Chicago: Northwestern University Press, 1969), 133. See also Barbara Swain, *Fools and Folly During the Middle Ages and the Renaissance* (New York: Columbia University Press, 1932); Enid Welsford, *The Fool: His Social and Literary History* (London: Faber and Faber, 1935), esp. chap. 3; and Sandra Billington, *A Social History of the Fool* (New York: Saint Martin's Press, 1984).

3. Willeford, *Fool and His Scepter,* 158.

4. Although the town Sut lives in (or near) is never named and seems to be near Knoxville, we know that Harris met the historical Sut Miller in a place called Ducktown, in the southeastern corner of Tennessee. In order to emphasize the historical dimension of Sut's role as comic preacher, I will refer to his community as Ducktown. See Ben Harris McClary, "The Real Sut," in this volume, and Robert E. Barclay, *Ducktown Back in Raht's Time* (Chapel Hill: University of North Carolina Press, 1946). I follow Victor Turner's use of liminal: "Liminal to Liminoid in Play, Flow, Ritual: An Essay in Comparative Symbology," *Rice University Studies* 60 (1974): 53–92; and *The Ritual Process: Structure and Anti-Structure* (1969; reprint, Ithaca: Cornell University Press, 1977).

5. Ernest E. Leisy, "Jesse Holmes, The 'Fool Killer,'" *Publications of the Texas Folklore Society* 8 (1930): 152–54, and Ralph S. Boggs, "Running Down the Fool Killer," *Publications of the Texas Folklore Society* 14 (1938): 169–73, discuss a particular fool killer in nearby North Carolina, Jesse Holmes, who was popular particularly during the Civil War but also in the late 1850s. The fool killer is mentioned twice in *Yarns:* "Trapping a Sheriff" (264) and "Sut Lovingood's Chest Story" (h). In "Sut Lovingood Come to Life," Harris's first postwar Sut sketch, Sut is appointed "fool killer Gineril." The piece appeared originally in the *Nashville Union and American,* 3 May 1866. See M. Thomas Inge, ed., *High Times and Hard Times: Sketches and Tales by George Washington Harris* (Nashville: Vanderbilt University Press, 1967), 276–81.

6. Donald G. Mathews, *Religion in the Old South* (Chicago: University of Chicago Press, 1977); John B. Boles, "Evangelical Protestantism in the Old South: From Religious Dissent to Cultural Dominance," in *Religion of the Old South,* ed. Charles R. Wilson (Jackson: University of Mississippi Press, 1985), 13–34; David Edwin Harrell, Jr., "The Evolution of Plain-Folk Religion in the South, 1835–1920," and Wade Clark Roof, "Religious Change in the American South: The Case of the Unchurched," in *Varieties of Southern Religious Experience,* ed. Samuel S. Hill (Baton Rouge: Louisiana State University Press, 1988), 24–51, 192–210. Compare to the way ritual clowns function in Pueblo Indian communities: Louis A. Hieb,

"Meaning and Mismeaning: Toward an Understanding of the Ritual Clown," in *New Perspectives on the Pueblos*, ed. Alfonso Ortiz (Albuquerque: University of New Mexico Press, 1972), 163–95.

7. See Benjamin Franklin Fisher IV's article in this collection, "George Washington Harris and Supernaturalism."

8. Compare to Rickels's idea of Sut and religion: "Sut exists outside Christianity" (100); "Sut escapes the Christian conception of man. . . . He is the creator of his own being" (101)— both comments are in the selection for this collection; and Elmo Howell, "Timon in Tennessee: The Moral Fervor of George Washington Harris," also in this volume.

9. By 1850 only 20 percent of the clergy had any formal training. See Mathews, *Religion*, 23, 30, and esp. 85, 96. Also see *The Autobiography of Peter Cartwright, The Backwoods Preacher*, ed. W. P. Strickland (New York: Carlton and Porter, 1856), 4–7.

10. Biblical allusions include a light hidden under a basket (269), girding one's loins (191), and the call from labor to refreshment (119). Other references include Judas Iscariot (38), Job (76), Belteshazzar, comically spelled Beltashashur (79, 119), Joseph and Potiphar's wife (87–88), Beelzebub (83), Samson and the Philistines (191).

11. In medieval and Renaissance traditions, a "natural" fool is someone who is mentally defective, an idiot. Clearly, Sut is not an idiot in this sense, which makes him an "artificial" fool, acting foolishly for the entertainment and possible edification of others. See Welsford, *The Fool*, and Heather Arden, *Fool Plays: A Study of Satire in the "Sottie"* (Cambridge: Cambridge University Press, 1980). Rickels, *George Washington Harris*, sees Sut as closest to this artificial or court fool (105), yet he also thinks Sut personifies "mindlessness" (98). Noel Polk criticizes Rickels, saying, "Sut is not mindless and he is no fool," in "The Blind Bull, Human Nature: Sut Lovingood and the Damned Human Race," which is reprinted in this collection. Polk sees the phrase "nat'ral born durn'd fool" as ironic self-deprecation and Sut as a backwoods Socrates, a moral gadfly. This claim, however, does not exclude Sut from the role of the artificial fool. Sut may be, as many have argued, a backwoods version of the "wise fool" so favored by Renaissance writers,

but the degree of intention in any show of wisdom or satiric moral fervor is debatable. In my view, the fool figure always embodies the potential for exhibiting mindless clowning as well as wisdom. Compare to M. Thomas Inge, "Sut Lovingood: An Examination of the Nature of a 'Nat'ral Born Durn'd Fool,'" *Tennessee Historical Quarterly* 19 (1960): 231–51.

12. See Mathews, *Religion,* 86, for the Methodist habit of riding circuit for a while before marrying—often, a woman of means.

13. "Sut Lovingood's Chest Story," f. Inge's facsimile edition includes this tale left out of the original and paginates it with letters. See his "A Note on the Text."

14. Barclay characterizes the mining boom as follows: "the year 1850 . . . ushered in a decade that proved to be the most interesting and the most exciting that Ducktown had seen. . . . Every element which entered into similar stampedes throughout mining districts of the West in later years was present in the rush to Ducktown. Here was the scene of one of the most hectic scrambles of fortune seekers in the South" (*Ducktown,* 38). By 1854, the year Harris probably met Sut (Rickels, *George Washington Harris,* 28–29), the area was "thronged to overflowing with ardent speculators" (31–32).

15. The text also refers to this character as Squire Hanley.

16. See Mathews, *Religion,* for the role of women in the churches, 101–20.

17. Compare to Polk's description of Wirt and Susan. It is interesting that the snatch of a drinking song Wirt sings as part of his ring-tailed roarer's exhibition is called by Sut "one vearse ove the sixteen hundred an' ninety-ninth *hyme*" (251, emphasis added).

18. Lynn, *Mark Twain,* 137. The idea of the comic as a kind of ugliness is found in Aristotle's "Poetics" (1449a, 32–37). The word he uses, "to geloion," is usually rendered as "the ridiculous," but it could be translated as "the laughable." See the Revised Oxford Translation of *The Complete Works of Aristotle,* ed. Jonathan Barnes, Bollingen Series 71, 2 vols. (Princeton: Princeton University Press, 1984), 2:2319. A discussion of the values of the Old South leads into a number of debates. The ground of these discussions is whether or not the antebellum South possessed a "character" distinctive from the North and thus generative of its own values. For a good overview of the

historians' debate on this issue see Drew Gilpin Faust, "The Peculiar South Revisited: White Society, Culture, and Politics in the Antebellum Period, 1800–1860," in *Interpreting Southern History*, ed. John B. Boles and Evelyn Thomas Nolen (Baton Rouge: Louisiana State University Press, 1987), 78–119. Influential in making the argument for a distinct southern world view is the work of Eugene Genovese, starting with *The Political Economy of Slavery: Studies in the Economy and Society of the Slave South* (New York: Pantheon Books, 1965). Faust lists Genovese's later work. See also Edward Shapiro, "Frank L. Owsley and the Defense of Southern Identity," *Tennessee Historical Quarterly* 36 (1977): 75–94; Bertram Wyatt-Brown, *Southern Honor: Ethics and Behavior in the Old South* (New York: Oxford University Press, 1982); Randolph B. Campbell, "Planters and Plainfolks: The Social Structure of the Antebellum South," in Boles and Nolen, *Interpreting Southern History*, 49–77; and Grady McWhiney, *Cracker Culture: Celtic Ways in the Old South* (Tuscaloosa: University of Alabama Press, 1988). Eugene Current-Garcia argues that Sut symbolizes the Old South's "vigor and fertility." See "Sut Lovingood's Rare Ripe Southern Garden," *Studies in Short Fiction* 9 (1972): 129.

19. Leisure as a value has generated its own debate, one that is, again, intimately bound up with definitions of North and South. See David Bertelson, *The Lazy South* (New York: Oxford University Press, 1967); D. D. Bruce, Jr., "Play, Work and Ethics in the Old South," *Southern Folklore Quarterly* 41 (1977): 33–51; and C. Vann Woodward, "The Southern Ethic in a Puritan World," in his *American Counterpoint: Slavery and Racism in the North/South Dialogue* (New York: Oxford University Press, 1983). Bertelson and Woodward cast the debate about leisure versus laziness in the broad terms of Weber's analysis of capitalism and protestantism. For McWhiney, attitudes about work and leisure constitute the single most discernible cultural difference between North and South (*Cracker Culture,* 49).

20. Regardless of what might be said about the fictional character's work habits, Sut Miller, upon whom Sut Lovingood is based, was not a vagabond. McClary, in "The Real Sut," points out that Miller's farm was valued at $400 in the 1850 census.

Blanche Henry Clark, *The Tennessee Yeoman, 1840–1860* (Nashville: Vanderbilt University Press, 1942), also uses 1850 census documents to establish the number of small or non-slaveholding farmers in the state. Miller's farm places him squarely in the yeoman class and probably makes him a member of the "Celtic" economy of farmers who were oriented as much toward grazing as farming and more toward self-subsistence than markets. McClary notes that Sut Miller's farm was planted mainly in corn, not unusual of course, but one might speculate how much of that corn became whiskey and how much that conversion (again, not unusual) influenced Harris's conversion of Sut Miller to Sut Lovingood. If Sut Miller had a still, then Sut Lovingood as still operator and distributor in the town seems likely. In any case, Ducktown in the 1850s saw "a great deal of drunkenness, fighting, debauchery, and other ill conduct" (Barclay, *Ducktown*, 39). An enterprising man with a good supply of corn and his own still could make hard cash selling whiskey to the miners.

21. Since Jeannette Tandy first spoke of Sut as a "debased country boy" in *Crackerbox Philosophers in American Humor and Satire* (New York: Columbia University Press, 1925), 93, many critics refer to Sut as a young man. Inge, in "Examination of the Nature of a 'Nat'ral Born Durn'd Fool,'" makes the best argument for Sut being an adult. The ambiguity of his age fits his role as fool.

Uneasy Laughter

Sut Lovingood—Between Rip Van Winkle and Andrew Dice Clay

Sanford Pinsker

One could argue that Sut Lovingood is American humor's litmus test, the character who most divides readers into those appalled by his deadly, antisocial antics and those who find him "funny." Among the former one can list not only those contemporary students who complain that Sut's dialect makes for tough sledding but also the likes of Edmund Wilson, who wrote Sut down with these oft-quoted, uncomplimentary words: "a peasant squatting in his filth." Among the latter one can list not only those who pioneered Sut Lovingood study (e.g., Walter Blair, Milton Rickels, M. Thomas Inge) but also a growing band of hearty souls who assign such chestnuts as "Parson John Bullen's Lizards" or "Sicily Burns's Wedding" to their American literature classes and who dare the campus "thought police" to haul them in on charges of being racist, sexist, anti-Indian, anti-Semitic, or just plain un-American. The "one" who is going to argue all this—and to place Sut Lovingood somewhere between the subversive humor of Rip Van Winkle and the tirades of Andrew Dice Clay—is, of course, myself.

Let me begin by suggesting a few guiding principles: (1) that humor often goes for the bawdy or the body and most often for both at once, (2) that humor brings out Queen Victoria's magisterial dismissal—"We are not amused"—in those with pinched faces or political agendas and most often for those with both, (3) that humor, for all its tendency toward anarchism, is likely to be deeply conser-

vative beneath the skin, and (4) that humorous incidents thrive on
a wide range of incongruities but that humor itself often revolves
around the incongruity between wishful projection and a restrain-
ing environment.

That much said, consider Washington Irving's "Rip Van Winkle,"
a tale in which the battle of the sexes is given a distinctly American
spin. Rip, of course, is the quintessential henpecked husband, and
the revenge he perpetrates with his "tall tale" about a ten-year ben-
der in the Kaatskills is of a piece with later avatars on the same
theme—say, James Thurber's "The Unicorn and the Garden" or any
stand-up comic who punctuates his shtick with variations of Henny
Youngman's "Take my wife, please!" As Diedrich Knickerbocker,
Irving's seriocomic historian/narrator puts it, in an elevated diction
designed to convey both sobriety and verisimilitude:

> I have observed that he {Rip} was a simple, good-natured man; he was,
> moreover, a kind neighbor, and an obedient, henpecked husband. Indeed,
> to the latter circumstance might be owing that meekness of spirit which
> gained him such universal popularity, for those men are most apt to be ob-
> sequious and conciliating abroad who are under the discipline of shrews at
> home. Their tempers, doubtless, are rendered pliant and malleable in the
> fiery furnace of domestic tribulation, and a curtain lecture is worth all the
> sermons in the world for teaching the virtues of patience and long-suffering.
> A termagant wife may, therefore, in some respects, be considered a tolerable
> blessing; and if so, Rip Van Winkle was thrice blessed.

Granted, the other women in the village "took his part in all family squabbles and never failed, whenever they talked those matters
over in their evening gossipings, to lay all the blame on Dame Van
Winkle"—all of which serves to isolate Rip's wife from the community and to raise Judith Fetterley's feminist hackles:

> But what is a woman to do with "Rip Van Winkle"? How is she to read
> our "first and most famous" story in which that American imagination is
> born if the defining act of that imagination is to identify the real American
> Revolution with the avoidance of women, which means the avoidance of
> one's wife? What is the impact of this American dream on her? The answer
> is obvious: disastrous. . . . The woman who reads "Rip Van Winkle" finds
> herself excluded from the experience of the story. She is no part of the act
> of resistance, nor does she recognize herself in that which is being resisted.[1]

There is little question, I think, that Dame Van Winkle is cast as
the tale's comic butt. That she dies by breaking a blood vessel "in a
fit of passion at a New England peddler" (no doubt some cousin of
Sam Slick, the first in a long line of Yankee conmen) is seen as po-

etic justice for a life of combing poor Rip all to thunder. As Fetterley would have it, the tale's subtext places female readers in the untenable position of participating, and then approving, in her comic demise. Sisterhood, after all, should be stronger.

But my students—both male and female—tell me otherwise. For them, Rip suggests the very antithesis of Benjamin Franklin's earnest, hard-plugging heroes. He is a man who much prefers goofing off to keeping his eye fixed on the main chance. In short, Rip is a "simple, good-natured man" rather than a shark, the sort of person who "would rather starve on a penny than work for a pound." It is not so much that he has an aversion to work—indeed, he "would never refuse to assist a neighbor even in the roughest toil"— but, rather, that he shied away from any labor Franklinesque sorts would call "profitable."

Rip, in a word, stands four-square for *vacation,* and it is in that spirit that my students identify with his "foolish, well-oiled dispositions to take the world easy." Such respites from routine, I would argue, are hardly drawn along sexual lines; and if it is true that Rip's program seems thoroughly masculine—flying kites, shooting marbles, fishing, hunting—it is equally true that my female students usually have no trouble in making the appropriate translations.

On this level, then, when those students who know their Flaubert exclaim, "Rip, *c'est moi!*" the remark strikes me as entirely in order, although I hasten to add that the identifications suggested by Irving's subversive tale run deeper and that they have more to do with a masculine flight from domesticity and the responsibilities of parenthood than with androgynous "vacations." Granted, what Rip charts out is the essential rhythm of pastoral as William Empson defines the term—that is, as a movement from the complex to the simple. If the inside of his house is filled with hectoring, the outside is not only "the only side which, in truth, belongs to a henpecked husband" but also the side that includes the bench outside the village's small inn (where "sages, philsophers, and other idle personages" swapped stories or jawed over the events of the day) and, of course, the wilderness.

Dame Van Winkle can intrude upon the former but not the latter. And it is to wilderness—to Nature, as it were—that Rip flees and where he hatches up his liberating "tall tale." Interestingly enough, Rip's dreamscape is filled with authority figures, with strange, bearded men who reminded him "of the figures in an old Flemish painting." Art, in effect, comes springing to life as the odd crew "desisted from their play and stared at him with such fixed, statuelike gaze and such strange, uncouth lackluster countenances that his heart turned within him and his knees smote together." Indeed, Irving's tale revolves around "authority" in a wide variety of guises—from the patriarchal Nicholas Vedder (whose opinions are signaled by his pipe smoke) to the hallucinatory Dutch Masters whose bowling sends thunderclaps across the Kaatskills; from Dame Van Winkle's oppressive "petticoat government" to the appeal, and power, of Rip's "story."

Those with a mind to probe the details of Rip's protracted slumber hardly need break a sweat: Freudians, for example, can fix on the phallic possibilities of a Rip who awakens to find "an old firelock lying by him, the barrel encrusted with rust," while classicists can point out that Rip's twenty-year "odyssey" in the woods reduplicates the adventures of Odysseus. The rub, of course, is that deep readings can miss the story's central point: if anything, Rip *returns* a more masculine figure than when he departed and, unlike Odysseus, his "adventures" are a study in protracted stasis. Rather, what Rip's "story" accomplishes is nothing less than a victory over responsibility itself, whether defined as patriot or citizen, parent or spouse.

More than a hundred years after Irving's *The Sketch Book* (1820), Delmore Schwartz would write a troubling account of a young artist's coming of age entitled "In Dreams Begin Responsibilities"; I would argue that "Rip Van Winkle" suggests precisely the opposite—namely, how in dreams responsibilities can *end:* "Rip's daughter took him home to live with her; she had a snug, well-furnished house, and a stout, cheery farmer for a husband, whom Rip recollected as one of the urchins that used to climb upon his back. As to Rip's son and heir, who was the ditto of himself, seen leaning against the tree, he was employed to work on the farm, but evinced a hereditary disposition to attend to anything else but his business."

Rip's strange tale in effect becomes his ticket to the good life Dame Van Winkle's nagging had denied him, and "whenever her name was mentioned . . . he shook his head, shrugged his shoulders, and cast up his eyes, which might pass either for an expression of resignation to his fate or joy at his deliverance." The ambiguity eludes Knickerbocker (who, after all, is only interested in establishing the truthfulness of Rip's tale) but not, I would argue,

Irving himself. What he understands—and what subsequent writers would exploit—is the power of an unbridled imagination. To
Southwest humorists, the result was the tall tale, unraveled by grad-
ual increments and told with a poker face; to contemporary South
American writers, the impulse transmogrified into magical realism.
The essential point, however, remained much the same—namely,
that the whopper well told could make comic artists out of wastrels,
cultural heroes from certifiable ne'er-do-wells.

George Washington Harris's Sut Lovingood is, of course, an exaggerated case, for if "Rip Van Winkle" could exercise a Judith Fetterley, one can only imagine what an ornery, thoroughgoing sexist
like Sut might occasion. After all, the ring-tailed roarers we meet in
southern humor were hardly as docile, as passive, or (Fetterley
notwithstanding) as lovable as Rip. And if it is true that their words
often spoke more loudly than their actions (see, for example, the
battle between the Pet Child of Calamity and Sudden Death and
General Desolation in "The Raftsman Passage" of Mark Twain's *Life
on the Mississippi*), it is equally true that these backwoods behe-
moths knew how to eye-gouge and hair-tug.

For such characters, a good joke maimed its victim, a great one
killed him. And in this violent universe, Sut Lovingood may well be
the hands-down winner. Here, for example, is Sut's account of how
he terrorized Doctor Gus ("Gut Fatty") Fabin by blowing up a chest
in which the unfortunate doctor is hiding:

> I hearn him groan an' he trimbled till he shuck the chist, but he sot intu
> prayin fur the heathen, an' spread ove the gospil, like a hoss. I know'd that
> I hed planted a big skeer an' that hit would bar fruit afore moon down, so I
> jist snatched up a chunk ove fire ofen the hath an' toch off the powder on-
> der the tail ove the old hoss. Now I'll jist be continentally an espesially
> durned ef that chist didn't go outen the door breast high, an' the fus time hit
> struck the yeath wer forty feet down the hill. . . . The chist tuck down the
> mountin; I seed hit's course by the lite ove the cane squib an' the fox fire, an'
> every now an' then the hoss fotch a yell—hit won't a squeal, ur a bray, but
> sorter between the two: a orful sound. I've never hearn eny thing make jist
> that nise afore or sence, an' I swar I dont want tu.[2]

Sut, of course, is lathered up and seeking revenge against Sicily
Burns for pumping him full of soda (she had hoodwinked him into
thinking it was an aphrodisiac), and the unfortunate doctor—who
is also Sicily's adulterous lover—gets caught in the cross fire. But
other than to point out that Sut also has his moments on the receiving end of elaborate, debilitating pranks and to suggest that

there is often a measure of method, even of poetic justice, in Sut's madness, what makes the otherwise "unacceptable" acceptable (and indeed, what makes it enjoyable as *humor*) is nothing more, or less, than the language served up generously in yarn after yarn. What Irving's mannered, scrupulously "historical" narrator tries to keep in check, Harris unleashes in one outrageous yarn after another.

To be sure, there is a distance between "George," the framing narrator of the Sut Lovingood yarns, and Sut himself, but it is largely a matter of correct diction versus dialect rather than the more typical case in southern humor of a dandyish narrator utterly appalled at the amorality and viciousness of the tale to which he has been privy. "George"—who is virtually indistinguishable from George Washington Harris—neither judges Sut's mean-spiritedness nor does he present alternatives. In fact, "George" shares his liquor, his tobacco, and on occasion, tries to spin his own yarns, only to have Sut make it abundantly clear that "George" is no match. And given Sut's earthy poetry, his metaphysical capacity to pump an image into baroque proportions, Sut may just be right. Here, for example, is how he describes New York dandies:

> They skims an' flutters roun' fool-wimmin, jist like li'tnin-bugs roun' a tuft ove hollyhocks, only the bugs am six tu thar two, an' hes the deal at that on the amount ove fire they kerries, an' whar they kerries hit. I never sees one but what I wants him atween these yere thumb nails—the human way ove killin' all sich insex. Well, arter his laigs were ontangled, hit sed I had insulted hit, and wanted satisfackshun. Now the idear ove me, a nat'ral-born durn'd fool, insultin' ove enything what c'u'd talk, sounds sorter like a hog insultin' ove a settin' hen, by tearin' up her nest an' eatin' the aigs; 'twer mons'ous like fool talk. But I tho't I'd gin hit satisfackshun, enyhow, so I drapp'd ontu my all-fours, sorter behind hit, fotch a rale fightin'-hoss squal, an' landed both my hine feet onder the fork ove hits cotetail.[3]

Plunk a rustic down on Gotham's pavements and the appeal—as the recent films about Mick ("Crocodile") Dundee demonstrate—is automatic, which is to say, sentimental. Sut is a darkly comic, even anti-Romantic, version of the scenario. To put it mildly, he is scarcely the stuff of which matinee idols are made. Not only is Sut what he labels himself—a natural durned fool, lacking a soul and eschewing a heaven—but his very appearance also works against him: "a queer looking, long legged, short bodied, small headed, white haired, hog eyed, funny sort of a genius, fresh from some bench-legged Jew's clothing store" (*Yarns*, 19). If he is a "child of nature," it is a nature more bellicose and mean-spirited than, say, Rousseau imagined.

At the same time, however, when Sut rails against progress in general and machinery in particular, he gives voice to a conservatism that one can detect in humorists from Charlie Chaplin (*Modern Times*) to Russell Baker. Here, for example, is Sut's description of Horace Greeley, a man whose belief in progressive movements and scientific advancement earns him the dubious title of being "the only man in New York what kin hold a candil fur me to act durn'd fool by":

> He printed sumthin', nex' day in his paper about "Free Love an' Human Progress"; sed he believed that crosses yet would be made atween animals an' varmints, an' sutin mersheans, what would perjuce somethin' tu answer in place of humans—(Dad tried that explite once, durn his pot-heded soul! an' Ise a kerrien the consekenses)—that he hed seed, the day afore, the projuce ove a cross atween a broken-laiged kangeroo and a fust class mowin'-mershean. (*High Times*, 142)

In short, Sut *is* his voice—one forever railing less at the injustices of the world than at the universe itself, which is also to say that Sut is neither a "patient" Job nor a prophetic one. Rather, he exists outside all moral boundaries, more akin to the cartoon world of Roadrunners and Wiley Coyotes than to flesh-and-blood "characters." Does all this excuse Sut, or perhaps more to the point, make him more palatable to modern readers who must plod their way through his path of destruction? If, as Fetterley suggests, readers are manipulated into participating in Dame Van Winkle's comic death, do they also join in Sut's mutilations of women and innocent children, of blacks and Jews, of Indians and God only knows who else? Does it help, for example, to point out that Sut himself apparently does not expect anybody to believe a word of his outrageous yarns because he "aint spected tu act ur talk like a human no how"? Does it help to suggest that Sut represents a phenomenon simultaneously above and beyond, below and outside, the human continuum: "I's nuffin but sum new-fangil'd sort ove beas', a sorter cross atween a crazy ole monkey an' a durn'd wore-out hominy-mill" (*Yarns*, 107)? Or is it that, on a level only explored by certain of our darkest twentieth-century writers (say, the Kafka who turns Gregor Samsa into the bug he has, in fact, always been), Sut is *us*, albeit on a lower frequency and in an idiom we recognize as simultaneously illiterate and oddly eloquent?

As I said when I began this piece, Sut Lovingood is arguably American humor's litmus test. His only competitors strike me as Johnson J. Hooper's Simon Suggs and William Faulkner's Flem Snopes, and even they pale when compared yarn by yarn, hatred by hatred, injury by injury, death by death. The person who can abide large doses of Lovingood is likely to have not only the historical sense necessary to appreciate southwestern humor as it thrived in its time, its place, but also a considerable taste for the rancid, the sour, and the just plain stomach-turning; the person who would champion Sut, who would argue that his malevolence constitutes "humor" must have, in addition to the items listed across the semi-colon, a feeling for the chaos, disruption, indeed, for the sheer subversiveness that so often hides just beneath the folds of comic action.

After all, it takes precious little to push Sut's button. Merely point out that there is an apparent inconsistency in one of his yarns, as a pedantic encyclopedia salesman once did, and Sut responds with the chilling retort—"Yu go tu *hell*, mistofer; yu bothers me" (*Yarns,* 232)—that has dogged his heels as a trademark ever since. No doubt this article, and this mistofer/author, would earn the same contempt. But no matter. Despite everything, Sut makes me laugh. Sometimes it is simply the elegance of his excess. Here is a man who knows how to give mournful spots the description they richly deserve:

> Well, Bull's Gap am a bottomless mud hole, twenty odd miles long, mixed with rocks, logs, brush, creeks, broken stages, dead hosses, mean whiskey, cold vittils, an' cross dogs. Me an' about forty other travelers wer a-makin the trip amongst all this mixtry, while hit would fust rain the best six outen eleving; then hit would snow awhile tu rest hitself, then sleet a littil jist tu show what hit could du, freeze awhile an' begin anuther rainin match, an' a-doin wun ur turther all the time es hard es a shoemaker workin by the job ur the devil a-splittin fat pine tu lite up a new comer, an' him a Congrisman ur a suckit rider.[4]

He is also a man who knows that swearing is not for amateurs (something Mark Twain was always pointing out to his wife, Livy)—that it is an art. At Bull's Gap, the forty or so travelers accompanying Sut set off to swearing up a storm ("sum a cussin that are shanty tavrin, sum a cussin fur supper, sum a cussin the strike nine snake whisky, an all a cussin thar levil best")—all of which sets Sut to wondering just how good these swearers are:

I axed the tavrinkeeper how he liked that cussin es a specimint ove the gift in perfecshun. Oh, he sed, hit wer ornary, not third rate in quality, an' wantin powful in quantity; hardly listened tu hit; in fac, hit didn't even warm him up; wouldn't du as a sampil ove the art at all; an' axed me ef I hadn't been fotched up by monsous pius pussons ni untu a church, for hit wer clar I wer a poor judge ove cussin. Sed he hed a crowd the nite afore what onderstood the business—sixty-seven ove em; an' they wer so well trained that hit sounded like one man, only sixty-seven times louder. Sed they cussed hum pussonely, till his jackit buttons flew off an' the ainds ove his har cotched fire; then they turned in ontu a stage agent an' cussed him into a three week's spell ove fits an' diarrear, but he hadn't much ove a constitushun, no how; an' then finished off by cussin wun ove the stage waggins ontil hit run off inter the woods without eny hosses tu hit. (*High Times,* 145–46)

Cantankerousness, I would add, is also an art, and those who practice it would be well advised to cover their bile with a full arsenal of similes, extended metaphors, analogies, and perhaps most of all, the special lilts of dialect. The last item is especially important because Sut's speech turns black-and-white cinematography into whole swatches of brilliant local color. Granted, Sut's description of a bullfrog paddling away with an iron teaspoon would be funny even if rendered in standard English, but its comic ante raises considerably when the scene tumbles—by slow increments—from his low-falutin' mouth:

He {the "all-firedest, biggest, spottedest, long laigedest bull frog I ever seed"} hed a iron teaspoon crosswise in his mouf, an' he struck out an' swum tu a injun rubber over shoe what wer floatin about boat-fashion loose. He climbed aboard, an' sot in tu paddlin hissef wif his spoon, injun way, fust one side ove the keel and then tuther, across that ar pond. The cussin hed stopped by this time, an' I never seed es meny big eyes afore; they wer es round an' big es ef their heds hed been stretched over martingil rings an' durn the word wer spoke. He steered fur the bluff bank ove an old har trunk, an' clomb tu the top ove hit wif his spoon in his mouf agin, an' then tuck its bowl in his paws, stood up on his hine laigs, an' scratched his back overhanded with the handil. Arter he satisfied hissef at that devarshun, he tuck aim at me (he'd been a-watchin me afore), an' fired his durned ole rusty spoon at my hed. I hearn hit whiz a-pas' my year. (*High Times,* 146–47)

Even more important, perhaps, dialect serves to create a necessary distance—at once aesthetic and psychological—between the bigoted Sut and his more enlightened readers. Anti-Semitic ranting, for example, makes us uncomfortable, and for good reason. Ezra Pound springs quickly to mind as our century's most infamous example, although he is hardly an isolated case among modernist writers. But long before the likes of highbrows such as Henry Adams or Henry James, D. H. Lawrence or T. S. Eliot, Sut also knew how to bait Jews with the best of them. Moreover, as the opening lines of "Sut Lovingood's Hog Ride" demonstrate, Harris makes it abundantly clear that "George" shares in Sut's bigotry:

> Here came an "Israelite, in whom there was *much* guile," hatless, breathless, coatless, as fast as his abridged legs would allow, protesting most vociferously that he "vash *not* Levi Shacobs." Sut was in hot pursuit, with a table knife in his mouth and a clothes line in his hands. He would throw the coils over the Jew's head, lariat fashion, with great precision of aim, and he, with equal dexterity, would shed them off again, increasing his speed and his protestations against the "Shacobs" charge.
>
> Sut would shout furiously in reply, "Yes, you am Jacobs. Whar's my breetches, yu durn close clipt, Ch——st killin, hog hatin, bainch laiged son of a clothes hoss? I means tu fust circumsize yer snout, an' then hang yer arterwards. *Yeres* the tools," brandishing the knife and rope.[5]

Those scholar-critics of a mind to "defend" Sut against charges of anti-Semitism argue from the historical record—namely, that Nashville (where the story is set) had precious few Jews during the period and that it is unlikely that Harris had much, or even any, contact with them. But the more salient point might well be the one Mark Twain made when he was "congratulated" for not peppering his works with negative stereotypes of Jews. As he put it in an article for *Harper's* (September 1899): "I am quite sure that (bar one) I have no race prejudices, and I think I have no color prejudices nor caste prejudices nor creed prejudices. Indeed, I know it. I can stand any society. All that I care to know is that a man is a human being— that is enough for me; he can't be any worse." Sut might argue that he hates women, Indians, blacks, Jews, his immediate family, and damn near anybody else equally. Indeed, the only difference between Sut and other natural durned fools is that they do not know what they are, and Sut does. Socrates apparently felt the same way about his Athenian society, although he preferred irony to venom, Socratic "questions" to litanies of cussing.

The result for Socrates was a life spent in pursuing the truth and especially in trying to determine how a good man should live; for Sut, the result was an unshakable conviction that life is nasty, brutish, and short—and above all else, *not* available to the corrections Thomas Hobbes imagined might make it otherwise. Small wonder, then, that Sut's dark vision can take a suicidal bent, that he thinks about bust-

ing his head open "agin a bluff ove rock," only to add—significantly—that I "jis' wud du hit, ef I warnt a cussed coward" (*Yarns*,
97). From such a driven character, one can expect the wide streak of
meanness, the uncompromisingly grim attitude, and the frenetic energy that infuse his yarns. If the satirist means to "pull down vanity,"
one could argue that Sut means to pull down the world itself, to reduce even the smallest trace of human nobility to ash.

Put another way, Sut pushes the realist's war against sentimentality to a new, shivery dimension. Here, for example, is how Sut responds to the death of his father: "Thar never wer a man yet, so
mean, but what some time, or other, done at least one good thing.
Now, my Dad put off doin his good thing, for an awful long time,
but at last he did hit, like a white man. He died, by golly! perfectly
squar—strait out, an' for keeps."[6]

In the long, complicated history of Oedipal struggles no rebel-
lious son has ever been so matter-of-fact about a father's demise—
and no son has been less attentive about the decorum normally surrounding burial rites. When Dad dies, Sut "liberates" a couple of
Old Stump Snodgrass's steers and hitches them to a big shingle shed
as a practical way of toting the remains to the cemetery. Unfortunately, Sut forgets that steers have a habit of being spooked by the
smell of death, and the result is yet another occasion when all hell
busts loose:

> So, jist es soon es they cotch the first whiff . . . they snorted—bawl'd—histed
> their tails up strait, an' with one mind, run away, hoss fashion. I be dam, if
> they dident git frum thar, like they tho't that dad wud be too late fur the boat.
> When I look'd up in the air at the wavin' tails, wif the tassels hangin' the
> wrong way, I tho't ove the plumes ove a hearse, an' their bellerin' minded me
> ove the brass horns, blowin' some ove the Dead March in Saul, an' dad shave
> me, ef I dident feel proud agin. Thar was *some* style about us, ef we wer
> nothin' but Lovingoods. (*High Times*, 209)

Sut's "style," of course, is bedlam, anarchy of the go-for-broke variety. Neil Schmitz argues that the results are less "tall tales" than a
series of what Sut calls "skeers": "Each 'skeer,' both in the tale and
the telling, is carefully crafted, painstakingly constructed. Harris
had numerous careers—mechanic, planter, merchant, factory
owner, superintendent of a glass-works. He was, it would seem,
above all, a mechanic, something of an engineer curious about the
production of 'special effects.' He liked to imagine things splinter-
ing, breaking, smashing. He liked to write about things flying

apart."[7] One sees this temperament at work when the Lovingood cortege finally arrives at the cemetery (death serving Sut as the ultimate crack-up), and Harris waxes macabre in ways that would only be matched when Faulkner sent the Bundrens on their darkly comic journey in *As I Lay Dying:*

> I found that the dad rabbited steers wer aimin' tu run plum a-stradle ove the grave. So, I tho't I'd improve the occasion, tu save some liftin'. Jist es the sled flew over hit, wif a slider on each side, I turned roun'—sot my foot agin dad's hed, an' done jist *so*. Hit shot him out, like an arrow, an' he chug'd in, es plum an' strait, es an 'oman lays a baby in the cradle. Bomp: I never hearn sich a jolt, he wer yearnist dead, ur that fall wud a sot him tu kicken'. (*High Times*, 210–11)

Whatever else they might be, Sut Lovingood's yarns are *not* for the fainthearted. Much the same thing could be said of Andrew Dice Clay's stand-up monologues. If Sut opines that "Men wer made a-purpus jis' tu eat, drink, an' fur stayin awake in the yearly part ove the nites: an' wimen wer made tu cook the vittils, mix the sperits, an' help the men du the stayin awake" (*Yarns*, 88), Andrew Dice Clay would insist that, women's lib notwithstanding, nothing much has changed—at least so far as Real Men like himself are concerned. When he finishes screwing a broad, he's *finished*. There's no need for further talk, and certainly not for any guilt. "Whadda ya need?" the Dice Man asks incredulously, "Cab fare? It's on the counter. And on the way out, make me a sandwich, bitch."

Granted, Clay (né Andrew Clay Silverstein) means to come off as a tough-talking, New York Italian street punk, circa 1950, rather than as a Tennessee redneck. And as such, he is a study in exaggeration, from his black leather jacket with grotesque rhinestone trimming and oversized collar, black pants and t-shirt, fourteen-inch bejeweled belt buckle, and omnipresent cigarette to a speech pattern generously peppered with "OOHHs" and obscenities. Who else would begin a stand-up monologue with "So I got my tongue up this chick's ass, see" and who else would argue that what woman *really* want is to be "hammered like chopped meat"? In short, Dice Clay cuts through the liberal bullshit—about how one should treat homeless panhandlers ("Spare change? Whadda ya gonna do, open up a store with a quarter?"), about Japs and Chinks ("Same thing"), about immigrants from the Mideast ("They're not black, they're not white—they're sorta urine-colored"), about gays ("I don't see how a guy looks at another guy's hairy ass and says: 'I gadda have *that.*'"), and, of course, about women. The result be-comes an extended exercise in dividing the world into those who hoot their approval and those so outraged that they want to shut Andrew Dice Clay down.

How, then, to explain his appeal—much less to make an aesthetic judgment about his material—for the packed audiences who cackle when he puts down Puerto Ricans, Asians, homosexuals, and, most of all, women? No doubt a sociologist would argue that the Dice Clay cult is partly backlash, partly camp. He is the embodiment of every attitude liberals should eschew in the 1990s, the antithesis, as it were, of a cuddly, right-thinking type like Alan Alda. And while I have no doubt that many of those who egg Dice Clay on subscribe to his hate-ridden agenda, I also suspect that many regard his con-certs as a species of "vacation," a way of escaping from the heavy, pinch-faced burden of "proper attitudes" as they are defined by the self-righteous Left. Dice Clay, in short, offers the same chance to be outrageous that the late, unlamented *Morton Downey, Jr., Show* served up under the guise of spirited debate—and my hunch is that he will last about as long.

None of this, of course, is much solace to those who find Dice Clay's antics deeply offensive. But as Nora Dunn, the *Saturday Night Live* regular player, discovered, nothing attracts attention, or mud-dies the comic waters, more quickly than efforts at censorship. And this is especially true when those who delight in goring other peo-ple's oxen complain that *their* ox is receiving unkind, ungentle treatment.

In the case of Andrew Dice Clay, I suspect that the best response is to hand him endless amounts of rope and then to watch as he hangs himself—as he clearly did in a weepy, self-serving tirade on the *Arsenio Hall Show* and, more spectacularly, in his first (and probably last) feature-length motion picture, *Ford Fairlane.* After all, one can count on *People* magazine to find other, newer oddities for next month's issue and absolutely bank on Andrew Dice Clay as yet another phenomenon that proves Andy Warhol's thesis about contemporary fame lasting fifteen minutes.

Even the Dice Man's most enthusiastic fans are likely to find themselves soon bored silly by his narrow range and witless "wit." After all, the Dice Clay you see at one concert is pretty much the Dice Clay you will see at the next one. Consider, for example, his ribald nursery rhymes. Granted, the Dice Man gives them his distinctive, exaggerated touch, but the material itself ("Jack and Jill went up the hill / Each had a buck an' a quarter / Jill came down with two-fifty—YEOUW, the whore") is what passes—indeed, what *passed*—as racy stuff in the fifth grade. Dice Clay's recitation is, at best, but a small improvement.

The same thing is true of Dice Clay's "attitude." As he puts it, in an effort to divide the world further between hard-core fans and dissenters, "I know what you're thinkin'—cute comic but he's got an attitude. Well, FUCK YOU!" Here one is reminded of what Sut observed about cussin'. Most of the time—and here I would include the likes of Richard Pryor and Eddie Murphy—sheer repetition devalues whatever power a word such as *fuck* might legitimately pack. Real humorists know that humor is made of sterner, more durable stuff. And that, of course, is the central difference between Dice Clay's ranting and Sut Lovingood's comic tirades. The former is designed exclusively for "performance" while the latter is slated for the printed page. Thus, George Washington Harris exploits the full resources of imagery and metaphor, whereas Dice Clay tries to hold together a string of one-liners (e.g., "So the teacher asks me: 'What's the fuckin' difference between 2/8 and 3/8?' That's what I said— what's the fuckin' difference?") by the force of "personality" alone. Andrew Dice Clay may insist that he is *not* his persona and that any effort to confuse the two misses the point, but the deeper, sadder truth is that he has become the Dice Man in yet another instance of the Frankenstein monster hopping off the laboratory table and pursuing its creator.

Both Washington Irving and George Washington Harris used narrative techniques to avoid this fate. But, then again, they were artists who knew that humor requires artfulness of a high degree and, moreover, that a genuinely subversive humor—one that earns its uneasy laughter—must probe more deeply, more darkly, into the respective societies at which they poked fun. For Irving's Rip Van Winkle, what this came to was a mythopoeic grasp of our need to take respites from responsibility and how essential "story" was to that process. For Harris's Sut Lovingood, it was an understanding of how tenuous, how desperate, the world of the Old Southwest really was. Both, I suspect, would not have been much amused by Dice Clay's description of women dolled up in their "fuck-me" pumps and teased hair who operate on the premise that "Somebody's gonna treat me like the pig I am."

Notes

1. Judith Fetterley, *The Resisting Reader* (Bloomington: Indiana University Press, 1978), 9–10.

2. "Sut Lovingood's Chest Story," in George Washington Harris, *"Sut Lovingood. Yarns": A Facsimile of the 1867 Dick and Fitzgerald Edition,* ed. M. Thomas Inge (Memphis: Saint Luke's Press, 1987), f–g. This story was added to the facsimile edition and therefore is paged with letters rather than numbers. All references to Harris's published collection will be to this edition and will be hereafter noted in the text.

3. "Sut Lovingood's Adventures in New York," originally in *New York Atlas,* 8 August 1858. See M. Thomas Inge, ed. *High Times and Hard Times: Sketches and Tales by George Washington Harris* (Nashville: Vanderbilt University Press, 1967), 136. Other citations will refer to this edition and will be noted in the text.

4. "Sut Lovingood at Bull's Gap," in Inge, *High Times,* 144. Other citations will be noted in the text. Originally in *New York Atlas,* 28 November 1858.

5. "Sut Lovingood's Hog Ride," in Inge, *High Times,* 157. Originally in *Nashville Daily Press and Times,* 14 September 1865.

6. "Well! Dad's Dead," in Inge, *High Times,* 207. Other citations will be noted in the text. Originally in *Knoxville Daily Press and Herald,* 15 November 1868.

7. Neil Schmitz, "Forms of Regional Humor," in *Columbia Literary History of the United States,* ed. Emory Elliott (New York: Columbia University Press, 1988), 322.

A Bibliography of George Washington Harris

M. Thomas Inge

Works by George Washington Harris

"Sporting Epistle from East Tennessee." *New York Spirit of the Times: A Chronicle of the Turf, Agriculture, Field Sports, Literature and the Stage,* 11 February 1843, 596–97. Hereafter referred to as *Spirit of the Times.*

"Quarter Racing in Tennessee." *Spirit of the Times,* 15 April 1843, 79.

"Sporting Epistle from East Tennessee." *Spirit of the Times,* 17 June 1843, 187.

"Sporting Epistle from East Tennessee: A Quarter Race—Corn Shucking—Quilting—Log Rolling." *Spirit of the Times,* 2 September 1843, 313.

"The Knob Dance, A Tennessee Frolic: Dick Harlan's Story." *Spirit of the Times,* 2 August 1845, 267.

"The Snake-bit Irishman: An Original Tennessee Hunting Incident." *Spirit of the Times,* 17 January 1846, 549–50. Revised for *Sut Lovingood. Yarns Spun by A "Nat'ral Born Durn'd Fool." Warped and Wove for Public Wear.* Hereafter referred to as *Yarns.*

"A Sleep Walking Incident." *Spirit of the Times,* 12 September 1846, 343.

"There's Danger in Old Chairs!" *Weekly Nashville Union,* 6 October 1847, 3.

"How To Marry." *Spirit of the Times,* 21 October 1854, 422.

"Sut Lovengood's [sic] Daddy, Acting Horse." *Spirit of the Times,* 4 November 1854, 447–48. Revised for *Yarns.*

"Playing Old Sledge for the Presidency—Dream of Sut Lovingood's." *Nashville Union and American,* 18 October 1856, 2.

"Sut Lovengood [sic] Blown Up." *Savannah Morning News* [edited by William Tappan Thompson], date unknown. Reprinted in *Nashville Daily Gazette,* 21 July 1857. Revised for *Yarns.*

"Sut Lovengood's [sic] Shirt." *Nashville Union and American,* 1 May 1857. Revised for *Yarns.*

"Sut Lovingood's Lizzards." *Nashville Union and American,* 15 November 1857. Revised for *Yarns.*

"Sut Lovingood's Dog." *Nashville Union and American,* 8 January 1858. Revised for *Yarns.*

"Sut Lovingood at Sicily Burns's Wedding." *Nashville Union and American,* 15 April 1858. Revised for *Yarns.*

"Old Burns's Bull Ride." *Nashville Union and American,* 22 April 1858. Revised for *Yarns.*

"Letter from Sut Lovingood of Tennessee." *Nashville Union and American,* 16 June 1858, 2.

"Letter from Sut Lovingood of Tennessee." *Nashville Union and American,* 24 June 1858, 2.

"Note from Sut Lovingood." *Nashville Union and American,* 27 June 1858, 2.

"Sut Lovingood's Chest Story." *Nashville Union and American,* 30 June 1858, 1.

"Letter from S——l, of Tennessee." *Nashville Union and American,* 7 July 1858, 2.

"The Doctor's Bill." *Nashville Union and American,* 10 July 1858, 1.

"Sut Lovingood Escapes Assassination." *New York Atlas,* 11 July 1858, 6.

"Sut Lovingood's Adventures in New York." *New York Atlas,* 8 August 1858, 1.

"Sut Lovingood at Bull's Gap." *New York Atlas*, 28 November 1858, 6.

"The Cockney's Baggage." *New York Atlas*, 9 January 1859.

"She had the Slows." *New York Atlas*, 6 February 1859, 4.

"Sut Lovingood and the Locomotive." *New York Atlas*, 6 February 1859, 4.

"How to Gain your Seed Oats." *New York Atlas*, 20 February 1859, 3.

"A Strange Breed of Cats." *New York Atlas*, 20 February 1859, 3.

"Sut Lovingood's Love Feast ove Varmints, I." *Nashville Union and American*, 19 April 1859, 2.

"Sut Lovingood's Love Feast ove Varmints, II." *Nashville Union and American*, 21 April 1859, 2.

"Sut Lovingood's Love Feast ove Varmints, III." *Nashville Union and American*, 30 April 1859, 1.

"Sut Lovingood's Love Feast ove Varmints, IV." *Nashville Union and American*, 3 May 1859, 1.

"Sut Lovingood Travels with Old Abe as his Confidential Friend and Advisor." *Nashville Union and American*, 28 February 1861, 2.

"Sut Lovingood with Old Abe on His Journey." *Nashville Union and American*, 2 March 1861, 2.

"Sut Lovingood Lands Old Abe Safe at Last." *Nashville Union and American*, 5 March 1861, 3.

"Sut Lovingood's Hog Ride." *Nashville Daily Press and Times*, 14 September 1865, 1.

"Sut Lovingood Come to Life." *Nashville Daily Union and American*, 3 May 1866, 1.

"The Coat of Faded Grey." *Nashville Union and American*, 1 July 1866.

"Sut Lovingood's Big Dinner Story." *Nashville Union and American*, 10 August 1866, 4.

"The Rome Egg Affair." *Nashville Daily Union and American*, 2 September 1866, 4.

"Sut Lovingood, on the Puritan Yankee." *Nashville Union and American*, 16 October 1866, 4.

"Sut Lovingood's Dream: Tartarus, and What He Saw There." *Lynchburg Daily Virginian*, 23 January 1867, 1.

Sut Lovingood. Yarns Spun by a "Nat'ral Born Durn'd Fool." Warped and Wove for Public Wear. New York: Dick and Fitzgerald, 1867.

"Saul Spradlin's Ghost." *Chattanooga Daily American Union*, 31 October 1867, 1. [A second installment of this story is not extant.]

"Sut Lovingood Reports What Bob Dawson Said, After Marrying a Substitute." *Chattanooga Daily American Union*, 27 November 1867, 1, and 28 November 1867, 1.

"Sut Lovingood's Big Music Box Story." *Chattanooga Daily American Union*, 11 December 1867, 1, and 12 December 1867, 1.

"Sut Lovingood's Hark from the Tomb Story." *Chattanooga Daily American Union*, 17 March 1868, 1.

"Sut Lovingood, a Chapter from His Autobiography." *Chattanooga Daily American Union*, 31 March 1868, 1, and 2 April 1868, 1.

"Correspondance Extraordinary. The Forthcoming Early Life of Sut Lovingood, by his Dad. Negotiations Completed." *Knoxville Press and Messenger*, 30 April 1868, 1.

"The Early Life of Sut Lovingood, Written by his Dad, I." *Knoxville Press and Messenger*, 7 May 1868, 1.

"The Early Life of Sut Lovingood, Written by his Dad, II." *Knoxville Press and Messenger*, 14 May 1868, 1.

"The Early Life of Sut Lovingood, Written by his Dad, III." *Knoxville Press and Messenger*, 21 May 1868, 1.

"Bill Ainsworth's Quarter Race: A Story of the Old Times (1833) in East Tennessee." *Knoxville Press and Messenger*, 4 June 1868, 1.

"Sut Lovingood's Allegory." *Knoxville Press and Messenger*, 17 September 1868, 1.

"Well! Dad's Dead." *Knoxville Daily Press and Herald*, 15 November 1868, 3.

"Sut Lovingood on Young Gals and Old Ones." *Knoxville Daily Press and Herald,* 13 May 1869, 3.
"Sut Lovingood 'Sets Up with a Gal—One Pop Baily.' " *Knoxville Press and Messenger,* 29 September 1869, 1.

Modern Collections of George Washington Harris

Inge, M. Thomas, ed. *Sut Lovingood's Yarns: Edited for the Modern Reader.* New Haven, Conn.: College and University Press, 1966.

————. *High Times and Hard Times: Sketches and Tales by George Washington Harris.* Nashville: Vanderbilt University Press, 1967.

————. *"Sut Lovingood. Yarns": A Facsimile of the 1867 Dick and Fitzgerald Edition.* Memphis: Saint Lukes Press, 1987.

Parks, Edd Winfield, ed. *Sut Lovingood Travels with Old Abe Lincoln.* Chicago: Black Cat Press, 1937.

Weber, Brom, ed. *Sut Lovingood.* New York: Grove Press, 1954.

Works on George Washington Harris

ANNUAL
Ben Harris McClary, ed. *The Lovingood Papers.* Knoxville: University of Tennessee Press, 1962–67.

DISSERTATIONS AND THESES
Barry, Linda Anne. "Old Southwestern Humor as a Genre and Five of its Writers." Master's thesis, University of West Florida, 1986.

Black, William P. "Sut Lovingood as Seen by George Washington Harris." Master's thesis, Duke University, 1966.

Boykin, Carol. "A Study of the Phonology, Morphology, and Vocabulary of George Washington Harris's *Sut Lovingood. Yarns.*" Master's thesis, University of Tennessee, 1966.

Brown, Carolyn S. "Petrified Truth: The Tall Tale in American Folklore and Literature." Ph.D. diss., University of Virginia, 1983.

Burton, Linda. "An Anthology of Tennessee Short Fiction." Ph.D. diss., University of Tennessee, 1981.

Crouch, Howard G. "George Washington Harris: Southwestern Humorist and Creator of Sut Lovingood." Master's thesis, Radford College, 1965.

Day, Donald. "The Life and Works of George Washington Harris." Ph.D. diss., University of Chicago, 1942.

Gentry, Robert B., Jr. "The Animal Motif in the Sut Lovingood Yarns." Master's thesis, University of Tennessee, 1967.

Gooch, Margaret McDiarmid. "Point of View and the Frontier Spirit in the Old Southwestern Tales of Baldwin, Longstreet, Hooper, and G. W. Harris." Ph.D. diss., University of North Carolina at Chapel Hill, 1968.

Gray, Joanne. "George Washington Harris's Sut Lovingood and Johnson Jones Hooper's Simon Suggs: Picaroons of the Old Southwest. A Study in Literary Continuity." Master's thesis, Jacksonville State University, 1973.

Harrison, Louis B. "The Influence of George Washington Harris in the Writings of Mark Twain." Master's thesis, University of Texas at Austin, 1963.

Heflin, John J., Jr. "George Washington Harris ('Sut Lovingood'): A Biographical and Critical Study." Master's thesis, Vanderbilt University, 1934.

Hess, Bertha R. "Backwoods Humor of the South." Master's thesis, Auburn University, 1933.

Inge, M. Thomas. "A Study of the Sut Lovingood Yarns and Other Writings of George Washington Harris." Master's thesis, Vanderbilt University, 1960.

————. "The Uncollected Writings of George Washington Harris: An Annotated Edition." Ph.D. diss., Vanderbilt University, 1964.

Kerlin, Charles Martin, Jr. "Life in Motion: Genteel and Vernacular Attitudes in the Works of the Southwestern Humorists, Mark Twain, and William Faulkner." Ph.D. diss., University of Colorado, 1968.

Latta, Charles M. "Reason in Fooldom: George Washington Harris's Sut Lovingood." Master's thesis, University of Louisville, 1967.

Lipper, Mark Mario. "Comic Caricatures in Early American Newspapers as Indicators of the National Character." Ph.D. diss., Southern Illinois University, 1973.

Mace, Jennings Roy, II. "Simon Suggs, Madison Tensas, and Sut Lovingood: Human Nature and Three Characters from the Humor of the Southwest." Ph.D. diss., University of North Carolina at Chapel Hill, 1979.

Milner, Joseph O'Beirne. "The Social, Religious, Economic, and Political Implications of the Southwest Humor of Baldwin, Longstreet, Hooper, and George Washington Harris." Ph.D. diss., University of North Carolina at Chapel Hill, 1970.

Newton, David Wayman. "Voices Along the Border: Cultural Identity, Social Authority, and the Idea of Language in the Antebellum South." Ph.D. diss., Emory University, 1993.

Plater, Ormonde. "Tall Tales and Tall Talk in the Sut Lovingood Stories: An Oral Tradition Influences a Literary Tradition." Master's thesis, Tulane University, 1965.

———. "Narrative Folklore in the Works of George Washington Harris" Ph.D. diss., Tulane University, 1969.

Sexton, Mark Stephen. "Vernacular Religious Figures in Nineteenth-Century Southern Fiction: A Study in Literary Tradition." Ph.D. diss., University of North Carolina at Chapel Hill, 1987.

Simpson, Douglas G. "The Needlers: America's Journalistic Satirists." Master's thesis, University of Washington, 1969.

Stewart, James E. "George Washington Harris: A Critical Study." Master's thesis, Kansas State College at Pittsburg, 1963.

Stilley, Hugh M. "William Faulkner and George Washington Harris: Frontier Humor in the Snopes Trilogy." Master's thesis, University of British Columbia, 1965.

Williams, Cratis D. "The Southern Mountaineer in Fact and Fiction." Ph.D. diss., New York University, 1961.

ARTICLES AND BOOKS
*indicates reprinting in this volume
*Anonymous. "New Books." *Nashville Union and American,* 25 April 1867.
*Anonymous. "New Publications." *New York Times,* 8 April 1867.
Arnold, Saint George Tucker, Jr. "Sut Lovingood, The Animals, and the Great White Trash Chain of Being." *Thalia: Studies in Literary Humor* 1 (1978–79): 33–41.

———. "Stumbling Dogtracks on The Sands of Time: Thurber's Less-Than-Charming Animals and Animal Portraits in Earlier American Humor." *Markham Review* 10 (1981): 41–47.

Bain, Robert. "George W. Harris." In *Antebellum Writers in New York and the South,* edited by Joel Myerson, vol. 3 of *Dictionary of Literary Biography.* Detroit: Gale Research Co., 1979. 138–43.

Bass, William W. "Sut Lovingood's Reflections on His Contemporaries." *Carson-Newman College Faculty Studies* 1 (1964): 33–48.

Bier, Jesse. "'Southwestern' Humor." In *The Rise and Fall of American Humor.* New York: Holt, Rinehart, and Winston, 1968. 52–76.

Blair, Walter. "Sut Lovingood." *Saturday Review of Literature.* 15 (7 November 1936): 3–4, 16.

*———. *Native American Humor, 1800–1900.* New York: Alfred A. Knopf, 1937. Reprint, with new material, as *Native American Humor.* New York: Harper and Row, 1960. 96–101.

Blair, Walter, and Hamlin Hill. *America's Humor: From Poor Richard to Doonesbury.* Oxford: Oxford University Press, 1978. 213–21.

Blount, Roy, Jr., ed. *Roy Blount's Book of Southern Humor.* New York: W. W. Norton, 1994. 235–41.

Boykin, Carol. "Sut's Speech: The Dialect of a Nat'ral Borned Mountaineer." In *The Lovingood Papers,* edited by Ben Harris McClary. Knoxville: University of Tennessee Press, 1965. 36–42.

Bridgman, Richard. *The Colloquial Style in America.* New York: Oxford University Press, 1966. 23–31.

*Brown, Carolyn S. "Sut Lovingood: A Nat'ral Born Durn'd Yarnspinner." *Southern Literary Journal* 18 (1985): 89–100. Revised for *The Tall Tale in American Folklore and Literature.* Knoxville: University of Tennessee Press, 1987. 74–88.

*Brown, J. Thompson, Jr. "George Washington Harris." In *Library of Southern Literature,* 16 vols., edited by Edwin A. Alderman, Joel Chandler Harris, and Charles W. Kent. Atlanta: Martin and Hoyt, 1907–09. 5:2099–102.

Bungert, Hans. "Re: Stark Young's Sut Lovingood." In *The Lovingood Papers,* edited by Ben Harris McClary. Knoxville: University of Tennessee Press, 1965. 53–54.

Casey, Janet G. "Newly Discovered Reprintings of George W. Harris's Tales and Letters." *Studies in American Humor* 5 (1986): 89–91.

Cohen, Hennig. "Mark Twain's Sut Lovingood." In *The Lovingood Papers,* edited by Ben Harris McClary. Knoxville: University of Tennessee Press, 1962. 19–24.

Cohen, Hennig, and William B. Dillingham, eds. *Humor of the Old Southwest.* 3d ed. Athens: University of Georgia Press, 1994. 193–246.

Covici, Pascal, Jr. *Mark Twain's Humor: The Image of a World.* Dallas: Southern Methodist University Press, 1962.

Current-Garcia, Eugene. "Sut Lovingood's Rare Ripe Southern Garden." *Studies in Short Fiction* 9 (1972): 117–29.

Day, Donald. "The Humorous Works of George W. Harris." *American Literature* 14 (1943): 391–406.

———. "The Political Satires of George W. Harris." *Tennessee Historical Quarterly* 4 (1945): 320–38.

*———. "The Life of George Washington Harris." *Tennessee Historical Quarterly* 6 (1947): 3–38.

———. "George Washington Harris." *Encyclopedia Britannica.* Vol. 11. Chicago: Encyclopedia Britannica, 1960. 217.

———. "Searching for Sut." In *The Lovingood Papers,* edited by Ben Harris McClary. Knoxville: University of Tennessee Press, 1965. 9–15.

Estes, David C. "Sut Lovingood at the Camp Meeting: A Practical Joker Among the Backwoods Believers." *Southern Quarterly* 25 (1987): 53–65.

*Fisher, Benjamin Franklin, IV. "George Washington Harris and Supernaturalism." *Publications of the Mississippi Philological Association* 1 (1982): 18–23.

Flautz, John T. "The Dialect Sermon in American Literature." In *Popular Literature in America,* edited by James C. Austin and Donald A. Koch. Bowling Green, Ohio: Bowling Green State University Popular Press, 1972. 129–45.

Gardiner, Elaine. "Sut Lovingood: Backwoods Existentialist." *Southern Studies: An Interdisciplinary Journal of the South* 22 (1983): 177–89.

Gray, R. J. "Southwestern Humor, Erskine Caldwell, and the Humor of Frustration." *Southern Literary Journal* 9 (1975): 3–26.

Griffith, Nancy Snell. *Humor of the Old Southwest: An Annotated Bibliography of Primary and Secondary Sources.* Westport, Conn.: Greenwood Press, 1989. 83–109.

Hansen, Arlen J. "Entropy and Transformation: Two Types of American Humor." *American Scholar* 43 (1974): 405–21.

Hauck, Richard Boyd. *A Cheerful Nihilism: Confidence and "The Absurd" in Humorous American Fiction.* Bloomington: Indiana University Press, 1971. 74–76.

*Howell, Elmo. "Timon in Tennessee: The Moral Fervor of George Washington Harris." *Georgia Review* 24 (1970): 311–19.

Howland, Hewitt H. "The Selection of Irvin S. Cobb: Sut Lovingood's Daddy, Acting Horse." In *Humor By Vote.* New York: Laugh Club, 1933. viii, 22–31.

Inge, M. Thomas. "Sut Lovingood: An Examination of the Nature of a 'Nat'ral Born Durn'd Fool.'" *Tennessee Historical Quarterly* 19 (1960): 231–51.

————. "William Faulkner & George Washington Harris: In the Tradition of Southwestern Humor." *Tennessee Studies in Literature* 7 (1962): 47–59.

————. "A Personal Encounter with George Washington Harris." In *The Lovingood Papers,* edited by Ben Harris McClary. Knoxville: University of Tennessee Press, 1963. 9–12.

————. "George Washington Harris and Southern Poetry and Music." *Mississippi Quarterly* 17 (1963–64): 36–44.

————. "Stark Young's Sut Lovingood." In *The Lovingood Papers,* edited by Ben Harris McClary. Knoxville: University of Tennessee Press, 1964. 45–46.

————. "George W. Harris's 'The Doctor's Bill': A Tale about Dr. J. G. M. Ramsey." *Tennessee Historical Quarterly* 24 (1965): 185–94.

*————. "Sut and His Illustrators." *The Lovingood Papers,* edited by Ben Harris McClary. Knoxville: University of Tennessee Press, 1965. 26–35.

————. "The Satiric Artistry of George W. Harris." *Satire Newsletter* 4 (1967): 63–72.

————. "Early Appreciations of George Washington Harris by George Frederick Mellen." *Tennessee Historical Quarterly* 30 (1971): 190–204.

————. "The Appalachian Backgrounds of Billy DeBeck's Snuffy Smith." *Appalachian Journal* 4 (1977): 120–32.

————. "George Washington Harris." In *American Literature to 1900,* edited by James Vinson. New York: Saint Martin's Press, 1980. 149–50.

————. "George Washington Harris." In *Fifty Southern Writers Before 1900,* edited by Robert Bain and Joseph Flora. Westport, Conn.: Greenwood Press, 1987. 220–26.

————. "George Washington Harris." In *Reference Guide to American Literature,* edited by D. L. Kirkpatrick. Chicago: Saint James Press, 1987. 260–61.

————. "Sut Lovingood and Snuffy Smith." In *Comics as Culture.* Jackson: University Press of Mississippi, 1990. 68–77.

————. *Faulkner, Sut, and Other Southerners.* West Cornwall, Conn.: Locust Hill Press, 1992. 51–104.

————. "George Washington Harris." In *The Mark Twain Encyclopedia,* edited by J. R. LeMaster and James D. Wilson. New York: Garland, 1993. 349–50.

————. "Sut Lovingood and Snuffy Smith." In *Barney Google and Snuffy Smith: 75 Years of an American Legend,* edited by Brian Walker. Wilton, Conn.: Comicana Books, 1994. 100–105.

————, ed. *The Frontier Humorists: Critical Views.* Hamden, Conn.: Anchor Books, 1975. 69–74, 118–69, 266–80, 315–17.

Inscoe, John C. "Faulkner, Race and Appalachia." *South Atlantic Quarterly* 86 (1987): 244–53.

Keller, Mark."That George W. Harris 'Christmas Story': A Reconsideration of Authorship." *American Literature* 54 (1982): 284–87.

Knight, Donald R. "Sut's Dog Imagery." In *The Lovingood Papers,* edited by Ben Harris McClary. Knoxville: University of Tennessee Press, 1965. 59–60.

Leary, Lewis. "The Lovingoods: Notes Toward A Genealogy." In *Southern Excursions: Essays on Mark Twain and Others.* Baton Rouge: Louisiana State University Press, 1971. 111–30.

Lenz, William E. "The Identity of George W. Harris's 'Man in the Swamp.'" *Notes on Mississippi Writers* 13 (1981): 14–17.

*————."Sensuality, Revenge, and Freedom: Women in *Sut Lovingood's Yarns* [sic]." *Studies in American Humor,* n.s., 1 (1983): 173–80.

——. *Fast Talk and Flush Times: The Confidence Man as a Literary Convention.* Columbia: University of Missouri Press, 1885. 106–17.

Long, Hudson. "Sut Lovingood and Mark Twain's *Joan of Arc.*" *Modern Language Notes* 64 (1949): 37–39.

Lynn, Kenneth S. *Mark Twain and Southwestern Humor.* Boston: Little, Brown, 1959. 130–39.

McClary, Ben Harris. "Sut Lovingood Views 'Abe Linkhorn.'" *Lincoln Herald* 56 (1954): 44–45.

*——. "The Real Sut." *American Literature* 27 (1955): 105–06.

——. "Sut Lovingood's Country." *Southern Observer* 3 (1955): 5–7.

——. "George and Sut: A Working Bibliography." In *The Lovingood Papers,* edited by Ben Harris McClary. Knoxville: University of Tennessee Press, 1962. 5–9.

——. "Sanky and Sut." *Southern Observer* 9 (1962): 13.

——. "On Quilts." In *The Lovingood Papers,* edited by Ben Harris McClary. Knoxville: University of Tennessee Press, 1965. 61–62.

——. "George W. Harris's New York *Atlas* Series: Three New Items." *Studies in American Humor,* n.s., 2 (1983): 195–99.

——. "George W. Harris's 'Special Vision': His *Yarns* as Historical Sourcebook." In *No Fairer Land: Studies in Southern Literature Before 1900,* edited by J. Lasley Dameron and James W. Mathews. Troy, N.Y.: Whitson Publishing Co., 1986. 226–41.

McKeithan, D. M. "Mark Twain's Story of the Bull and the Bees." *Tennessee Historical Quarterly* 11 (1952): 246–53.

——. "Bull Rides Described by 'Scroggins,' G. W. Harris, and Mark Twain." *Southern Folklore Quarterly* 17 (1953): 241–43.

*Matthiessen, F. O. *American Renaissance.* Oxford: Oxford University Press, 1941. 641–45.

Meine, Franklin J. "George Washington Harris." In *Dictionary of American Biography.* New York: Scribner, 1932. Vol. 4, pt. 2, 309.

——, ed. *Tall Tales of the Southwest: An Anthology of Southern and Southwestern Humor, 1830–1860.* New York: Alfred A. Knopf, 1930. xxiii–xxiv.

*Mellen, George F. "Sut Lovingood's Yarns." *Knoxville Sentinel,* 11 February 1909.

——. "George W. Harris." *Knoxville Sentinel,* 13 February 1909.

——. "Lovingood's Settings." *Knoxville Sentinel,* 7 March 1911.

——. "Sut Lovingood." *Knoxville Sentinel,* 8 January 1914.

Micklus, Robert. "Sut's Travels with Dad." *Studies in American Humor,* n.s., 1 (1982): 89–101.

Nilsen, Don L. F. "Linguistic Humor in Western Literature." *Southwest Folklore* 5 (1981): 15–51.

Parks, Edd Winfield. *Segments of Southern Thought.* Athens: University of Georgia Press, 1938. 215–22.

Penrod, James. "Folk Humor in *Sut Lovingood's Yarns* [sic]." *Tennessee Folklore Society Bulletin* 16 (1950): 76–84.

Plater, Ormonde. "Before Sut: Folklore in the Early Works of George W. Harris." *Southern Folklore Quarterly* 34 (1970): 104–15.

——. "The Lovingood Patriarchy." *Appalachian Journal* 1 (1973): 82–93.

*Polk, Noel. "The Blind Bull, Human Nature: Sut Lovingood and the Damned Human Race." In *Gyascutus: Studies in Antebellum Southern Humorous and Sporting Writing,* edited by James L. W. West. Atlantic Highlands, N.J.: Humanities Press, 1978. 13–49.

Ragan, David Paul. "At the Grave of Sut Lovingood: Virgil Campbell in the Work of Fred Chappel." *Mississippi Quarterly* 37 (1983): 21–30.

Rickels, Milton. "The Imagery of George Washington Harris." *American Literature* 31 (1959): 173–87.

*——. *George Washington Harris.* New York: Twayne Publishers, 1965.

——. "Sut Lovingood's Yarns." *Mississippi Quarterly* 21 (1967): 80–82.

——. "Elements of Folk Humor in the Literature of the Old Southwest." *Thalia: Studies in Literary Humor* 4 (1981): 5–9.

———. "George W. Harris's Newspaper Grotesques." *University of Mississippi Studies in English* 2 (1981): 15–24.

———. "George W. Harris." In *American Humorists, 1800–1950, Part I: A–L.* Vol. 11 of *Dictionary of Literary Biography,* edited by Stanley Trachtenberg. Detroit: Gale Research Co., 1982. 180–89.

———. "The Grotesque Body of Southwestern Humor." In *Critical Essays on American Humor,* edited by William Bedford Clark and W. Craig Turner. Boston: G. K. Hall, 1984. 155–66.

Rose, Alan Henry. "Characteristic Ambivalence in the Yarns of George Washington Harris." *Tennessee Folklore Society Bulletin* 41 (1975): 115–16.

———. "'A Plan to Wake the Devil': Race and Aesthetics in the Tales of George Washington Harris." In *Demonic Vision: Racial Fantasy and Southern Fiction.* Hamden, Conn.: Anchor Books, 1976. 63–71.

Ross, Stephen M. "Jason Compson and Sut Lovingood: Southwestern Humor as Stream of Consciousness." *Studies in the Novel* 8 (1976): 278–90.

Rourke, Constance. *American Humor: A Study of the National Character.* 1931. Reprint, New York: Harcourt, Brace, Jovanovich, 1959. 311.

Royot, Daniel. "A Nat'ral Born Durn'd Fool: L'Irresistible decheance de Sut Lovingood." *Caliban* 26 (1989): 57–64.

Schmitz, Neil. *Of Huck and Alice: Humorous Writing in American Literature.* Minneapolis: University of Minnesota Press, 1983. 30–64.

———. "Forms of Regional Humor." In *Columbia Literary History of the United States,* edited by Emory Elliott. New York: Columbia University Press, 1988. 306–23.

Starr, William J. "An Unknown Tale by George Washington Harris." In *Gyascutus: Studies in Antebellum Southern Humorous and Sporting Writing,* edited by James L. W. West. Atlantic Highlands, N.J.: Humanities Press, 1978. 159–72.

Stewart, Randall. "Tidewater and Frontier." *Georgia Review* 13 (1959): 296–307.

Tandy, Jeannette. *Crackerbox Philosophers in American Humor and Satire.* New York: Columbia University Press, 1925. 93–94.

Thorpe, Willard. "Suggs and Sut in Modern Dress: The Latest Chapter in Southern Humor." *Mississippi Quarterly* 13 (1959): 168–75.

*Twain, Mark. "Sut Lovingood." *San Francisco Daily Alta California,* 14 July 1867.

Watterson, Henry. *Oddities in Southern Life and Character.* Boston: Houghton Mifflin, 1882. 415.

———. *The Compromises of Life.* New York: Fox, Duffield, 1903. 66.

*Weber, Brom. "A Note on Edmund Wilson and George Washington Harris." In *The Lovingood Papers,* edited by Ben Harris McClary. Knoxville: University of Tennessee Press, 1962. 47–53.

Wenke, John. "*Sut Lovingood's Yarns* [sic] and the Politics of Performance." *Studies in American Fiction* 15 (1987): 199–210.

Williams, Cratis. "Sut Lovingood as a Southern Mountaineer." *Appalachian State Teacher's College Faculty Publications* 44 (1966): 1–4.

*Wilson, Edmund. "Poisoned!" *New Yorker,* 7 May 1955, 138–46. Reprinted in *Patriotic Gore.* New York: Oxford University Press, 1962. 507–19.

Young, Thomas Daniel. *Tennessee Writers.* Knoxville: University of Tennessee Press, 1981. 5–11.

———. "A Nat'ral Born Durn'd Fool." *Thalia: Studies in Literary Humor* 6 (1983): 51–56.

Ziff, Larzer. "The Fool Killer: George Washington Harris and Sut Lovingood." In *Literary Democracy: The Declaration of Cultural Independence in America.* New York: Viking Press, 1981. 181–94.

Contributors to "New Perspectives"

SHELLEY ARMITAGE is Professor of American Studies at the University of Hawaii at Manoa where she teaches courses in regionalism, folk and popular arts, and women's studies. She has published six books in these areas as well as two on comic art. In 1995 she was the Dorrance D. Roderick Professor of English at University of Texas El Paso where she taught cultural studies.

PASCAL COVICI, JR., E. A. Lislly Professor of English at Southern Methodist University, was born and grew up in New York City. He first encountered Sut Lovingood in graduate school at Harvard University, where he received all of his degrees (1952, 1955, 1957). At SMU since then, he has written *Mark Twain's Humor: The Image of a World* (1962) and edited five volumes, with introductions, among them the Viking *Portable Steinbeck* (1971) and the Penguin American Library edition of Stephen Crane's *The Red Badge of Courage and Other Stories* (1991). At present he is working on a book-length manuscript concerning American ambivalence toward psychological and cultural independence as reflected in our literature, particularly nineteenth-century fiction. His essay in this volume arose from that interest. He was vice-president and president of the Mark Twain Circle of America from 1988 to 1992.

HERSHEL PARKER is H. Fletcher Brown Professor of American Romanticism at the University of Delaware and Associate General Editor of the Northwestern-Newberry Edition of *The Writings of Herman Melville* (12 volumes to date, most recently *Moby Dick, Journals, Clarel,* and the *Corrrespondence*). He is the editor of the 1820–66 section of the widely used *Norton Anthology of American Literature*. Northwestern published his *Flawed Texts and Verbal Icons* (1984) and *Reading "Billy Budd"* (1990). Current projects include a two-volume biography of Melville, the first volume (900 pages) due out early in 1996 and the second volume in 1997 or 1998. He is expanding Jay Leyda's documentary life into three or four volumes of *The*

New Melville Log. Recent publications include "Deconstructing *The Art of the Novel* and Liberating James's Prefaces," in the *Henry James Review.*

SANFORD PINSKER is Shadek Professor of Humanities at Franklin and Marshall College. He writes widely on American literature and culture for journals such as the *Georgia Review,* the *Virginia Quarterly, Modern Fiction Studies,* and *Salmagundi.* Recent books include studies of Cynthia Ozick and Joseph Heller. In addition, he is coeditor of *Jewish-American History and Culture: An Encyclopedia* (1992). A current project is entitled *Representative Humorous Men: Benjamin Franklin, Mark Twain, James Thurber, and Woody Allen,* to be published by Wayne State University Press.

NANCY A. WALKER is Professor of English and Director of the Women's Studies Program at Vanderbilt University. Her fields of interest are American humor, American women writers, and autobiography. She is author of *A Very Serious Thing: Women's Humor and American Culture* (1988), *Feminist Alternatives: Irony and Fantasy in the Contemporary Novel by Women* (1990), *Fanny Fern* (1992), and *The Disobedient Writer: Women and Narrative Tradition* (1995). She has coedited an anthology of American women's literary humor and has edited a critical edition of Kate Chopin's *The Awakening.* Among current projects, she is editing a collection of articles from leading women's magazines from the 1940s and 1950s.

The Editors

JAMES E. CARON is an Associate Professor of English at the University of Hawaii at Manoa where he maintains his interest in comic art, popular culture, literary naturalism, and Mark Twain. He is a contributor to the *Mark Twain Encyclopedia* (1993) and has published in *Nineteenth-Century Fiction, Studies in American Humor, Texas Studies in Literature and Language,* and *Modern Language Studies.* He is working on a book that will use a multidisciplinary approach to analyze comic art forms.

M. THOMAS INGE is Robert Emory Blackwell Professor of Humanities at Randolph-Macon College. He is editor of more than thirty-five volumes, including *Sut Lovingood's Yarns.* In addition, he serves as series editor for volumes on popular culture and reference books on American literary criticism. His most recent publications as author include *Great American Comics* (1990), *Comics as Culture* (1990), *Faulkner, Sut, and Other Southerners* (1992), and *Perspectives on American Culture: Essays on Humor, Literature, and the Popular Arts* (1994).

Index

328 Index

—WRITING OF: exaggeration, 81, 83, 86, 90, 94, 102, 106, 149, 208, 211; folk elements, 18, 87–89, 91, 113, 122, 182, 184, 193, 200–201, 203–209, 212, 229–30, 234–35, 239, 241, 274, 283–84; realism, 81–82, 94, 104, 152, 176, 186, 234, 309; sentiment, 58–61, 84–85, 146, 171, 223–24, 256–57, 291;

—TITLES: "Bart Davis's Dance," 211, 221, 269; "Bill Ainsworth's Quarter Race," 59; "Blown up with Soda," 52, 128, 142, 192, 211, 221, 233; "The Cockney's Baggage," 53; "Contempt of Court—Almost," 101, 120, 153, 155, 168, 220–21, 223, 225, 276, 286; "Dad's Dog School," 86, 118, 158–62, 166, 204–206, 211, 269, 276, 281, 283; "The Doctor's Bill," 54; "Eaves-dropping a Lodge of Free Masons," 85, 178, 203, 222, 246, 251, 267, 275; "The Early Life of Sut Lovingood, Written by his Dad," 59; "Frustrating a Funeral," 154, 172, 184, 186, 222, 279, 285; "Hen Baily's Reformation," 20, 123, 154, 205; "How to Marry," 50; "The Knob Dance," 44, 122, 235; "Letter from S——l," 53–54; "Mrs. Yardley's Quilting," 110, 154, 191, 222, 261; "Old Abe on His Journey," 56; "Old Abe Safe at Last," 56, 120; "Old Abe's Confidential Friend and Advisor," 56; "Old Burns's Bull Ride," 53, 117, 131, 154, 157, 205–206, 208, 233; "Old Skissim's Middle Boy," 122, 151, 154, 177; "Parson John Bullen's Lizards," 53, 132, 137, 154, 191, 202, 211, 237, 266; "Playing Old Sledge for the Presidency," 51; "Quarter Race in Tennessee," 41; "Rare Ripe Garden-Seed," 118–19, 152, 194–96, 220, 223–24, 265–66, 269, 286; "A Razor Grinder in a Thunder-Storm," 154, 211; "Saul Spradlin's Ghost," 59, 181; "Sicily Burns's Wedding," 53, 117, 123, 132, 150, 154, 156, 191, 202, 207, 233, 266, 272; "A Sleep Walking Incident," 45; "The Snake-bit Irishman," 5, 49, 154, 181, 209; "Sporting Epistle" (11 February 1843), 41, 181; "Sporting Epistle" (17 June 1843), 42; "Sporting Epistle" (2 September 1843), 42; "Sut Assisting at a Negro Night-Meeting," 154, 206, 265; "Sut Lovingood 'Sets Up

With a Gal—One Pop Baily,'" 61; "Sut Lovingood at Bull's Gap," 54, 306; "Sut Lovingood Come to Life," 57; "Sut Lovingood on Young Gals and Old Ones," 61; "Sut Lovingood Reports What Bob Dawson Said," 59, 237; "Sut Lovingood, A Chapter from his Autobiography," 59; "Sut Lovingood, on the Puritan Yankee," 142; "Sut Lovingood's Adventures in New York," 54, 122, 127, 232, 304; "Sut Lovingood's Allegory," 60, 146; "Sut Lovingood's Big Dinner Story," 57; "Sut Lovingood's Big Music Box Story," 59; "Sut Lovingood's Chest Story," 53, 182, 194, 262; "Sut Lovingood's Daddy, Acting Horse," 50, 116, 128, 130, 132, 141, 150, 156, 158–59, 161–62, 202, 211–12, 222, 231–32, 238, 268, 280; "Sut Lovingood's Dog," 53, 154–55, 167–68; "Sut Lovingood's Dream," 57; "Sut Lovingood's Hark from the Tomb Story," 59; "Sut Lovingood's Hog Ride," 308; "Sut Lovingood's Love Feast ove Varmints," 55; "Sut Lovingood's Sermon," 58, 103, 171, 275; "Sut's New-Fangled Shirt," 52, 117, 128, 130, 164, 167, 205, 211, 221, 238, 240, 268, 279–81; "Taurus in Lynchburg Market," 156–57, 160, 165–67, 169, 205, 211; "There's Danger in Old Chairs," 45; "Trapping a Sheriff," 84, 145, 195–96, 203, 211, 220, 223, 227, 256, 269, 286; "Tripetown: Twenty Minutes for Breakfast," 171, 275; "Well! Dad's Dead," 61, 106, 121, 180, 238, 309; "The Widow McCloud's Mare," 154. See also Sut Lovingood
Harte, Bret, 190
Hawthorne, Nathaniel, 15, 198 (n. 2), 218
Hennessy, William J., 128, 130
Hershfield, Leo, 135, 137
Holland, Josiah G. ("Timothy Titcomb"), 251, 256
Holley, Marietta, 22, 261–64, 266–68
Hooper, Johnson J., 7, 10, 13, 115, 122, 130, 247, 249–51, 257, 306. See also Simon Suggs
Howard, Justin H., 130, 132, 137, 239
Howells, William Dean, 9–12, 198 (n. 2)